Perils of the Night

Perils of the Night

A Feminist Study of Nineteenth-Century Gothic

Eugenia C. DeLamotte

New York Oxford
OXFORD UNIVERSITY PRESS
1990

Oxford University Press

Oxford   New York   Toronto
Delhi   Bombay   Calcutta   Madras   Karachi
Petaling Jaya   Singapore   Hong Kong   Tokyo
Nairobi   Dar es Salaam   Cape Town
Melbourne   Auckland

and associated companies in
Berlin   Ibadan

Copyright © 1990 by Oxford University Press, Inc.

Published by Oxford University Press, Inc.,
200 Madison Avenue, New York, New York 10016

Oxford is a registered trademark of Oxford University Press.

Library of Congress Cataloging-in-Publication Data
DeLamotte, Eugenia C.
Perils of the night : a feminist study of nineteenth-century
Gothic / Eugenia C. DeLamotte.
p.   cm.
Bibliography: p.
Includes index.
ISBN 0-19-505693-0
1. English fiction—19th century—History and criticism.
2. Gothic revival (Literature)   3. Feminism and literature—
History—19th century.   4. Women and literature—History—19th
century.   5. American fiction—19th century—History and criticism.
6. Horror tales—History and criticism.   7. Brontë, Charlotte,
1816–1855—Criticism and interpretation.   I. Title.
PR868.T3D45   1990
823'.0872—dc19   88-30489   CIP

2 4 6 8 9 7 5 3 1

Printed in the United States of America
on acid-free paper

For My Parents
Roy and Araminta DeLamotte

Preface

This study is an interpretation of the Gothic "myth" as both the original
creators of the genre and later writers in the Gothic tradition used it.
Central to every aspect of my argument is the perception that the Gothic
vision has from the beginning been focused steadily on social relations
and social institutions and that its simultaneous focus on the most private
demons of the psyche can never be separated from this persistent preoccupation with the social realities from which those demons always, in
some measure, take their shape. That is why the last two chapters of the
book center on the work of Charlotte Brontë, who of all nineteenth-
century exploiters of the Gothic tradition saw most clearly, and portrayed
most brilliantly, what the Gothic had always known: the way the perils
of the soul in its darkest night reflect, in magnified and revealing forms,
the quotidian realities of life in the daylit world of money, work, and
social rank.

The introduction locates the central focus of the book in the context of
changing critical trends in the definition of the genre "Gothic," places
my interpretation of the Gothic in the context of other readings of the
Gothic myth, and argues against a tendency, in many otherwise provocative explorations of the genre, to masculinize the Gothic canon. In subsequent chapters every reading of later uses of the Gothic tradition begins
with an analysis of the often-neglected, original Gothic dominated by
women readers, writers, and protagonists in the 1790s. Consequently, the
book contains analyses of a number of works by writers—especially
women—whose fiction has not been the subject of much serious explo-

ration. In my discussions of the original Gothics I have also tried to contribute to a much-needed analysis of the formal aspects, particularly the narrative methods, of the genre: the complex relation of its pastoral and Gothic settings; its status as novel or romance, which has much to do with the way the social, as opposed to the psychological, content of the Gothic should be read; the differences between Gothic tragedy and comedy; and the role in Gothic narratives of such allegorical techniques as the substitution of temporal connection for causality or the division of one psychological event into two apparently different stories. This study also explores the meaning of several Gothic conventions whose significance has not previously been recognized, among them the strange convention of the heroine's refusal to exonerate herself and the convention of the "educational idyll" (a term Mary Jacobus uses in another but interestingly related context) that conceals a mystery. Aside from the fact that the early popular Gothic deserves more analysis than it has received, my approach also has the advantage of analyzing from a new vantage point how writers like Melville and Brontë were working in the Gothic tradition.

Part I locates the Gothic myth at the heart of an anxiety about the boundaries of the self and explores four contexts in which that anxiety appears in Gothic romance: self-defense, knowledge, repetition, and transcendence. Part II uses those contexts to explore further the question why the Gothic has been so preeminently a woman's genre. Central to the answer are two perceptions: first, that women's Gothic was from the beginning obsessed with the interrelated social and psychological constraints on women's freedom to make themselves known through the act of "speaking 'I,' " and, second, that women's Gothic participated only partially in a vision of the evil Other as a disguised version of the self. That vision is often assumed to be a hallmark of the most sophisticated and psychologically perceptive Gothic, especially by critics who place works by and about men at the center of the Gothic canon. Certain conventions of women's Gothic do point toward the writers' suspicion of a desiring, dissatisfied self buried within even good women—a self that contemporary ideologies of womanhood would not permit them to acknowledge overtly. Indeed, the subject of fear in women's Gothic is, again and again, a disguise for that of anger. On the other hand, a major source of this anger is a perception that in an important sense, the evil Other the Gothic heroine confronts is not a hidden self at all but is just what it appears to be: an Other that is profoundly alien, and hostile, to women and their concerns.

Once again the work of Charlotte Brontë serves as the culmination of my argument, because one of her great achievements was to reveal the latent content—especially the latent anger—of the women's Gothic tradition preceding her. One of the remarkable aspects of Brontë's reading and writing of women's Gothic in *Jane Eyre,* for example, is the way the heroine's definitive acts of self-defense rely on her ability to see through a mystification that had obscured the true meaning of much earlier women's Gothic: to see that what appears to women in the guise of transcendence may be only a version of that old Gothic peril, domestic entrapment. The final section of the chapter on *Jane Eyre* approaches from this new perspective the novel's notoriously problematic ending, redefining the nature of its contradictions in terms of those inherent in Brontë's special subversion of Gothic romance. Having unveiled some aspects of women's experience that women's Gothic before her had known only in disguise, Brontë was forced into another set of disguises that reveal much about the limits she set on her own transcendent visions. In *Villette,* a novel bitterly angry at those very limits, Brontë pushed even further the implications of her Gothic vision: focusing more centrally on the heroine's difficulty "speaking I" and defining that difficulty in terms of the way women fight their psychological battles both against and on behalf of a self on which an alien, oppressive Other has been superimposed.

As this description suggests, much of my study is devoted to reading texts, both popular and literary. These readings are intended to cast new light on the many facets of the Gothic myth; on the social and psychological functions of the popular Gothic, especially for women; on many hitherto-ignored continuities between popular and "high" Gothic; on the structural as well as thematic aspects of the genre; and on the rich array of formal techniques available to nineteenth-century writers who knew the popular Gothic tradition well. Most of these texts have been read as "Gothic" before; by illuminating the Gothic itself in a new way, I hope to provide some perspectives from which such works as *Pierre, The Recess, The Portrait of a Lady, The Mysteries of Udolpho, Melmoth the Wanderer, The Marble Faun,* and "The Yellow Wallpaper" may be usefully reexamined. Thus, these readings are also intended, quite simply, to cast new light on the texts themselves.

Bahama, N.C.   E.C.D.
August 1989

Acknowledgments

The generous support of many people has gone into writing this book. I am grateful for permission to consult the collections of the Bodleian and British Libraries, for the extraordinary resourcefulness of the interlibrary loan staff at Odense University, and for the kind assistance of Frank Walker of the Fales Library at New York University. Grants from the American Council of Learned Societies and the Bowdoin College Faculty Research Fund gave me the time to complete the project. Jacob Kinnard, Helaine Olen, and Jeffrey Olsen provided valuable research and clerical assistance. Students from my courses at Bowdoin will recognize in this book many of the ideas we discussed at length; my debt to them—for their criticism, insights, and provocative questions—is incalculable. The women's studies research group at Bowdoin—whose members include Susan Bell, Lynn Bolles, Barbara Weiden Boyd, Helen Cafferty, Liliane Floge, Marya Hunsinger, Sarah McMahon, and Marilyn Reizbaum—gave patient and creative attention to my work in progress and generously shared their perspectives, drawn from a variety of disciplines.

Many other teachers, colleagues, and friends contributed advice, comments, and encouragement at various stages of the project. I would especially like to thank Warner Berthoff, Randy Fertel, Robert Griffin, James Henderson, Buford Jones, Joseph Litvak, Elizabeth McKinsey, Ellen Peel, Gail Rickert, Jane Tompkins, and Susanne Wofford. I owe special debts to Marion Wash and Naomi Williams, who first interested me in literature and taught me to write; to my parents; and to Rebecca DeLamotte.

Contents

I

BOUNDARIES OF THE SELF
AS A GOTHIC THEME

. . . this problem of the possible reconcilement of this world with our own souls. . . .

MELVILLE

Introduction: The Genre, the Canon, and the Myth

> With deepest sympathy I accompanied the prayer against the perils of darkness—perils that I seemed to see, in the ambush of midnight solitude, brooding around the beds of sleeping nations; perils from even worse forms of darkness shrouded within the recesses of blind human hearts; perils from temptations weaving unseen snares for our footing; perils from the limitations of our own misleading knowledge.
>
> DE QUINCEY, *Confessions of an English Opium Eater*

I

A Gothic parody of 1813 portrays a well-read "Heroine" in raptures over a newly acquired ruin. In her excitement she sends out immediately for a set of appropriate furnishings, including "painted glass enriched with armorial bearings," "pennons and flags stained with the best old blood;—Feudal if possible," "antique tapestry sufficient to furnish one entire wing," "an old lute, or lyre, or harp," "a bell for the portal," black hangings and curtains, and a velvet pall. Unfortunately, the man dispatched on the errand has surprising trouble finding in town these items available everywhere in romance. He gets an old pall from an undertaker; otherwise Cherubina must do what she can with a few shabby substitutes (Barrett 3: 22–23, 70–71).

Barrett's account of this shopping expedition belongs to the first wave of satires, prefaces, reviews, and literary essays that, in the late eighteenth and early nineteenth centuries, established the practice of grouping together the works we now term *Gothic*. Writers of the period associate these works on the basis of various similarities: the portrayal of "Gothic" times or "Gothic superstitions"; a debt to German horror romance or the romances of Ann Radcliffe; the descent from Walpole's "Gothic Story" *The Castle of Otranto*.[1] Fundamentally, however, most of these characterizations boil down to versions of Cherubina's shopping list. They are enumerations, examples, and parodies of the many and much-used conventions associated with the new vogue for "stories of haunted castles and visionary terrors" (*Critical Review* 16: 22, quoted in Lévy 251).

Barrett's book assembles a dazzling collection of those conventions. There are the desperate villains Daggeroni, Stiletto, and Poignardi; the Marquis de Furioso; the Lady Sympathina; the Baroness De Violenci; the ill-fated Lady Hysterica Belamour; the aged retainer Whylome Eftsoones. There is a sliding panel and a "moth-eaten parchment" containing tantalizing clues: "Murd——Adul——" (2: 183). There is "Ossianly" thunder "on a nocturnal night in autumnal October" (2: 170), a ghost at midnight, "an extraordinary rencontre" (2: 188), "a tender dialogue" (2: 185), "an interesting flight" (2: 185). There is the clairvoyant dream, as the lid of a pot rises, and a "half-boiled turkey" emerges to lead the heroine to its head and feathers in the yard (1: 19–20). There is the obligatory lament for the glories of the past, when an ancient servant observes that what seems a fresh pool of blood has been there "these fifty years," like the evidence that lasts conveniently for centuries in Gothic romance. "But, alas-o-day! modern blood won't keep like the good old blood" (3: 202). And of course, "On the rocky summit of a beetling precipice, whose base was lashed by the angry Atlantic," there is Il Castello di Grimgothico. "As the northern tower had remained uninhabited since the death of its late lord, Henriques De Violenci, lights and figures were, *par consequence,* observed in it at midnight" (2: 172).

Even before Radcliffe had made her own best use of them in 1794, such materials were clichés. Indeed, as Kiely says, some of her techniques "were clichés before they had time to become conventions" (65). By 1801, the *Monthly* needed only to list the ingredients of William Henry Ireland's *Rimualdo* to indicate what kind of book the reader could expect: "unnatural parents,—persecuted lovers,—murders,—haunted apartments,—winding sheets, and winding stair-cases,—subterraneous passages,—lamps that are dim and perverse, and that always go out when they should not,—monasteries,—caves,—monks, tall, thin, and withered, with lank abstemious cheeks,—dreams,—groans,—and spectres." "Such," the reviewer says, "is the outline of the *modern* romance . . ." (34: 203).

From its beginnings in the dream of an antiquarian collector, Gothic romance has lent itself to such descriptions by inventory.[2] For this very reason, perhaps, critics did not, for a long time, seek much further for a definition: the genre was simply accounted for as the sum of its conventions. Thus, for example, when Lundblad set out in 1946 to examine Hawthorne's debt to the Gothic tradition, she made a checklist of conventions and looked for them in each of his works: the manuscript, the castle, the crime, religion, Italians, deformity, ghosts, magic, nature, armored knights, works of art, blood (17–24). Her study made an important case for the pervasive influence of Gothic romance on almost all of Hawthorne's work, but the full meaning of that influence remained obscure.

The shopping-list approach to a definition of Gothic romance lasted until the 1960s, when several new works initiated a different kind of inquiry. What was really behind the black veil of Udolpho—and all the moldering castle walls, the secret doors, the masks and cowls and rotting tapestries? What fear, what longing, what faith, or what despair found their expression in Gothic romance? And why did so many later writers, seeking a fresh language for "the truth of the human heart," begin with the tired vocabulary of Gothicism? Works that ask such questions have attempted, for example, to define a Gothic "monomyth" and relate it to "dark Romanticism" (Thompson); to explain "the coherence of Gothic conventions" (Sedgwick) or the "deep structures" of the genre (Lévy); to trace, in later works, the development of its symbolic resources (Nelson); to place the Gothic in the context of women's psychology and social status (Doody, Fleenor, Gilbert and Gubar, Holland and Sherman, Kahane, Moers, Nichols, Ronald, Wolff); to trace a persistent Gothic tradition in England (Wilt), America (Fiedler, Ringe), or the twentieth-century South (Malin).

To engage in such inquiries is to look for what, in Guillén's description of genre, would be called the Gothic myth: that aspect of the genre that has become "a kind of permanent temptation to the human mind" ("Toward a Definition of the Picaresque" 99). The myth of a genre involves a sense, "independent of any particular work, of the theme as a whole" (100). It is "an essential situation or significant structure derived from the [works] themselves" (71), which consist of two groups: a first circle that deserves the name of the genre "in the strict sense—usually in agreement with the original . . . pattern"—and a second circle that belongs to the genre "in a broader sense," failing to include some characteristics of works in the inmost circle but nonetheless exhibiting certain "indispensable" traits (93). The genre itself Guillén distinguishes both from its exemplars and the myth: it is "an invitation to the actual writing of a work, on the basis of certain principles of composition," and no one example embodies it completely (72).

As critical attention has come to focus more and more on the myth, and accounts of the genre have moved further from mere inventory, the term Gothic has come to embrace an increasingly wider range of works.[3] As a result, some novels recently read as Gothic or as part of a Gothic tradition contain neither winding sheets nor winding staircases. Such items can perhaps be dispensed with. But what if the work labeled Gothic also has no castle; no midnight bell; no banditti; no frightened heroine; no ghosts, storms, corpses, manuscripts? How many conventions of this "conventional genre par excellence" (Sedgwick, "Character" 266) can be missing from a work before its description as Gothic—and the category itself—begins to lose force and meaning? Should Gothic, by definition, imply some indispensable conventions? Or could a work with no Gothic stage props at all enact, nonetheless, the Gothic drama? In generic criticism there is always some interplay between readings of the myth and characterizations of the original pattern. Sometimes the most interesting incarnations of the myth appear in works far removed both in time and content from the inmost circle. The discovery in these later works of a new reading of the models of the genre may alter our own reading of those models and thus alter some initial premises about the genre itself. On the other hand, consideration of the myth has sometimes ended in fundamental premises about the genre that have little relation to its original pattern.

In the case of Gothic romance, this pattern has been best described by Maurice Lévy,[4] who makes a convincing case for limiting the term Gothic to the substantial, but historically restricted, body of fiction he discusses in *Le Roman "gothique" anglais, 1764–1824*. Unrivaled in its comprehensiveness, Lévy's account describes an inmost circle created over a period of fifty years in English literary history. This circle consists of a massive group of works so close in their manipulation of certain conventions of plot, setting, and character that they may be identified as an eminently recognizable and coherent genre, the Gothic romance. Lévy's canon can be usefully accepted as a basis for establishing the original Gothic pattern, and even the most remote concentric circles should be viewed from the perspective of that center. Even so, this perspective presents some problems. Following Roudaut ("Pas un roman noir . . . sans un château" [716]), Lévy insists on architecture as the key to Gothicism. Indeed, he chooses the term *Gothic romance* rather than *roman noir* because "le genre créé par Walpole se caractérise, de façon primor-

diale à nos yeux, par le rôle déterminant qu'y jouent les *demeures*. L'im-
aginaire, dans ces romans, est toujours *logé*" (vii). This emphasis excludes from Lévy's discussion *Caleb Williams* and *Frankenstein,* which
belong to the same historical period as does the Gothic he defines and
have been central to some provocative explorations of the Gothic myth.[5]
It excludes as well almost all the American works ever read as Gothic,
since in late eighteenth- and nineteenth-century America the "prestigieux
vestiges du passé" (Lévy 7) that inspired Walpole and Radcliffe were not
so easy to come by as were those writers' romances.[6]

It is not mere chance that the first works of criticism to pull away
significantly from the inventory approach to Gothicism dealt with American literature.[7] American writers' own struggle to work what they had
learned from Gothic romance into a cultural context that, by its very
nature, excluded many Gothic materials, itself prepared the way for an
approach to Gothicism other than list making. American writers like
Brockden Brown and Hawthorne—to the extent that they used the Gothic
tradition—were engaged precisely in trying to disentangle the Gothic myth
from its Old World conventions in order to free it for use in an American
context. They were reacting to the same "invitation to form"[8] that excited
English writers, but the same materials were not available to them.

As late as 1859 Hawthorne was worrying about the absence of Gothic
materials—shadow, antiquity, mystery, ruin—in his (blessedly) sunny native
land. How was one to write romance without them? (*Marble Faun,*
"Preface" 590). Brockden Brown, whose career as a novelist coincided
with the heyday of Gothic romance in England, seems to have wrestled
with a similar problem in his earliest novel. The advertisement for *Sky
Walk* in the *Weekly Magazine* of March 17, 1798, assures the prospective
reader both that the author uses native materials, "paint[ing], not from
books, but from nature," and that his story will have attractive affinities
with certain "popular tales" that, albeit exciting, serve only to "amuse
the idle and thoughtless." "A contexture of facts capable of suspending
the faculties of every soul in curiosity, may be joined with depth of views
into human nature and all the subleties [*sic*] of reasoning," he says (*Uncollected Writings* 136). To suspend the faculties of every soul in curiosity is not one of the goals Fielding mentions in his preface to *Joseph
Andrews,* and as Johnson said, "[I]f you were to read Richardson for the
story, your patience would be so much fretted that you would hang yourself" (Boswell 190). It was Radcliffe who, as J. M. S. Tompkins points
out, first made reading "an exercise to be undertaken with bated breath"
(250). In the light of such evidence that American writers like Hawthorne

and Brown wanted, at least in some sense, to use the Gothicists' techniques, if not all of their materials, critics of American literature have
looked not only for Gothic elements in certain texts but also for displacements or "transpositions" of those elements.[9] Fiedler gave impetus to this
search with his perception that in American literature the wilderness is a
substitute for the haunted castle (160).

Lévy's definition of Gothic insists on the centrality of the very prop
most difficult for an American romancer to procure for an American tale.
On the other hand, the study of American uses of the Gothic tradition is
especially perilous precisely because it tends to lure readers away from
strenuous, constant attention to the original models of the genre. These
classic models[10] present enough problems for a study of the Gothic myth.
First, they are themselves in some ways not so coherent a group as their
common stage properties might suggest. There are many Gothic works
of which, for all their tedious similarities, it is yet strangely difficult to
speak in the same breath. Aside from a few ghosts and groans and old
buildings, how much do the works of such writers as Clara Reeve and
Charles Maturin really have in common? Differences among the original
models themselves mean that generalizations about the genre are often
tacitly rooted in the works of one particular author and not necessarily
transferable to those of another. The figure of Maturin, for example, looms
particularly large behind considerations of Gothic romance as "quest romance,"[11] a rubric less easily applied to Radcliffe's *A Sicilian Romance*
or *A Romance of the Forest*.

Second, the central figures of Radcliffe, Walpole, Reeve, Maturin,
M. G. Lewis, Godwin, and Mary Shelley account for only a fraction of
the works written between 1764 and 1824 that can be classified as Gothic.
Theoretically the term applies to hundreds of volumes, a thorough consideration of which would involve all the difficulties attendant on any
study of popular novels. These difficulties include not only the inaccessibility of the texts and their sheer numbers but also the fundamental
problem of what attitude criticism should take toward this fiction and its
relations to elite literature. The Gothic romance in the 1790s was one of
the first varieties of mass-market fiction, associated with William Lane's
profitable and prolific Minerva Press and with the relatively new phenomenon of circulating libraries. Peacock called this a literature "completely
expurgated of all the higher qualities of mind,"[12] and it was suggested
that the press could perhaps have found a more appropriate symbol than
Minerva—a goose (Blakey 59). Many twentieth-century critics of Gothicism betray a certain defensiveness about the supposedly lowly status of

their subject, an attitude that results, once again, in an almost exclusive focus on works at the periphery of the genre and, consequently, in the occasional inapplicability of theories of the Gothic myth to the primary works that might be supposed to have generated it.

One could argue that—at least for the purposes of studying such writers as Brockden Brown, Hawthorne, and Melville—what counts is not the vast body of popular works but a few select flowers of the tradition. These authors must have recognized such classics as interesting versions of what was otherwise a cliché, and there is good evidence that they read them. Brockden Brown in his advertisement for *Sky Walk,* however, was clearly thinking not only of *Caleb Williams* but, more generally, of the "popular tales" based on suspense—tales that were a staple in the circulating library of Caritat, who published *Wieland* and *Ormond.*[13] Melville apparently felt convinced enough of the popular affinities of *Pierre* to think that he had written a potboiler.[14] Any reader of *Blackwood's*—and Hawthorne for a time seems to have been a regular one (Kesselring 45)—would have been conscious not only of the few strikingly original Gothic romances but also of their wider popular context.

Even so, why protest the neglected state of all those Gothic courtyards where the "rank luxuriant grass" has not been trampled by a hoard of critics? To read one of these works is to read them all. To embark on yet another quest for the elusive "spirit-spout" is both more interesting and more important than to follow yet another mysterious blue light down yet another dark and winding staircase to the inevitable heap of old bones. *Moby-Dick* is always new, and Gothic romance was old almost before it began. The very sameness of the productions of Regina Maria Roche, Anna Maria Mackenzie, Eliza Parsons, "Rosa Matilda," and the "Lady" who wrote so many tales that harrow up the soul contributes to an impression that we know *that* Gothic already, and only too well. Thus it makes but a ghostly appearance in many discussions of Gothicism, lurking in the shadows of some other, later, and presumably superior literature. References to this latter category as "high" or "literary" render the other variety all the more unmentionable.

But merely to recognize the sameness of a certain kind of fiction is not to explain its myth. There are many ways in which "low" or "nonliterary" Gothic has hardly been explored. In particular, there is the suspicious fact that when terms like "high Gothic" are used, they inevitably refer to a canon that is almost exclusively male, even though women were (and are) the primary readers, protagonists, and creators of the genre. Only recently has serious attention been called to what should have been a striking fact: most of these books are about women who just can't seem to get out of the house. The anxiety to distinguish a canonical tradition from a popular one is always based on a strangely limited view of the way a writer's imagination works. In the case of the Gothic, such a broadly popular genre, it is particularly distorting.[15] The task is not to prove Melville's or Emily Brontë's work superior to its popular origins but to illuminate their work by placing it in the light of the whole tradition: a task that will be easier when the whole tradition is illuminated.

Radcliffe must be regarded as the center of the Gothic tradition, if only for the central place she held in the minds of critics and writers alike during the flood tide of Gothic romance. Even if Horace Walpole, Clara Reeve, Sophia Lee, and Charlotte Smith assembled the materials of Gothicism, no one so much as Ann Radcliffe issued the "invitation to form" itself.[16] It is useful to locate her among the three phases that Fowler distinguishes in the development of a genre. First is the assembling of a "genre complex" until the emergence of a "formal type." Then comes the development of a " 'secondary' version" consciously based on the primary version, which the author makes "an object of sophisticated imitation, in the Renaissance sense," while nonetheless "retaining all its main features, including those of formal structure." Finally there is a tertiary phase, which occurs with the radically new use of a secondary version and is often a form of "interiorizing" (90–91). In these terms, Radcliffe's *The Mysteries of Udolpho* emerges at the end of the primary phase; *Melmoth the Wanderer* is a secondary version of the same formal type; and *Caleb Williams* and *Frankenstein,* especially because of their interiorizing of Gothic motifs, can be seen as part of a tertiary phase, despite their early date.

Two passages in Maturin and Hawthorne illustrate the differences among primary, secondary, and tertiary forms of Gothic. Just as we are about to descend with Alonzo di Monçada into the subterranean passageways of the convent in *Melmoth the Wanderer,* the narrator stops to remind us that we have read about such things before: "Romances have made your country, Sir, familiar with tales of subterranean passages, and supernatural horror. All these, painted by the most eloquent pen, must fall short of the breathless horror felt by a being engaged in an enterprise beyond his power, experience, or calculation . . ." (191). In many ways *Melmoth* might be seen as tertiary, but this passage indicates what it is for the most part—secondary Gothic. For all his complexity, there is a fundamental sense in which, for whatever reason (money?), Maturin is engaged primarily in trying to scare the reader out of his or her wits. On the threshold of his descent to Avernus, Alonzo announces that the reader who was frightened by subterranean passages in Radcliffe hasn't seen anything yet.

Hawthorne's very different handling of the subterranean scene in *The Marble Faun* is instructive. Miriam disappears, and the reader has a brief moment to wonder where she is. Almost immediately, however, Hawthorne interrupts the excitement: "And, not to prolong the reader's suspense (for we do not particularly seek to interest him in this scene, telling it only on account of the trouble and strange entanglement which followed), they soon heard a responsive call, in a female voice" (605). As Jameson says, "Genres are essentially contracts between a writer and his readers; or rather, to use the term which Claudio Guillén has so usefully revived, they are literary *institutions,* which like the other institutions of social life are based on tacit agreements or contracts" ("Magic Narratives" 135). In his description of subterranean fright, Hawthorne deliberately evokes a certain literary institution and then deliberately violates the first article of its contract: the agreement that the reader of Gothic romance will be kept in terrible suspense. Suspense, says Hawthorne in effect, is exactly *not* the reason he has brought us to these dark passageways—although there is an implicit joke that, even so, up to this point we will already have reacted to the scene as would any naïve reader of primary Gothic.

The purpose of these distinctions among primary, secondary, and tertiary Gothic is not to suggest that there are sharp and obvious borderlines between them,[17] but to emphasize that even a writer like Maturin was invoking a well-established literary institution rather than creating one. It was Radcliffe who, as her earliest readers knew, first codified the original provisions of the "contract" on which that institution was based. Her contemporaries recognized her as, if not the fountainhead, at least the opener of the floodgates for those tales with which, according to the *Critical Review* in 1796, the press had been inundated since "Mrs. Radcliffe's justly admired and successful romances" (16: 22, quoted in Lévy 251).[18] *The Mysteries of Udolpho,* in particular, attained a special status not only in the development of Gothic romance but in literary history more generally. The governess in *The Turn of the Screw* had apparently read it (28); Jane Austen allowed the sensible Henry Tilney to praise it (*Northanger Abbey* 85–86); when Cherubina's father burned her romances, at least one volume of *The Mysteries of Udolpho* somehow "escaped the conflagration" (Barrett 1: 19). M. G. Lewis finished his own influential work under the impetus of having read it (Lévy 328–29); literally hundreds of other novelists and romancers seem to have had it in mind when they poured forth their own effusions for the circulating libraries.[19] A reference in 1795 to the originator of Radcliffe's type of fiction necessitated a footnote to explain that the writer thus designated was Horace Walpole, but the allusion to Radcliffe herself was so obvious as not even to require the mention of her name.[20] *Melmoth the Wanderer* begins with a somewhat defensive preface explaining, among other things, why the "Spaniard's Tale" is not, as readers might at first assume, a mere revival of "Radcliffe-Romance" (5). "One of the most famous romances which ever was published in this country" was how Thackeray described *The Mysteries of Udolpho* in 1860,[21] and in 1888 Oscar Wilde said of Radcliffe that she "introduced the romantic novel, and has consequently much to answer for . . ." ("English Poetesses" 119).

It is necessary to insist on the centrality to the genre of Radcliffe in general and of *The Mysteries of Udolpho* in particular, precisely because of the masculinization of the canon—both in terms of a tendency to see the "high" form of Gothic as written by men and of a tendency to see Gothic in its fullest development as centering on a male rather than a female protagonist. By these terms Radcliffe and her most famous work are easily relegated to the periphery of the genre she herself did most to define. Thus in Fiedler's view, for example, the Gothic reveals the collective "soul of Europe" in flight from "its own darker impulses" (129). "These deeper implications are barely perceptible," he says, "in the gently spooky fiction of Mrs. Radcliffe" (129). The "deeper implications" of Radcliffe's own fiction, connected as they are to the lot of women, are left unexplored, as Radcliffe herself, the great inaugurator of the genre, is defined out of it: "[T]he fully developed gothic centers not in the heroine . . . but in the villain . . ." (128). It is telling that Fiedler also defines "society" out of the Gothic: "The flight of Clarissa . . . takes place in society. . . . The flight of the gothic heroine is out of the known world into a dark region of make-believe . . . through a world of ancestral and infantile fears projected in dreams" (128). In one sense this is true, but in another it lacks much as a description, at least of women's Gothic after Radcliffe, in which the "region of make-believe" is also a picture of "the known world," but in the form in which women "know" it. Similarly, in Day's reading of Gothic, "the most important aspect of the conventions governing the Gothic protagonist" is not the presence of a certain kind of woman, but the absence of a certain kind of man: "the disappearance of the romance hero" (16). This reading of the heroine herself as absence recalls those readings of Gothic that see Gothic itself as quest romance, a vision that tends to blank out the female Gothic altogether.[22] The real clue to the mystery of the genre will not explain the woman out of its center but will solve the special mystery of her place there.

What was the source of Radcliffe's extraordinary influence, of the deep impress made by Gothic romance on some of the greatest literary imaginations of the nineteenth and even the twentieth century? In the past thirty years, criticism has offered some important clues to the answer. One group of these clues centers on the "oneiric" quality of the Gothic world (Roudaut and Lévy); another, on perceptions that the genre "gives shape to concepts of the place of evil in the human mind" (MacAndrew 3) or suggests "a mythology of the mind" that can confront the problem of evil (Nelson). Another focuses on the religious dimension of the Gothic: on perceptions, for example, that its iconography is the iconography of the Age of Faith (Thompson, "Introduction" 2); that it is an essentially Protestant, even Calvinist, genre (Porte, "In the Hands"); that the sense of mystery it evokes is a response to the "numinous" (Varma, Varnado); or that the Gothic "treats of the separated one" and works out a "mystic theoretic of . . . the search for a community of individuals" (Wilt 19, 5).[23] Another set of clues focuses on power as a Gothic issue, seeing that a "fear of power" is central to Gothic plots (Ridgely 85), that the Gothic finds "larger powers . . . in places outside (or inside) the scope of everyday life . . . in places apparently abandoned but secretly tenanted" (Wilt 295). Still another set of clues places "the divided self" at the center of Gothic romance (Miyoshi Chap. 1), revealing that its "dialectic of fear and desire" is related to the problem of individual identity (Day). Another centers specifically on the Gothic concern with women's selves, arguing that the genre gives "visual form" to women's "fear of self" (Moers 107); that it speaks for the special psychological and social concerns of women (Doody, Fleenor, Gilbert and Gubar, Holland and Sherman, Moers, Nichols, Ronald); that the mystery of female sexuality (Wolff) or, more broadly, of female identity itself (Kahane) is at its heart.

What my study has in common with these will become evident in subsequent chapters; most important for this context is the fact that it is based on a spatial model of the Gothic similar to that proposed by Sedgwick. Sedgwick points out that although the model for most psychoanalytic criticism of the Gothic is based on metaphors of depth, it is more accurate to see Gothic anxiety as focused on "interfacing surface[s]" (*Coherence* 26).[24] A similar spatial model forms the basis of my study, which begins from a perception that Gothic terror has its primary source in an anxiety about boundaries and that Gothic romance offers a symbolic language congenial to the expression of psychological, epistemological, religious, and social anxieties that resolve themselves most fundamentally into a concern about the boundaries of the self.[25] This language consists of conventions: stage properties, character types, plot patterns, episodes, and situations. The image of boundaries or barriers is central to this language, but the original models of the genre differ in the extent to which and the emphasis with which they use its vocabulary to address the issue of the boundaries of the self. Later writers used the Gothic tradition to investigate the issue more vigorously and perceptively than did most of the original Gothic romancers, but the works of the "original pattern" inaugurated those later explorations in some ways that have not yet been examined.

Throughout this study, I shall use the term Gothic romance only for a certain class of works published during a specific historical period, roughly the one that Lévy defined as the heyday of the genre, 1764 to 1824. I shall use the term Gothic tradition in a broader sense to refer not only to these early works but also to the uses that later authors made of Gothic romance. Many critics have contributed to a characterization of the inmost circle of works,[26] and so there is little need to rehearse once more the often enumerated elements of the genre, except insofar as it is necessary to indicate the different emphasis my view of the genre occasionally gives them. The discussion that concludes this chapter outlines only my most basic assumptions; the remainder of the book expands on both my definition of the genre and my reading of the myth, in each case moving from central works of the original pattern outward into the expanding circle of their influence.

II

The primary subject and object of Gothic romance is that kind of terror best characterized in James's description of what he had attempted to study in "The Jolly Corner": "the spirit engaged with the forces of violence" ("Preface," *Novels and Tales* 17: xvi). The word *engaged* is particularly apt, implying as it does either antagonism or attraction, or both, as the basis for the relations between the spirit and these "forces." This is the theme, in some sense, of many works of literature, among them many of James's own works besides his ghost stories. But what characterizes Gothic romance specifically is the way it presents the "engagement." In Gothic romance of the inmost circle, this special mode of presentation usually, although not always, centers on the dominant presence in the narrative of a certain kind of architecture,[27] first represented in Walpole's description of the Castle of Otranto. This kind of architecture is the repository and embodiment of mystery. Specific secrets are hidden in it, and to discover them one must confront the mystery of the architecture itself: its darkness, labyrinthine passageways, unsuspected doors, secret staircases, sliding panels, forgotten rooms. The architecture is also a repository and embodiment of the past. It contains evidence of specific life histories: a skeleton stashed beneath the floorboards or locked in a chest, a prisoner shut away in a dungeon, a manuscript reporting a crime, an ancestral portrait revealing the hero or heroine's true lineage, the ghost of a previous occupant, an aged retainer who remembers certain sinister events of long ago. The building itself embodies the past more generally—the historic past; the collective past of the readers and often of the characters. As Tompkins says, "The castles of Gothic romance, unlike those of mediaeval romance, are never new. The tale may play in bygone centuries, but they are more ancient still . . ." (267).

These two aspects of the architecture are related in a complicated way. As the repository of mystery, the architecture contains the past in the form of what has been deliberately "lost" by the villain in an act symbolic of repression and must be retrieved by the hero or heroine in order to remedy another form of loss of which this place is also a symbol: the loss of an Edenic world associated with an innocent childhood past, of which the architectural place is a nightmarish obverse. In some cases, the physical loss of the pastoral world threatens to be also a psychological and spiritual loss through the discovery that the mystery of the Gothic place may well have some sinister bearing on, or even for a time be identical with, another mystery connected with that pastoral world itself. The potential for this psychological and spiritual loss is in some sense a potential for self-loss, represented emblematically in the fact that the hero or heroine tends to become lost in this place of mystery. The architecture, in turn—by virtue of the threat it represents that she will never get out—stands also for the danger that she herself, and the virtues she stands for, will be lost to history, just as the secret of this place has been lost.

The protagonist's adventures in this architectural setting, or in a series of similar settings, are an objective correlative for the terrors of "the spirit engaged with the forces of violence." These forces may manifest themselves in the arbitrary tyranny of a wicked prioress, priest, or parent; in the rampages of a wanton libertine or lust-crazed monk; in the hellish machinations of a woman scorned. But there is always in Gothic romance a sense that the danger exceeds any that human agency alone can bring about. Just as the architectural setting is both the repository of specific mysteries and embodiment of Mystery, repository of histories and embodiment of History, so in its dominant human occupant the architecture contains a specifically threatening personality while in its atmosphere embodying a vaster, vaguer threat. At the Castle of Udolpho, Emily feels herself "surrounded by vice and violence" (*Mysteries of Udolpho* 329). "O that I was out of this house," cries another heroine in a similar plight, ". . . danger and death surround me on every side" (Roche, *Clermont* 3: 42).

Vice, violence, danger, death—the abstract nature of the terms is significant. So is the vague premonition, the indefinable feeling of dread that possesses the heroine as she crosses the threshold of the castle. Although this feeling could easily be credited to the operations of reason, it almost never is. The heroine rarely deduces—from the lateness of the hour, the remote situation of the house, and evil glint in the villain's eye—that some foul plot is afoot. Instead a vague dread comes over her; an unaccountable terror grips her; without knowing why she is suddenly afraid.[28] The reader could think of a dozen reasons; strangely, heroines often fail to produce a single one. This relation between the heroine and the setting of her terror points to the superpersonal aspects of the danger she confronts. At the threshold, the heroine does not speculate on the intentions of the person who brought her there; rather, she responds to the atmosphere of his house.

The perils of the night often have names in Gothic romance: Schedoni, Manfred, Montoni, Manfroné, Sanguedoni, Schemoli.[29] But they also have a local habitation that helps render "nameless" the dread such villains inspire. "Nameless dread" may describe the fear of possibilities no decorous heroine would name even in her mind. But it also implies the dread that is nameless because its object is diffuse, unclear, insusceptible to definition. The vast, mysterious castle tends to depersonalize the threat of violence, diffusing the titanic, villainous personality into something even larger—and more obscure. The villain represents the threat of evil in a particularly vivid and concentrated form, but behind him the menacing darkness of his castle represents—in the plural and in the abstract—the "forces" of violence itself.

The uncanny diffusion of these forces takes place in two directions. Especially when the supernatural is part of the castle's atmosphere, a specifically evil character may seem only a personal concentration of more vaguely menacing forces that transcend the merely human. But the personal concentration of the forces of violence tends also to be an embodiment of larger forces in another sense: mammoth social institutions whose power transcends that of any individual. The church, the courts, the Inquisition, and the family are such institutions. They too are often embodied architecturally: in the cathedral or convent, the prison, the dungeons of the Inquisition, or the stronghold of a tyrannical father or husband. Here too, individual oppressors appear against a vast background: the abbess reigning in her dark, immeasurable architectural domain; the Inquisitor leading his victim through a labyrinth of stairs and passageways. This vast background is not merely architectural: there is also the abbess as a member of a larger order, the hooded Inquisitor among all the other hooded Inquisitors, and the sinister individual who is finally revealed as merely one member of a secret society. Like the architecture in Gothic romance, as Lévy describes it, these social institutions are frightening because they are not "à la mesure de l'homme."[30] Alonzo asks in *Melmoth the Wanderer*, ". . . When I consider the omnipotence of the ecclesiastical power in Spain, may I not address it in the language applied to Omnipotence itself: 'If I climb up to heaven thou art *there*;— if I go down to hell, thou art *there* also;—if I take the wings of the morning, and flee unto the uttermost parts of the sea, even there—" (180). Alonzo's persecutor taunts him for trying to escape from his convent:

> "And you dreamt," he cried, "in your temerity, you dreamt of setting the vigilance of a convent at defiance? Two boys . . . were fit antagonists for that stupendous system, whose roots are in the bowels of the earth, and whose head is among the stars,—*you* escape from a convent! *you* defy a power that has defied sovereigns! A power whose influence is unlimited, indefinable, and unknown, even to those who exercise it, as there are mansions so vast, that their inmates, to their last hour, have never visited all the apartments. . . ." (219–20)

In this description the vague "stupendous system," of which the convent is only a small visible part, seems to have escaped human control altogether and taken on a life of its own: a power whose influence is unknown even to those who exercise it. The "fear of power" embodied in Gothic romance (Ridgely 85) is a fear not only of supernatural powers but also of social forces so vast and impersonal that they seem to have supernatural strength.

The context that depersonalizes and diffuses the forces of violence in

Gothic romance may well be a specific architectural place or natural place—forest or cave—with features similar to those of the haunted castle. But this context need not be a physical milieu; a persistent attribution of strange, mysterious, seemingly supernatural characteristics to the villain or villainess can have the same effect. Such is the case with Godwin's Falkland, Dacre's Zofloya, Maturin's Orazio, and Melmoth the Wanderer. Works without a primarily architectural setting could be relegated to a second circle of Gothic romances, but in practice such a distinction proves difficult to maintain and not particularly useful. It is significant that as Lévy's description of Gothic romance moves from Walpole to Maturin, architecture moves increasingly away from his primary focus and into the "deep structures" of his own argument.

There are, in fact, two classic situations that should be recognized as Gothic. One of them is architectural, as it were, and is illustrated in Emily St. Aubert's description of her plight midway through *The Mysteries of Udolpho*: "in a foreign land—in a remote castle—surrounded by vice and violence" (329). The other is epitomized in Annibal's situation, as his pursuer Orazio describes it: "[T]hink on your wanderings, your persecutions, your fear-spent, spectre-ridden life" (*Montorio* 3: 276). Both these passages describe the experience of being at the same time cut off, hemmed in, and in danger of being broken in on by some outside force. The picture of an innocent young woman trapped in a haunted house at the mercy of a ruthless villain is a literal rendering of that experience; the description of Annibal's "fear-spent, spectre-ridden life" is its metaphorical equivalent.

Both Emily and Annibal are cut off by virtue of their separation from home: "in a foreign land," "your wanderings." The terrifying events at the core of Gothic romance take place in an alien world set apart from normal quotidian experience and from the logical and moral laws of everyday reality (Roudaut 723–25; Lévy 408). It is also separated from the usual social relations of life in its outward forms, although—and this fact has never been adequately recognized—those relations reappear in this alien world in disguise and are in many ways its primary subject. The Gothic place apart, with its "oneiric" atmosphere, may be a remote castle, but it may also be everyday reality as experienced by the mind obsessed. Both the wanderer and the prisoner, shut into this alien world, are thereby shut out from ordinary life. "A fugitive, an exile, a dependant, the outcast of your family," Orazio calls Annibal (*Montorio* 3: 277). And thus set apart, they are nonetheless hemmed in: Annibal by the seeming omnipresence of his persecutor; Emily by the castle walls and the evil "surround[ing]" her. Both passages evoke the sense of a self trying to shut out something alien to self—specters; vice and violence. In each case, this threat is concentrated in a single human figure of extraordinary evil, but in both descriptions the evil is also vague and diffuse: vice and violence are abstractions; specters have no substance.

The psychological, moral, spiritual, and intellectual energies expended in the engagement with the forces of violence are generated by an anxiety about boundaries: those that shut the protagonist off from the world, those that shut the protagonist in, and those that separate the individual self from something that is Other.[31] A locus classicus of the Gothic shows how this anxiety dominates the "fear-spent, spectre-ridden life." As the shades of evening close in, a small party of travelers wind their way toward the Castle of Udolpho, its splendid battlements gleaming high above them in the last rays of the sun. When they arrive at the top of the precipice, the massive walls are already partially obscure in twilight. A huge gate is drawn back; the carriage rolls through a gloomy courtyard and another gate; and Emily St. Aubert, seized with unaccountable dread, is led into the dim Gothic domain of the sinister Montoni. By lamplight she investigates the remote bedchamber he has assigned her and finds that it has two doors. One leads out to the labyrinthine corridors of Montoni's stronghold; the other opens on a stairway leading down into the dark. The first door she locks, but at the second door she makes a terrible discovery: its lock is on the other side (*Mysteries of Udolpho* 226–35).

The precipice cuts Emily off from hope of rescue and from the world as she has previously experienced it. The massive walls, reminding her of a prison, ensure that once she is inside, it will be almost impossible to get out. The series of thresholds emphasizes her passage from the daylight world she has known to a mysterious and threatening world she has never seen. The twilight, boundary between day and night, marks her passage from a daylit to a nocturnal reality. The two doors to her chamber suggest the threat of intrusion. These boundaries and barriers are the focus for her anxieties and fears, which derive their force both from the terrors of separateness and the terrors of unity: the fear of being shut in, cut off, alone; the fear of being intruded upon.

Boundaries and barriers, after all, are the very stage properties of Gothic romance: veils, masks, cowls, precipices, black palls, trap doors, sliding panels, prison walls, castle ramparts. As Lévy says, "the traditional obstacles to the happiness of the couple in the sentimental romance took quite a literal form in Gothic romance" (268). And these "obstacles of stone" are by no means the only translations of metaphorical barriers into physical ones. All the major Gothic conventions involve either literal or metaphorical boundaries, and sometimes both. Most obviously this is true of the architectural settings. Castle walls isolate an inside world from an outside world, preventing intrusion from without and escape from within. To mark the transition between these worlds, Gothic narratives linger for a moment at the dividing line between them, evoking what Lévy calls "anxieties of the threshold" (405): "The heavy door, creaking upon its hinges, reluctantly yielded to his hand—he applied his shoulder to it and forced it open—he quitted it and stept forward—the door instantly shut with a thundering clap. Sir Bertrand's blood was chilled—he turned back to find the door, and it was long ere his trembling hands could seize it—but his utmost strength could not open it again" (Aikin, "Sir Bertrand" 131). That cliché of the horror movie, the sound of a door grating on its hinges, was first a cliché of Gothic romance, used then as now to mark every state of anxiety associated with boundaries. Nathan Drake's exemplary "Gothic Tale" of 1798 exploits all of these anxieties in rapid succession. As the hero explores a mysterious castle, there opens before him "a ponderous iron door, slowly grating on its hinges." No sooner has he crossed this threshold than the iron door rushes closed "in thunder" and shuts him in. Venturing further into the darkness, he thinks he hears the door creak open again behind him ("Henry Fitzowen" 120–22).

The Gothic convent evokes the same set of anxieties. Alonzo di Monçada stands by his "chained, barred and bolted" convent door, "the door that shut me out from life" (*Melmoth* 174). Even the trees in the convent garden seem to close him in: "I saw the moonbeams through the trees, but the trees all looked to me like walls. Their trunks were as adamant, and the interlaced branches seem'd to twine themselves into folds that said, 'Beyond us there is no passing' " (102). The convent is effectively a prison; deep inside it there are likely to be other prisons. To one of these Monçada is brought by five monks: "It was a long time before they could open it; many keys were tried . . . my cries were drowned in the jarring of the heavy door, as it yielded to the efforts of the monks, who, uniting their strength, pushed it with extended arms, grating all the way against the floor of stone" (144). In the Protestant Gothicists' eyes, those immured in such convents are, for the most part, thereby shut off even from true devotion. Separated from nature, they are also separate from God: "Who could first invent convents? . . . and to make religion a pretence, too, where all that should inspire it, is so carefully shut out!" (*Mysteries of Udolpho* 475). The conventual life prevents the "effusions" of "divine philanthropy" as well: instead of moving outward in charity, the soul is shut away in "selfish apathy."[32] And yet for all the ways it isolates its victims, the convent also subjects them to the most terrible invasions of individual privacy—by spies who report to the abbott or abbess; by eerie pseudosupernatural manifestations that intrude on the monk's cell, perhaps even on his dreams (*Melmoth* 156–57); or by the intervention of a hierarchical power in the most intimate concerns of a young woman's life—her romantic attachments, the choice of a suitable husband (Fuller, *The Convent;* Radcliffe, *The Italian*). "I knew I had no lock to my door," says Monçada, "and could not prevent the intrusion of any one into my cell who pleased to visit it" (*Melmoth* 154).

Castles and convents, in addition, are filled with labyrinthine passageways: nightmarish proliferations of walls, gates, gratings, and doors separating the wanderer both from the hidden center and the exit. Such barriers may also prevent return to the entrance, as in *A Sicilian Romance,* in which that unfortunate device, the spring lock, ensures that some crucial doors will open only from one side (2: 124–25; 2: 159).

Ghosts and other supernatural beings defy both physical boundaries and the boundaries whereby daylight reason distinguishes one thing from another. The tomb cannot contain them; they cross the border between the living and the dead; notoriously, they walk through walls. Thus the old servant describes her encounter with Melmoth: "[A]t that moment she saw the figure of a tall man cross the court, and go out of the court, she knew not where or how, for the outer gate was locked, and had not been opened for years" (23).

Caves and caverns evoke a double terror associated with boundaries: the fear that the walls may have no opening; the fear that the cavernous space is limitless and that one will never find a wall.[33] Vampirism (a convention established later in the Gothic tradition) represents the threat of physical violation—a transgression against the body, the last barrier protecting the self from the other. Bondage or enthrallment poses the similar threat of spiritual or psychological violation and the fusion of two separate identities into one. Transformation, a common Gothic motif, is a figurative crossing of boundaries. What was x becomes y, the line dividing them dissolving. Sedgwick points to another metaphorical boundary: the "barrier of unspeakableness" that again and again prevents the revelation of truth: "an interpersonal barrier where no barrier ought to be—language is properly just the medium that should flow between people, mitigating their physical and psychic separateness . . ." (*Coherence* 17).

The mysterious crime at the heart of most Gothic plots is a transgression of legal barriers as well as, in many cases, a transgression of the stronger barriers of taboo—incest, the murder of a brother, patricide. The titanic hero-villain, or heroine-villainess, of many Gothic works is fashioned after Prometheus or Faust,[34] archetypal transgressors of the dividing line between the human and divine. It is striking how often the ambitions of such characters are expressed metaphorically in terms of boundaries and barriers. Sanguedoni sets "no limits to his wishes, no bounds to their enjoyment" (Curties, *Monk of Udolpho* 2: 148). To Dacre's Victoria, Zofloya represents means by which "every barrier to the gratification of her wishes would ultimately be destroyed" (*Zofloya* 2: 115). Montorio loves "to enter on the very confines of intellect" (Maturin, *Montorio* 1: 11). Frankenstein sees life and death as "ideal bounds, which I should first break through" (Shelley 314).

Incest, that typical Gothic obsession, blurs the distinctions between two kinds of love. In *The Monk,* Antonia responds instinctively to Ambrosio with sisterly affection, and sisterly affection alone. Ambrosio has a similar instinctive response to her, but his brotherly love soon begins to shade over into the most brutal lust. For him these feelings seem to be on a continuum, without clear demarcations between them. As Miyoshi says, "The incestuous relation, in dissolving the usual familial as well as extrafamilial bonds between individuals, finally dissolves the identifying masks distinguishing one individual from another." The result is a "double perspective" in which "clear borderlines of things shift and blur. Not only the familial identities of persons, which shift from daughter to mistress, or son to lover, in relation to the incestuous parent, but the moral categories derived from the family structure begin to transfuse—love into lust, kindness into cruelty" (11–12).

"Clear borderlines of things shift and blur." In the world of Gothic romance, the physical and metaphorical boundaries that one ordinarily depends on prove unstable, elusive, ineffective, nonexistent. A secret panel opens in the solid wall; the bed curtains move; a door gives way; the dead come to life; portraits leave their frames; a brother murders his sister; events that should have an end seem endless. At the same time, other boundaries appear unexpectedly. A door slams shut behind the timid explorer; the path of escape ends abruptly at a locked gate (Radcliffe, *The Italian* 138); the victim in flight comes to the edge of a precipice (Dacre, *Zofloya* 3: 101).

Two fears dominate this Gothic world, the fear of terrible separateness and the fear of unity with some terrible Other.[35] They are embodied in two classic formulas of the ghost story: the heroine's terrifying discovery that she is all alone and her subsequent discovery that—horror of horrors!—she is *not* alone. Although much Gothic fiction exploits those fears on a relatively simple level, a number of nineteenth-century British and American writers used the same conventions to explore a metaphysical version of the same theme. Transferred to a psychological, religious, and epistemological context, the terrors of unity and separateness revolve around a question central to Romanticism. What distinguishes the "me" from the "not-me"?[36] Where, if they exist at all, are the boundaries of the self?

From this perspective on Gothic romance, both the Gothic "monomyth" and the "coherence of Gothic conventions" can be seen to involve what Melville called the "problem of the possible reconcilement of this world with our own souls." Because the question of the distinction between the me and the not-me is central to light as well as "dark" Romanticism, the definition of Gothicism as fundamentally concerned with the boundaries of the self provides another way of looking at the connection between the Gothic tradition and the Romantic tradition. And because the dividing line between the world and the individual soul has had, from the inception of the Gothic craze, a special relevance to the psychology and social condition of women, this interpretation of the "deep structures" of Gothicism provides a new explanation of the appeal the genre has always had for women readers and writers.

III

This study is presented in two sections. Part I examines the way that Gothic romance—and a group of nineteenth-century works in the Gothic tradition—explore four issues related to the problem of the boundaries of the self: self-defense, knowledge, repetition, and transcendence. From the beginning, many Gothicists exploited a version of the fears of unity and separateness that centers almost exclusively on issues of physical safety. In sentimental Gothic romance, for example, anxieties about boundaries usually originate in the fear of physical violation. Chapter 1 begins by examining the subject of the self and its boundaries in such works, focusing on the theme of "conscious worth" as a heroine's defense against Gothic villainy. It ends with a discussion of how Charles Brockden Brown and Henry James used Gothic conventions to explore some of the more ambiguous psychological and moral dimensions of self-defense.

Chapter 2 turns to the epistemological perspective of Gothic romance, from which the boundaries of the self can be seen to pertain to the division, or lack of division, between the perceiving subject and the object perceived. Because *not knowing* is the primary source of Gothic terror, the essential activity of the Gothic protagonist is interpretation. The relations among reason, faith, and imagination are a crucial focus of Radcliffe's work in particular. The chapter accordingly examines knowledge as a Gothic theme in "Radcliffe-Romance" and then, by way of Maturin and Mary Shelley, considers how Melville used the Gothic to explore the mystery of knowledge itself.

One of the problems of knowledge that Gothicists investigate is the dilemma of the self unable to perceive anything but its own reflection. Reflection is one of many forms of repetition in Gothic romance; indeed, repetition is so central an aspect of the genre that it may be considered one of its major conventions.[37] Chapter 3 explores Hawthorne's theme of "deadly iteration" as the key to his Gothic vision of the boundaries of the self: a double vision in which the reflections of the "Haunted Mind" take on the aspect of both claustrophobic isolation and transcendent unity. The psychological, moral, and epistemological context of that examination places Hawthorne in what Ralph Waldo Emerson called "the party of memory"—that version of "dark" or "negative"[38] romanticism opposed to Emerson's own "party of hope." The issue of the self and its boundaries is a major interface between these two parties: it represents the point at which optimistic Romanticism is most often on the edge of despair and pessimistic Romanticism on the verge of transcendence. Chapter 4 investigates this interface with special reference to the question of how Gothic romancers—and Emily Brontë in her use of the Gothic tradition—view the possibilities of transcendent "egress" from the self.

Part II addresses more specifically the question of the Gothic as a women's genre, explaining that phenomenon in terms of the centrality of boundaries of the self to women Gothicists' presentation of their central issues: self-defense, knowledge, repetition, and transcendence. From the time Radcliffe made popular the proudly silent heroine who knows herself innocent but will not defend herself verbally, those central issues became linked in women's Gothic to a persistent, though often merely implicit, concern: the problem of making oneself known to others through language. In *Villette*—perhaps the fullest exploitation in the nineteenth-century novel of the tools Gothic romance provided for exploring the moral, social, psychological, and epistemological dilemmas of women— Charlotte Brontë makes this problem of "saying 'I' " her explicit focus both formally and thematically. Lucy Snowe's difficulties in defending herself, knowing and being known, avoiding entrapment in her own version of deadly iteration, and achieving transcendence all are related to it. By setting the problem of self-assertion so clearly in the foreground of Lucy's Gothic adventure, Charlotte Brontë creates an audacious revisioning and demystifying of women's Gothic. As a consequence, her novel, more fully than any other in the tradition, illuminates the reasons why women writers before and after her have so often chosen to say "I" in the form of Gothic romance.

That men's and women's Gothic shares many common concerns—most notably an obsession with the problem of the boundaries of the self—is one of the conclusions of this study and will be obvious in my analyses of the Gothic as Maturin, Melville, James, and Hawthorne used it. That not all women writers take the same approach to this crucial issue for women is equally obvious, as is the fact that some of them, like Mary Shelley and Emily Brontë, choose to view it through a male, rather than a female, protagonist. But what becomes evident in the analyses of male and female Gothicists writing about both women and men and the boundaries of the self is that the problem of the boundaries of the self was a crucial issue for women in some special ways—ways that sometimes manifest themselves even in a woman's portrayal of a male protagonist and that sometimes do not manifest themselves fully even in the most sensitive Gothic portrayals, by male writers, of that issue as it applies to women.

The ways in which the feminist orientation of this study informs its interpretation of the boundaries of the self as a Gothic theme can be illustrated by a comparison of my "spatial model" of the Gothic with the one it most closely resembles, that of Sedgwick.[39] Although in Sedgwick's model the individual "units" are not always equivalent to "the fictional 'selves' in the novels," when a fictional self is a subject of the conventions she discusses, her conception of the way it is "spatialized" is akin to my description of the self and its boundaries as Gothic romance presents them:

It is the position of the self to be massively blocked off from something to which it ought normally to have access. . . . Typically . . . there is both something going on inside the isolation (the present, the continuous consciousness, the dream, the sensation itself) and something intensely relevant going on impossibly out of reach. While the three main elements (what's inside, what's outside, and what separates them) take on the most various guises, the terms of the relationship are immutable. The self and whatever it is that is outside have a proper, natural, necessary connection to each other, but one that the self is suddenly incapable of making. The inside life and the outside life have to continue separately, becoming counterparts rather than partners, the relationship between them one of parallels and correspondences rather than communication. This, though it may happen in an instant, is a fundamental reorganization, creating a doubleness where singleness should be. And the lengths there are to go to reintegrate the sundered elements— finally, the impossibility of restoring them to their original oneness—are the most characteristic energies of the Gothic novel. (Sedgwick, *Coherence* 13)

Sedgwick's spatial model is very close to that on which my own read- ing of the Gothic is based, with the important difference that whereas her model is focused on "the sudden, mysterious, seemingly arbitrary, but massive inaccessibility of those things that should normally be most ac- cessible" (14), mine includes also the image of the division between self and Other as a focus of the anxiety to make oneself inaccessible to the outside world. This other side of the image of the self "massively blocked off" from what is beyond it is particularly important, as one of the chief subjects of the Gothic is the vulnerability of women to intrusions from an outside world to which, in another sense, they have frustratingly little access. Often there is an important inequality of meaning in which the same barrier represents something quite different for the woman on one side of it and the man, whether hero or villain, on the other side. The fact that the barrier does not mean the same thing for the man and the woman reflects the inequality between their respective control over those boundaries, and the inequality of their access—physical, social, psycho- logical, intellectual—to each other.

In addition, I regard even the image of the self "massively blocked off" from a different perspective. In Sedgwick's interpretation, "the bar- rier between the self and what should belong to it can be caused by anything and nothing" (14), and the "seemingly arbitrary" nature of the cause is emphasized by the fact that what the self is blocked from are the very "things that should normally be most accessible." My interpretation assigns a different emphasis and meaning to the terms "seemingly" and "should normally." Sedgwick describes the "something" from which the self may be blocked: "This something can be its own past, the details of its family history; it can be the free air, when the self has been literally buried alive; it can be a lover; it can be just all the circumambient life, when the self is pinned in a death-like sleep" (13). Any reader of the Gothic will appreciate the aptness of these images, yet the substitution of the pronoun *she* for *it,* in another list, yields quite a different result: This something could be her own mother *(Sicilian Romance),* the details of her own identity *(Romance of the Forest)*, a knowledge of the larger world outside the limited sphere to which she has been assigned from birth (Lee, *The Recess*), a lover from whom decorum cuts her off *(The Italian)*, her own anger.

All these are things to which the self should indeed normally have access, and any barrier cutting the self off from them might well seem arbitrary. On the other hand, in women's experience, as much feminist theory since the time of Mary Wollstonecraft has suggested, such things are what women are normally cut off from, even though they "ought" to have access to them as a matter of course. The "interfacing surfaces" to which Gothic anxiety is attached represent the social norms that cut women off from their history, the larger world, even from what Mary Daly would call their "authentic sel[ves]" (4). The female protagonists of Gothic romance do experience these barriers as "seemingly arbitrary," but it is suggestive that the particular quality of the arbitrariness consists in the injustice of their sudden, perverse appearances in a world in which the heroine would otherwise be quite content. The strong affect associated with these barriers—a piercing sense of injustice—points to the fact that their apparent arbitrariness masks a set of causes too dangerous for Gothicists to contemplate directly. In the plot the barriers are experienced as arbitrary, but what they represent in reality is a set of boundaries that have an all-too-specific origin in the social and economic institutions of patriarchy and their psychological consequences for women. It is indeed strange to find oneself suddenly and arbitrarily separated from a lover by a convent wall, as Ellena does in *The Italian,* but it is also normal for a woman to be bounded, in her relations with a suitor, by the kinds of decorum the convent often represents. It is unsettling to discover, as the girls do at the beginning of *The Recess,* that from birth one has apparently been assigned to struggle for self-realization in an artificially enclosed world completely set apart from the larger events in society. But women's autobiographies are full of accounts of precisely that realization. The sudden whisking away of Emily St. Aubert to Udolpho—and her seclusion there in a room with one door she has no way of keeping locked— is indeed sudden, surprising, and absurdly out of the ordinary. But what it stands for is the most ordinary—and absurd— fact of women's lives: their vulnerability; their unequal control, in comparison with men, over what keeps them from the world and what keeps the world from them. As Holland and Sherman say, "[T]he gothic novel provides a polarizing of inside and outside with which an adult woman, particularly in a sexist society, might symbolize a common psychosocial experience: an invaded life within her mind, her body, her home, bounded by a social structure that marks off economic and political life as 'outside' " (288).

In women's Gothic, what Sedgwick calls the "proper, natural, necessary connection" between the self and what it is blocked from is not "one that the self is *suddenly* incapable of making," (italics added); it is, on the contrary, a connection that women are not ordinarily able to make, because of the social forces and the psychological consequences of women's experiences of those forces that define women's relation to the world beyond them. The suddenness with which these barriers appear in the Gothic reflects a sense of the meaninglessness and arbitrariness of the normal barriers for which they are a disguised representation. Thus the "fundamental reorganization" at the heart of the Gothic plot—that instantaneous transformation of unity to separateness of which Sedgwick speaks—represents no re-organization at all; it stands simply for the organization of society as women experience it. In the Gothicists' picture of that organization, the normal is masked as abnormal—a disguise that points out the injustice, abnormality, and arbitrariness of women's ordinary experiences. Nor does "the barrier of unspeakableness" (20) involve, in its special application to heroines rather than heroes, an arbitrary or inexplicable blocking. It is an image of women's problem saying "I" in a world where, confined to their "proper sphere," they have been assigned to correspondence rather than communion, forced to be counterparts rather than partners.

The Gothic, as Wilt says, "treats of the separated one" (19), but most often this is true not in its study of "the self-separated one, the hero/villain" (19) or "guilt-haunted wanderer" (Nelson 237), as striking as the individual figures of Ambrosio, Melmoth, or Frankenstein may be. The isolato at the heart of the Gothic is not one of those singular individualists, but the many Emilys, Emilias, Matildas, and Julias who stand, in their very interchangeability, for Woman—the true "separated one" at the heart of a social order whose peculiar disorder it is to make *her* the fearful Other.

1

Self-Defense in the Gothic Tradition: Radcliffe, Brockden Brown, Henry James

Perils . . . in the ambush of midnight solitude . . . perils from even worse forms of darkness shrouded within the recesses of blind human hearts . . .

DE QUINCEY

I

". . . and when, with fainting spirits, you attempt to fasten your door, you discover, with increased alarm, that it has no lock" (Austen, *Northanger Abbey* 128). With these words Henry Tilney evokes the classic scenario of Gothic terror. The heroine trembles at a door as footsteps approach. The door is locked and she cannot open it; or it is unlocked and she cannot fasten it; or it is fastened with a lock that is rusty and insecure; or she fastens it only to hear the ominous creak of yet another door.[1] On the simplest level of plot, this nightmarish scene describes the most fundamental anxiety about boundaries of the self: fear of physical violation. *The Mysteries of Udolpho* provides some classic examples of the terror evoked in such scenes. In the first one, Emily St. Aubert is alone in a chamber with two doors, one leading to a corridor and the other to a private staircase. Radcliffe pictures the heroine late at night, alarmed by noises first at one door and then at the other, torn between her desire to escape and her fear of venturing out in either direction. At the corridor door she hears breathing; at the other she hears footsteps. Between them she trembles in indecision until she and the reader are exhausted with anxiety.

In the evening, Emily had passed some melancholy hours with Madame Montoni, and was retiring to rest, when she was alarmed by a strange and loud knocking at her chamber door, and then a heavy weight fell against it, that almost burst it open. She called to know who was there, and receiving no answer, repeated the call; but a chilling silence followed. It occurred to her—for, at this moment, she could not reason on the probability of circumstances—that some one of the strangers, lately arrived at the castle, had discovered her apartment, and was come with such intent, as their looks rendered too possible—to rob, perhaps to murder, her. The moment she admitted this possibility, terror supplied the place of conviction, and a kind of instinctive remembrance of her remote situation from the family heightened it to a degree, that almost overcame her senses. She looked at the door, which led to the staircase, expecting to see it open, and listening, in fearful silence, for a return of the noise, till she began to think it had proceeded from this door, and a wish of escaping through the opposite one rushed upon her mind. She went to the gallery door, and then, fearing to open it, lest some person might be silently lurking for her without, she stopped, but with her eyes fixed in expectation upon the opposite door of the stair-case. As thus she stood, she heard a faint breathing near her and became convinced, that some person was on the other side of the door, which was already locked. She sought for other fastening, but there was none.

While she yet listened, the breathing was distinctly heard, and her terror was not soothed, when, looking round her wide and lonely chamber, she again considered her remote situation. As she stood hesitating whether to call for assistance, the continuance of the stillness surprised her; and her spirits would have revived, had she not continued to hear the faint breathing, that convinced her, the person, whoever it was, had not quitted the door.

At length, worn out with anxiety, she determined to call loudly for assistance from her casement, and was advancing to it, when, whether the terror of her mind gave her ideal sounds, or that real ones did come, she thought footsteps were ascending the private stair-case; and, expecting to see its door unclose, she forgot all other cause of alarm, and retreated towards the corridor. (299–300)

Radcliffe's long-windedness—or, rather, her ability to remain breathless for surprisingly long stretches of narrative—makes such scenes difficult to read out of context. However, it also renders them impossible to paraphrase, and they are so central to her art that one more such scene is worth quoting in Radcliffe's own words. This one takes place earlier in the same room:

A return of the noise again disturbed her; it seemed to come from that part of the room, which communicated with the private staircase, and she instantly remembered the odd circumstance of the door having been fastened, during the preceding night, by some unknown hand. Her late alarming suspicion, concerning its communication, also occurred to her. Her heart became faint with terror. Half raising herself from the bed, and gently drawing aside the curtain, she looked toward the door of the stair-case, but the lamp, that burnt on the hearth, spread so feeble a light through the appartment, that the remote parts of it were lost in shadow. The noise, however, which, she was convinced, came from the door, continued. It seemed like that made by the undrawing of rusty bolts, and often ceased, and was then renewed more gently, as if the hand, that occasioned it, was restrained by a fear of discovery. While Emily kept her eyes fixed on the spot, she saw the door move, and then slowly open, and perceived something enter the room, but the extreme duskiness prevented her from distinguishing what it was. Almost fainting with terror, she had yet sufficient command over herself, to check the shriek, that was escaping from her lips, and, letting the curtain drop from her hand, continued to observe in silence the motions of the mysterious form she saw. It seemed to glide along the remote obscurity of the apartment. . . . but then, advancing slowly towards the bed, stood silently at the feet, where the curtains, being a little open, allowed her still to see it. . . .

Having continued there a moment, the form retreated . . . and then again advanced. . . . and, springing toward the bed, Emily discovered—Count Morano!

She gazed at him for a moment in speechless affright, while he, throwing himself on his knee at the bed-side, besought her to fear nothing, and, having thrown down his sword, would have taken her hand, when the faculties, that terror had suspended, suddenly returned, and she sprung from the bed, in the dress, which surely a kind of prophetic apprehension had prevented her, on this night, from throwing aside. (260–61)

The source of these scenes is not far to seek. Radcliffe may have taken her underground passageways from Walpole and her deserted suite from Reeve (Tompkins 230, 261), but her most brilliant contribution to Gothic romance was the idea of combining such stage properties with what she had learned from Richardson. From him she got the atmosphere of *Clarissa*—the claustrophobic sense of Otherness, pressing in on the solitary individual who tries, despite it, to keep a distinct selfhood intact. Lovelace traps Clarissa in a world exclusively expressive of his own ego, peopled only by his creatures, who manifest not their personalities but his, by playing the parts he assigns them.[2] The Castle of Udolpho—solitary, powerful, attractive, ruined—expresses Montoni's personality in a similar way. His will impinges on Emily in the very atmosphere of the castle, just as everything around Clarissa reflects Lovelace's one purpose.

The Gothic villain always has control of the physical barriers between himself and the woman he pursues. The castle is his; the key is his; the strength is his; he knows the secret door. Schedoni steals into Ellena's bedroom while she sleeps (Radcliffe, *The Italian*); Manfroné invades Rosalina's room through a sliding panel she knows nothing about (Mary-Anne Radcliffe, *Manfroné* 3–7). Monimia fastens her door "as well as I am able" (Smith, *Old Manor House* 375); Emily St. Aubert pushes against hers all the furniture she can move (*Mysteries of Udolpho* 320). None of these heroines will be safe if she has nothing more to depend on. As Radcliffe delicately hints through Emily's anxiety about her bedroom doors and as Richardson illustrates more bluntly, the best of heroines ultimately has no physical power against a determined villain. But she does, in the tradition Richardson initiated, have another kind of power. Wealth, social position, brute strength—all advantages of the typical Gothic villain—crumble before this, the maiden's one capacity for self-defense. Richardson devoted chapters to it; his successors celebrated it in scenes like the one in which Adeline wards off the Marquis de Montalt:

> He threw his arm around her, and would have pressed her toward him; but she liberated herself from his embrace, and with a look, on which was impressed the firm dignity of virtue, yet touched with sorrow, she awed him to forbearance. Conscious of a superiority, which he was ashamed to acknowledge, and endeavouring to despise the influence which he could not resist, he stood for a moment the slave of virtue, though the votary of vice. (Radcliffe, *Romance of the Forest* 2: 116)[3]

Clarissa devotes all of her energies to the quality that cows the villain in such scenes, the "dignity of virtue" or, as it is also called, "conscious innocence" or "conscious worth." On a stage where everyone else speaks Lovelace's lines, Clarissa must fight just to speak with her own voice and not his. She maintains her separateness through a vigilant consciousness of her worth and his moral inferiority—a consciousness so strong that Lovelace himself quails, again and again, before a sense of her inviolable otherness. In the last emergency the heroine's only defense is to make the villain perceive so vividly the spiritual barrier between him and her that he will be abashed into maintaining a physical distance as well.

To be inviolably and consciously Other than her pursuer is a strenuous task for the heroine, and to believe in the barrier thus created is sometimes an even more strenuous task for the reader. No one after Richardson dared to leave the heroine alone so often or so long with a villain, her conscious worth, and no help on its way to the rescue. His successors the sentimental Gothicists devote some theoretical praise to conscious worth, in passages whose motto might well be taken from Milton: " 'Tis chastity, my brother, chastity: / She that has that, is clad in complete steel . . ." (*Comus* ll. 420–21).[4] But Monimia's letter to Orlando is more expressive of the heroine's practical situation: "I have fastened the door as well as I am able, and would secure that below if I knew how: but it is not possible for me to do it myself . . ." (Smith, *Old Manor House* 375). In sentimental Gothic fiction, conscious worth protects the heroine until something or someone intervenes, and just in the nick of time.

These timely interventions show a sad decline from the patient art of Richardson, who boldly sent to Clarissa's aid no hero, but only poor humbled Belford, and long after the crucial moment was past. Richardson, however, genuinely believed Clarissa's spiritual power superior even to Lovelace's physical power, as he set out so laboriously to prove in the last volumes. This is the point of Clarissa's scrupulous meditations on her possible complicity in the rape. It is crucial for her to determine, and for Richardson to establish, that the *spiritual* barrier between her and Lovelace is still intact. In other words, Clarissa must prove for herself and the reader that she did not in her own mind first open the door to Lovelace.

In his analyses of the issue, Richardson comes close to suggesting that Clarissa did open the door, and modern readers are often quick to agree.[5] But to such interpretations it is often added that here Richardson wrote a better book than he knew, or expressed an idea he was not conscious of expressing, or suggested an interpretation of Clarissa more profound than his own. This caveat is important, because Richardson's own opinion is clearly that Lovelace has, paradoxically, been defeated despite his success. Hence the villain's dissatisfaction with his supposed victory: his victim was unconscious, but it was her *conscious* virtue he sought to subdue. At the end, Lovelace fades away as a physical power; Clarissa's spiritual power is apotheosized. She has defended the barriers between them, and she has won.

Perhaps Richardson's Gothic successors were not dedicated to so complicated a gospel, or perhaps he had exhausted the only means available for illustrating it through plot. At any rate, they contented themselves with doing obeisance to the heroine's spiritual power while defending her without ultimate recourse to it. Emily departs in triumph from an encounter with Montoni, filled with "sacred pride," resolved to endure his oppression heroically, and rejoicing in her superiority (*Mysteries of Udol-*

pho 381–82). But a few coincidences and the help of Ludovico remove her from Montoni's power. Decked out in the whole armor of God, Radcliffe's heroines are hurried off the battlefield. Who would have won?

The sentimental Gothicists avoid a direct answer, and the result is a curious double message. Rejoice, young ladies—you are tremendously powerful, but watch out—you are defenseless. This double message comes through most clearly in examples like those just cited, when conscious worth provides direct, physical, and extremely temporary protection from the villain. But it comes through, as well, in other variations on self-defense. In some passages, for example, as in a key confrontation between Emily and Montoni, conscious worth is described in physical metaphors but actually operates on a spiritual plane of which the villain may not even be aware. Thus Montoni cannot correctly interpret Emily's proud silence, born of "the consciousness of having deserved praise, instead of censure": "[H]e was a stranger to the luxury of conscious worth, and therefore, did not foresee the energy of that sentiment, which now repelled his satire" (*Mysteries of Udolpho* 270). Montoni's satire is "repelled" by "conscious worth"; however, since he is in certain ways not even capable of realizing that an act of self-defense is taking place, the value of the act derives not from its effect but from the meaning the heroine gives it in her own mind. In her mind she may be powerful, but Montoni's essential apprehension of her relative weakness does not change.

In other passages the defense provided by conscious worth is an even more psychological one, merely enabling the heroine to maintain that "patient fortitude" which, as Tompkins points out, is the favorite virtue of female authors in this period (270). Such is the resistance Ellena di Rosalba offers the wicked abbess in *The Italian,* her "conscious innocence" enabling her to maintain "an air of dignity" in the face of oppression (85). In still other passages, conscious worth defends the heroine simply by constituting her claim on the protection of Providence, which will intervene to rescue her in the end. The idea that the powers of darkness cannot ultimately harm the good is central to the sentimental Gothic tradition, whose first article of faith is expressed at the end of *A Sicilian Romance:* "[T]hose who do only THAT WHICH IS RIGHT, endure nothing in misfortune but a trial of their virtue, and from trials well endured, derive the surest claim to the protection of Heaven" (2: 192).

Indeed, behind all the versions of conscious worth as self-defense, including even those in which it has an actual physical efficacy, is the faith that God ultimately looks after his own. The Duke of Orleans tells Cicely of Raby that her virtue for a while awed him into maintaining his distance, after which time "providence was your guard, miraculously were you preserved" (Musgrave, *Cicely of Raby* 3: 4, 66, 65). Emily's conscious worth may "repel" Montoni's satire, but Providence finally intervenes to repel Montoni himself.

Thus there is always a central ambiguity implicit in Gothic portrayals of women engaged in the act of self-defense—engaged, that is, in an act by definition incompatible with the realities of their physical and social situations. Charles Brockden Brown and Henry James examined some important aspects of this ambiguity in their uses of the Gothic tradition.

II

Brockden Brown's fiction embodies simultaneously several different responses to Gothicism, which was in its period of greatest popularity during his career as a novelist. The preface to *Edgar Huntly* condemns "Gothic castles and chimeras" as a means of producing terror (29), but that terror was a means of interesting the reader is something the author takes for granted. Whole scenes from *Wieland* could have come straight from the pages of Radcliffe, whom Brown certainly admired,[6] and the prose of his novels is full of the rhetoric of Gothic suspense: "Fear and wonder rendered him powerless. An occurrence like this, in a place assigned to devotion, was adapted to intimidate the stoutest heart. His wandering thoughts were recalled by the groans of one near him" (*Wieland* 19). "She was tortured with impatience, and uncertainty. . . . An half hour passed away in this state of suspense" (*Wieland* 18). "The door below creaked on its hinges. . . . Footsteps entered, traversed the entry, and began to mount the stairs" (*Wieland* 110).

On the one hand, Brown seems to have played the Gothic vogue for all it was worth,[7] even tossing into his plots some random Gothic ingredients for good measure: strange resemblances between characters, for example, or the fact that Stephen Dudley stole his wife from a convent (*Ormond* 193). On the other hand, like his mentor Godwin, who adapted a popular form to his own ends, Brown occasionally showed a striking disrespect for the romance reader's expectations. He hides Carwin in the closet but allows the heroine boldly to go in and fetch him out, then deprives him of the only sensibly villainous motive for having been there in the first place. He allows his heroine Constantia to stab her persecutor and then, having omitted a hero, sends a woman to the rescue. Unlike Richardson's virtuous Clarissa, whose passive resistance to a cruel brother

never violates womanly decorum, Brown's Clara actually considers killing her brother in self-defense. Furthermore, this heroine, in a manner
inconceivable of the proudly virtuous Ellena, Emily, Emmeline, or Monimia, bursts out in a fit of morbid introspection, ". . . I acknowledge
that my guilt surpasses that of all mankind . . ." (*Wieland* 249).

Brown adopted the sentimental Gothicists' interest in conscious worth
as he adopted much else that was Gothic, changing its context and its
meaning. As a feminist, he was interested in the issue of self-defense in
the context of a threatened woman's response to her oppressor; he was
also interested in self-defense in a broad moral and political context that
included the problem of self-protection against tyranny and injustice. Clara
Wieland declares with bold rationalism that women should kill their attackers, not themselves. Brown then puts the theory to the ultimate test
by making the attacker her brother, and Clara recoils in horror from
her clearheaded resolution. Constantia presents another variation on the
theme. Shocked earlier by Martinette's unwomanly participation in the
violence of the French Revolution, she ends by killing Ormond in a
"momentary frenzy," having fully intended to use the knife on herself
instead.

Brown, like Jane Austen, was clearly dissatisfied with the manner in
which the Gothic heroine was supposed to behave. But he was ambivalent about the alternatives. His heroines, although models of virtue and
endowed with names to prove it, do not therefore fortify themselves with
a consciousness of their superiority and stare the villain down. Far from
maintaining a kind of spiritual class barrier between themselves and their
attackers, they blur the moral distinctions between them by attacking, or
planning to attack, in return. By killing for her liberty, Constantia com-
mits an apparently necessary act that has nonetheless been discussed earlier as a morally equivocal one. She thereby negates part of the distinction between herself and the morally equivocal characters Martinette (whom
she also resembles physically) and Ormond. Perhaps in her "momentary
frenzy" she is even giving in to one of the arguments Ormond himself
made against suicide in self-defense: "Poor Constantia! . . . To escape
this injury . . . thou wilt . . . put an end to thy activity in virtue's
cause; rob thy friend of her solace, the world of thy beneficence, thyself
of being and pleasure?" (234–35). In a sense, although not the sense
Ormond intended, Constantia finally accepts his argument that such a
suicide would be unreasonable.

It is worth recalling Brown's disapproval of Clarissa, who he said "died a victim to errors, scarcely less opprobrious and pernicious than those of her tyrants and oppressors" ("Walstein's School" 156). Not surprisingly, conscious virtue as a technique of self-defense makes its least impressive showing in Gothic or Gothic-influenced works that lean away from a conservative ethos. In Radcliffe, the innocent display their conscious worth to show their colors, as it were, and their ally Providence does the rest. In some highly improbable scenes, for example, the hero of *The Italian* uses the tactics of conscious innocence against the Inquisition, thereby marking time until, with a little prompting from the author, evil finally recoils upon itself and he is rescued. In her first book, Radcliffe allowed the hero to kill his enemy, but as her methods became more subtle, her good characters became more passive. Ellena and Vivaldi steel themselves to endure tyranny—to resist it mentally, to keep it from making inroads on their moral nature—not to fight it. *The Mysteries of Udolpho* concluded with the lesson that those who are good and "supported by patience" win in the end (692). Because direct action against injustice is not necessary in Radcliffe's philosophy or her plots, the boundaries between good and evil characters are neatly preserved. The villains destroy themselves or each other, and the possibility of the good sullying their hands in defense of goodness never seriously arises.

Brown, like his contemporary Godwin and his successor Melville, is more interested in conflicts that blur the lines between contenders. Can Caleb Williams attack his attacker without becoming as guilty as he? Can the oppressed defend themselves without becoming the oppressors? Can goodness strike a blow against evil without destroying the distinctions that give the blow its meaning?

"As the absence of discriminated feeling and character was necessary to the completeness of the effect Mrs. Radcliffe sought to produce," said her first biographer, "so she was rather assisted by manners peculiarly straight-laced and timorous. . . . A moral paradox could not co-exist with a haunted tower in the mind of her readers " (Talfourd 120). Thus a secure sense of identity always underlies a secure consciousness of worth in Radcliffe's romances. The one thing that never surprises the heroine is herself.[8] But in *Wieland* and *Ormond* the very process of self-defense redefines the self that is at stake. Emily and Adeline are shocked to find someone unexpected in their bedchambers. Clara and Constantia are shocked to find someone unexpected in themselves. "I hope," says Sophia after the catastrophe of *Ormond,* "that nothing has happened to load you with guilt or with shame."

"Alas! I know not," Constantia replies. "My deed was scarcely the fruit of intention" (240). Like Clara Wieland, another paragon of rationalism, she has found that "ideas exist in our minds that can be accounted for by no established laws" (*Wieland* 99). As Emily Dickinson said,

> Ourself behind ourself, concealed—
> Should startle most—
> Assassin hid in our Apartment
> Be Horror's least.

III

In his works most influenced by Gothicism, Charles Brockden Brown wrote about self-defense, but not about conscious worth as a means to that end. It was Henry James who gave American literature its richest exploration of conscious virtue as a defense against Gothic villainy. *The American* and *The Portrait of a Lady* are meditations on the previously unexploited potential of that theme. Both novels raise the issue by means of a catastrophe undreamt of in Radcliffe's philosophy but perhaps prepared for by Richardson's. What would happen, James asks, if the hero renounced his opportunity to rescue the victim or the victim renounced her opportunity to escape? Might not the Gothic villain still be defeated in some way? Might not the renunciation itself be a victory for conscious worth?

The American contains quite a collection of Gothic conventions: a gloomy old house, decayed aristocratic villains, a mysterious crime, ruins, imprisonment in a convent, a manuscript revealing its author's murder, an atmosphere of suspense. On the surface, these conventions are no better than they should be. But one anomaly makes them new. The imprisoned heroine is disposed of in none of the usual ways. No crazed monk kills her to complete the tragedy;[9] she is not rescued from the convent at the last minute;[10] the villains do not solve her problems by doing away with themselves and/or one another;[11] no accomplice leads her through an underground labyrinth to freedom.[12] The hero could rescue her by using blackmail and thus forfeiting the goodness that makes him the hero in the first place; so he does not. Claire could escape by rebelling against her wicked relatives, but like the ancestor to whom she presumably owes her name, she regards filial obedience as a categorical imperative. Indeed, her voluntary immurement might have shamed even Ellena di Rosalba, who merely considered refusing an indecorous rescue from a convent (*The Italian* 122–23).

It could be argued that Claire and her suitor win anyway, by refusing to compromise their virtue. They transgress none of their principles in the struggle with those who have transgressed all of them, and thus maintain the boundary between themselves and what is evil. The walls of Claire's convent are a symbol of those boundaries; they ensure a safe separation from the evil in her family as well as protection against the internal evil that might tempt her, against her conscience, to a union with Christopher Newman. By resisting the temptation to do evil in order to fight evil, Claire and Newman defend themselves against it, even though those who are themselves evil seem outwardly to triumph.

In many ways the novel invites such an interpretation; on the other hand, James is never so unsubtle a moralist or even so unsubtle a storyteller. Encrusted as it is with the easily definable clichés of old romance, the plot of *The American* still somehow slips through one's fingers, recalling William James's comment that among the conventions his brother defied in another of his novels was the convention of telling the story.[13] Did Claire choose the convent, or did her relatives force her into it? Was she in love with Newman? Did she regard immurement in a convent with the same loathing as did her Protestant lover, or the Protestant readers of Gothic romance? Were the relatives really wicked, and is Newman really a hero?[14] The image of Christopher, belated discoverer of the Old World and its fabulous wealth, staring in bewilderment at the convent walls, has after all its comic side. The New World millionaire is baffled of his purchase by shockingly old-fashioned villainy and incomprehensibly Catholic piety—together the quintessence of the Europe from which he will always be shut out. Paradoxically, its very inaccessibility affirms his own worth, but even that may be a dubious prize—the weapon his enemies relied on for his defeat.

James suggests that perhaps Claire either chose or did not resist the convent in order to protect herself against an inclination of her own to which she felt it would be wrong to yield. The focus, however, is not on the victim but on her potential rescuer, Newman. *The Portrait of a Lady* makes richer the ambiguities surrounding the Gothic theme of conscious worth, by focusing on a heroine's renunciation of escape rather than the hero's renunciation of a plan to rescue her and by developing more fully the suggestion in the earlier work that defense of oneself may rest ironically on a defense against oneself.

In *The Portrait of a Lady* James introduces Gothic conventions more subtly than in *The American;* they belong, for the most part, to the metaphorical rather than the physical level of action.[15] For that reason they are also in the eye of the beholder, recalling Donatello's realization, after the fall, that his own castle is a dismal one (Hawthorne, *Marble Faun* 716). Unlike other heroines, Isabel does not see a ghost the first night she sleeps in a strange house, but only at the end of the novel. Italy is filled with ruins, but Isabel is not conscious of them as *ruined* until her vision has been educated by suffering. Rosier recognized Osmond's palace as "a kind of domestic fortress, which bore a stern old Roman name, which smelt of . . . crime and craft and violence . . ." (336). But the fact that she is imprisoned by a Gothic villain comes to Isabel's consciousness only gradually:

> [W]hen, as the months elapsed, she followed him further and he led her into the mansion of his own habitation, then, then she had seen where she really was. She could live it over again, the incredulous terror with which she had taken the measure of her dwelling. . . . It was the house of darkness, the house of dumbness, the house of suffocation. Osmond's beautiful mind gave it neither light nor air; Osmond's beautiful mind, indeed, seemed to peer down from a small high window and mock at her. (395–96)

This metaphor of Osmond's personality as a suffocating mansion turned prison reveals James's perception of the symbolic content latent in much Gothic romance. Isabel is surrounded by an alien personality who crushes in upon her, mocks her, suffocates her, and is all the while trying to erase the boundaries between her and him, to remake her in his image.

In the long series of "lurid flashes" (515) at the climax of the novel, Isabel wakes to the Gothic horrors that have so long surrounded her. She sees herself in a dark prison with Osmond as jailer; she sees that Rome is filled with ruins; she sees the "ghost" of Gardencourt. Heiress of an Emersonian faith in self-reliance, Isabel has never doubted her reality as a distinct individual. Now she finds that her very feelings have not been her own; the boundaries of her self were violated before she recognized a threat. "What have you to do with me?" she asks Osmond's accomplice Madame Merle, who answers, "Everything!" (477).

Isabel discovers too late the assassin hid in her apartment, but that is not the worst horror. "Ourself behind ourself, concealed—Should startle most—." Caspar Goodwood's kiss, "like a flash of lightning," provides that final revelation. The additions James made in the New York edition at this point make clearer that the "lightning" illuminates Isabel's own

hitherto-unacknowledged sexuality. Discovering the force of Caspar's offer, she also discovers what she must do: renounce the temptation he
represents. By doing so, she is, like Christopher Newman, resisting the
temptation of yielding to evil in order to fight it. The encounter with
Caspar, presented in such erotic imagery, establishes that Isabel is fully
conscious of what she is rejecting. She runs in terror, not from her own
sexuality, as is sometimes suggested, but from what it might have led her
to do. Her flight therefore reveals her strength by announcing her refusal
to stoop to Osmond's level in order to escape him. She has been shocked
at Osmond's cavalier attitude toward marital infidelity; now she is shocked
that she herself almost yielded to it. Osmond's power has been manifested in his slow transformation of Isabel into someone more and more
like himself. When Isabel refuses what would in her eyes have been an
illicit sexual relationship, she is holding herself back from the center of
Osmond's own life, warding off the insidious encroachment of his personality on hers, evading the last transformation.[16]

Appropriately, the image of Isabel at her final moment of illumination
is the image of a woman with her hand on the latch of a door. Behind
her is the darkness; inside the house she is about to enter is light; she
stands at the threshold. This final portrait recalls other images of doors:
Osmond's sinister comparison of himself to a rusty key turning in the
lock of Isabel's intellect; the grim image of Isabel "framed" in his gilded
doorway, "the picture of a gracious lady" (239, 339). It also recalls a
particularly evocative image from the days of Isabel's earliest acquaintance with Pansy. In that earlier scene, before Isabel's marriage, Pansy
stood in Osmond's doorway looking wistfully out as Isabel took leave of
her. "I am only a little girl," she said, "but I shall always expect you."
Then from the darkness of the house her father had forbidden her to
leave, Pansy watched Isabel go out: "[A]nd the small figure stood in the
high, dark doorway, watching Isabel cross the clear, grey court, and disappear into the brightness beyond the big *portone,* which gave a wider
gleam as it opened." "I have promised papa not to go out of this door,"
Pansy had explained (293–94).

The Gothic novelist always pauses at the threshold of the villain's dim
domain, allowing the heroine and the reader to shudder with sudden,
intuitive horror.[17] In this pause at the *portone* of Osmond's villa, the
reader shudders but the heroine misses her chance. Only from Pansy's
vantage point is the meaning of the threshold clear. It is perhaps this
vantage point that Isabel has in mind in the last scene when she chooses
to return; she did, after all, promise Pansy to come back. The final image

of Isabel thus reverses the earlier one and yet repeats it in one significant detail. Once again the freedom to cross the threshold is hers.

Charles Brockden Brown rejected the easy doctrine of conscious worth as self-defense in order to present on the one hand his feminism and on the other his Calvinistic sense that a true sight of the self one is defending may be the real horror.[18] James's approach is different. He unites the theme of conscious worth with that of self-knowledge, presenting self-discovery as the basis of a new, stronger self-defense. By renouncing rescue, Isabel achieves it, because her renunciation is based on James's version of conscious worth: the virtue of those who are "finely aware and richly responsible." The final scene between Isabel and Caspar belongs to an old Gothic tradition. Terror stricken, a woman flees through the darkness from her pursuer. But this time it is the rescue she flees, and the possibility arises that the woman in flight may at last have the power to defend herself.

In exploiting the potential of the Gothic theme of conscious worth, however, James also exploited its ambiguities. The doubt that the last image of Isabel evokes in the reader's mind is in part the doubt evoked in all those Radcliffean scenes in which the very splendor of the heroine's spiritual power raises the question of its practical efficacy in the real world. It is easy to imagine that a new, stronger Isabel will go back to Rome and, as the Countess Gemini once imagined, draw herself up "the taller spirit of the two" (414). It is more difficult to imagine how. In addition, the question arises of where the ultimate power lies. Did Isabel, after all, have a choice? Or is the final image of her just one more image of a frightened woman at a door that represents her vulnerability?

Isabel has promised Pansy to come back, but she has also implied to Henrietta that she needed an excuse (520–21). As in the case of many a Gothic heroine before her, Isabel's final consciousness of her virtue is wedded to her consciousness of the proprieties. To do, at the crucial moment, what is conventional is an act loaded with significance in a novel in which the conventions of European society have a force like fate. Perhaps the final scene with Caspar represents Isabel's definitive demarcation from Osmond; it could, on the other hand, represent the collapse of her last fortification against the man who is, in his own words, "convention itself" (288). Or perhaps it is just that, like Clarissa's triumph, Isabel's final victory is rooted in her final defeat: her defeat by life or experience or fate or simply, as Godwin would have said, "things as they are."

2

The Mystery of Knowledge:
Frankenstein, Melmoth, Pierre

. . . perils from temptations weaving unseen snares for our footing;
perils from the limitations of our own misleading knowledge.

DE QUINCEY

I

Richardson was undoubtedly the inspiration for the passages cited at the
beginning of the preceding chapter, but Radcliffe added to the formula
she learned from him something special to Gothicism: the fact that in
neither of these scenes does the heroine know who or what threatens her.
In Richardson the heroine and the reader know only too well who it is at
the door—the same person it has been for hundreds of pages and will be
for hundreds more. Radcliffe's heroines hear breathing, see something
move, discern a shape indistinctly; they are not sure. Constantly they
guess, imagine, surmise; and the mental processes they go through in
their uncertainty are under constant surveillance by the omniscient author.
Describing Emily's dilemma between the two doors, for example,
Radcliffe supplies a simultaneous evaluation of the heroine's mental activities. "It occurred to her—for, at this moment, she could not reason
on the probability of circumstances. . . . terror supplied the place of conviction. . . . whether the terror of her mind gave her ideal sounds, or
that real ones did come . . ." (299–300). These comments imply that
Emily is not using her reasoning powers to their full advantage. Falling
prey to that excessive sensibility her father warned against, she has allowed terror to distort her perceptions. In Radcliffe's romances, not knowing
is a source of terror, but terror is also a source of not knowing. The
revelation that the ominous breathing at the corridor door was only An-

43

nette is typical. (This is one of many reminders that Radcliffe herself invented the satirical scenes in which Catherine Morland's imagination runs away with her.) But the fact that we never learn whether there was anyone at the other door is also typical. Someone did come through that door in another scene; maybe, in this case too, Emily's fearful imaginings were right.

Similarly, when Morano steals into Emily's bedroom she misses her chance to discover his identity, because terror has "deprived her of the power of discrimination" (261). Not in possesssion of her reason, Emily cannot even see clearly. On the other hand, some faculty hardly akin to reason has provided her with "a kind of prophetic apprehension" (261) that she should not undress. This piece of information might be dismissed as a mere requirement of decorum were it not that prophetic apprehensions are present elsewhere in Radcliffe's works. Adeline, for example, has a clairvoyant dream, and the heroines' terror-inspired guesses are often right.[1]

At first glance, Radcliffe's view of the relationship of reason, imagination, and knowledge seems self-contradictory. She praises Emily's curiosity about the black veil, for example: "But a terror of this nature, as it occupies and expands the mind, and elevates it to high expectation, is purely sublime, and leads us, by a kind of fascination, to seek even the object, from which we appear to shrink" (248). In this elevated state of mind, however, Emily sees something that is not there; "her delusion and her fears would have vanished together" (662) if she had dared to investigate more closely. The reference to sublime terror recalls Radcliffe's famous distinction between horror and terror:

> "They must be men of very cold imaginations," said W____, "with whom certainty is more terrible than surmise. Terror and horror are so far opposite, that the first expands the soul, and awakens the faculties to a high degree of life; the other contracts, freezes, and nearly annihilates them. I apprehend, that neither Shakespeare nor Milton by their fictions, nor Mr. Burke by his reasoning, anywhere looked to positive horror as a source of the sublime, though they all agree that terror is a very high one; and where lies the great difference between horror and terror, but in uncertainty and obscurity, that accompany the first, respecting the dreaded evil?" ("On the Supernatural" 150–51)

Here are high claims for those whose imaginations are not "cold," for whom terror provoked by "uncertainty and obscurity" is "a source of the

sublime." Why then is Vivaldi's enjoyment of "the region of fearful sublimity" (*The Italian* 58) an object of Radcliffe's gentle satire? His meditations on the nature of his strange visitant are described with some ambivalence:

> He was awed by the circumstances which had attended the visitations of the
> monk, if monk it was . . . and his imagination, thus elevated . . . was
> prepared for something above the reach of common conjecture, and beyond
> the accomplishment of human agency. His understanding was sufficiently
> clear and strong to teach him to detect many errors of opinion, that prevailed
> around him, as well as to despise the common superstitions of his country,
> and, in the usual state of his mind, he probably would not have paused for
> a moment on the subject before him; but his passions were now interested
> and his fancy awakened, and, though he was unconscious of this propensity,
> he would, perhaps, have been somewhat disappointed, to have descended
> suddenly from the region of fearful sublimity, to which he had soared—the
> world of terrible shadows—to the earth, on which he daily walked, and to
> an explanation simply natural. (58)

Despite the references to "errors of opinion" and "an explanation simply
natural," Radcliffe clearly feels, and makes her readers feel in this passage, the attraction of "the world of terrible shadows." But she undercuts
Vivaldi's sublime enthusiasm with humor: he *was* a bit inclined to ignore
"the earth, on which he daily walked." When Vivaldi later leans increasingly toward interpreting the monkish apparition as supernatural, the reader
is presumably intended to remember the hero's charming tendency to get
carried away. On the other hand, the experience that leads him into "the
region of fearful sublimity" is described in a passage surely reminiscent
of Mr. Burke's reasoning and one of Milton's "fictions": "It stood at the
dusky extremity of the avenue, near the stair-case. Its garments, if garments they were, were dark; but its whole figure was so faintly traced to
the eye, that it was impossible to ascertain whether this was the monk. . . .
When he reached the head of the stair-case . . . the form, whatever it
might be, was gone" (74).

What accounts for the apparent contradictions in Radcliffe's judgments
on the perceptions inspired by sublime curiosity? First, she is under a
moral obligation to stress for her impressionable readers the enlightened
nature of her Catholic heroes and heroines. Their Catholicism, she implies, is a mere accident of time and place; they are not really duped by
"monkish superstitions." But the rich half-light of Catholicism is so
suggestive! Like all the Protestant Gothicists, Radcliffe felt the attraction

of the religion that sees through a glass darkly but celebrates its mysteries in such glorious art. She shares the state of mind that led one Gothic enthusiast to a double encomium on English ruins: they are the pride of the nation that (1) can display such picturesque monuments and (2) reduced to ruin such abominable relics of superstition.[2] Radcliffe, too, expresses both views.

In addition, Radcliffe believed that terror could stretch the faculties of the mind, expanding its capacity for religious apprehensions. But imagination is, in her view, an instrument for experiencing reality, not for creating it. In this she agreed with the Scottish commonsense philosophers that "God was creative and man was inventive, with the imagination locked inside a reality which it did not create and was constrained to use according to certain principles."[3] God himself, of course, is part of that reality. Thus, to see God in the misty Apennines is evidence of a soul expanded and awakened to eternal verities, because God exists prior to the imagination that perceives his presence. To see an evil supernatural "it" in the shadows of a Gothic fortress is merely error, because such things do not exist apart from the imagination. Delusion at its worst is a product of "passion, inflaming imagination, bearing down the boundaries of reason and living in a world of its own" (*Mysteries of Udolpho* 329). In Radcliffe's novels, to be and to be perceived are emphatically not the same. The wanderer in the gloom of the woods may feel "that high enthusiasm, which wakes the poet's dream" and so "send forward a transforming eye into the distant obscurity" (*Mysteries of Udolpho* 15), but the transformation is poetry, a legitimate response of the imagination to God's world. Both a temporal and an eternal world exist independent of the mind; the scenes in which the Something at the Door is comically revealed to have no relationship to the heroine's imaginings are Radcliffe's way of kicking the rock.

But Radcliffe comes close to presenting the idea, if not stating it directly, that the imagination, though it cannot create real things, can provide valid insights through the delusions it produces. First, the success of her art depends on the gullibility of the reader, who is not supposed to reason calmly but to be frightened like the overly susceptible heroes and heroines.[4] The contrast with Charlotte Smith's brief Gothic excursions is instructive; here is a writer who takes no chances with her readers' nervous susceptibilities. Monimia's Gothic terrors jostle in the same pages with Orlando's educated laughter at her "simplicity" (*Old Manor House* 40, 41), and the reader has little time to make any wild surmises before the mystery is dispelled. In Radcliffe the aura of mystery lingers long after the mystery itself is finally explained.[5] As her biographer Talfourd asked,

> What reader would bear to be told that the black veil, from which his imagination has scarcely been allowed to turn for three volumes, conceals a waxen image; that the wild music, which has chanced to float on the air, in all the awful pauses of action, proceeded from an insane nun, permitted to wander about the woods; and that the words, which startled Montoni and his friends, at their guilty carousals, were uttered by a man wandering through a secret passage almost without motive; unless the power and sweetness of the spell remained after it was thus rudely broken? (129).

All of Radcliffe's proofs that perception distorted by emotion is not reliable, all her disquisitions on the virtues of reason, tend to pale beside the convincing evidence of a world in which reason does not seem to apply and imagination seems to give more direct access to truth.[6] Is what Emily imagines behind the black veil any less true than the fact of its being waxwork? Montoni does murder a woman, in essence, and he does treat her corpse with shocking disrespect. The unspeakable sight that Emily, overstimulated with sublime curiosity, thinks she sees behind the veil coincides with her growing surmise about Montoni: he is unspeakably evil. And that surmise is correct.

There is no doubt in Radcliffe's works that objective reality exists outside the mind. On the other hand, as Roudaut and Lévy point out, the world of the Gothic castle asserts, *ipso facto,* another kind of reality. "Pénétrer dans un château c'est devenir personnage d'un rêve; c'est être livré, tout en restant soi, et en le sachant, à des forces libres de toute détermination logique et morale . . ." (Roudaut 725). In a moment of authorial self-consciousness about this strange state that she is presenting as "real," Radcliffe has Emily meditate on the seeming unreality of the experiences she has had at Udolpho, events that "seemed more like the visions of a distempered imagination, than the circumstances of truth" (329). And yet, the author seems to assure us, life sometimes does resemble the visions of a distempered imagination; there are circumstances in which what seems most unreal is the only reality. Even if the supernatural is explained away at the end of the book, it has been demonstrated that the possibility exists of having experiences that have little connection with the earth on which we daily walk.[7]

The revelation that the dusky figure that rustled in a corner and finally pressed itself into Emily's chair was only a dog (95) is not after all the kind of thing that keeps Radcliffe's readers turning the pages. The life of her work emanates from the moment before such revelations—the moment of not knowing for sure, when everything, including the mind, is neither–nor. That is the moment of imagination, when the boundary between the self and the other has no meaning, the moment when what matters is not reality but the heroine's projection outward of her fears of reality: the moment, in short, of negative capability. The haunted mind, Hawthorne says, exists in a state somewhere between what has been and what will be, "an intermediate space, where the business of life does not intrude" ("Haunted Mind" 411): a borderland, in other words; a "neutral territory" (*Scarlet Letter* 105). This borderland is the realm of romance, and that is why, whatever rationalism Gothic novels of the *surnaturel expliqué* may purport to espouse, to the extent to which they evoke the state of being neither–nor, when imaginary reality supersedes objective reality, they espouse a philosophy subversive of enlightenment rationalism.

That moment when "nothing is, but what is not" is the essence of Gothicism, because not knowing for sure is the primary source of Gothic terror. An essential activity of the Gothic protagonist is therefore interpretation. What was that noise? What does the veil conceal? Whose foot is on the stair? The appeal of Poe's Dupin and his descendants is that in the midst of the most confusing and contradictory appearances, they have a foolproof method of knowing the truth. They are the descendants of the protagonists Radcliffe did not create—the Vivaldis who deduce rationally the identity of the shape before them in the dusk, the Emilys who reason calmly that the breathing at the door must be the maid's. The heroes and heroines she did create have their descendants too, however; and the authors who inherited her legacy inherited as well the questions her romances raise about the relative merits of reason, imagination, and faith. In this sense it is not so far from the "mysteries of Udolpho" to the "mystery of Isabel," except that Melville took the mystery a step further. The terror he portrays is not just the terror of *not knowing,* but of *not knowing how to know.*

"A wild, bewildering, and incomprehensible curiosity had seized him, to know something definite of that face" (*Pierre* 63). The passion Isabel arouses in Pierre is, among other things, a passion for knowledge. "For me, thou hast uncovered one infinite, dumb, beseeching countenance of mystery, underlying all the surfaces of visible time and space" (70). The desire "to know something definite" becomes a mania with Pierre. "From all idols, I tear all veils; henceforth I will see the hidden things . . ."

(91). "Pierre saw all preceding ambiguities, all mysteries ripped open . . ." (118).

Such metaphors link Pierre with the many characters in Gothic fiction who, in pursuit of knowledge, draw aside veils, lift palls, wrench open chests and coffins, rip up floorboards and wainscotting, venture through any door they happen to find ajar, and force their way through many that are not. As part of the mise-en-scène, such barriers represent—literally— the separation of the inquisitive mind from the object of its speculation. Metaphorically, the pursuit of knowledge is often described in Gothic romance in similar terms. Frankenstein speaks of his desire to "step within the threshold of real knowledge" (300), to unveil the face of Nature (299), to enter its "citadel" despite "fortifications and impediments" (299), to "break through" the "ideal bounds" of life and death "and pour a torrent of light into our dark world" (314). In such images as these, the question of how human beings know is less at stake than is the question of whether some things ought to be known at all. The scenes in which Radcliffe's heroes and heroines must imagine what is on the other side of the door present only one of many aspects of the theme of knowledge as she and other Gothic romancers explored it. Before the theme of knowledge as Melville himself explored it in *Pierre* can be placed in its full Gothic context, some of these other aspects must be elucidated.

Much of the complexity of knowledge as a Gothic theme derives from the fact that the word *knowledge* itself has meaning in two contexts. There is knowledge in the sense of learning: abstract knowledge attained by education, scientific investigation, study, and exploration—the kind of knowledge for which Faustean characters sell their souls. And there is the knowledge that is part of human intimacy: the confidences of lovers and friends, "knowledge" in the sense of sexual relations. These two meanings are closely interwoven in Gothic romance, in which *Love, Mystery, and Misery*[8] are so often the soul of the plot. The terrors of knowing and not knowing, the perils of the heart unable to make itself known and the heart exposed to the knower's gaze—all are aspects of the theme of knowledge as Gothicists explore it. This theme itself is one of the many facets of the central theme on which the "Gothic imagination" is always turning its dark light—the boundaries of the self. How individual romancers treat the theme of knowledge in the context of this other theme varies greatly. It is nonetheless possible to make some broad generalizations, the broadest of which is that how this theme in Gothic romance is treated depends on whether the vision of the writer is tragic or comic. Whether a Gothic romance ends happily or not depends on and ultimately defines the role that knowledge plays in the plot. At issue in both kinds of Gothic plot are the moral status of curiosity and the means of access to knowledge, the consequences of the knowledge of evil, and the role "abstract" knowledge plays in the context of the "social" knowledge involved in human relationships.

In Gothic plots that end happily, the hero or heroine's access to knowledge may derive from a variety of sources. Among these are informative dreams, especially those that providence "impresses . . . upon the imagination" (*Gabrielle de Vergy* 1: 19); mysterious lights that guide the way through treacherous passages; those "stately, deputed spectres" (Tompkins 293) who provide information on the villain's guilty past; and, when all else fails, sheer irrepressible curiosity. From a moral point of view, all of these sources of knowledge are unexceptionable, including the last, which is continually associated in Gothic comedy with the protagonist's courage, capacity for sublime awe, humane sympathy, or receptivity to providential inspiration.

At a crucial but potentially problematic moment in Emily's history, for example, Radcliffe emphasizes the heroine's gentle sympathy as she looks in on her father reading in his private closet. Having come to see whether he is ill, she remains out of "a mixture of curiosity and tenderness. She could not witness his sorrow, without being anxious to know the subject of it . . ." (*Mysteries of Udolpho* 26). When he takes out a miniature of a woman and sighs over it in anguish, Emily stays long enough to see, "having looked repeatedly" (26), that the woman in the portrait is not her mother. Then with characteristic delicacy, she retires: "At length St. Aubert returned the picture into its case; and Emily, recollecting that she was intruding upon his private sorrows, softly withdrew from the chamber" (26). Radcliffe's mastery of tone (best illustrated in the word *softly*) allows her, by sheer force of gentility, to carry off such a scene without casting aspersions on the inquisitive heroine. In other scenes Emily's curiosity is a positive virtue: her drawing aside of the black veil is associated with her capacity for sublime awe (248), and her drawing aside of the curtain in Volume 3, Chapter 1 is something she forces herself to do out of duty to her aunt (348).

For the most part, however, Emily St. Aubert exhibits an appalling self-restraint, most memorably in the scene in which she burns her father's mysterious papers without reading them. " 'Let me hasten to remove the temptation, that would destroy my innocence, and embitter my life with the consciousness of irremediable guilt, while I have strength to reject it' " (103), she says. Radcliffe is obviously conscious that the temptation of knowledge must, as the source of the Fall, be handled with some delicacy. In Gothic comedy, heroines may fall from a state of ignorant childhood happiness to the suffering wisdom of adulthood, but their access of knowledge is never a fall from innocence.[9] Here Emily resists the primal temptation, and throughout the rest of the book her detective work, when she undertakes it, is carried out on the nicest moral principles. She declines, for example, to stoop so low as to "tempt" an "innocent girl to a conduct so mean, as that of betraying the private conversation of her parents" (418). Such scruples, if carried too far, would of course bring the narrative to a grinding halt, so for mere petty fact finding and rumor mongering, the author provides the servant Annette. Fortunately for the reader, Emily's amusement at Annette's tendency to be ever "on the wing for new wonders" (299) is balanced by her own half-fearful curiosity to learn the many secrets of which Annette manages to make herself the repository. This curiosity, Radcliffe makes clear, is not wholly admirable, but it is a subject for a condescending authorial smile, not condemnation.

Radcliffe's command of her art by the time she wrote *The Mysteries of Udolpho* allowed her to accommodate the heroine's curiosity in a moral framework that, while vindicating that curiosity, nonetheless presents the desire for knowledge as cause for ethical choices. Few Gothicists had the skill to maintain such a balance if they wanted to; in comic Gothic the moral status of curiosity is usually handled in other ways. Sometimes a bold inquisitiveness is simply part of a hero's complement of knightly virtues. As Drake's Henry Fitzowen drew near a ruined castle among the elms, moaning with "a sullen and melancholy sound" in the fitful moonlight, "ardent curiosity mingled with awe dilated his bosom, and he inwardly congratulated himself upon so singular an adventure" ("Henry Fitzowen" 118). Characters of courage and humanity will always investigate mysterious groans; when groans are not forthcoming, such characters may feel the subtle promptings of providence. Rosetta Ballin's heroine finds her imprisoned lover by following the promptings of an overpowering inquisitiveness. "My heart was bent on a discovery, and an inexpressible something drew me to it" (*Statue Room* 2: 62); "an inexpressible something revived me, and bid me proceed" (2: 69). Barrett satirized this kind of curiosity in *The Heroine,* in a passage describing how Lord Theodore, passing a lighted window in a dark alley one night, was struck with inspiration: "An indescribable sensation, an unaccountable something, whispered to him, in still, small accents, 'peep through the pane' " (2: 188).

The fact that in Gothic comedy the voice of curiosity speaks for the noblest sentiments and often turns out to be the still, small voice of God himself is indicative of the role knowledge plays in such works generally. Even when ignorance is associated initially with pastoral bliss, not knowing in Gothic comedy almost always involves some degree of pain, if only the vague sense of loss that clouds the seeming Edens of a fallen world. In *Udolpho* and *Clermont,* for example, the heroine's Arcadia centers on a beloved father touched by the melancholy derived from his experience in some other, sadder world. Although she does not know the cause, the heroine too is touched by his sorrow, and the happy ending exorcises precisely this vague mystery that was part of her innocent youth. At its worst, the condition of not knowing in these romances is a condition of terror, isolation, and the threat of madness. The crisis of the protagonists' fortunes in Gothic comedy involves temporary imprisonment in a place one of whose prime characteristics is that it cannot be fully known.[10] After nightmarish struggles, the hero or heroine finds— either here or in some related place—the evidence of someone else's sin. This evidence discloses the secret of his or her hereditary wrongs and the key to his or her true identity. The "identity" is identity in the sense of social position,[11] and the crucial act of knowledge in Gothic comedy is a social act, in that it brings to light a crime against the social order, most often usurpation.[12] Knowledge of the long-hidden secret exorcises evil and reestablishes social unity, chiefly by making possible the marriage of hero and heroine and returning money and property to their rightful, virtuous owners.

Not surprisingly, education tends to play an important role in such works, which portray the enlightened mind as a crucial defense against superstitious terror, and eloquence as a chief weapon against tyranny. St. Aubert, who enjoys "the treasures of knowledge" (2) in his pastoral retreat, makes a point of giving his daughter a good education. "A well-informed mind . . . is the best security against the contagion of folly and of vice. The vacant mind is ever on the watch for relief, and ready to plunge into error, to escape from the languor of idleness. Store it with ideas, teach it the pleasure of thinking; and the temptations of the world without, will be counteracted by the gratifications derived from the world within" (6). Emily's stay at Udolpho is a test of whether her "world within" is sufficient to withstand the "world without"—of whether her reason is strong enough to overcome the temptations of superstition and her wit and eloquence will be proof against the persecutions of Montoni.

In addition, education in Gothic comedy includes knowledge in both its abstract and social meanings, as education in these works is so often an act of love. A message that the reader of books by women Gothicists could hardly escape is that the generous education of a daughter is one of the surest indices of parental affection. Emily St. Aubert has been "tenderly educated" (329) by her father. Her lover in turn shows himself worthy of St. Aubert's daughter by courting her with conversation on sublime nature and extracts from the best authors. His admiration for good literature, his delight in sharing it with Emily, and his ever-so-slight superiority in these matters (he sometimes corrects her taste) prove him deserving of her love. He and Emily come to know each other in the social sense by sharing the "treasures of knowledge" so dear to both of them.

The relation between love and education in such works is illustrated by the Gothic episodes of Charlotte Smith's *An Old Manor House.* The hero discovers a secret door to the turret where the beautiful Monimia is imprisoned every night by her aunt. The villain later shows his colors by snooping around, discovering this door, and trying to get in. The hero, however, knows its right use. Late at night he conducts Monimia through it, via some frightening passageways, to the aristocrat's library from which her lowly status has shut her out. Here he carries on an ardent but decorous courtship mingled with the education that is "to render her mind as lovely as her form" (28). He lends her books, discusses them, and supplements her learning, *en passant,* with rationalistic arguments against the Gothic terrors that assault his beloved in their progress through the gloomy house. Her aunt has dissuaded her from wandering about the house by telling her ghost stories, but Orlando explains that this was a means to "fetter" (44) Monimia in ignorance: " '[L]ike all other usurped authority, the power of your aunt is maintained by unjust means, and supported by prejudices, which if once looked at by the eye of reason would fall. So slender is the hold of tyranny, my Monimia!' " (44).

These scenes are an emblem of the role played by knowledge generally in Gothic comedy. Monimia's ignorance is her prison room; not knowing is associated with fear, domination, and isolation. Knowledge, in contrast, means freedom, unity, and love. When knowledge does bring terror in such works, the terror is temporary, and often the "knowledge" proves merely to have been a form of ignorance. In Musgrave's *The Solemn Injunction,* for example, three people venture into a secret closet and discover a manuscript proving incestuous the central passions of their lives. At last the heroine herself explores the closet and discovers the truth, which is that no one has in fact committed incest and that they are all entitled to live happily ever after. Typically of the comic Gothic plot, what the heroine discovers is the story of another woman's guilt, which clarifies her own identity and brings to light her hereditary wrongs. The other explorers thought they had discovered their own identities and hereditary sin, a discovery that, had it proved true, would have given the plot a shape more characteristic of Gothic tragedy.

The plots of most Gothic romances exhibit the essential outlines of the hero-journey, as Joseph Campbell describes it. The basic pattern of this myth is the crossing of a threshold from the ordinary daylight world into a fabulous unknown world where, after various difficulties, the hero manages to acquire some essential boon. He then recrosses the threshold, bringing back the boon to benefit the world where the journey originally began (30, 245–46). This is essentially the pattern of Gothic comedy, in which the knowledge discovered at the heart of the alien world turns out to have some redemptive use in the ordinary world and indeed, on a symbolic level, is precisely what makes possible recrossing the threshold—going home.

Tragic Gothic romance, on the other hand, tells the story of hero-journeys that fail to work. In these plots, the threshold is crossed initially for the wrong reasons, and the knowledge discovered in the dark alien world is such that it renders a return to the daylight world meaningless or impossible. In Maturin's *Montorio,* for example, once Ippolito has allowed his curiosity to lead him into the underground vault of what seems to be a satanic society, he can never leave it psychologically. His guide's threat is prophetic: " '[F]rom henceforth it shall ever seem as if this vault indeed engulphed you, as if your view was bounded by its darkness . . .' " (3: 85).

Although in Gothic comedy, curiosity may well be the voice of God prompting the explorer toward redemptive knowledge, in Gothic tragedy it is just the reverse—an echo of the tempter's voice in Eden. Even education is suspect in these works. Melmoth's temptation of Immalee in her island paradise, for example, begins with instruction in comparative religion, and her desire to know more of the world ends in her participation in its suffering. " '[T]o think, then, is to suffer—and a world of thought must be a world of pain!' " (288), Immalee concludes. And yet, she realizes, the pain itself is compensation for the loss of ignorance: " '[T]here is a pain sweeter than pleasure, that I never felt till I beheld him. Oh! who would not think, to have the joy of tears?' " (288). Falling in love with Melmoth and learning to think are the same for Immalee; here love is associated with education, but both are a form of suffering. In this

Gothic vision, "the treasures of knowledge" are ambiguous, indeed. They may be associated with love, but far from facilitating redemptive marriages and the reestablishment of social order, knowledge and the thirst for it bring isolation that is yet no protection from terrible unity, and parodic unities that are merely versions of isolation.

Underlying this version of curiosity is the old association of a lust for knowledge with sexual lust. In the background of the tragic Gothic version of knowledge is Marlowe's Faustus, whose attraction to Hellenic learning was expressed in a longing for Helen herself. In that background, too, are Milton's Adam and Eve, whose transgression replaced conjugal unity with separation, desire, and the egotistical sexual union that provides relief from neither. Thus illicit knowledge in tragic Gothic is often associated with illicit passion. Ambrosio's first use of Matilda's illicit knowledge, for example, is to procure through her magic a glimpse of the woman he desires (Lewis, *The Monk* 208). In Maturin's Gothic romances, curiosity itself is described as a kind of lust: a "feverish thirst . . . consuming [the] inmost soul" (*Melmoth* 58), a "fatal thirst of invisible knowledge" (*Montorio* 3: 448), "wild wishes to attain the secrets and communion of another world" (*Montorio* 1: 2).

The "communion" illicit knowledge brings in tragic Gothic is usually a horrific parody of the normal human intimacy—the normal form of social "knowledge"—that lust for abstract knowledge precludes. Maturin's Annibal, having made his way through a door that, as a nervous servant says, was intended to be closed "for *ever*" (*Montorio* 1: 148), finds himself in possession of "knowledge . . . without bounds" and thus "fear . . . without hope" (2: 3). He regrets bitterly the eagerness that led him to the knowledge of someone else's guilt: "These things do not come in quest of us; 'tis our fatal curiosity that removes the natural barrier of separation" (2: 233). This removal of natural barriers leads, ironically, to a separateness aptly represented in the first serious consequence of Annibal's knowledge: imprisonment. "In a moment the door was closed on me. The human faces were shut out. Their very steps seemed to cease at once; door after door closed at successive distances . . ." (2: 25). At the same time, his isolation is an unholy union. He is "mated and leagued with these horrors, blended in unhallowed intimacy with what it is frightful and unlawful for human nature to know" (2: 232). The ultimate symbol of this unholy intimacy is Annibal's passion for his own sister, a passion discovered in the course of his quest for knowledge. Incest, as is often pointed out, is an emblem of solipsism—the narcissistic love that is merely another version of confinement in the self.[13]

One reason the possessor of illicit knowledge finds himself or herself isolated is that the knowledge must be hidden; it cannot be shared like the "treasures of knowledge" St. Aubert imparts to his daughter. Annibal's brother Ippolito, because of a passion for forbidden knowledge, becomes the victim of a man referred to as "the stranger" or "the unknown" or sometimes "the tempter," whom he both flees and pursues out of terror and curiosity. This pursuit assimilates him into "the unknown," alienating him increasingly from other people but at the same time making that alienation desirable by causing him to fear that his own secret may be known. The horrible unity and separateness that come to characterize his life are made particularly vivid when he asks a servant whether he has seen the stranger. Terrified at Ippolito's proximity, the man answers oddly. Ippolito presses him about the appearance of the being he is pursuing: " 'I should wish to know him, should it be my chance to encounter him,' " he says. " 'You will easily know him by yourself, Signor,' " replies the servant, " 'he is just your stature and figure' " (2: 323). Ippolito himself has become, for other people, the stranger, the unknown, the object of fearful speculation. And he is afraid they may have discovered what he wishes to conceal: "Suspicion haunted his footsteps; the relentless vigilance of superstition had an eye on him for evil, and not for good. . . . His dark and secret trials were known . . ." (2: 327). His horror of being known and his strange relationship with "the unknown," whom he flees and pursues, separate him increasingly from normal relations with other people. Even his sufferings cannot be fully communicated to another soul. "Every ear is deaf, and every heart is iron to me," he says, ". . . but you, Oh, you! may you one day know what it is to knock at the human heart, and find it shut!" (2: 446).

This last metaphor reflects the fact that the only "communion" Ippolito has attained in his search for knowledge is a form of alienation. By allying himself with "the unknown," he has forfeited the sympathy of humanity, the privilege of being able to make his suffering known to another heart. The paradox of Ippolito's separateness in unity and unity in separateness is expressed on the metaphorical level of many Gothic romances, in that the curiosity they portray simultaneously destroys and creates barriers. Frankenstein's success, for example, involves a number of ironic reversals of the boundary metaphors in which he expressed his aspirations. The man who wanted to look upon nature's face "unveiled" (299) wakes to find his discovery beside the bed, holding up the curtain and gazing at him (319). The man who wanted to "step within the threshold of real knowledge" shudders to hear the creaking of his door in the dead of night as the monster steals into his house. The man who broke through the "bounds" of life and death (314) finds "an insurmountable barrier" between him and his "fellow men" (427). The man who wanted to let a "torrent of light into our dark world" (314) feels "a kind of panic," as he hangs over the corpse of his bride, when a ray of moonlight illuminates the room. His creature, at the open window, has thrown back the shutter to look in on Frankenstein's handiwork (468).[14]

To learn nature's secret, Frankenstein makes himself into a man who cannot confide his own secret, even to his best friend. His renunciation of knowledge in its most pleasant social senses—the confidences of family and friends, sexual relations with his new bride—leads to an experience of social knowledge in its most unpleasant context: the prying of the legal investigator who wants to solve his mystery, the constant intrusions of the only creature who does know his secret and who longs to be acknowledged by his creator. Frankenstein brings all this on himself by divorcing scientific knowledge from its proper social context. In order to burst through the "bounds" that keep him from nature's mystery, he must begin by imposing boundaries on himself, shutting himself up "in a solitary chamber, or rather cell, at the top of the house, and separated from all the other apartments by a gallery and stair-case . . ." (315). His seclusion in such a cell for such a purpose is an ominous prediction of the double terrors of unity and separateness in which his lust for knowledge involves him. In that cell he creates the monster who intrudes on him wherever he goes and, as Wilt points out, "proceeds with dreamlike thoroughness to cut off all those whom Frankenstein cut off from his affections while he fed his obsession . . ." (66).

The creature's solitary life of peeping and prying is itself an emblem of the monstrous distortion, in Frankenstein's own life, of legitimate human aspiration for "knowledge" in both of its contexts. Like his creator, Frankenstein's monster desires abstract knowledge—an education—and like him he suffers a futile desire to make himself known to other people. The representation of these two desires for knowledge, and of their intimate relationship in Mary Shelley's Gothic vision, is the monster's position outside the wall of the De Lacey family. Through a chink in that wall he looks in enviously on what is surely, here in the central narrative of the novel, the author's own vision of abstract knowledge in its proper social context. From beyond the wall, Frankenstein's monster observes a family circle into which a "stranger," Saphie, is being incorporated by means of education (383ff). As he peers in on these scenes, Frankenstein's monster—the great scientific discovery—longs "to discover

[him]self" (379) to the family he watches so curiously. "I was shut out from intercourse with them, except through means which I obtained by stealth, when I was unseen and unknown . . ." (387). But there is no true social intercourse without being known, and as the monster soon learns, he is doomed to fail in his intrusion on this family circle. Both Frankenstein and his monster, having long had for human relations only their hateful and torturous mutual confidence, do at last manage to confide in someone else. Ironically, the recipient of their confidences is the explorer Walton, a man who longs for two things: knowledge and a friend. Especially, he says, a friend who would help him "regulate" his mind and thus overcome the bad effects of his solitary education (273–74).

Frankenstein's monster is one of the many alienated characters in Gothic romance who are "secret witnesses," able to know other people only "by stealth." Because their human relationships are based on spying and eavesdropping, they gain access to other people's lives solely through intellectual knowledge, never through the knowledge associated with love. Prominent among these figures is the ubiquitous father confessor of Gothic romance: Manfroné, Schedoni, Schemoli, Udolpho, the odious confessor in *Melmoth* who gets Senora Monçada's secret out of her and uses it to torture her and her family. The confessor's job is to hear secrets, but he is often to be found augmenting his knowledge after hours by means of sliding panels and secret doors. Lurking in shadows, hiding behind a cowl (in Manfroné's case, a cowl and a mask), he conceals the hideous secrets of his own heart while prying relentlessly into those of others. The most extreme version of this unholy combination is the figure of the hooded Inquisitor, prying anonymously into the guilt of other souls.

Brockden Brown's Ormond, the "secret witness" who spies on Constantia from behind an "unsuspected door" (*Ormond* 232), is a version of this figure. So is Carwin, who, with his strange mixture of wickedness and rather touching curiosity about other people's lives, seems to derive something both from sinister spies like Schedoni and the more pitiable figure of Caleb Williams. So are Hawthorne's unpardonable sinners, including Roger Chillingworth, who, in order to pursue knowledge without being known, casts off his name, trading his marriage for the cold intimacy of leech and patient. In her encounter with him after seven years, Hester notices his "searching . . . yet carefully guarded look. It seemed to be his wish and purpose to mask his expression with a smile . . ." (*Scarlet Letter,* 184). Hawthorne gives a vivid description of Chillingworth's search for knowledge:

He now dug into the poor clergyman's heart, like a miner searching for gold; or, rather, like a sexton delving into a grave, possibly in quest of a jewel that had been buried on the dead man's bosom, but likely to find nothing save mortality and corruption.

. . . . .

Then, after long search into the minister's dim interior, and turning over many precious materials . . . all of which invaluable gold was perhaps no better than rubbish to the seeker,—he would turn back discouraged, and begin his quest towards another point. He groped along stealthily, with as cautious a tread, and as wary an outlook, as a thief entering a chamber where a man lies only half asleep,—or, it may be, broad awake,—with purpose to steal the very treasure which this man guards as the apple of his eye. (160)

The success of Chillingworth's search gratifies not only a lust for illicit knowledge but also a passion for hiding what he knows: "All that guilty sorrow, hidden from the world, whose great heart would have pitied and forgiven, to be revealed to him, the Pitiless, to him, the Unforgiving! All that dark treasure to be lavished on the very man, to whom nothing else could so adequately pay the debt of vengeance!" (166). Chillingworth's power over Dimmesdale ends only when he can no longer gloat in secret over this "treasure," because Dimmesdale himself has shared it with the world.

The search Hawthorne describes in these passages is that of all those Gothic confessors and inquisitors who seek a knowledge of the heart without the heart's special knowledge. The descriptions of Chillingworth's pursuits bear a striking resemblance to the passage in Maturin's *Montorio* describing Ippolito's attack on the Inquisitors, who see him merely as "a hoard of dark secrets, which can never be exhausted" (2: 513):

And why confess to *you?* What claim have you from nature, or from confidence for the demand, or do you ground it upon the absence of all? Are we to repose in you a trust, witheld from all mankind beside, because you have less motive of solicitude, less claim on confidence, less power or wish of sympathy than all mankind? Are *you* like the ocean, to engulph in silence and darkness, the treasures intended to be shared with affection and sympathy? Is confidence like the ebony, the growth of subterrene darkness, the nursling of a dungeon? No, it is your greedy, furtive, serpent curiosity, that longs to wind itself about the tree of knowledge; 'tis the ambition of a fiend, counterfeiting the aspirations of an angel, like the impure priests of a pagan idol, ye love to prey on violated purity, that as yet has never sacrificed to nature or to passion, and to call it a rite of religion. (2: 488–89)

In this image of the Inquisitor, the ultimate "secret witness," the theme of the search for abstract knowledge intersects with the theme of knowledge as a form of human relationship. The lust for knowledge is here specifically associated with sexual lust and opposed to the love that shares the "treasures" of confidence. The knower refuses to be known; he disguises his motives to gain knowledge and hides his prize—engulfs it "in silence and darkness"—when he succeeds. This figure stalks through the pages both of Gothic comedy and tragedy, but in Gothic comedy he loses at the end. His own secret is finally made known, as in Schedoni's case, or the victim's self-knowledge in the form of conscious innocence holds him at bay. Maturin's comment on this vision of conscious worth as self-defense is found in Monçada's account of his encounter with the Holy Office: "I knew myself innocent, and this is a consciousness that defies even the Inquisition itself; but, within the walls of the Inquisition, the consciousness, and the defiance it inspires, are alike vain" (*Melmoth* 232).

Maturin's own most mature Gothic exploration of the theme of knowledge merits discussion. His achievement in developing the potential of the theme as he found it in earlier Gothic romance is worthy of attention in its own right; it also deserves attention as the single development of the theme that is most obviously behind Melville's use of the Gothic in *Pierre*. The themes that Maturin had explored in the story of the Montorios—the consequences of aspiring to the "secrets and communion of another world," the knowledge that brings both inescapable unity and immitigable isolation—received their final elaboration in the story of Melmoth.

II

On a dark and stormy night in Spain during August 1677, an Englishman sought shelter in a remote and solitary house on the plains of Valencia. The manuscript that records what happened next is unfortunately damaged; indeed, it is "discoloured, obliterated, and mutilated beyond any that . . . ever before exercised the patience of a reader" (28). Just as an old woman reluctantly admits the traveler, a hiatus occurs: "[T]he house was handsome and spacious, but the melancholy appearance of desertion _____." The next readable passage finds the Englishman on his way through the house. He hears a shriek. " 'Don't heed it,' said the old woman, lighting him on with a miserable lamp—'it is only he_____' " (31–32).

The terrors of not knowing are the subject of this fragment in several ways. The manuscript itself tells of a man led by a stranger through a dark house in a foreign country. Making his way through the manuscript is a young man suffering a "feverish thirst of curiosity" (58). Reading about this reader of the manuscript is the reader of the book, eager to know what will happen. And behind the mystery is the author himself, lighting the reader on with the most miserable lamp he can provide. The damaged manuscript, he eventually reveals, tells part of the story of Melmoth the Wanderer, who to relieve his "desperate curiosity" (541) sold his soul to the devil. As is usually the case with these bargains, the deal turned out to be a bad one, and Melmoth, having traded the miseries of ignorance for the miseries of knowledge, finds himself an outcast incapable of love, "knowing all, and known to none" (397).

We first meet Melmoth the Wanderer in two fleeting moments. He appears to his descendant John Melmoth, whom he beckons mysteriously and inspires with intolerable curiosity; he appears in the midst of a storm, laughing demoniacally at the fate of two lovers blasted by lightning. We see him next at a wedding feast, where his presence disturbs one of the guests, a priest. " 'Who knows him?' exclaimed Olavida, starting apparently from a trance; 'who knows him? who brought him here?' " (35). When the other guests disclaim any knowledge of the stranger, Father Olavida poses the same question to them individually: " 'Do you know him?' 'No! no! no! was uttered with vehement emphasis by every individual. 'But I know him' said Olavida . . ." (35). And the priest, bending forward and pointing to the Englishman with an expression of "rage, hatred and fear" (35), announces, " 'He is—he is_____' " and drops dead (35). An acquaintance explains later why Olavida died: " 'He sought the knowledge of a secret withheld from man' " (38). Melmoth disappears in the confusion, and the wedding guests sit up late discussing what they should do. Suddenly a scream of horror is heard from the bridal chamber, where the wife is found dead in her new husband's arms.

Thus, in his first appearances Melmoth is alternately associated with the lure of illicit knowledge and with the destruction of love. He preys on the desire for knowledge—the insane desire for knowledge about *him*—which his presence inspires in certain people. He thereby causes isolation, like that of the Englishman Stanton, who, having heard the story of the wedding feast, sets out in an insane quest of Melmoth that ends with his confinement in a madhouse. Melmoth causes this kind of separateness, and he preys on it. He arrives in Stanton's madhouse to offer him liberation at the price of his soul; he arrives in the prisons of the Inquisition to offer escape to Alonzo di Monçada; he arrives to offer riches to the unhappy Walberg, whose poverty has isolated him from his family to such an extent that he tries to murder his children. Were he to succeed in these temptations, Melmoth would drive his victims into even worse isolation, for his whole object is to persuade someone to trade destinies with him, a man who is, as Hawthorne would have said, "the Outcast of the Universe" ("Wakefield" 926).

At the center of Melmoth's own history is the tale of his torturous relationship with Immalee, the innocent child of nature whom he educates on her tropical island. Despite her "ardent curiosity" (286) about almost everything, Immalee asks no questions about Melmoth's dark secret. Unlike all those people who respond to him with feverish curiosity about his strange nature, Immalee responds to him with love alone. Tortured momentarily by this innocent trust, Melmoth tells her that she cannot love him; he is "hated and hateful" (318). Not by her, Immalee objects. "Yes, by you, if you knew whose I am and whom I serve." To this Immalee responds, "Who you are, I know not—but I am yours" (318). In his agony of pity and despair, Melmoth almost confides in her, beginning by saying that he is a man "separated from life and humanity by a gulph impassable," and continuing, "a disinherited child of nature, who goes about to curse or to tempt his more prosperous brethren; one who—what withholds me from disclosing all?" (319). But here a flash of lightning cuts him off, and it seems the Devil intervenes in answer to the question, thus illustrating the truth of what Melmoth has said. He is separated from humanity, including Immalee, by an impassable gulf.

Immalee's acceptance of Melmoth without any impulse to pry into his secret remains steadfast even after she leaves her island and becomes Isidora in Spain.[15] This acceptance is reflected in her offer to marry him: "to be yours amid mystery and grief" (366). Even as she offers herself to a man who has sold himself to the Devil, the offer, uniting passion with innocence, is itself a sign of her purity. Indeed, Maturin, with a clever twist on the theme of conscious innocence, presents her passion for this damned soul as, by its very nature, a defense against damnation: "There was a grandeur, too, about her slender form, that seemed to announce that pride of purity,—that confidence in external weakness, and internal energy,—that conquest without armour,—that victory over the victor, which makes the latter blush at this triumph, and compels him to bow to the standard of the beseiged fortress at the moment of its surrender'' (366). Melmoth responds to this spectacle of beauty, devotion, and "pure and perfect innocence" with "one generous, one human feeling" (366) and tears himself away from her. Ironically, such separation is the only expression of love of which he is capable. But he comes back at last to offer her "a union with the man who cannot love" (375).

Their wedding ceremony solemnizes this bizarre unity in separateness, at the heart of which is the demonic knowledge that prevents Melmoth from loving, and the love that induces Isidora to accept a man she does not know:

> The place, the hour, the objects, all were hid in darkness. She heard a faint rustling as of the approach of another person,—she tried to catch certain words, but she knew not what they were,—she attempted also to speak, but she knew not what she said. All was mist and darkness with her,—she knew not what was muttered,—she felt not that the hand of Melmoth grasped hers,—but she felt that the hand that united them, and clasped their palms within his own, was *as cold as that of death.* (394)

For Isidora, the wedding is a nightmare of not knowing, but this separateness at the heart of her marriage is her salvation: an aspect of what Maturin elsewhere calls her "impregnable innocence" (286). When at the end of her life Melmoth finally tells Isidora his secret, she does, as he predicted earlier, reject him. The "impassable gulph" between Melmoth and her is a result of his satanic bargain for illicit knowledge, a bargain that enables him to pass through any door or wall, to get through the rocks and breakers that set Immalee's island apart from the world, to enter the cells in the prisons of the Inquisition, even to see into the minds of his victims. His illicit knowledge gives him access everywhere; yet because of it there is nowhere he belongs. The moment at which he tells his secret is always the moment of his rejection; the man to whom no wall is a barrier is everywhere shut out.

The image of Melmoth's isolation is reinforced by Maturin's narrative technique, which repeatedly shuts off the reader from the central character. Melmoth's history is revealed by means of an elaborate system of framing devices that holds the reader apart from him. We do not learn his secret—the details of his bargain of his soul for knowledge—until near the end of the novel, and there it is enclosed in a remarkable system of Chinese boxes.[16] The Spaniard tells his story, within which he recounts the details of a manuscript he read, which told the story of Immalee, within which her father heard from Melmoth the story of Elinor and John, a story within which a clergyman told the story of Melmoth's personal history. At the heart of this labyrinth of tales and tellers is Melmoth's own personal narrative, but told by Melmoth at second hand, in the voice of someone else.

The barrier this narrative framework sets up between reader and protagonist is reflected in the relation between Melmoth and his final interpreters in the novel. The climax of Melmoth's tragedy occurs in a room that these characters, young John Melmoth and Alonzo di Monçada, are forbidden to enter. " 'Remember,' " says Melmoth, " 'your lives will be the forfeit of your desperate curiosity. For the same stake I risked more than life—and lost it!' " (541). Although the reader has been allowed to see Melmoth's dream the night before, the final drama of Melmoth's life is played out behind a closed door.

In his decision to pose as an author who either does not know or will not let the reader know the full details of his story, Maturin was responding to one of the central narrative dilemmas of the Gothic romancer, who constantly finds herself or himself in the position of having in some way to reveal events purportedly belonging to the category of which no human being has certain knowledge. From the time Walpole appeared in the double role of superstitious teller and enlightened translator of a monkish tale, there were various solutions to the problem. The device of *surnaturel expliqué* is one way out of the dilemma: the author reveals superhuman events or beings and later reveals that they were only human after all. The problem with any revelations is that as Bachelard says, a closed box will always have more in it than will an open one (88). The attraction of mystery stories is not the solution at the end but the mystery itself. This is a fact of which Maturin was well aware, as his descriptions of the Montorios' curiosity make clear. Annibal describes his "pursuit of something I could not well define, but whose importance was increased by its obscurity" (*Montorio* 1: 36). Ippolito pursues "invisible knowledge" (3: 448). Both descriptions make it clear that although the Montorios hunger for illicit knowledge, it is really mystery itself they are after. They desire knowledge, but it is the experience of *not* knowing that they find exhilarating. The desire not to know is one of the great appeals of Gothic romance; behind it, perhaps, is a hope that there may be something, after all, that cannot be known.

III

Pierre opens with the image of nature taking refuge in silence from a sudden consciousness of her own mystery (1). It ends with an image of the hero "arboured" in the "ebon vines" of Isabel's hair (505), symbol throughout the book of her mystery. The last words spoken are Isabel's enigmatic comment on Pierre's tragedy: " 'All's o'er, and ye know him not' " (505). Between the mysteries of the beginning and the end are the "ambiguities" advertised in the subtitle, ambiguities that come to focus on the issue of knowledge itself. It is not surprising that for such a book Melville turned to the resources of Gothic romance, a genre that offered a highly developed vocabulary of images, scenes, and plots already associated, in some cases quite subtly, with the theme of knowledge.

Among the Gothic writers Melville probably read were those who had explored that theme most consciously and with the greatest complexity: Godwin, Radcliffe, Mary Shelley, and Maturin (see Arvin, "Melville and the Gothic Novel" 33–35). Regardless of the extent to which he may or may not have been specifically influenced by any or all of them, it is at least clear that Melville saw in the conventions of Gothic romance some of the same potential for exploring the theme of knowledge that they had seen. The Gothic writers to whom he refers directly in *Pierre* are those whose "countless tribes of common novels . . . and dramas" "laboriously spin veils of mystery only to complacently clear them up at last" (199). The contemptuous reference to these lesser writers points to Melville's own intention of writing a mystery with no solution and would show, if nothing else did, that the Gothic tradition was consciously in his mind as he wrote *Pierre*. In fact, there is much to show it; the plot is full of Gothic conventions and effects.

This Gothic plot revolves around the theme of knowledge in both its abstract and social meanings. Love itself is presented from the beginning as a form of knowledge in the abstract: "Looking in each other's eyes," Melville says, "lovers see the ultimate secret of the worlds" (45). And yet it is also presented as a form of not knowing: "Love is built upon secrets, as lovely Venice upon invisible and incorruptible piles in the sea" (113). The complication of the plot is introduced in a discussion between Pierre and Lucy about the proper relationship of confidence and love. "Oh, never should Love know all" (50), says Pierre, whereas Lucy maintains that love endures "only in unbounded confidence" (50) and asks Pierre to swear that he will never keep a secret from her (51). He refuses, already under the influence of that "inscrutable dark glance" toward which he will turn from the "all-understood blue eyes of Lucy" (181). Like Maturin's Annibal, he is pursuing something whose importance is "increased by its obscurity."

Pierre's love for Isabel begins as "a wild, bewildering, and incomprehensible curiosity" (63), a desperate desire to know what secret is hidden in her eyes. The intensity of this desire is reminiscent of the lust for knowledge that possesses so many of Maturin's characters, but the fact that it is directed toward a woman integrates the two meanings of knowledge in a way that Maturin did not, and generates many of the "ambiguities." As in the case of Maturin's characters, the "secrets and communion" Pierre seeks with and through Isabel are, on one level, "of another world." Isabel affects Pierre like a haunting "phantom" (73); she seems "not of woman born" (160). Pierre's burning desire "to know something definite of that face" (63) is expressed metaphorically in a desire to see behind a veil: "If thou hast a secret in thy eyes of mournful mystery, out with it, Pierre demands it: what is it that thou hast veiled in thee . . . ye sovereign powers. . . . I conjure ye to lift the veil; I must see it face to face" (56).

The biblical allusion to the final solution of mysteries links the particular mystery of Isabel, "the unknown" (72), to the mystery of some greater Unknown, just as Maturin's frequent repetitions of "the unknown" in references to Orazio make that character a symbol of the cosmic secrets Ippolito wants to learn. But the allusion also shows that, like Father Olavida in *Melmoth,* Pierre seeks "the knowledge of a secret withheld from man." It is not "now" but "then" that St. Paul anticipates seeing things "face to face." The frustrations inherent in trying to see them now are represented in the problem Pierre confronts when he tries to gain more than mortal knowledge through the knowledge of a mortal. Not surprisingly, Pierre's anticipation, as he waits for the hour of his rendezvous with Isabel, "that face to face, that face must shortly meet his own" (156) ends merely in an encounter, face to face, with mystery.

Merely is the appropriate word only from one perspective. In one sense, Pierre, who arrives at his tryst with Isabel in the hope of gaining knowledge about her, is disappointed. "Her light was lidded, and the lid was locked" (199). She can provide him only with a spoken counterpart of the mutilated manuscripts so many Gothic protagonists must struggle to interpret. In another sense, however, her very mystery is a revelation. "For me," Pierre has said of her mysterious face, "thou hast uncovered one infinite, dumb, beseeching countenance of mystery, underlying all the surfaces of visible time and space" (70).

This image of the specific mystery that unveils all mystery points to the paradoxical nature of the gnosis that Pierre experiences, or thinks he experiences, through Isabel. Through her he gains a knowledge of the unknowableness of the world, a revelation of the mystery underlying all appearances. The knowledge Isabel offers Pierre is the knowledge of mystery; the unity that results from and accounts for this gnosis is thus a union with mystery. This paradoxical unity is expressed in the strangely illogical metaphor of Pierre joined to "wondering": "The intuitively certain, however literally unproven fact of Isabel's sisterhood to him, was a link that he now felt binding him to a before unimagined and endless chain of wondering" (195). Pierre's strange union with mystery through, on the one hand, an intuitive knowledge of his relation to Isabel and, on the other, a knowledge through her of the world's unknowableness is embodied in his acknowledgment of a sister whose secret he cannot know. "Her light was lidded, and the lid was locked. *Nor did he feel a pang at this*" (199, italics added). Pierre's union with Isabel is based on an essential separation, a determination "to pry not at all into this sacred problem" (199). In her eyes he sees the mystery of the worlds; their love is built on secrets, as lovely Venice is built on invisible piles in the sea.

It is this strange relationship that generates the Gothic plot of *Pierre*. At the heart of Pierre's tragedy is the simultaneous unity and separateness that Isabel causes in his life, represented in the imagery of barriers broken down by their relation and barriers thereby created. These boundaries and barriers at the heart of the Gothic plot are the boundaries of the self: self defined as perceiver and knower of the world external to it; self knowing and known in the social sense. Ultimately the theme of knowledge in both senses comes to center on Pierre's novel, emblem of the artist's imagination—"that power," as Radcliffe's biographer said, "whose high province is to mediate between the world without us and the world within us . . ." (Talfourd 108).

Pierre's acknowledgment of Isabel as his sister is represented in several metaphors of barriers broken through or boundaries crossed. All of them appear in complicated reworkings of Gothic scenes. The first group of these metaphors describes Isabel's initial effect on Pierre: his resolve to have knowledge at any cost. The metaphors are set in a Gothic context of mysterious occurrences that evoke the difficulties both of making oneself known and of knowing. A "hooded and obscure looking figure" (84) accosts Pierre with a mysterious letter from Isabel. This is a stock figure from Gothic romance, but infused with symbolic significance: in a book so much of which is about the terrors and difficulties of making oneself known to the outside world, it is revealing that Isabel should have to have her letter delivered by a messenger whose face can be seen only "indistinctly" (84). The letter itself, like so many manuscripts in Gothic romance, is stained and in places "almost illegible" (89), the difference being that unlike the crumbling manuscripts of Gothic romance, this one has just been written. Lucy has told Pierre that he is welcome to unlock her portfolio and "read [her] through and through" (54), but even when Isabel writes a letter to reveal her secret, she cannot make herself completely legible. The partial concealment associated with Isabel's first revelation foreshadows her later attempts at self-expression through language, which, when she uses it, tends to disintegrate into confusion and silence. This confusion results partly from the fact that she knows so little about herself and partly from the fact that what she does "know" is a mystery, which finally cannot be expressed in words at all. She expresses this mystery most effectively in music. It is part of Pierre's tragedy that the only means of self-expression available to him is the lesser medium of language.

The "truth" revealed in the darkness by the hooded messenger and Isabel's partly obscure letter moves Pierre to a passion for knowledge. This passion he describes as impiety; as in many Gothic romances, the ambition to "see the hidden things" is the prelude to a tragedy of the impious mind seeking to know more than it should.

> Well didst thou hide thy face from me, thou vile lanterned messenger. . . .
> Doth Truth come in the dark, and steal on us, and rob us so, and then depart.
> . . . . .
>
> Thou Black Knight, that with visor down, thus confrontest me, and mock-
> est at me; lo! I strike through thy helm, and will see thy face, be it Gorgon!
> . . . From all idols, I tear all vails; henceforth I will see the hidden things;
> and live right out in my own hidden life? [*sic*]—now I feel that nothing but
> Truth can move me so. This letter is not a forgery. (90–91)

In this metaphor, Pierre seems to associate the boundary that keeps him from knowing the "hidden things" with the boundary that keeps his own "hidden life" from being known. Thus he resolves at the same time to tear all veils from all idols and "to live right out in my own hidden life." At first sight this intriguing phrase appears to be a resolve to acknowledge to the world something hidden inside him. The juxtaposition of *out* and *in,* however, obscures the logic. How can Pierre live "right out" *in* his "hidden life"? Although much of the near-hysterical, melodramatic rhetoric of the novel does not bear close scrutiny, this resolve of Pierre's is a good description of what he actually tries later to do and of the logical contradictions in the enterprise that make it fail. It describes his bizarre acknowledgment of Isabel as his wife in order to hide the fact that she is his sister while at the same time "living out" his brotherhood. It describes the marriage that is a living out of Pierre's desire, still hidden, really to be Isabel's husband. Furthermore, it describes his attempts as an author to live out, in a novel, an inner life that in many ways he would prefer to keep hidden and that in some senses cannot be made known, anyway: "With the soul of an Atheist, he wrote down the godliest things. . . . For the pangs in his heart, he put down hoots. . . . and everything he disguised . . ." (472). "And the great woe of all was this: that all these things were unsuspected without, and undivulgible from within . . ." (471).

Pierre's initial reaction to Isabel's letter, the resolve to tear down the barriers that have kept him from knowing the hidden things and to live "out in" his hidden life, culminates in quite a literal image of what Berthoff refers to as "the prime Romantic subject of the 'growth of the mind' " (49).[17] Realizing that the walls are closing in on him, Pierre rushes from his ancestral mansion. "He could not stay in his chamber; the house contracted to a nutshell around him; the walls smote his forehead; bare-headed he rushed from the place, and only in the infinite air, found scope for that boundless expansion of his life" (91). The mind bursts from its container; inner space explodes into the infinite air; and Pierre, one assumes, finally succeeds, as the chapter title announces, at "Emerg[ing] from his Teens."

A second group of metaphors of boundaries destroyed by Pierre's acknowledgment of Isabel as his sister is associated with the Gothic scene of his midnight vigils before his father's picture:

> Thus sometimes in the mystical, outer quietude of the long country nights; either when the hushed mansion was banked round by the thick-fallen December snows, or banked round by the immovable white August moonlight; in the haunted repose of a wide story, tenanted only by himself; and sentinelling his own little closet; and standing guard, as it were, before the mystical tent of the picture; and ever watching the strangely concealed lights of the meanings that so mysteriously moved to and fro within; thus sometimes

stood Pierre before the portrait of his father, unconsciously throwing himself open to all those ineffable hints and ambiguities, and undefined half-suggestions, which now and then people the soul's atmosphere as thickly as in a soft, steady snowstorm, the snowflakes people the air.

. . . . .

But now, now!—Isabel's letter read: swift as the first light that slides from the sun, Pierre saw all preceding ambiguities, all mysteries ripped open as if with a keen sword, and forth trooped thickening phantoms of an infinite gloom. (117–18)

Conflated in this scene are the Gothic conventions of the mysterious ancestral portrait and of "haunted" apartments where mysterious lights are seen to move to and fro. The mysterious lights, however, are here represented as emanating from the ancestral portrait itself, described metaphorically as a tent. The metaphor will echo later in the description of Isabel's tentlike hair, black veil of her mystery as she kneels at the casement window (210). Among the extraordinary aspects of Melville's manipulation of Gothic elements here is the way his conflation of metaphors moves the scene back and forth between inside and outside. This movement suggests a breaking down of several kinds of barriers: barriers inside Pierre, barriers outside him, barriers between his innermost self and the outside world.

The midnight vigil is, on the one hand, an image of extreme inner seclusion: inside the house, alone in the haunted story, the house itself shut in by snow or "immovable" moonlight. Within this "walled isolation" (120), Pierre nonetheless occasionally "throws himself open" in such a way that it snows *inside* him. But this phenomenon is only temporary. "Pierre would regain the assured element of consciously bidden and self-propelled thought; and then in a moment the air all cleared, not a snowflake descended . . ." (118). Thus the image of Pierre shut into his own room is an image both of the mind communing secretly with itself and the mind susceptible to intrusion from without. Pierre, banked round by snow, is "unconsciously . . . open" to the possibility of an *interior* snowstorm.

But inside the haunted wing he is also outside the picture, the "tent," guarding it. Inside his innermost private room, that is, Pierre guards something even further inside. And yet the image of guarding a tent is an image of being completely *outside*. The source of the paradox is that the mystery of the portrait is, after all, a mystery of the world outside Pierre at the same time that it is his own. Thus the ripping open of the mysteries is an event inside Pierre, an event outside him, and an event that destroys the distinction between inside and outside. It recalls his double resolution to tear the veils from all idols and to live out his hidden life, and it is explained by an earlier passage in the novel: "From without, no wonderful effect is wrought within ourselves, unless some interior, responding wonder meets it" (70).

Isabel's letter, obscure though it is, has ripped open the mysteries. Here is a good ending for a Gothic romance: the source of the mysterious lights in a haunted wing is revealed; the combination of an ancestral portrait and a manuscript reveals the orphan's identity; and proper social relations can be restored. But Pierre's revelation is devastating precisely because it shows that proper social relations can never be restored. He cannot claim his sister without disowning his father; he cannot be a brother without finding his mother's door shut against him; he cannot be a husband without denying a sister. The source of these problems is the America depicted so scathingly in *Pierre:* a class-ridden society in which there are no proper social relations, a "green and golden" (1) Eden that, like so many childhood pastorals of Gothic romance, turns out to have fallen long ago, if only the protagonist had known. The snake had been there all the time, and Pierre finally recognizes it after reading Isabel's letter: it is his aristocratic mother, with her "scaly, glittering folds of pride" (126). The "green and golden" New World of Pierre's happy family life is revealed as the same Old World of his sister's childhood isolation: a world of "greenish" foundations and yellow, rotting sills (161); a world of decay and death. And so in *Pierre* the ripping open of mysteries produces, instead of explanations, more phantoms: "thickening phantoms of an infinite gloom" (118).

Pierre enters Isabel's world in a third Gothic metaphor of the removal of barriers, namely, his crossing the threshold of the house where she is staying. "He stands before the door; the house is steeped in silence; he knocks; the casement light flickers for a moment and then moves away; within, he hears a door creak on its hinges; then his whole heart beats wildly as the outer latch is lifted; and holding the light above her supernatural head, Isabel stands before him" (156–57). By the time Pierre goes to his first appointment with Isabel, her allure has been described both in physical and metaphysical terms. Thus this scene is at the same time a metaphysical and overtly sexual rendering of the characteristic pause at the threshold before the Gothic protagonist crosses the border of the dark, mysterious world. Lévy praises Maturin for restoring to the Faustean legend its proper dignity: "Lewis l'adolescent, et à sa suite Charlotte Dacre et quelques autres imitateurs, avaient faussé la légende Faustienne, et

substitué au drame de la connaissance celui plus ordinaire de la chair"
(584). In *Pierre* the two dramas are the same. Pierre's desire for Isabel
is a whole complex of longings, the object of all of them being knowledge. The epistemological passion she inspires in him—"to know something definite of that face" (63), to tear the veil from all hidden things—
is also a physical passion for her. Pierre's desperate desire to know Isabel—to know her in the sense of becoming acquainted with her, to know
her story, to know her secret, to know her sexually—leads him, in this
central Gothic episode, across her threshold. The setting, like many settings for corresponding scenes in Gothic romance, evokes the Fall, but
in such a way as to "make strange" the Gothic convention by broadening
its meaning and making it more ambiguous.

Pierre approaches the house when Gothic protagonists so often approach them, "at fall of eve" (153). From the forest's "owl-haunted depths
of caves and rotted leaves, and . . . overgrowth of decaying wood . . .
came a moaning, muttering, roaring sound: rain-shakings of the palsied
trees, slidings of rocks undermined, final crashings of long-riven boughs
and devilish gibberish of the forest-ghosts" (154). The images of falling
that permeate this description are a version of circumstances associated
with many Gothic protagonists' initiation into the dark world of terror
and desire. The architectural embodiment of this world is often set in
natural surroundings suggesting the danger of a fall.[18] Often the Gothic
castle is set high on a precipice (Lévy 407). As MacAndrew says, "[A]t
the most intense moment of moral danger, there . . . appears in [the
Gothic] landscape the terrible abyss of damnation" (49). The bandit's
hideout in Maturin's *The Albigenses,* for example, is set on a spectacular
eminence, and one of the first things the imprisoned heroine notices from
her casement window is what a long way down it is (2: 234). In the
bowels of this hideout is the lycanthrope, whose descent from man to
beast is another metaphor for the same danger. In most cases, the building itself is also falling, piecemeal. It is in a state of collapse and yet at
the same time gives the impression of irresistible strength, as if its ruin,
like that wrought by the Fall itself, were here to stay. Inside there is a
concentration of "vice and violence" (*Mysteries of Udolpho* 329). Gothic
interiors are places where goodness is imprisoned: "Misery yet dwelt in
the castle of Dunbayne, for there the virtues were captive, while the vices
reigned despotic" (Radcliffe, *Castles of Athlin and Dunbayne* 39). The
settings of such buildings evoke the perpetual imminence of a fall; the
buildings themselves, in their outward appearance and inner life, evoke
the Fall in its permanence.

All these elements are present in Pierre's first visit to Isabel but are mixed and transformed in many ways. First, in Melville's version of the crossing of the threshold, what is usually the decayed aspect of the architecture is imputed to the landscape itself. The forest is not, like the precipices of Gothic romance, a place from which one can fall; it is itself decayed and decaying, fallen and falling. The house itself is "ancient" (156), and its roof and north side are "moss-encrusted" (156)—qualities one associates with the mossy ruins of Gothic romance. But it is also a farmhouse set on a "mild lake" (154) in a "verdant spot" (154) near cornfields, and the prisoners there are "gentle and contented captives— the pans of milk and the snow-white Dutch cheeses in a row, and moulds of golden butter, and the jars of lily cream" (154).[19] As it turns out, however, there is also another prisoner—the mystery of the pastoral house, as it were: Delly, the fallen woman. She is locked into a room upstairs, where she paces back and forth, treading the "gushing grapes" of the words Isabel utters in the room below (166). In this bizarre image of Delly's suffering producing the wine of Isabel's verbal communion with Pierre, Melville invokes both the Fall and the Fortunate Fall. In keeping with the ambiguity of that double resonance, Pierre's entry into this world and his subsequent communion with Isabel, expressed symbolically in their "sacrament of the supper" (228), release Delly from her imprisonment. Having decided to "live right out in [his] own hidden life," Pierre, in an act that could equally well be symbolic of salvation or damnation, liberates the fallen woman from the house where Isabel is staying.

By crossing Isabel Banford's threshold, Pierre releases into the outer world the "hidden life" of the house. He also finds himself in an inner world he has not known before. What world his desire for knowledge has opened to him is indicated in part by another Gothic scene involving boundaries. In this scene Isabel, concealed by the black "veil" (210) of her hair and kneeling at an "obscurely open window" as if at a "shrine," initiates Pierre into the dark mysteries of which she seems the priestess (210). Beyond the window is the "ebonly warm and most noiseless summer night" (210), lit erratically with heat lightning. Isabel, associated constantly with interiors, is nonetheless priestess of nature. Again, as in the scene in which Pierre meditated on the portrait, the imagery shifts between a world within and a world without, suggesting that the mysteries of the darkest interior of the heart are also the mysteries of the universe. And again, Pierre's new knowledge is not the kind of knowledge that Radcliffe's heroines ultimately discover—or that Maturin's heroes ultimately discover, for that matter—but the revelation of mystery itself.

All four of these Gothic metaphors, or groups of metaphors, of barriers removed, crossed, or broken down represent unities in which the "knowledge" that Isabel is his sister has involved Pierre. He is united with mystery, with nature, and with his own hidden life, and all these unities are represented in the communion with Isabel to which his wild curiosity has led him. The sexual imagery associated with this communion, however, suggests that it is incestuous. At the heart of *Pierre* is the tragic Gothic vision that sees knowledge as disaster and the unity it brings as a form of alienation. Like the love Annibal found by opening doors supposedly shut "for *ever,*" Pierre's knowledge may be not a transcending of his own boundaries but a solipsistic imprisonment in self that only appears to be a unity with something beyond him.[20] This possibility is strongly suggested by the fact that as in the cases of Frankenstein, the Montorios, and Melmoth, the unity Pierre achieves through the knowledge that removes barriers is also a form of isolation, manifested in the appearance of other barriers that the search for knowledge creates.

Pierre bursts into the infinite air as his mind expands beyond his mother's closed aristocratic world. But in the American society Melville portrays here, to leave that world is to belong nowhere. This first departure from his mother's house foreshadows Pierre's final departure, when he leaves as an outcast, tripping on the threshold as if he had been thrown out (258). As he and Isabel enter the city, they hear "the locking, and bolting, and barring of windows and doors . . ." (322). To be united with Isabel is to be, like her, completely separate, "thrust out of all hearts' gates" (223). "Thus, in the Enthusiast to Duty, the heaven-begotten Christ is born; and will not own a mortal parent, and spurns and rends all mortal bonds" (149). Pierre's escape from the contracting walls of his maternal house foreshadows the final rending of the bonds linking him with his parents and his past. The cause of this rending is his union with Isabel, who seems to bind him to her by some spell (213). Ironically, the bond proves literally to be mortal. The scene in which Pierre crosses Isabel's threshold is a partial explanation of the paradox. If in his enthusiasm Pierre resembles the second Adam who, in two senses, "rends all mortal bonds," in his lust for knowledge he also resembles the first Adam, whose transgression was the source of Christ's *Todesbanden* and of that primal separation, the exile beyond the walls of paradise.

By allying himself with "the unknown" (72), Pierre, like Ippolito, forfeits the sympathy of a world that cannot know him. And—as in the case of Frankenstein, the Montorios, and Melmoth—the reason the world cannot know him is partly that he is afraid it will. Pierre's first reaction to his new "knowledge" of his relation to Isabel is to hide it from everyone else. "What inscrutable thing was it, that so suddenly had made him a falsifyer . . . to his own . . . confiding mother?" (69).[21] His "very soul was forced to wear a mask" (255). His first response to the ripping open of his father's mystery is to lock up the evidence, the ancestral portrait, in a chest. Locking up the evidence, hoarding knowledge, is an act Gothic villains are always perpetrating; Pierre follows this act with others also reminiscent of Gothic villains, and of Gothic hero-villains who fail to bring their abstract knowledge into proper relation with social knowledge. He hides a corpse: ". . . Pierre went forth all redolent; but alas! his body only the embalming cerements of the buried dead within" (132). He buries his mother and Lucy, prematurely, somewhere deep in his own psyche: "At last he dismissed his mother's memory into that same profound vault where hitherto had reposed the swooned form of his Lucy. But, as sometimes men are coffined in a trance, being thereby mistaken for dead; so it is possible to bury a tranced grief in the soul . . ." (399). He casts Lucy, secretly, into a deep inner dungeon: "[S]o, deeper down in the more secret chambers of his unsuspecting soul, the smiling Lucy . . . was being bound a ransom for Isabel's salvation" (148).

All of these metaphors show that although Pierre's new knowledge is self-knowledge—the destruction of barriers that kept his own mystery locked up inside him—it also necessitates new repressions. He locks up the portrait so that he will not see it; he hides a corpse inside himself. Later he must place a curtain over his window to keep the strange Plotinus Plinlimmon from looking in; Pierre is obsessed with the idea that Plinlimmon, knowing his secret, leers at him. Of course, says Melville, "the Kantists might say, that this was a *subjective* sort of leer in Pierre" (409). This is in one sense a joke on Plinlimmon's own Transcendentalism, but it points also to a truth about Pierre. Melville suggests that perhaps Pierre only pretended to himself not to understand Plinlimmon's pamphlet, because he could not afford to admit that it told him something he already knew about himself (409–10). Thus the drawing of the curtain between Pierre and Plinlimmon is also in one sense a form of repression: Pierre does not want to see staring him in the face a reminder of the self-knowledge he is trying to hide from himself. This attempt to veil himself from Plinlimmon's inquisitive eyes is described as the curtaining of a portrait (409), a simile calling to mind Pierre's concealment—from himself—of his father's picture, and his meditation on Lucy: "[L]et me upon her sweet image draw the curtains of my soul" (259).

Thus Pierre's revelation, a source of unity with his own hidden self, with Isabel, and with some cosmic Other beyond the casement, is also a source of his separateness—from Lucy, his mother, his past, and even, ironically, from his own innermost self. This paradox of separateness in unity and unity in separateness is embodied most strikingly in his bizarre "marriage" with Isabel. On the one hand this marriage is described in images suggesting sexual union; on the other hand it amounts to a vow of celibacy. Melville describes Pierre's pious fraud as "an act, which would prospectively and forever bar the blessed boon of marriageable love from one so young and generous as Pierre, and eternally entangle him in a fictitious alliance which, though in reality but a web of air, yet in effect would prove a wall of iron" (244).

This "wall of iron" sets Pierre apart from the world and unites him with Isabel in "continual domestic confidence" (267), but the union itself, being "fictitious," is merely separateness. What kind of "confidence," after all, is based on mystery? Here Melville's ambiguity regarding Pierre's actual relation with Isabel helps to evoke the double horrors of unity and isolation. Is, or is not Pierre committing incest? In fact it appears that he is engaged both in a horrifying union with a woman he believes to be his sister and a torturous, frustrating separation from her. When he asks Isabel how one can sin in a dream, he appears to have plunged "deep down in the gulf of the soul" after hovering "on the verge" (382), but much later he is still teetering on the "verge" of "a black, bottomless gulf of guilt" (469). The ambiguities clouding our vision of the relationship mean that we see it both ways, which would appear to be the point. Pierre is involved in a marriage based on a vow of celibacy, and as is so often the case in Gothic romance, this vow produces "strange, *unique* follies and sins, unimagined before" (296).

As in Gothic romances, too, the vow implies religious orders. Pierre's initiation into the mysteries of which Isabel is priestess leads him to the Church of the Apostles. Architecturally, this building is a symbol of what should be a unity but in fact is separateness, as it used to be a church but has been "divided into stores; cut into offices . . ." (370). The order of Apostles itself is also separateness masquerading as unity, for its chief figure, Plotinus Plinlimmon, is characterized by an "essential unresponsive separateness" (Wadlington 111), a certain quality of "non-Benevolence" (404). Around this sinister figure eddies an "inscrutable atmosphere" (406), and his very clothes, yes, even his face, seem to disguise him (404). Pierre suspects Plotinus of duping Charlie Milthorpe into thinking he knows Plotinus "thoroughly" when in fact he knows him not at all (407). Despite his inaccessibility, Plotinus is apparently the type who pries into other hearts, since he seems often to be meditating on Pierre. In all this he is a Transcendental version of the bogus religious figures of Gothic romance who veil their own mysteries but display an unholy interest in those of others. This cold interest is presumably part of Plinlimmon's non-benevolence. "For that face did not respond to any-thing. Did I not say before that that face was something separate, and apart; a face by itself? Now, anything which is thus a thing by itself never responds to any other thing. If to affirm, be to expand one's isolated self; and if to deny, be to contract one's isolated self; then to respond is a suspension of all isolation" (409).

By responding to Isabel, Pierre experienced a "boundless expansion of his life," and yet somehow it has led him to the haunts of Plinlimmon, the very image of separateness. It is appropriate that Pierre's separateness in unity with Isabel—his incestuous and hence solipsistic union, his mar-riage that is not a marriage—should have just this place as its setting, because Plinlimmon's world is a version of Isabel's. The "inscrutable atmosphere" (406) around him recalls Isabel's "mysterious haze" (191) and the "haze of ambiguities" (213) in which she involves Pierre. Plin-limmon gives the appearance of great knowledge, and yet he may be a great humbug. Isabel claims to know with certainty that she is Pierre's sister, and yet she may not be. Like Isabel, Plinlimmon seems to have no relations, and as in her case, this state of unrelatedness seems to tran-scend mere ordinary orphanhood. She seems "not of woman born" (160); he seems "to have no family or blood ties of any sort" (405). Recognizing the orphan Isabel as his sister, Pierre recognizes the "divine unidentifi-ableness" in himself: a "feeling entirely lonesome, and orphanlike" (125). Transcendentalism is the religion of the divine unidentifiableness in the soul; appropriately, Pierre, by discovering his orphanhood, becomes a Transcendental "Apostle."

In Isabel's life, the problem of relatedness is bound up with the prob-lem of knowledge. "I never knew a mortal mother" (160), she begins her story. The key issue in the Gothic plot is what Pierre calls "the grand governing thing of all—the reality of the physical relationship" (195). Can Pierre and Isabel really know, without clear proofs, that they are related? The issue of relatedness is in turn connected, through the figure of Plotinus Plinlimmon, to the philosophical problem of knowledge. Plotinus's name perhaps points to the reason for his state of extreme separateness: an epistemology that, Melville implies, locks up the mind in itself by insisting that real knowledge is intuitive and need have no corresponding evidence in the outside world.[22] This is the epistemology to which Isabel, by persuading Pierre not to weigh her evidence in the "dull head['s]" "cold courts of justice" (98), has temporarily converted him. Pierre's conversion to the mystery of which Isabel is priestess and to the philosophical stance of those who believe in intuitive knowledge as immediate access to truth leads him—as of course it would—to this haunt of Transcendentalists, with its secret society presided over by a solitary, unknown and unknowable man. It is here that Pierre comes to hide away his knowledge—that Isabel is his sister—from other people, and it is here that he finds himself "hemmed in" by ambiguities, "the stony walls all round that he could not overleap" (469).

It is here too that he becomes "unwilling states-prisoner of letters" (473) in the attempt to translate his gnosis—the knowledge of the hopelessly insoluble mystery of the world— into the "inventional mysteries" (493) of a novel. Like all Gothic protagonists, Pierre becomes "gradually separated from the world and imprisoned within [his] own consciousness" (Kiely 77).[23] It is Melville's innovation to make this imprisonment in the Gothic edifice of the self an imprisonment in a religion and epistemology that preclude the mind's contact with anything beyond the self (represented not only in Plinlimmon but also in Pierre's incest, so often an image of entrapment in self) and, furthermore, an imprisonment in the writing of a novel.

Gothic romances are replete with characters telling their stories or writing them down. It is typical, for example, that when Cicely of Raby makes her way into the haunted castle, she should find a "ghostly" veiled figure sitting at a table "covered with written paper and writing implements" (Musgrave, *Cicely of Raby* 4: 62). The manuscript turns out to be the story of a woman who shut herself up, "amidst ruins, solitude, and misery" (4: 100) and wrote her memoirs. The veiled figure is her skeleton, still, it seems, unable to leave the writer's desk. In *Melmoth the Wanderer,* Alonzo di Monçada, locked up in his convent, arouses suspicion by his "absurd and perpetual demand for paper" (132). He is writing his case for the benefit of the outside world, and he hopes by so doing to rejoin it. Pierre has something in common with these characters: as an "unwilling states-prisoner of letters" (473) he writes desperately from a (metaphorical) prison, and he is writing a personal narrative. But he is also different. First, there is never any doubt that once allowed pen and ink, most of these other Gothic characters will be able to tell their stories. They write (literally, of course), with the same facility that seems to have characterized the authors who produced the multi-volume works in which we meet them. Ippolito, allowed to write his defense for the Inquisitors, has no trouble doing so. He has a straightforward if extraordinary tale to tell, and it is a relief to write it down. Narratives like the one he writes explain mysteries. But Pierre, shut up in the states-prison of letters, is trying, by *writing* "mysteries" (493), "to open," as Hawthorne would say, "an intercourse with the world."

In his juvenile productions, Pierre gained quite a reputation: as a well-known writer he was invited, for example, to speak to the *Urquhartian Club for the Immediate Extension of the Limits of all Knowledge, both Human and Divine* (351). Now, however, he discovers that he was not quite so well known as he thought, and he discovers furthermore that he is incapable of making himself known, not only in the sense of establishing a literary reputation, but even in the sense of translating his ideas onto paper.[24] From the depths of his isolation in the Church of the Apostles, Pierre writes a novel, the one point of contact between him and the outside world, his one hope of making himself known. And yet it is also the emblem of his "great woe": the fact "that all these things were unsuspected without, and undivulgible from within . . ." (471).

As Harry Levin says, the fiction Pierre is writing "has its inspiration and its obstacle in his marital obligations—or rather, in the unhallowed family ties that they mask" (186). Pierre's problem as a writer derives from the fact that his inspiration is Isabel: source of his quest for knowledge, of his exultation and despair in the insoluble mystery of the world, of his terrible self-knowledge and self-deception, of his desire to open an intercourse with the world while keeping the world away from his secret. It is hard for a man who is trying both to reveal his cosmic knowledge and to hide the personal knowledge that inspired it to do either successfully, especially when his book itself is a search for truth despite its "everlasting elusiveness" (472) and when he is trying to communicate both his knowledge and his search for knowledge through the medium of "mysteries." Furthermore, Pierre is trying to make public a knowledge the public cannot appreciate anyway, and his very publishers are in the end an insuperable barrier of "Steel, Flint & Asbestos" (497). Not surprisingly, Pierre's novel, the interface between his inner life and the outer world, becomes, like Isabel's own attempts at self-expression, a kind of anticommunication. It is a mask and a prison: a barrier between him and the world with which it should connect him.

Now he gave jeer for jeer, and taunted the apes that jibed him. With the soul of an Atheist, he wrote down the godliest things; with the feeling of death and misery in him, he created forms of gladness and life. For the pangs in his heart, he put down hoots on the paper. And everything else he disguised under the so conveniently adjustable drapery of all-stretchable Philosophy. For the more and the more that he wrote, and the deeper and the deeper that he dived, Pierre saw the everlasting elusiveness of Truth; the universal lurking insincerity of even the greatest and purest written thoughts. (472)

Here the quest for knowledge, the attempt to express knowledge, and the attempt to conceal it are all one. The writer's prison is the prison of the self: the self in the act of knowing, the self both fearing and longing to be known.

Isabel inspires Pierre with a passion for knowledge; she converts him from an epistemology that demands evidence to one that relies on the heart's intuition; she initiates him into a gnosis that, paradoxically, is the knowledge of mystery; she inspires him with a passion to make his knowledge known; she inspires him with a fear that someone knows his secret. In all of this Isabel is an embodiment of knowledge, or at least the appearance of knowledge, and Pierre's relation to her resembles the unities in separateness that such tragic Gothic figures as Caleb Williams, the Montorios, and Frankenstein experience in their relations with the figures who represent their illicit knowledge—Falkland, Orazio, Frankenstein's creature. But Isabel also represents not knowing, in all its Gothic terror and glory.

Gothic romance in general presents two versions of not knowing: not knowing as a source of pain and horror, of mere confusion, and not knowing as the source of sublime exaltation. The extent to which these two kinds of mystery are linked depends on the Gothicist. One reason Radcliffe does not fully condemn Vivaldi's tendency to see the supernatural when he cannot see clearly, or Emily's tendency to believe herself visited by the spirit of her father, is that these tendencies are part of the characters' susceptibility to a real supernatural, manifest in the natural mysteries of His world. Early in *The Mysteries of Udolpho* we hear how the obscurity of the woods drew forth Emily's poetic imagination. At the close of that scene Radcliffe quotes Thomson's lines: "A faint erroneous ray / Glanced from th'imperfect surfaces of things, / . . . flung half an image on the straining eye . . ." (17). Here the state of not knowing in which the "straining eye" can make out only partial images is sublime; later, in the obscurity of Emily's room at Udolpho, it will be horrific.

The casement windows of the villain's haunted castle, however, open out on the sublimities of God's world; Radcliffe's Emily and Ellena look out from the darkness and confusion of the villain's mysteries toward the sublime obscurities of nature and nature's God. The half-images—the mysteries—of both worlds appear in some sense to be two versions of the same thing. Radcliffe herself would not have made the connection consciously, but her first biographer saw it in her work: "The tremblings of the spirit, which are base when prompted by anything earthly, become sublime when inspired by a sense of the visionary and immortal. They are the secret witnesses of our alliance with power, which is not of this world. We feel both the fleshly infirmity and our high destiny, as we shrink on the borders of spiritual existence" (Talfourd 107).

Maturin, a bolder writer than Radcliffe, made the connection overtly, announcing in the preface to *Montorio* that he had chosen as his subject the passion of fear—a passion that might be traced "to a high and obvious source" (1: v). Melville was bolder still, uniting the two versions of not knowing in one character and declining to provide a philosophical framework that would resolve the resulting ambiguity. This center of the not knowing in *Pierre* is Isabel, who, depending on how one sees her, is either the priestess of mystery, embodying the allurements of the "secrets and communion of another world" (*Montorio* 1: 2), or a confused young woman, victim of not knowing as a source of alienation and despair. Correspondingly, Pierre's relation with her, depending on the perspective from which one views it, looks both like cosmic unity and cosmic alienation, both like contact with the profoundest mystery and mere ignorance.[25]

Both versions of Isabel's mystery are represented in Gothic stage settings. The cosmic mystery into which she initiates Pierre is represented in the stormy night scene at the casement when Pierre visits to hear the second part of her story. The horror of mere confusion and disorientation in her life has objective correlatives in the strange house she remembers as her first home and in the madhouse to which she was sent later. In addition, both the positive and negative versions of mystery are embodied in the version of Gothic pastoral with which Melville begins the book.

Isabel's earliest memory is of the starkest, bleakest alienation, at the heart of which was the experience of not knowing. Her story begins, "I never knew a mortal mother" (160) and is interspersed with statements that even now she does not know whether what she says is true: "Scarce know I at any time whether I tell you real things, or the unrealest dreams" (165). The objective correlative of this nightmarish experience of alienation and not knowing is a version of the haunted house. As Tompkins says of Radcliffe's Gothic edifices, one of their essential characteristics is that they are never "fully known, even to their inhabitants, whose steps are always liable to stray, as in a dream, into unfamiliar apartments and down crumbling stairways" (257). The Gothic heroine's lack of knowledge isolates her not only from the physical world around her in the Gothic castle but also from the mental world of its chief inhabitants. One thinks of Emily's speculations on Montoni: " 'O could I know,' said she to herself, 'what passes in that mind; could I know the thoughts, that are known there . . .' " (243). But Isabel's haunted house represents an experience of isolation and not knowing, the completeness and horror of which Emily St. Aubert could never have dreamed.

> My first dim life-thoughts cluster round an old, half-ruinous house . . . a wild, dark house, planted in the midst of a round, cleared, deeply sloping space. . . . Ever I shrunk at evening from peeping out of my window, lest the ghostly pines should steal near to me, and reach out their grim arms to snatch me into their horrid shadows. In summer the forest unceasingly hummed with unconjecturable voices of unknown birds and beasts. In winter its deep snows were traced like any paper map, with dotting night-tracks of four-footed creatures, that, even to the sun, were never visible, and never were seen by man at all. In the round open space the dark house stood . . . shadeless and shelterless in the heart of shade and shelter. Some of the windows were rudely boarded up . . . and those rooms were utterly empty, and never were entered, though they were doorless. But often, from the echoing corridor, I gazed into them with fear; for the great fire-places were all in ruins; the lower tier of back-stones were burnt into one white common crumbling; and the black bricks above had fallen upon the hearths, heaped here and there with the still falling soot of long-extinguished fires. Every hearth-stone in that house had one long crack through it; every floor drooped at the corners; and outside, the whole base of the house, where it rested on the low foundation of greenish stones, was strewn with dull, yellow moulderings of the rotting sills. (160–61)

Part of the originality of this description is that while clearly owing something to the Gothic tradition of dark, unknowable, ruined castles, it presents total desolation and knowinglessness not by means of obscure suggestion but with uncanny clarity. In addition, this ruined house, instead of being a place, as in most Gothic romance, where we meet the heroine just emerging into maturity, is the scene of her childhood. The fearful state of not knowing is not something Isabel must encounter as a well-educated young woman; it is the fundamental condition of her life.[26]

Another unusual aspect of this place is that it is a Gothic house without something they always have—clues. "No name; no scrawled or written thing; no book, was in the house; no one memorial speaking of its former occupants. It was dumb as death" (161). There were no gravestones outside it. These details are the more striking for their absurdity in realistic terms. Are we to assume that as a small child who was an absolute paragon of ignorance, Isabel was searching her Gothic homestead for *written* clues as to its "former" owners, when not only could she not read, she did not even understand who its *present* owners were? In an ordinary Gothic romance, someone would eventually go back to this old house and find a manuscript or pile of bones revealing everything. But Isabel's account rules that out. There are no clues in the house, and there is furthermore no way of getting to it. It exists on no map; Isabel does not even know in what country it was situated or whether, in fact, it ever existed at all.

Whether this house existed in fact, it is clear that for Isabel it exists as a mental state. In her experience, not knowing is a nightmare of alienation, a state of cosmic unrelatedness. Not to know who you are or where you are is to belong nowhere and to no one. The extreme of not knowing who you are is madness. In the madhouse, Isabel says, there were many people, "but for the most part they lived separately" (166). Separateness is Isabel's great source of suffering, and she longs for its exact opposite: "I feel that there can be no perfect peace in individualness. Therefore I hope one day to feel myself drank up into the pervading spirit animating all things" (167). In order to be related to someone else, however, she must know that she is related. "I never knew a mortal mother." Gothic romance is filled with orphans who finally succeed in proving, by means of a crucial ancestral portrait, a birthmark, or some other token that in fact they belong to someone. Despite what they originally thought, they have, after all, a family, a family history, an identity, a social role. It is one of Isabel's strange characteristics that although she is someone whose identity can never be known with objective certainty, who describes her life as a nightmare of confusion and bewilderment, and who refers to herself repeatedly as not knowing anything, she claims to have certain knowledge—and proof—of this one fact: her relation to Pierre. These proofs are of striking dubiousness, and Pierre challenges her about them. How, for example, did the guitar come to be at Saddle Meadows? To this question Isabel responds, "[F]ar sweeter are mysteries than surmises . . . " (215). Even Isabel's "knowledge" of her relation to Pierre is based on mystery. But as Pierre's own subsequent experience shows, mysteries are not always sweet, and they can be a source of isolation that is the opposite of the universal relatedness Isabel desires.

The two versions of mystery represented in Isabel's life—the positive version, a source of exaltation, and the negative version, a source of pain—are intertwined throughout the Gothic plot. Indeed, they are already present together in the version of Gothic pastoral with which the book begins. *Pierre* opens with a description of nature seemingly overcome by a sudden consciousness of her own mystery and seeking refuge from it in silence: hence the "wonderful and indescribable repose," the "trance-like aspect of the green and golden world" (1). This world is Melville's version of the Gothic protagonist's childhood Arcadia which turns out to have been Eden only in the sense that the child did not know about the Fall, the evidence of which was to be found in some aspect of the Eden itself. Behind Melville's version of pastoral there is, of course, a long tradition to which all Gothic pastorals belong, and in that tradition the hint of something amiss is a common feature of the description of Arcadia.[27] What specifically links Melville's "green and golden world" to the Gothic tradition of pastoral is the presence of mystery as the discordant element. The central mystery in Pierre's innocent world will come to be associated with his father's past, as is so often the case in Gothic romance; the snake in his Eden will turn out to be his mother (126). What is interesting about the first paragraph of *Pierre* in the context of Gothic uses of pastoral is that before any mention of the mystery of Isabel or the mystery of Pierre's father, the mystery of this Eden is associated with the landscape itself. The very source of the pastoral beauty, in fact, is nature's need for refuge from a consciousness of her own mystery. This mystery is ambiguously described. It produces the "wonderful and indescribable repose" of the pastoral world, but it is also something from which "refuge" is necessary. And it is the source of slightly sinister stasis: the grass seems to have ceased to grow. Grass cannot be observed in the process of growing, as grass or trees or flowers can be seen stirring in the wind; the grass that seems to have stopped growing is thus not a logical image in the context of the surprising *visible* stillness of Pierre's world. On the one hand this is an image of nature "breathless with adoration," but on the other it is an image of lifelessness. The fact that the grass does not seem to be growing presents a decided contrast with the imagery in at least one literary paradise Melville knew well: Milton's Eden, where the only labor consists in trying to restrain the wondrously generative vegetation.

Furthermore, Melville says that Pierre seems as if "bewitched by the loveliness of this silence" (1). In this initial context, before the introduction of Isabel, "bewitch" seems a relatively neutral term. Later it takes on a range of positive and negative connotations. In the descriptions of Isabel there is much to reevoke the whole atmosphere of this first pastoral scene: her "mystery," her acute consciousness of it, her tendency to seek refuge from it in silence and stillness, her "bewitchingness" (199), and the remarkable stasis associated with her "sweet and awful passiveness" (268). Into her silence and stasis she seems to draw Pierre, whose moments of physical passion with her are always associated, paradoxically, with muteness and motionlessness.

These correspondences are some of the many linking Isabel's mystery with the mystery of nature, in both its beauty and its horror. The mystery of her face is the mystery of the "Eolean pine" (55); her "bewitchingness" is like that of "the mysterious vault of night" (199); she opens to Pierre the dark mysteries beyond the casement window. Her effect on Pierre is, ironically, to lead him away from nature and into the enclosed world of the city. Ultimately, however, his meditation on the mysteries into which she has initiated him leads him back to the topography of his childhood, as from his cold Inferno in the city he revisits that lost landscape in a waking dream. In this dream vision he climbs the mountains bounding the pastoral world of Saddle Meadows, penetrating the purple haze to their real meaning, embodied in the image of Enceladus, "son and grandson of an incest" (483). Thus Pierre deciphers one of nature's mysteries and at the same time one of his own: the face of the incestuous Titan is his.

This vision is the counterpart of the final revelation in Gothic romances when the hero or heroine realizes what it all meant; the mysteries of the childhood world are elucidated, and Paradise (at least in Gothic comedy) can be regained. Alicia goes back to her old home and finds the real history of of her family, the source of her father's disappearance and her mother's mysterious grief (Musgrave, *Solemn Injunction*). Emily learns the source of her father's sorrow *(Mysteries of Udolpho);* Madeline Clermont learns the real story of her father's life (Roche, *Clermont*). Julia Mazzini, after a long underground journey, finds herself back home, in an underground chamber where she recovers her lost mother (Radcliffe, *Sicilian Romance*). The revelation is always associated with the protagonist's family history, but the landscape of childhood is not implicated in the revelation. This is one reason Paradise can be regained at the end. Pierre's elucidation of the mysteries of his own family is produced through an elucidation of the mysteries of the landscape itself. And like many tragic Gothic characters before him, what Pierre discovers is that his own and his family history is bound up with incest. By locating the mystery in the natural world, Melville broadens the meaning of the mystery and of the knowledge at stake. The mystery of Isabel that is the mystery of Pierre's family is also the mystery of nature itself. Pierre elucidates this mystery, not by going back home and reading some papers[28] or by hearing the confession of a dying relative,[29] but by finding the "hidden life, curtained by that cunning purpleness" (479). And again, as in the case of the midnight vigil, the barrier preventing him from knowing what was beyond himself was also the barrier concealing his own inner secret.

Ironically, what this final unveiling of the landscape and of Pierre's own face reveals is another barrier: the rock in which Enceladus-Pierre is trapped, "writhing from out the imprisoning earth" (480). Here is another image of the isolation and despair into which Isabel has initiated Pierre. The final secret his knowledge of her reveals is the secret meaning of his incestous communion with her, that meaning being that he is irrevocably locked into his own mortality, despite his "appetite for God" (480). The nature into which Isabel has liberated him through knowledge is only a prison: the prison of not knowing that is his mortal nature.

The image of Enceladus "writhing from out the imprisoning earth" is a culmination of the imagery of impassable barriers: the "iron wall" of Pierre's marriage, the "stony walls" of ambiguities that hem him in, the states-prison of letters where he is trapped in himself. The sum of all these walls is "the wall of the thick darkness of the mystery of Isabel" (238). At one time Pierre thought that he saw glowing on this wall, "recorded as by some phosphoric finger . . . the burning fact, that Isabel was his sister" (238). Thus he did not care that "her light was lidded and the lid was locked." But having for so long accepted the validity of the intuitive knowledge that told him, without any proofs, Isabel was his sister and having believed that through her he had come to a knowledge of mystery, Pierre suddenly stumbles on the mystery of knowledge itself. This discovery occurs in an ironic reversal of a scene often associated with revelations in Gothic romance, the scene in which someone looks at the picture of what ought to be a stranger and recognizes it. Dorothée notices that Emily wears a picture of Dorothée's own dead mistress *(Mysteries of Udolpho);* Schedoni sees his own picture on Ellena's bosom *(The Italian);* Matilda and Ellinor weep inexplicably over the picture of a stranger who turns out to be their mother (Lee, *The Recess*). Pierre goes to an art gallery where he discovers the picture of a stranger who somewhat resembles his father. But there is no one to say who the subject of the picture is; its label reveals that it is *"A stranger's head, by an unknown hand"* (487). And instead of elucidating the mysteries, it calls everything into question: "How did he know that Isabel was his sister?" (492).

By the time Pierre experiences this negative revelation, as it were, portraits have taken on a significance they do not have to any great extent in Gothic romance. Ancestral portraits usually exist in the Gothic to establish rightful heirs in their proper family relationships. But Melville has throughout the book, and especially in the passages describing Pierre's struggle to write, linked the quest for knowledge with the quest to express knowledge in art. Pierre's portrait of his father was introduced by a story suggesting that its painting was an act of knowledge on the artist's part and that Pierre's father feared a portrait might reveal his secret. Pierre is struck by two things at the art gallery: the fact that he cannot really know Isabel is his sister and the fact that "[a]ll the walls of the world" seem hung with pictures "grandly outlined, but miserably filled" (487). The latter thought recalls Enceladus, image of the writer struggling toward heaven but trapped in the "imprisoning earth." The image of the "walls of the world" is one of the last images of the conflation of the quest to know and the quest to make one's knowledge known through art. Pierre looks at a picture and realizes that he cannot know his relation to Isabel; he looks at pictures and realizes that the walls of the world are hung with artists' failures. And the "walls" of the world—the "imprisoning earth"—are exactly the reason for both dilemmas.

Knowing is as much a source of terror in Gothic romance as is not knowing. Pierre's final horrifying revelation combines both terrors in his sudden realization that he does not even know how to know. Is knowledge possible? The arrival of Lucy at the Apostles' suggests for a brief moment that it is. Lucy's relation to Pierre comes close to being a redeemed version of his relation to Isabel. It is another religious vow, since Lucy wants to be regarded as a nunlike cousin, and it is another expression of love through a vow not to marry. It is also another renunciation of love's right to confidence. Lucy has accepted Pierre's mystery as he accepted Isabel's; she acknowledges that he was right in saying that love should never "know all." Her refusal to pry into his secret takes its strength from her conviction that she possesses, through love, an intuitive knowledge of him. In the same way, Pierre's refusal to pry into Isabel's mystery was based on a conviction that he could intuitively know his relation to her. At first Lucy does seem to have an intuitive knowledge of Pierre's spiritual plight. But then she has a revelation that makes the reader wonder how much, and what, she really knows. Isabel throws open a door, and Lucy is struck with "a sudden irradiation of some subtle intelligence—but whether welcome to her, or otherwise, could not be determined . . ." (463–64). Melville's own refusal "to complacently clear up" his mysteries in the end means that the reader never knows whether or not such knowledge exists as Lucy seems for a moment to represent.

Whatever the status of Lucy's knowledge, she ends, like everyone else, in the prison whose walls enclose the book's final mysteries and revelations. In the cell are a group of friends, lovers, and enemies whose proper relations are hidden in darkness. At last it is revealed that Lucy is dead and that Pierre is dead. Isabel, dying, manages to say, "All's o'er, and ye know him not!" (505)—Melville's version, perhaps, of the many nonrevelations made by all those characters in Gothic romance who die in the act of telling what they know.[30] The book ends with a final barrier: Isabel's black hair, which has "veiled" her throughout the book, falls over Pierre as well.

Pierre has been the Gothic hero who brings dark knowledge to light; the Gothic villain who locks up secrets; the Gothic hero-villain who sells his soul for knowledge and then fears to be known; the Gothic victim for whom not knowing is a source of terror and despair; the Gothic heroine who, through the sublime mysteries of nature, apprehends the unknown. And the ambiguities resulting from his playing all these roles make him also—to a much greater extent even than Melmoth—the Gothic protagonist from whom the reader is ultimately shut out. Early in their relationship, Isabel embraced Pierre "so convulsively, that her hair sideways swept over him, and half concealed him" (265). From whom? There was no one else there. Melville seems here to imagine the readers as an audience at a play, an audience that suddenly finds the protagonist half-concealed from its view. At the end of the book, Pierre is "arboured" (505) by Isabel's hair, and the audience no longer sees his face.

Were the book a drama, the actress who played Isabel would be hard pressed to know exactly how to deliver her last line. Is it spoken in despair? In resignation? In relief? Is it a bare statement of fact, without emotion? Or is there, perhaps, a note of triumph? In the first discussion of the relation between love and confidence, Lucy described the pleasures of knowing one's beloved: ". . . Love is vain and proud; and when I walk the streets, and meet thy friends, I must still be laughing and hugging to myself the thought,—They know him not;—I only know my Pierre . . ." (51). Whether or not Isabel is hugging to herself this thought at the end of the book, it is easy to picture Melville doing so. Isabel is right: no one knows Pierre, including the reader, and it is with relief that one sees Melville at last taking refuge in silence from his own mystery. It is hard to escape the sense, as the novel nears its close, that Melville does not want the reader to understand Pierre after all and that the many Gothic props have been brought on stage partly for camouflage. Certainly Melville used Gothic elements to better effect in the works in which he used them more sparingly. The mysteriously inscribed coffin at the end of *Moby-Dick* is an example. Most Gothicists recognize that there is indeed more in a closed box than in an open one; nonetheless, in Gothic romance the presence of a closed box and a puzzling inscription cannot but lead at last to their being emptied of mystery. In *Moby-Dick* the coffin is inscribed with the unreadable secret of the universe (399), and it is precisely the fact of its being sealed shut that saves Ishmael from death. The author opens neither the coffin nor its text, because the central mystery of his book cannot, like Gothic mysteries, be "elucidated." Many of the Gothic devices in *Pierre* are used to a similar end: the ancestral portrait that can never be tortured into answering Pierre's question, even were it "hung up in the deepest dungeon of the Spanish Inquisition" (116); the haunted house that can never be explored and contains no clues anyway; the antirevelation of the portrait in the art gallery of a stranger who must remain just that. But these devices come after a while to resemble rather cynical melodramatic jokes, whose effect is far from the generous tragic humor of *Moby-Dick.*

In *Moby-Dick* the "drama of knowledge" is played out on a cosmic scale big enough to accommodate both an exuberant delight in the encyclopedic amassing of facts and an exultation in the ultimate mystery they cannot explain. Ahab's story is told with both a comic sense of the impossibility of knowledge and a tragic appreciation of the heroic nature that destroys itself in the effort to know. The sealed coffin with its unreadable inscription is the final embodiment of this double vision of mystery: it is the ever-turning wheel of Ixion but also the "still point of the turning world"—the unopened box that buoys the solitary self amid the "heartless . . . immensities."[31]

What Melville does with this Gothic device is a good emblem of what he does with all the Gothic devices in *Moby-Dick:*[32] the power of his imagination liberates them, allows them to float free of their old context. *Pierre,* on the other hand, conveys a sense of the Gothicist trapped in his own devices, however brilliantly he may use them. This sense derives in part from the more constraining scope of domestic drama in comparison with the vast setting of *Moby-Dick*. And in part it derives from the fact that in *Pierre* the exultation associated with not knowing is clearly subordinate to its torments. The central symbol of mystery in *Moby-Dick* appears at the end of the novel in a dazzling apotheosis, but in *Pierre* the very priestess and emblem of mystery comes more and more to look like a bewildered young woman, trapped in the pain and loneliness of mere mundane confusion.

In the cold stasis of Pierre's private Inferno, in the horrors of his consummated or unconsummated guilty passion, and in his final imprisonment, one senses the claustrophobia of Melville's increasing confinement, as the book goes on, in his own psychic darkness. The horror and frustration that permeate the last half of the novel perhaps derive from the fact that the mysteries Melville was dealing with there, as so many readers have suspected, were his own private mysteries and not, after all, the mysteries of the universe.

A reader of Radcliffe, Godwin, Mary Shelley, and Maturin must have realized what potential the genre of Gothic romance offered as a instrument of knowledge: knowledge of the irrational, of the psyche in its hidden depths. The early Gothicists are often praised for having made the treasures of this knowledge available to later novelists—for having pursued, in an age of reason, what Pierre himself determined to pursue before everything else: "The heart! the heart!" (*Pierre* 127). Their works are often compared with the eruption of the id into rational discourse, an analogy consonant with their "oneiric" quality. But to this should be added that like dreams in Freud's account of them, Gothic romance both expressed and masked the hidden life.

"And here it may be randomly suggested, by way of bagatelle, whether some things that men think they do not know, are not for all that thoroughly comprehended by them; and yet, so to speak, though contained in themselves, are kept a secret from themselves?" (*Pierre* 410). The oneiric quality of Gothic romance often gives one a sense in reading it that the "inventional mysteries" are not only personal mysteries of the author but also mysteries *to* the author. And this accounts, perhaps, for the way Gothic romancers so consistently lose control over their material. Having summoned up the powers of darkness, they are forced to turn and run. To say this is not to scoff at the genuine pain and anguish such works represent, but only to say that even the worst anxiety dreams may be most fundamentally engaged, as Freud said all dreams are, in preventing the disruption of sleep.

Romancers like Spenser and Ariosto use dreamlike images and narrative techniques reminiscent of dream logic,[33] but they do so in order to address issues that cannot be otherwise addressed.[34] At its worst, Gothic romance presents symbolic situations resembling nothing so much as the wish fulfillments whereby the dreaming mind flees the consequences of its knowledge. Freud compared the wish fulfillment in one of his own dreams to the joke about a man who borrowed a kettle and returned it damaged. In his defense, the man explained that (1) the kettle was in perfect condition when he returned it; (2) it already had the hole when he borrowed it; and (3) he never borrowed it anyway (*Interpretation of Dreams* 153).

In Freud's dream, the triple defense was designed to mask a feeling of guilty responsibility. The plots of many Gothic romances use the same kind of defense. In *Montorio,* for example, two brothers are driven by the diabolical persecutions of a mysterious monk to kill their father, a cruel tyrant who, by almost anyone's standards, richly deserves it. In a sense they do this, despite their moral revulsion, of their own free will. The murder occurs when, without a word but with an identical impulse, they rush into the room where their father kneels and attack him simultaneously. It is later revealed, however, that this was not their father after all; their real father is in fact the very man who incited them to the crime. The court rules that for this he deserves to die. Thus Maturin presents the story of two sons who, in a scene of shocking violence, murder their father. However, (1) it was not really their fault; (2) it was not really their father; and (3) it was really their father's fault. Not surprisingly, one of the author's preoccupations in this romance is the danger of self-knowledge.

An admirer of Walpole's *Mysterious Mother*[35] could hardly have been unaware of the depths into which he was plunging by treating the theme of incest. But perhaps Melville was aware too that he had chosen for his own *Familienroman* a form well adapted not only to discovering knowledge but also to concealing it. His awareness of the potential of fiction in general for evasion rather than confrontation is obvious in his central image of the writer Pierre, with his passion for knowledge, his passion for mystery, his suspicions that nothing can be known, his self-knowledge and self-deception, his double wish to make known his gospel through the written word and to keep the public from knowing *him.* Melville himself complained bitterly of the necessity he felt for concealing himself from his readers.[36] Certainly it seems that in *Pierre* he found no way to tear all veils from all idols while still, as Hawthorne would have said, "keep[ing] the inmost Me behind its veil" (*Scarlet Letter* 85).

Pierre has long been recognized as the novel in which Melville made his most obvious and extensive use of Gothic materials. It has also long been recognized as a failure,[37] and these two characteristics, the failure and the Gothicism, have often been linked either implicitly or explicitly in criticisms of the novel. The Gothicism of *Pierre*, however, need not be associated merely with the spectacle of an exhausted Melville borrowing heavily and even desperately from a stock of popular devices, characters, and plots to make up for a temporary deficit of creative energy. Melville's originality in the use of Gothic materials to explore the theme of knowledge consists not only in the richness, complexity, and subtlety of the theme itself as he presents it but also in the daring with which he "made new" the Gothic legacy in the service of that theme. This transformation is arguably the most creative aspect of the novel, the one aspect that makes *Pierre*, undoubtedly a failure, something of the Titanic failure Melville himself seems to have felt it to be. The failure of *Pierre* is connected to its use of the Gothic tradition, but not because Melville chose to use that tradition or because he used it unimaginatively. In his wholesale use of Gothic materials in *Pierre*, Melville simply fell prey in the end to the fatal flaw inherent in wholesale Gothicism itself. It tends to become, through its dreamlike form and symbolism, a device for not knowing after all: a device for transcribing the author's most intimate personal suffering, rendered as fiction in the way that dreams are fiction, but untransmuted by art.

3

"Deadly Iteration": Hawthorne's Gothic Vision

perils . . . perils . . . perils . . . perils . . . perils

I

"What could be more absurd," thinks young John Melmoth, "than to be alarmed or amazed at a resemblance between a living man and the portrait of a dead one!" (Maturin, *Melmoth* 20). But the self-admonition fails to reassure him, and the reader knows better than to accept it: *all* resemblances are amazing or alarming in Gothic romance. They belong to the wider network of repetitions that, often in startling quantity, characterize even the shortest Gothic tales and "fragments."[1] Rescued from Udolpho, for example, Emily St. Aubert arrives at another castle, scene of the sufferings of yet another persecuted lady, who strangely resembled her. An old servant, telling the story of that other woman, frightens Emily by throwing a veil over her to enhance the likeness. Hawthorne's reworking of the scene depicts a similar thrill of horror. To Priscilla, suddenly caught beneath a veil once more, it seems the past is repeating itself, despite her naïve assumption that "the past never comes back again." "Do we dream the same dream twice?" she has asked. "There is nothing else that I am afraid of" (*Blithedale Romance* 484).

Gothic romance appeals to those who know what it is to dream the same dream twice. Emily St. Aubert flees not once but repeatedly through identical dark corridors and spends night after night in the room she cannot lock. In *The Monk*, the Bleeding Nun appears night after night to intone her repetitive refrain: "Raymond! Raymond! thou art mine! . . ." (123). The Monk meets his end, not simply by falling from a cliff, but by plunging "from precipice to precipice" (344). Maturin's Annibal is not merely locked in; he hears "door after door [close] at successive distances" (*Montorio* 2: 25). In works beyond the inmost circle of the genre, repetition may well be the major persistent preoccupation of the Gothic mode. Frankenstein and his alter ego flee in mutual pursuit over a monotonously repetitive icy landscape. His very name an echo of itself, William Wilson flees his double obsessively, only to meet him at every turn. Hepzibah Pyncheon, fleeing the House of the Seven Gables, finds "This one old house . . . everywhere" (398). Carwin's "biloquism" creates the illusion that Clara is in two places at once (Brown, *Wieland*). In *Edgar Huntly* there are two sleepwalkers, two panthers, two manuscripts, two secret boxes, twins.

Formally, such repetition is an inheritance from the narrative structure of the original "Gothic" romances—in eighteenth-century terms, the Renaissance romance of Spenser and Ariosto as well as medieval romance.[2] Holcroft saw an absence of "unity of design" as a characteristic distinguishing romance from the novel.[3] Hurd felt it especially necessary to defend the structure of Spenserian romance, in the course of the defense comparing it to Gothic architecture (*Letters on Chivalry* 61–67). Indeed, the basic principle of narrative technique in medieval and Renaissance romance, as Hauser says of Gothic art in general, is coordination rather than subordination:[4] numerous similar castles, similar adventures, characters in similar plights. Like Sir Thopas in Chaucer's parody, the knight is forever riding on and on, doing battle with one enemy after another, and riding on again.

Gothic romance tends to be similarly episodic and repetitious, but with a different and distinctive effect. The repetition of the Gothic romance is not merely that of the adventurer in transit from one peril to another, but of life in extremis. There is a sense of excess and hysteria, of events escaping from their ordinary temporal bounds. Lovers do not merely pledge each other in wine; they pledge "repeatedly in goblets of the most potent wine" (Dacre, *Zofloya* 2: 61). The climax of *Zofloya* involves not just the stabbing but the repeated stabbing of the villain.

Indeed, repetition is not an incidental formal element in Gothic romance, but a key means by which its essential elements are created.[5] First, repetition is an essential aspect of the architecture Gothicists devoted so much energy to describing. De Quincey in his *Confessions* compares his opium dreams with a scene in the "vast Gothic halls" of Piranesi's *Carceri:*

Creeping along the sides of the walls, you perceived a staircase; and upon it, groping his way upwards, was Piranesi himself: follow the stairs a little further, and you perceive it to come to a sudden abrupt termination, without any balustrade, and allowing no step onwards to him who had reached the extremity, except into the depths below. Whatever is to become of poor Piranesi, you suppose, at least, that his labors must in some way terminate here. But raise your eyes, and behold a second flight of stairs still higher: on which again Piranesi is perceived, by this time standing on the very brink of the abyss. Again elevate your eye, and a still more aerial flight of stairs is beheld: and again is poor Piranesi busy on his aspiring labors: and so on, until the unfinished stairs and Piranesi both are lost in the upper gloom of the hall.—With the same power of endless growth and self-reproduction did my architecture proceed in dreams. (106)[6]

Here repetition creates the element Carnochan finds in the *Carceri:* the double terror of boundedness and boundlessness, claustrophobia and vertigo.[7] In Gothic romance, as in the "vast Gothic halls" of Piranesi, one seems always to be running up against the same obstacle. Stairways, doors, iron gratings, and walls multiply in apparently endless profusion. Strangely, much of the feeling of claustrophobia derives from this sense of infinity: the sense that one will never come to an ultimate boundary dividing this place from some other place. Through other kinds of repetition, nonarchitectural Gothic romances (*Frankenstein*, for example, or *Caleb Williams*), render the double terror of boundedness and boundlessness as a state of mind. They describe the anxiety of the obsessed wanderer, lost in the universe, but trapped by "a sense of . . . universal persecution" (*Montorio* 2: 282). "I am so far *out,*" says Ippolito, "that even you who stand last and longest on the shore have ceased to see me in the distance" (*Montorio* 2: 298). And yet he cannot get away, for he sees the same thing everywhere he goes: " '[S]ee him,' he murmured, 'yes, I see him always; I see him now, I hear him; blindness cannot shut him out—I have lost myself, but I cannot lose him' " (2: 423).[8]
The horror of Piranesi's work and De Quincey's obsessive dreams derives not only from the multiplication of barriers in space but also from the infinite multiplication of what should be a discrete incident in time. In Gothic romance, too, devices and images of repetition suggest a double horror of boundedness and boundlessness in both spatial and temporal terms. The same events seem to recur again and again, trapping the protagonist in a single instant of time yet simultaneously evoking the nightmare of eternity. Through repetition, Gothic romance translates into sym-

bolic form what Kermode in *The Sense of an Ending* terms *chronos:* "purely successive, disorganized" time, unbounded by the "concords" beginnings and endings create (45–59). Suspense—the state of being intolerably in transition with no sense of what or where the end may be—is the subject and technique of Gothicism. Both "terror" Gothic and "horror" Gothic[9] play on the fear that there will be no decisive temporal boundary: one by the immediate introduction of new suspense as each mystery is solved; the other by a seemingly endless multiplication of loathsome details. Lippard's Gothic whorehouse is a proliferation of horrors, each room the scene of some gruesome spectacle. In Lippard, Lewis, and Maturin, one torment gives way to another and another, cumulatively evoking a sensation like that which terrified Jonathan Edwards's congregation:

> There will be no end to this exquisite horrible misery. When you look forward, you shall see a long for ever, a boundless duration before you, which will swallow up your thoughts, and amaze your soul; and you will absolutely despair of ever having any deliverance, any end, any mitigation, any rest at all. You will know certainly that you must wear out long ages, millions of millions of ages, in wrestling and conflicting with this almighty merciless vengeance; and then when you have so done, when so many ages have actually been spent by you in this manner, you will know that all is but a point to what remains. So that your punishment will indeed be infinite. ("Sinners in the Hands of an Angry God" 169)

Freud stresses the central role repetition plays in creating a sense of the uncanny. When a remarkable coincidence of "involuntary repetition" ("The 'Uncanny' " 237) occurs, the mind reverts to its primitive repertoire of animistic beliefs about the universe (247–48).[10] Why, indeed, should one be alarmed at a resemblance between a living man and the portrait of a dead one? Perhaps because of the mind's tendency, as Maturin would say, to remember involuntarily "the gossip's tale in solitude or in darkness" (*Montorio* 1: iv). Freud points out that this kind of repetition creates a sense of helplessness (236–37)—one of the horrors of "the spirit engaged with the forces of violence." He gives as an example his own experience, one hot summer day, of getting lost in a provincial Italian town. Alarmed to find himself in a quarter full of "painted women," he attempted to recover his bearings, only to find that, try as he might to go somewhere else, he invariably found himself back in this same street

(236–37). "Involuntary" repetition, indeed! Freud says in the same essay that what is most *unheimlich* turns out to be most *heimlich* in the end; what seems uncanny is most our own.

The world of Gothic fiction resembles nothing so much as the hall of mirrors in an amusement park horror house.[11] Lost in a labyrinth, the victim is confronted at every turn with variations on one endlessly reduplicated image. That the image is in some way his or her own makes the comparison particularly apt, for the essential quality of the haunted mind is an inability to see anything but itself.[12] What T. S. Eliot called "the awful privacy of the insane mind" results from the sick ego's tendency to expand its circumference to encompass the world. When Dimmesdale sees an *A* in the sky, Hawthorne comments, "In such a case, it could only be a symptom of a highly disordered mental state, when a man, rendered morbidly self-contemplative by long, intense, and secret pain, had extended his egotism over the whole expanse of nature, until the firmament itself should appear no more than a fitting page for his soul's history and fate!" (176). Here is the nightside of the Romantic vision of the expanding self that finds transcendent unity with everything. In this Gothic vision, egotism and anxiety expand the self to monstrous proportions, sucking everything into one vortex of horror, until there is no division between the me and the not-me. In Radcliffe's and Lewis's prisons there is at least the possibility of escape, but this prison offers its solitary inmate no walls to get beyond.[13]

The use of devices and images of repetition to explore anxieties connected with the problem of the boundaries of the self is central to all of Hawthorne's Gothic.[14] In Hawthorne's uses of the Gothic tradition, repetition is associated with the old Gothic problem of knowledge in both senses. This is the same issue central to Melville's Gothic, but their emphases are characteristically different. Melville tends to focus on the difficulty of knowing in cosmic terms: on the search for ultimate truth beyond the "pasteboard masks" of appearances. Hawthorne was more interested in the way guilt transforms the ordinary perceptions and relations of common life, weakening one's ability to know external reality in its true forms, diminishing the possibility of knowing and being known in human terms. Hawthorne was not an idealist.[15] In his view as in Radcliffe's, there is a reality outside the mind: other people to be known, external phenomena to be perceived. Much of the repetition in *The Mysteries of Udolpho* results not from the fact that the same incidents actually recur but from the fact that Emily's distorted perception causes her to interpret everything in the same way, whether the noise at the door is a dog, a maid, or an intruder. Radcliffe was interested in perception transformed by fear; Hawthorne, in perception transformed by sin and sorrow. In Hawthorne's Gothic it is the knowledge of evil that interposes a barrier between the inner and outer worlds, locking self into self-reflection, casting the individual out beyond the circle of human friendship. In his Gothic vision the potential for tragedy lies in the tendency of guilt to destroy at once the ability to see and to be seen. In "The Minister's Black Veil," Mr. Hooper, cut off by his sense of sin even from the woman who loved him, looks out from his deathbed and beholds "on every visage, a Black Veil" like his own (882). Perhaps he sees a truth about those other people, or perhaps he merely sees his own veil wherever he looks. At any rate, the veil keeps everyone else from seeing *him*.

"To the untrue man," Hawthorne says, "the whole universe is false,— it is impalpable,—it shrinks to nothing within his grasp" (*Scarlet Letter* 170). The man who fears to be known loses his ability to know; the universe fades away at his touch. After his fall, Donatello apparently perceives everything beyond his haunted mind as dim and "visionary" (705). And he shudders at Kenyon's speculations on the punishment of sin: not that it will be revealed to all the world but that the sinner will simply be "impermeable to light," alone because no one can see him (766). It would be even worse, Donatello suggests, to have one single companion and to see through eternity the same "weary, weary sin repeated in that inseparable soul" (766). To see the same "weary, weary sin repeated" is the essential Gothic horror portrayed in *The Marble Faun*. When Miriam recognizes in the dead Capuchin the very man she had thought to escape, Hawthorne says, "it was a symbol, perhaps, of the deadly iteration with which she was doomed to behold the image of her crime reflected back upon her in a thousand ways, and converting the great, calm face of Nature . . . into a manifold reminiscence of that one dead visage" (699).

This psychological phenomenon of "deadly iteration" is the central focus of Hawthorne's Gothic. Again and again, his work explores the way consciousness altered by guilt creates the self-iterative world of a "haunted mind," distorting that mind's ability to perceive the world outside it.[16] All of these transformations of consciousness and perception involve an alienation, caused in some way by sin, in which the self cannot reach beyond its own boundaries. Sin in Hawthorne's view, as in Jonathan Edwards's, is a form of separation. Hawthorne's sinners are afraid of revealing their secrets and therefore fear the intrusion of others into their private world. Thus they are cut off from other people, from nature in its true aspect, and from God. But their nightmarish separateness is, paradoxically, also a nightmarish unity. The whole world is a terrible oneness for them because it is a deadly iteration of their own perceiving minds, a multitudinous echo of the self.

II

The Marble Faun is Hawthorne's fullest rendering of this Gothic vision. As such, it shows most clearly the relations in Hawthorne's Gothic among the terrors of separateness and unity, the problem of knowledge, the theme of deadly iteration, and the motifs of barriers and boundaries. The complex interrelations of all these themes and motifs and their collective centrality to the work as a whole are illustrated by the way they occur together in similar configurations at moments of high drama. Most strikingly they do so in three crucial scenes: Miriam's disappearance in the catacombs, the commission of the crime, and Miriam and Hilda's encounter afterwards. All of these scenes rework and recreate classic elements of the Gothic romance.

The scene in the catacombs represents in physical terms a moral quality associated with Miriam in Hawthorne's first description of her. She is "the subject of a good deal of conjecture" (602), but no one really knows anything about her. "By some subtile quality, she kept people at a distance, without so much as letting them know that they were excluded from her inner circle" (601). This quality of separateness between Miriam and even her closest associates—a separateness connected with her mystery—is presented symbolically in the incident in the catacombs. Her companions stand in a small circular chapel surrounded by "great darkness . . . like that immenser mystery which envelops our little life, and into which friends vanish from us, one by one" (605). Miriam has somehow become lost in this darkness. When she reappears she points to the reason: the Model, whom we meet for the first time as he stands "just on the doubtful limit of obscurity, at the threshold of the small, illuminated chapel" (606). Miriam has a mysterious association with something just on the border of darkness, something beyond ordinary limits. Her vanishing beyond those limits reveals the "moral estrangement" (642) characteristic of her relation to the world when she is with the Model. "A solitude had suddenly spread itself around them," Hawthorne says of their encounter in Chapter 11:

It perhaps symbolized a peculiar character in the relation of these two, insulating them, and building up an insuperable barrier between their lifestreams and other currents. . . . For it is one of the chief earthly incommodities of some species of misfortune, or of a great crime, that it makes the actor in the one, or the sufferer of the other, an alien in the world, by interposing a wholly unsympathetic medium betwixt himself and those whom he yearns to meet. (642)

This medium prevents even the narrator from knowing exactly what the couple said in their conversation.

Miriam's union with the Model takes her beyond the limits of other fellowship, and his intrusion into her world involves her in obsessive repetition. He haunts her, following her in the streets, climbing her many steps and "sitting at her threshold." Often he comes into her studio, and his figure recurs again and again in her pictures (607). "A case of hopeless mannerism," according to rival artists, "which would destroy all Miriam's prospects of true excellence in art" (607).

Hilda's art also consists of repetition, because she is a copyist. But whereas Miriam's repetitious art is a symptom of her inability to escape her haunted mind, Hilda's results from exactly the opposite: a perfect ability to give herself over, as a medium would, to something beyond her—the spirit of other artists. Miriam's self-absorption confines her in repetition; Hilda's negative capability enables her, by repetition, to free old masterpieces from confinement. Through multiplication, she releases them from dark corners and guarded cabinets:

Since the beauty and glory of a great picture are confined within itself, she won out that glory by patient faith and self-devotion, and multiplied it for mankind. From the dark, chill corner of a gallery,—from some curtained chapel in a church, where the light came seldom and aslant,—from the prince's carefully guarded cabinet, where not one eye in thousands was permitted to behold it,—she brought the wondrous picture into daylight. . . . (624)

Here Hilda is associated with a "power of sympathy" directly opposed to the Gothic experience of alienation and confinement that characterizes Miriam's life. The Model draws Miriam out beyond the pale; he also traps her in a dungeonlike "dark dream" (637). To be cast out and locked in—old horrors of the Gothic heroine—are in Hawthorne's Gothic vision the rewards of the knowledge of evil. But Hilda too, despite her sympathies, is isolated—not by her knowledge but by her lack of knowledge, her innocence. She is set apart by her white robe and her virginal seclusion in the tower, high "beyond the limits" (708) bounding other people's lives. The central events at the climax of the romance have much to do with the barrier that separates the innocent Hilda from a guilty world. Suspecting some trouble in Miriam's heart, Hilda has turned back to find her and offer her a chance to confide. "The door of the little court-yard had swung upon its hinges, and partly closed itself. Hilda . . . was quietly opening it, when she was startled, midway, by the noise of a struggle within . . ." (688). The climactic chapter, "The Faun's Transformation," begins with the shutting of this door: "The door of the court-yard swung slowly, and closed itself of its own accord. Miriam and Donatello were now alone there" (689).

The ominous opening and closing of a door, which introduces so many Gothic scenes, is put here to unusually subtle use. In its immediate context, the closing of the door is an appropriate symbolic prelude to Hawthorne's long analysis of the effects of the Fall: the sudden receding of the outer world in the couple's first exhilaration of passion and guilt, their sense of seclusion in this wild and terrible unity, the desperate fear of isolation in their close embrace, the horrible perception that they are guilty not of a "little separate sin" but of all humanity's guilt, and the hint of the separateness that will soon shut them out even from each other (690–92). In a wider context the closing of the door belongs to a system of resonances throughout the romance: one thinks of the barring of the gate to Eden, mentioned in connection with Hilda's fall to sorrow (707); of the iron gateway to Donatello's domain, locked and bolted when Kenyon arrives (713); and of Hilda's shutting her window and drawing the curtain when Miriam calls up to her after the crime, "Pray for us, Hilda; we need it!" (692).

This closing of Hilda's window ends Chapter 19, just as the closing of the door began it. Although both point to Hilda's essential separateness from the guilt she has witnessed, the conclusion comes as a shock. Hilda has been continually associated with the Virgin, whose shrine she tends and to whom the plea "Pray for us" is traditionally addressed. The shock with which modern readers respond to Hilda's reaction is not merely due to their more general difficulties in appreciating her character. It results quite naturally from the way her unsympathetic response collides with the immense counterforce of those sympathies Hawthorne himself has just expended in this study of pain and guilt and passion. The scene is ambiguous, of course. "Whether Hilda heard and recognized the voice we cannot tell." But Hawthorne is careful to say that Miriam shouted loudly— "with the rich strength of her voice" (692). And the moral status of Hilda's virginal separateness is not merely a minor problem; it comes up again, this time as the central issue, in Miriam's encounter with Hilda the next day.

Approaching Hilda's tower, Miriam sees the "white window-curtain . . . closely drawn" (706). Inside, the intrusion of the knowledge of evil has rendered Hilda's closed world self-reflecting like Miriam's own studio. Hilda sits near the copy of the portrait of Beatrice, whose face Miriam's face once resembled. Now Hilda glances at the mirror and is struck with horror: for a moment, the look on Beatrice's face is repeated on her own. She remains deep in meditation until she hears someone coming up the stairs.

> It was long past noon, when a step came up the staircase. It had passed beyond the limits where there was communication with the lower regions of the palace, and was mounting the successive flights which led only to Hilda's precincts. Faint as the tred was, she heard and recognized it. It startled her into sudden life. Her first impulse was to spring to the door of the studio, and fasten it with lock and bolt. But a second thought made her feel that this would be an unworthy cowardice, on her own part, and also that Miriam—only yesterday her closest friend—had a right to be told, face to face, that thenceforth they must be forever strangers.
>
> She heard Miriam pause, outside of the door. (708)

The door swings open and Miriam steps in, holding out her arms to embrace her friend.

> Hilda was standing in the middle of the room. When her friend made a step or two from the door, she put forth her hands with an involuntary repellent gesture, so expressive, that Miriam at once felt a great chasm opening itself between them two. They might gaze at one another from the opposite side, but without the possibility of ever meeting more; or, at least, since the chasm could never be bridged over, they must tread the whole round of Eternity to meet on the other side. There was even a terror in the thought of their meeting again. It was as if Hilda or Miriam were dead, and could no longer hold intercourse without violating a spiritual law.
>
> Yet, in the wantonness of her despair, Miriam made one more step towards the friend whom she had lost.
>
> "Do not come nearer, Miriam!" said Hilda.
>
> Her look and tone were those of sorrowful entreaty, and yet they expressed a kind of confidence, as if the girl were conscious of a safeguard that could not be violated. (708–9)

The dominant tone of this scene is not one of suspense, but it is full of Gothic resonances: in the step on the stair, the reference to "terror," the image of the precipice, the suggestion that one or the other of the women is a ghost, Hilda's apparent consciousness of an inviolable "safeguard" that is, presumably, her innocence. Miriam here plays a version of the Gothic villain's role, coming up Hilda's stairs, entering against Hilda's true wishes, and trying in all her own guilt to embrace the innocent, unprotected orphan girl. Hilda, however, is defending herself not against a villainous stranger but against the woman whose best friend she has been. This variation on the old pattern generates a rich ambiguity. The complexity of Hawthorne's meditations here on the old themes of the Gothic villain's cosmic isolation and the Gothic virgin's self-defense is indicated by the fact that the safeguard protecting Hilda seems, at least for a moment, to be the same barrier that shuts Miriam out from humanity. Like Melmoth and other guilt-ridden figures of Gothic romance, Miriam finds herself separated by an impassable gulf from humankind. Her experience in this scene is a version of that experience Maturin's Ippolito described: "to knock at the human heart, and find it shut!" (*Montorio* 2: 446).

Hilda's heart is shut in self-defense, and Hawthorne clearly sympathizes with her desperate effort to maintain her purity in a fallen world. On the other hand, Miriam is also a sympathetic figure, and she blames her own tragic isolation on the "inviolable safeguard" that Hilda's conscious innocence has set up between them: " '[Y]our very look seems to put me beyond the limits of human kind!' " (709). No, Hilda says, Miriam herself is responsible. She has a point: we have seen Miriam beyond the limits before, alone with Donatello at the scene of their crime. The shutting of the courtyard door "of its own accord" represented a logical consequence of a sin such as theirs. The crime would, as a matter of course, cut them off from humanity anyway; Hilda's essential separateness from their act was a natural result of what they did, as well as a result of her own flight from the horror she had witnessed. But then again, Miriam was "beyond the limits of human kind" before she actually committed a crime, and the desperation that led to the crime resulted partly from her inability to find anyone receptive to her confidence. Her pause outside Hilda's door after the crime has its counterpart in a pause on Kenyon's stairs after he closed a door on her before the crime. Inspired by the knowledge of women that Kenyon's statue of Cleopatra seemed to reveal, Miriam tried to tell him her secret. But Kenyon blundered by assuming a tone of moral superiority, manifested in his offer, when she asked him to listen to her problem, to "help" her. She left without confiding. "After Kenyon had closed the door, she went wearily down the staircase, but paused midway, as if debating with herself whether to return" (664). Her final decision not to return is one of the several just-missed opportunities for confidence that give *The Marble Faun* so much of its tone of sadness and loss. There is throughout the work a sense that the "hunger of the heart, which finds only shadows to feed upon" (655) is an elemental part of human life; in the face of it, any deliberate refusal of communion looks a little cruel.

This sense contributes to the persuasiveness of Miriam's appeal to Hilda. She needs Hilda's help, she says, because she is fallen. (As Kenyon asks Donatello later, what mortal is not?) Hilda answers that she is only human. Her white robe could be stained, and her perception could be distorted. But these things happen anyway. Her fall to the knowledge of evil does, at least in one artist's eye, stain her robe with blood, and she loses her former ability for perceiving art with pure sympathy. Even before Miriam comes through Hilda's door, the isolated world of innocence she has tried to preserve by closing herself off has become the self-reflecting prison of a haunted mind. Her opening of the courtyard door has already involved her in a Gothic plot; drawing the white curtain cannot set her apart from it. She becomes conscious of her orphanhood and feels for the first time "the exile's pain" (787). She finds herself wandering miserably and endlessly through long galleries (783–87). She feels isolated, trapped in "a chill dungeon, which kept her in its gray twilight and fed her with its unwholesome air, fit only for a criminal to breathe and pine in! She could not escape from it. In the effort to do so, straying farther into the intricate passages of our nature, she stumbled, ever and again, over this deadly idea of mortal guilt" (780). In all this, Hilda repeats the Gothic experience of Miriam herself, who wandered in a "labyrinth of darkness" (604), felt herself an outcast, and was trapped in a "dungeon" (637). Like Miriam, Hilda cannot seem to see clearly; she experiences a form of deadly iteration, finding, for example, that she cannot concentrate on a picture by Leonardo because of "a fancied resemblance to Miriam" (780). Like Miriam she develops a desperate desire to make her secret known to someone else. Like the Model, who went from shrine to shrine doing penance, and like Donatello, who stops to pray before every shrine on his journey with Kenyon, Hilda goes "from gallery to gallery, and from church to church" (806) seeking release from her obsession. The climax of this Gothic plot is her disappearance into a convent and her final restoration to the world: "summoned forth from a secret place, and led we know not through what mysterious passages, to a point where the tumult of life burst suddenly upon her ears." She reappears, by way of a "great, gloomy hall" and a curtain, and is discovered standing on a balcony in a white domino (850–51).

Hilda's imprisonment in a convent is a literal version of the metaphorical entrapment and enclosure she has experienced since her knowledge of evil first forced her into a deceptive relation to the world. Miriam had warned her not to keep this knowledge "imprisoned" in her heart (711), but with no one to confide in, she was forced into the position of Dimmesdale, being untrue and so finding the whole world false. Since the incident in the catacombs, Miriam has been living in a Gothic world. One by one as the other three characters become involved in her life, they are sucked into the vortex as well. The climax of Hilda's involvement in this Gothic world occurs when she finally crosses the threshold of the Cenci palace, somehow mysteriously connected with Miriam, and ascends the steps toward a certain door (814). Thus on the one hand, her imprisonment represents the extremest form of her repetition of Miriam's own Gothic experience: the experience of being, like Beatrice, "all shut up within herself" (628)—an isolation brought about through the knowledge of evil and the consequent fear or inability to make oneself known. On the other hand, this imprisonment also represents an extreme version of Hilda's isolation through innocence. The white domino, presumably associated with some religious order, is a literal version of the metaphorical white robe she was so afraid of staining; her disappearance into a convent reveals the extreme tendency of her self-sufficient isolation in the tower where she burned oil before the Virgin's shrine.

Hilda's escape from a convent, after all, places her in a long line of Gothic heroines who narrowly escape imprisonment in perpetual virginity. Although the perils of Gothic heroines in many ways represent the perils of marriage,[17] Gothic heroines are also threatened by the possibility of not being married—by the perils of their great virtue, chastity. In *The Italian*, for example, Ellena di Rosalba finds herself torn from her betrothed during the wedding ceremony itself, accused of violating a nun's vow of chastity, and imprisoned in a convent. In order to escape, she must commit a breach of decorum by agreeing to flee with her lover—an act highly improper and fraught with shocking implications. But the situation is desperate; otherwise she must take the veil. And the breach of decorum, in fact, turns out to have no serious consequences. When Hilda's lamp goes out, an old woman predicts a terrible fall, but the tower does not in fact collapse. Apparently the Virgin's lamp did not really need to be tended forever.

Thus Hilda's final escape, like her closing of the window and her impulse to bar the door against her friend, raises once again the issue of the moral status of her isolation in innocence. The issue is an ambiguous one. Hawthorne provides several defenses of Hilda's severity toward Miriam: in the voice of Hilda, the voice of Kenyon, and his own voice. Hilda says, "If I were one of God's angels, with a nature incapable of stain, and garments that never could be spotted, I would keep ever at your side, and try to lead you upward. But I am a poor, lonely girl, whom God has set here in an evil world, and given her only a white robe, and bid her wear it back to Him, as white as when she put it on. Your powerful magnetism would be too much for me" (709). Kenyon tells Miriam, who agrees with him, that "the white shining purity of Hilda's nature is a thing apart; and she is bound, by the undefiled material of which God moulded her, to keep that severity which I, as well as you, have recognized" (756). Hawthorne himself says of Hilda's final conclusion that she "failed" Miriam "at her sorest need": "[W]e do not unhesitatingly adopt Hilda's present view, but rather suppose her misled by her feelings" (812). Another defense is probably inherent in the allusion to the parable of the wise and foolish virgins, as Bercovitch has shown ("Of Wise and Foolish Virgins").

But Hilda changes her mind about how she should have reacted to Miriam's plea for help, and Hawthorne himself, despite his (perhaps disingenuous) refusal to agree with her at that point, insistently raises the question of whether Hilda's viriginal isolation is really a good thing. Most notably the issue arises through the parallels between Donatello's and Hilda's experiences. Donatello's isolation in innocence is associated with a certain moral ambiguity, and because his and Hilda's falls from the bliss of Eden are so clearly parallel, the possibility arises that this moral ambiguity may apply to her case as well. Just as Hilda's innocence sets her high "beyond the limits" where other people live, Donatello has "an indefinable characteristic . . . that set him outside of rules" (598). Before his fall, he belonged to an Arcadia in the Apennines, a place where, "within circumscribed limits" (775), he knew joys that could be found nowhere else. But there is a suggestion of something a little too circumscribed about the limits of this paradise. The Monte Benis, when young, have a tendency to display delightful animal spirits like Donatello's but to become in later life "heavy, unsympathizing, and insulated within the narrow limits of a surly selfishness" (725). Donatello's fall, it seems, saves him from this confinement in self, moving him, after the first shock of his guilt, outward toward humanity. Is there something negative, too, about Hilda's isolation? Donatello's experience suggests that the knowledge of good and evil, while introducing into life a painful combination of isolation and unity, also paradoxically brings about the only escape from entrapment in self that is available in this world.

This world, after all, as Hawthorne never ceases to relate, fell long ago; innocence itself is thus in one sense a form of distorted perception. Hilda's miraculous insight into art turns out to have lacked a certain contact with "the truth of the human heart," which her Gothic vision gives her:

> On her part, Hilda returned to her customary occupations with a fresh love for them, and yet with a deeper look into the heart of things; such as those necessarily acquire who have passed from picture galleries into dungeon gloom, and thence come back to the picture gallery again. It is questionable whether she was ever so perfect a copyist thenceforth. . . . She saw into the picture as profoundly as ever, and perhaps more so, but not with the devout sympathy that had formerly given her entire possession of the old master's idea. She had known such a reality, that it taught her to distinguish inevitably the large portion that is unreal, in every work of art. Instructed by sorrow, she felt that there is something beyond almost all which pictorial genius has produced. . . . (806)

Donatello remembers a childhood Arcadia, but it turns out to have been a grim castlelike place in the Apennines, complete with a hideous memento mori bequeathed by an old sinner to his descendants (737). One thinks again of Emily's discovery of a mystery in her childhood Arcadia—a mystery intimately linked to that of Udolpho, the grim castle in the Apennines with its memento mori behind the black veil. Hawthorne goes further than Radcliffe by showing the childhood paradise and the grim castle to be one and the same.

Some women, Miriam told Kenyon, lead "high, lonely lives," with no need for "what is technically called love" (659–60). The indelicate phrase associates Hilda's isolation, if only for a moment, with something a little perverse. Fortunately Hilda, by discovering a need to confide in someone else, ultimately finds herself in need of "what is technically called love." Just as Donatello's sin brings him into real relation with humanity, so Hilda's discovery of sin—as well as her final decision to involve herself with Miriam's Gothic world by entering the Cenci palace—brings her down from the virgin's tower and into a human relationship.

When all of this is said, however, Donatello's and Hilda's experiences still differ in one essential respect. One suspects that in the final analysis this difference is simply that he is a man and she is a woman. Donatello falls to sin; Hilda falls not to sin but to sorrow, through the knowledge of another woman's sin. This is the only kind of fall characteristic of good women in Gothic comedy, as in *The Mysteries of Udolpho,* in which Valancourt discovers his own capacity for evil and Emily discovers that of someone else. Those old Puritans from whom Hilda claims her descent would no doubt have been surprised to hear anyone of either gender referred to as sinless, but good women in Gothic romances, including Hilda, simply are. Good and evil may battle for possession of their souls, but not within their souls. When a woman in Gothic romance genuinely feels evil impulses, it is a sure sign that she will give in to them. Milton's idea that "Evil into the mind of God or Man / May come and go, so unapprov'd, and leave / No spot or blame behind . . ." (*Paradise Lost* 5.117–19) has no place in the Gothicists' view of female virtue. Nor does the idea that a woman's knowledge of evil in her own heart can lead to anything but disaster.

One could argue that all romance tends toward an allegorical presentation of the good and evil impulses of the soul by means of separate characters. Gothic romance, however, flourished during a period of intellectual and cultural history in which increasing sentimentality about woman's supposed moral superiority to men made it easy to confuse the beau ideal of old romances with reality. As Tomalin says, an idealized view of women's spiritual nature—"a piece of chivalric nonsense"—was being "revived to do duty as a literal truth": the "perfectible woman" was being replaced by the "perfect lady" (309). The period to which she refers is that beginning just after Wollstonecraft's death in 1797. As she points out, by 1869 William Lecky could assert with confidence the current opinion that "[m]orally, the general superiority of women over men, is I think, unquestionable."[18] When real women are regarded as capable of a perfection almost allegorically single in its nature, it is hard to evaluate the role of female characters who, in traditional allegory, might represent only a single aspect of a complex personality. Although the dazzling paragons of female virtue who people Gothic romance are often shadowed by dark, passionate, wicked female counterparts, for example, it is often difficult to discern their relationship to these shadows. The heiress of Udolpho, who "suffered all the delirium of Italian love" (656), warns the virtuous Emily against "passions in your heart,—scorpions" (574) and asserts a kinship between her story and Emily's: "We are sisters, then indeed" (574).[19] But the woman who says these things is insane, and Emily's passion for Valancourt, which at this point in the story might be seen as a "scorpion" because of insinuations that he has lost his own moral purity, is vindicated when he turns out simply to have been the victim of slander.

It is hard to know whether Laurentini's story represents an aspect of Emily's own moral conflict. It could be that the shockingly wicked "sister" of the innocent Emily is merely an unconscious compensation for Radcliffe's own strenuously limited view of the good woman's inner life. Sentimental views of women's capacity for spiritual purity could not but involve a certain moral and psychological schizophrenia, especially in women writers. Twentieth-century women writers have testified to the lingering influence of these sentimental views. Whenever a woman sits down to write, Virginia Woolf said, the "Angel in the House" looks over her shoulder and does her best to interfere. "Above all, be pure," she warns ("Professions for Women" 285). Only recently, Fay Weldon began a discussion of her own work by citing this passage and concluding that the first requirement that liberates a woman to write is an ability to say, "I am bad, too."[20] Many women Gothicists seem to have been unable to say this directly, and yet indirectly their romances pose the question Milton posed with Eve's dream. How did such evil things get into an unfallen woman's mind? Or, in the Gothic mode, how does it happen that the purest woman's bedchamber has a door opening on the darkest subterranean depths?[21]

Hilda's room has no such door, and the fact that she gets lost in subterranean depths is, emphatically, someone else's fault. She says to Miriam not that she is only human and therefore a sinner but that she is only human and therefore susceptible of sin. The problem of interpreting Hilda is complicated by the fact that Hawthorne was concerned, as were Brockden Brown and Melville, with the question of whether innocence can ever actually engage with the forces of violence without forfeiting the qualities that give the struggle its meaning. Guido's archangel, Miriam thinks, should have ruffled feathers like the demon's own after such a ferocious conflict. Hilda's innocence is, like the angel's, "a thing apart" (756). Whether she is intended as a real woman, an allegory, or both, Hawthorne's depiction of her suffers from the difficulties attendant on most efforts to render such purity successfully. To imagine goodness in its essential, separate state is difficult. As C. S. Lewis says in his discussion of Milton's God, writers are always at a disadvantage and make their most damning self-revelations in trying to conceive of a character better than themselves (*A Preface to Paradise Lost* 100).

It is hard to escape the sense that Hawthorne's attempt to render this "thing apart" simply resulted in a rather limited character: a casualty, perhaps, of his attempt to put his own Angel in the House, Sophia, into a story of the ambiguous relations between sin and education. Despite Hilda's fall to knowledge, she remains innocent of much that Hawthorne's own work seems to know. It is disconcerting, for example, to find Hilda repudiating with horror the very moral toward which the romance seems to have been tending: "Is sin, then,—which we deem such a dreadful blackness in the universe,—is it, like sorrow, merely an element of human education, through which we struggle to a higher and purer state than we could otherwise have attained? Did Adam fall, that we might ultimately rise to a far loftier paradise than his?" (854). Some such notion must have enabled Kenyon to release Donatello from imprisonment in his tower; yet he hastens, under Hilda's influence, to repudiate the idea: "I never did believe it!" (855).

But this doctrine of the *felix culpa* is not, taken by itself, the moral of the tale. It is the "great mystery" on the verge of which Miriam delights to brood (840) but the mystery on which Hawthorne's Gothic broods is more complex. Miriam's formulation does, without giving a full answer, pose the question central to all of Hawthorne's Gothic: is any good to be gained from the knowledge of evil? In Gothic romance, the answer to this question tends to determine whether the ending will be happy or tragic. In Gothic comedy, the knowledge gained in the mysterious alien world enables the good characters to go home, get married, and live free of fear that the nightmare will repeat itself. But the knowledge at issue in these cases usually is limited: revelations of who murdered whom, who was related to whom, who was the rightful heir. And the happy endings often seem radically disjunct from the rest of the narrative, as the headlines of one work illustrate: *"Guilt, A Spectre, A Storm, A Frightful Abyss, The Cavern, The Rescue, A Coffin, A Corpse, The Lovers, Horrors, Surprise, Agony,* and finally, *Bliss, The Conclusion."* [22] In Shakespeare's romances, the final unities seem, in glorious paradox, to spring logically from suffering itself. The happy endings of Gothic romance have quite a different effect. The suffering comes to an end in much the same way that nightmares do—abruptly the dreamer wakes. This disjunction between intolerable agony and blissful conclusions suggests an underlying suspicion, even in Gothic comedy, that the problem of evil may have no satisfactory solution. In this sense even Gothic comedy participates in that tragic vision of the world as a "system of universal guilt and suffering from which there is absolutely no issue, no catharsis, no hope of redemption" (Porte, "In the Hands" 54).

Hawthorne's only unmitigated presentation of this tragic vision is to be found in the character of the monk in *The Marble Faun.* Haunting the empty catacombs like the ghost of an infidel, he represents the decaying religion that no longer believes in God but cannot stop believing in Hell. All he has left of religion, says Hawthorne, is the terror. Separated by faithlessness from his God, he is nonetheless bound to him in the useless penance that, without faith, can offer no escape from torment. It can only perpetuate itself in endless repetition, like the monk's progress "round the whole circle of shrines" (680) in the coliseum. This figure represents a tendency of Hawthorne's Gothic, but it is only a tendency. His broadest Gothic vision always sees a way out of the haunted world of deadly iteration.

The precise nature of this way out differs from romance to romance, but all Hawthorne's versions of it have one characteristic in common. Wherever in Hawthorne's romances there is an exit from the Gothic nightmare of sin and death, it results from the intimate relation between the knowledge of evil and another kind of knowledge: the power of sympathy. As a child, Pearl is caught up in an innocent repetition of Hester's own obsession. Because the scarlet letter is a mystery to her, she asks about it again and again, puzzling over its meaning. When the mystery is solved by her father's decision to make his guilt known—to share his "dark treasure" with the world—Pearl herself, the emblem of that treasure, is also brought into relation with the world beyond her. The knowledge of evil unlocks in her the capacity for knowledge through love. Unable to acknowledge her mother and father in the forest scene of Chapter 19, Pearl seemed set apart, as if she had "strayed out of the sphere in which she and her mother dwelt together" (207) and become trapped in some bright, otherworldly realm. In the fall to sorrow that enables her to weep, she loses forever the innocence that so sadly alienated her from the all-too-human sphere of her parents' guilt and love. No longer shut out, she need no longer be shut in; she is free to leave the confines of her mother's haunted world.

Donatello's knowledge of evil haunts and traps him until he can acknowledge his kinship with Miriam, accepting this dark reflection as his own. Until then, their unity is a tormented one, a terrible version of separateness. During the period of Donatello's worst despair, Miriam lives in his own house without overt recognition from him; on his journey with Kenyon, she glides along behind them like a ghost. Donatello's horror at seeing his "own weary, weary sin repeated in that inseparable soul" (766) prevents him from acknowledging her. When he finally does so, their union can be translated into a means of redemption. Miriam's suggestions that the woman who "beguiled him into evil" is the same woman who "might guide him to a higher innocence than that from which he fell" (753) recalls the redemptive form of repetition celebrated in Christian typology: the Second Eve, Mary, undoes the evil caused by the first.

Hilda's discovery of evil and her consequent inability to keep the knowledge locked inside her initiate the series of events that release her from her tower into the less austere world of human sympathies. As she emerges from depression, her initial impulse to separate herself from Miriam gives way to a sudden access of sympathy and to a deliberate assumption, as it were, of the burden of repetition. Before, she was horrified to see Beatrice's look reflected in her own face. Now, the thought that she was too hard on Miriam in her hour of need reminds her of a responsibility, and she goes with Miriam's package across the threshold of Beatrice's own "paternal abode" (814).

Miriam's unwelcome arrival at Hilda's door is juxtaposed, in the succeeding chapter, with Kenyon's arrival at Donatello's locked gate. Both Hilda and Donatello are prisoners in a tower, and both must be released from their isolation before the final unities can be created. Those unities represent loss as well as gain, as the double symbolism of the towers suggests: these prisons of the self are also the lost enclosed world of paradisal innocence. Outside the barred gates of Eden, all final unities include sin and sorrow as well as love; thus it is especially appropriate that Hilda receives as a bridal gift a reminder of Miriam's "sad . . . Mystery" (856). The bracelet is a circle—an old symbol of unity—but at the same time it is an emblem of deadly iteration: "[T]he Etruscan bracelet became the connecting bond of a series of seven wondrous tales, all of which, as they were dug out of seven sepulchres, were characterized by a seven-fold sepulchral gloom . . ." (855–56). The wedding gift implies that the sympathies awakened by Hilda's contact with Miriam's sorrow are a part even of her unity with Kenyon. Nonetheless, the couple will establish their unity in the New World rather than the Old.

In this ending Hawthorne seems to have been struggling especially with the problem of how to exorcise the repetition and bring home the virtuous characters without ignoring or devaluing the treasure unearthed in the Gothic world. Particularly in the character of Hilda, he seems to have been wrestling with the idea that it is possible both to look evil in the face—perhaps even one's own face—and to separate oneself from it ultimately: to go home without denying the knowledge gained in exile. Such is the suggestion in the scene at the end of the romance when Kenyon and Hilda encounter a figure whose face is "behind a veil or mask" (854) and who stands, metaphorically, "on the other side of a fathomless abyss" (855). They know the face, but they do not ask to see behind the veil. They have stood on the edge of the abyss themselves, but they accept Miriam's warning gesture to keep their distance from it (855).

Similarly, one projected ending of the "American Claimant" manuscripts, in which Middleton would at last have turned his back on the "fatal treasure" (9) of the reopened grave, suggests that one can come to terms with the guilty past—even one's own hereditary guilt—and then turn away to begin life anew. ". . . Middleton . . . resigns all the claims. . . . Thus he and his wife become the Adam and Eve of a new epoch . . ." (*American Claimant Manuscripts* 57–58). The hero is to find in the Old World the New World's own heritage but somehow go home to create the New Eden anyway. Perhaps the very recognition of the inheritance of sin and death is sufficient to keep the past from coming back. Or perhaps one can acknowledge the inheritance without accepting a legacy of guilt as a foundation for the remainder of one's life: "The moral, if any moral were to be gathered from these paltry and wretched circumstances, was 'Let the past alone; do not seek to renew it; press on to higher and better things—at all events to other things . . .' "(56).

To press on to other things is to escape repetition, yet in leaving the Old World for the New, Middleton will in one sense be repeating his guilty ancestor's own act. *The House of the Seven Gables* also ends with a repetition: Phoebe and Holgrave go away together to begin their wedded life in yet another old Pyncheon house. But this repetition, like the sevenfold gloom of Miriam's bracelet, is part of the happy ending. In each case the final unity is informed by the knowledge of evil but at the same time transforms that knowledge into something else. The central scene in *The House of the Seven Gables* celebrates the source of such transformations. In this scene the parlor becomes crowded with reflections, and reflections of reflections. Jaffrey Pyncheon, whose soul was earlier described as a corpse hidden in a house, has become the corpse hidden in a house: a physical reflection of the metaphorical state of his soul when he was alive. He sits beneath the portrait of the ancestral Pyncheon he so closely resembles, just as that Pyncheon sat dead beneath his own portrait long ago. The ghost of that original ancestor appears and examines his portrait; then the ghost of Jaffrey himself appears and examines it. Holgrave's two pictures of Jaffrey alive and dead prepare Phoebe to see the corpse itself. In the midst of this repetition, Phoebe and Holgrave's love creates an escape, through the sympathetic imagination, from the self-reflecting world of sin and death. At the very heart of the self-iterative world of the Pyncheon house, in the presence of a bloodstained corpse, Holgrave and Phoebe retransform the world originally transformed by the Fall. Holgrave's earlier assertion that in this world there are corpses everywhere you turn is not refuted; indeed, the setting confirms it. But the vision it represents no longer holds any terror. The scene is an exaltation of the power of sympathy to embrace the inevitably present past—the dream that always comes back—in a larger unity that can redeem it: "They transfigured the earth, and made it Eden again, and themselves the first two dwellers in it. The dead man, so close beside them, was forgotten. At such a crisis, there is no death; for immortality is revealed anew, and embraces everything it its hallowed atmosphere" (428).

Even in Hawthorne's darker versions of the Gothic mode, there is a close connection between the knowledge of evil and the power of sympathy: so close a connection that one seems the cause of the other. This relation stems from a paradox at the heart of Hawthorne's presentation of the self-reflecting world the knowledge of evil creates. Hawthorne's Gothic does explore the way that consciousness creates the self-iterative world of the "haunted mind." But it also explores—at the same time and through the same images—the question of whether certain kinds of distorted perception are a form of insight. Perhaps the self-reflecting world of the guilty soul mirrors something beyond the self as well, something otherwise inaccessible to the imagination.

The motif of reflection and repetition in *The Scarlet Letter* is introduced not in the story of Hester and Dimmesdale but in the Custom-House Sketch. There the imagination is compared to a mirror (104), and the mirror image of a moonlit room is said to bring things "one remove further from the actual, and nearer to the imaginative" (105–6). Here, as elsewhere in Hawthorne's romances, reflections—mirror images, photographs, portraits—are a kind of "neutral territory" between the physical and the spiritual, where the truths hidden by fact are made more plain. It is as if the reflection were a spiritual antitype revealing what the physical type only vaguely shadows forth. In Chapter 19 of *The Blithedale Romance,* for example, Coverdale catches in the mirror a prophetic glimpse of Zenobia's psychological state: her reflected face is "as pale, in her rich attire, as if a shroud were round her" (538). In *The Marble Faun*, the reflection in the mirror of Hilda's room provides a fleeting moment of insight, as an elaborate series of repetitions illuminates the mystery of Beatrice Cenci. In the mirror are reflected Hilda's face and her copy (a repetition) of a portrait (another repetition) of a real woman. The reflection of Hilda's face reflects Beatrice's face and, by implication, Miriam's, as her face once took on Beatrice's expression (628). The expression is that of a woman who fears to be known, but through these reflections the writer reveals her truth.

This scene provides a reminder that there are two different kinds of repetition in *The Marble Faun*. The romance is filled with the involuntary repetitions that characterize the mirror world of the haunted mind, but it is also filled with another kind of repetition: those images art makes of life. These two kinds of repetition intersect in some interesting ways. Hilda's room becomes a hall of mirrors when her life is drawn into Miriam's Gothic world. But at the center of the reflections is the portrait of Beatrice, a symbol of how art's reflections of life give access to spiritual truth. Miriam's art, degenerating into "hopeless mannerism," incessantly reproduces the Model. Her pictures are "not things that I created, but things that haunt me" (615). But Miriam's pictures are not the only ones that reproduce the Model; he is also to be found in Guido's picture of the Archangel and the demon. It is in the sketch, not the finished picture, that Donatello, Hilda, and Kenyon recognize the Model. Thus the recognition occurs in the context of Hawthorne's praise of the suggestive art that, in its incompleteness, calls forth the viewer's own creative powers (669). This discussion suggests that the supposed resemblance merely results from Donatello's, Hilda's, and Kenyon's obsession: already they are trapped in Miriam's haunted world. But on the other hand, it is reasonable that in the greatest art they should find a reflection of their own lives. The title of the book itself refers to the way art reflects life so as to reveal its hidden meaning. It is in a statue that Donatello's friends see him clearly for the first time, recognizing their conception of his moral nature in Praxiteles' conception of a faun. When Kenyon draws the veil from his statue of Cleopatra, Miriam seems to recognize some aspect of her own psychology. Hilda sees her own anguish in the portrait of Beatrice.

For Hawthorne as for Melville, art is itself an act of knowledge, revealing mysteries through reflections. Thus it is appropriate that works of art are themselves several times unveiled or uncovered in this romance—as in the uncovering of Hilda's portrait of Beatrice (628), the unveiling of Kenyon's Cleopatra (660), the drawing back of the curtain that hides Guido's picture (695), and the unearthing of the marble woman (833). To look at certain works of art is itself an act of unveiling, a revelation. Thus it is not surprising that the observer should find his or her own life reflected in a work of art. In the case of Guido's demon and Praxiteles' faun, this involuntary repetition is all the more reasonable because both of these works depict myths: archetypal patterns that repeat themselves again and again in human life. Hilda, Donatello, and Kenyon undoubtedly see the Model in Guido's sketch because they are accustomed to seeing him everywhere, as the "spectre" of their world. But Guido's sketch, by copying an archetypal pattern, also reflects their world truly.

The mirror, Hawthorne observes in *The House of the Seven Gables,* "is always a kind of window or doorway into the spiritual world" (412). In his Gothic vision this is true not only of art's mirror of life or of those haunted mirrors that open on the world of spirits but also of the mirror world of the haunted mind itself. In Hawthorne's romances, repetition shows how the haunted mind projects itself outward, recreating the world in its own image, rendering the not-me dim and "visionary." But repetition of this sort is visionary in a positive sense as well. In one way the knowledge of evil distorts the communications between the world of matter and of spirit, but in another way it intensifies them, because for Hawthorne the psychology of guilt is the psychology of imagination, of the "sympathetic imagination" both in moral and aesthetic terms. Even in Hawthorne's darkest Gothic, the mirror world of the self-reflecting ego is, like all mirrors, a door into the spiritual world. Such a door, it seems, opens two ways. Or rather, the image implies an identity between the glimpse inward toward the blind dark recesses of the human spirit and the gaze outward toward a realm of spiritual truth that transcends the human condition. The self-reflecting world of the guilty ego is a prison, but like so many Romantic prisons,[23] it somehow gives access—even special access—to what is beyond it. Brombert cites an example of this "happy prison" from Proust: "I understood then that Noah never saw the world so clearly as from inside the ark, though it was closed and there was darkness on the earth."[24]

Hawthorne's Gothic ultimately renders a similar perception: in its darkest night, the soul somehow sees most clearly—even what is beyond itself. The reason this escape through entrapment is possible is for Hawthorne a simple one. "The truth of the human heart," however hopelessly alone the individual may feel in "that saddest of all prisons" ("Minister's Black Veil" 880), repeats itself in every life, just as the Fall repeats itself again and again. Miriam's Model is in Guido's picture not only because the observers project onto it their own obsession but also because the specter that haunts them was alive in Guido's day. This discovery of Miriam's private obsession in a picture she did not paint is the counterpart in *The Marble Faun* of the revelation that other people besides Dimmesdale saw an *A* in the sky. Dimmesdale's interpretation of the letter reveals his colossal egotism, but it also reveals a spiritual truth. His hidden life is indeed written in the universe, because it is universal. Hester's tendency to see her own guilt reflected everywhere is a manifestation of her self-absorption, of the "awful privacy" of a mind unable to escape itself. But this distortion is also a kind of insight. One reason Hester sees her guilt reflected everywhere is that she herself, with her scarlet letter, reflects her society's guilt. The scene in which Dimmesdale, representing the Puritan state, preaches to Hester, the reflection of his own adultery, points to an inescapable unity that the Puritan society, in its isolation of Hester, has tried to deny. It is no accident that Hester sees the letter on her own breast reflected on the armorial breastplate of the governor himself or that the multitudinous accusing voice in the forest, directed toward the outcast woman, should be the voice of the very scarlet emblem of sin. The Puritans try to push Hester beyond the boundaries by which they define themselves, but they succeed only in making her a projection of their haunted minds. Her very separateness is a unity; her awful privacy, a "sisterhood with the race of man" (179).

4

Boundaries of the Self as Romantic Theme: Emily Brontë

For human beings are not so constituted that they can live without expansion."
MARGARET FULLER

There is no outside, no inclosing wall, no circumference to us.
EMERSON

I desire to speak somewhere *without* bounds. . . .
THOREAU

I am large, I contain multitudes.
WHITMAN

I

Before she saw St. Peter's, Hilda dreamed of it as a Gothic cathedral: "a structure of no definite outline, misty in its architecture, dim and gray and huge, stretching into an interminable perspective, and over-arched by a dome like the cloudy firmament. Beneath that vast breadth and height, as she had fancied them, the personal man might feel his littleness, and the soul triumph in its immensity" (*Marble Faun* 791). For some time after seeing the real thing, she continued to long for that dim, illimitable interior (791). Gothic romance also dreams of dim, illimitable interiors, focuses on them obsessively, and so contemplates again and again the finitude of mere "personal" man or woman. Like the tiny figure of Piranesi lost in "vast Gothic halls," the victims of "the forces of violence" are trapped by their own limitations, their imprisonment a metaphor for frustration with the littleness of the self. The plethora of boundaries and barriers reinforces this sense of frustration. Confronted with a prison wall, a locked door, a black veil, a mask, the edge of a precipice, the self runs up again and again against its mortality: the simple limits of what the human body can and cannot do in its defense, the limits of what the mind can know. Yet Gothic romance, despite its despairing fixation on the "littleness" of the individual, also asserts the triumph of the soul "in its immensity."

This characteristic of Gothic romance is most obvious in its preoccupation with hero-villains who defy or seem to defy the ordinary limitations of mortals. Often these figures are physically larger than lifesize—to such an extent, indeed, that other people wonder whether they are human at all. Some of them appear to be omniscient, omnipresent, immortal. Their victims sometimes speak of them as the Deity is spoken of: "But how can I contend with an inaccessible enemy, whose power is undefined, and whose duration is unimaginable?" (*Montorio* 2: 429). In architectural space their gigantic stature is increased by the vagueness of their outlines: their edges blur; they merge with the shadows; and the personal threat they represent is diffused into the vaguer, abstract threat of "the forces of violence." In natural spaces their stature and physical prowess suggest a human vastness commensurate with what is vast in nature. Frankenstein's monster and Zofloya stride over the mountains; Montoni's name suggests that his personality extends beyond his castle to encompass the mountainous landscape itself. To transcend their own littleness is often the great ambition of such figures. They want unlimited power; they want to live forever, to know more than humans are intended to know. Like Melville's Pierre, they suspect that mortal limitations are in some sense self-imposed and so can be eliminated by an effort of will: "Oh, men are jailors all; jailors of themselves . . ." (*Pierre* 127). Like Sanguedoni they set "no limits to [their] wishes, no bounds to their enjoyment" (Curties, *Monk of Udolpho* 2: 148). They dream, like Victoria, that "every barrier to the gratification of [their] wishes would ultimately be destroyed" (Dacre, *Zofloya* 2: 115).

The figure who Victoria dreams will help her accomplish this feat is himself larger than life: the apparently omnipotent Moor, Zofloya. Like other such gigantic figures (Orazio, for example), he seems to inhabit some border country between the human and superhuman. Just as Ippolito makes the mistake of thinking Orazio more than a man when he is not, Victoria makes the mistake of thinking Zofloya merely a dark man when he is the Prince of Darkness. The very ease with which the mortal can be confused with the immortal in Gothic romance signifies the soul's immensity. Seen from certain perspectives, in certain lights, the human figure itself looks vast, immaterial, otherworldly. And although on one level the device of *surnaturel expliqué* reveals that what seemed supernatural was natural after all, on another level it suggests that it was only natural after all to confuse the two.[1]

Even when the supernatural is not explained away, the role it plays in Gothic romance often asserts some intimate connection between the forces of the Beyond and the soul's own immensities. Zofloya, for example, turns out in the end to be the Devil, but because he so often appears in response to Victoria's thoughts, her imagination seems in some sense to have created him, even though he also exists independent of it. He first appears in her dreams after her long submersion in wicked fantasies culminates in a sensation of being "under the influence of some superior and unknown power" (2: 109). The increasing strength of Victoria's own evil desires coincides with an increasing obsession with Zofloya. He haunts her dreams; once, half-awake, she thinks she sees him beside her bed, whereupon he leaves her room by passing through a closed door (2: 134–35). She half sleeps again, and sees in "a grey silvery mist" the figure of Zofloya opening the curtains at the foot of her bed (2: 135). She is not certain he was there. Was it a dream, or not? Whether he came from within or without, there are no definite barriers between the Moor and Victoria's inner world of fantasy. His manner of arriving and departing suggests that here, at least, the perils beyond the sleeper's bed are the same perils lurking in the blind recesses of her heart. This identity makes the villainess-heroine's name appropriate despite its irony; her final defeat by the demon she has somehow conjured up is at the same time a victory of the part of her he objectifies: her soul's immense capacity for evil. The power of evil, traditionally represented in the figure of the Devil, is in this work a power of the human heart itself. And there is no mistaking the excitement with which Dacre adumbrates its dark magnificence.[2]

Few Gothicists rejoice quite so indiscretely as "Monk" Lewis or his disciple Charlotte Dacre (alias "Rosa Matilda," the demonic female spirit of *The Monk*), in the actual triumph of evil. Most Gothicists place their final emphasis on God's taking care of his own rather than on the Devil's arriving victoriously to claim his own. Nevertheless, even the primmest Gothic romancers tend covertly to celebrate the soul's immense capacity for evil, though deploring evil itself.[3] The thrill with which they contemplate human nature at its colossal worst is manifest most clearly in their association of Gothic villains with the sublimities of Salvator's landscapes and, by implication, with the ambiguous sublimities of his character. The same exultation underlies the nostalgia with which the more genteel and sentimental Gothic authors write of bygone "Gothic" times. Sophia Lee and Rosetta Ballin deplore Queen Elizabeth's villainy in no uncertain terms, but their outrage itself betrays some admiration: a shudder of awe at the very scope and grandeur of the tyranny that made the good old days so bad. "Personal littleness" could not inhibit the despot in those unenlightened times, even when she was a woman.

It is not only in titanic figures of evil that Gothic romance celebrates the immensities of the human soul. The figures such villains seek to dominate may seem appallingly little among the mountain crags and interminable archways, but at times they too are revealed in their spiritual immensity. Indeed, a dramatic recognition of personal littleness is often a prelude in these works to the soul's discovery of its true dimensions. The source of this paradox is found in the theory of the sublime that underlies so many descriptions of nature and architecture in Gothic romance.[4] In its experience of the sublime the soul "dilates," "distends," "stretches," "expands." The heroine, so small and vulnerable in the villain's domain, looks out on the landscape from her casement window, and suddenly in her ecstatic response to nature, the human soul is revealed in its magnitude. Such, at least, is the vision of Gothic comedy, in which humility in the face of one's mortality combines with awe in the face of sublime nature to dilate the soul with wonder and reverence. At such moments the imagination moves outward and upward through nature to nature's God. In more pessimistic versions of Gothic romance, the magnitude of the individual soul is attained only through strenuous contention against the limits of mortality; to reach its rightful dimensions the soul must transgress against the limits imposed by nature and nature's God, resist the constriction natural to the human state.

Whatever the moral evaluation associated with it, the soul's "voyage out" is everywhere the Gothicist's theme. Characters in Gothic romance are continually going on long journeys, escaping from confinements, looking out of prison grates and casement windows, longing to be free. It is hardly surprising that such images evoke *Alastor* and "The Prisoner of Chillon" as well as *The Mysteries of Udolpho,* for in all this, Gothic romance sounds a major theme of Romanticism: "the myth of the infinite self."[5]

"The only sin is limitation" (Emerson, "Circles" 171). "[T]o make the external internal, the internal external, to make nature thought, and thought nature,—this is the mystery of genius in the Fine Arts" (Coleridge, *Bio-*

graphia 2: 258).[6] "The great mission of our age is to unite the infinite and the finite" (Brownson 114). As these pronouncements of Emerson, Coleridge, and Orestes Brownson indicate, the boundaries of the self were not only a preoccupation of those Romantics who made deliberate and extensive use of the Gothic legacy but of Romanticism in general. This preoccupation links what are often seen as two opposing varieties of Romanticism: "dark" and "light" Romanticism, "negative" and "positive" Romanticism, or as Emerson called them, "the party of hope" and "the party of memory." Indeed, the issue of the boundaries of the self is the major interface between these two parties, the point at which optimistic Romanticism is most often on the edge of despair and negative Romanticism is on the verge of transcendence.

The term *negative Romanticism* comes from Morse Peckham's "Toward a Theory of Romanticism" and is used here with his discussion in mind. The emphasis of his definition of the term, however, is on lack of faith in "organicism"; here the term is intended to connote, more broadly, pessimism about the possibility of the kind of transcendence represented by escape from the boundaries of the self. In the background of this examination of the relation between a positive version of Romanticism and a negative version that owes much to the Gothic legacy are two studies in particular. The first is G. R. Thompson's anthology, *The Gothic Imagination: Essays in Dark Romanticism,* which defines dark romanticism as "the drama of the mind engaged in the quest for metaphysical and moral absolutes in a world that offers shadowy semblances of an occult order but withholds final revelation and illumination" (6).[7] The second is the controversy between Hume and Platzner about the distinctions set forth in Hume's "Gothic Versus Romantic: A Revaluation of the Gothic Novel." Platzner argues persuasively that "pursu[ing] the line of inquiry opened up by Northrop Frye" in *A Study of English Romanticism,* we should "locate the major thrust of *all* Romantic literature in the search for 'superior forms of consciousness and perception' (p. 29) which often involve some form or other of epistemological idealism. . . ." He points to the consequence of this Romantic preoccupation:

> [O]ne can therefore expect to find at stress points in either a Gothic Romance or a Keatsean ode an identification of consciousness and reality. That such a unification of self and object, however transitory, is achieved by both poet and romancer . . . should suggest that Gothic fiction and Romantic poetry represent cognate impulses of the visionary mind to repossess a universe it perceives as resistant or inimical to consciousness. That Byron and Coleridge

can be at once "Romantic" and "Gothic" or that individual poems like "The Ancient Mariner" or "Manfred" can project an image of the mind both alienated and transcendent, eluding thereby any rigid system of classification, should further suggest the degree of continuity that actually exists between Gothic quests and Romantic epiphanies. In fact, the persistent receptivity of the Gothic imagination to the affective or cosmic sublime can be seen as an almost Manichean struggle that embodies in mythic form a more familiar conflict of psychological states within the mind of the Romantic lyricist: the dialectic of dejection and joy. ("Rejoinder" 267–68)

That Gothic and Romantic in fact represent a number of "cognate impulses" is the subject of this chapter, which will examine the continuity between "Gothic quests and Romantic epiphanies" in terms of the ambivalent relation of Romantic writers in the Gothic tradition to the kinds of transcendence they aspire to and perhaps fear. At the center of the chapter is Emily Brontë, in whose work, of all other nineteenth-century novels, the paradoxical conjunction of transcendent aspiration and Gothic despair is most evident, and most evidently a subject of the text itself.

II

Most sources of terror in Gothic romance have positive as well as negative valences. The question of the soul's "immensity" is a case in point. From one perspective, the Gothicist regards the boundaryless self with horror: it is the amorphous Gothic villain whose personality, already diffused beyond him into the dark shadows of his castle, threatens to swallow up the tiny victim. But from another perspective, the very hugeness of the villain looks like the triumph of the "infinite self." Similarly, from one perspective the experiences of "danger and death . . . on every side," of not knowing, and of repetition look like the horrors and frustrations of personal littleness. All of these terrors involve a sense of being imprisoned in self, in the limitations of mortality. But as the first three chapters of this study have indicated, these very terrors may at the same time reveal the soul in its immensity. The potential victim, through a consciousness of those moral boundaries that set him or her apart from the villain, gains power to defy the forces of evil in all their vastness. Not knowing is a source of terror, but it may also be a condition of mystical unity with some ultimate reality beyond the self: an Other approached only through mystery. Deadly iteration is a nightmare, but the prison of self-reflection may reflect (and thereby give access to) something beyond it. In addition, those sources of terror examined in the first three chapters have positive valences because of their relation to three of Burke's requirements for the sublime: terror in the face of personal danger, obscurity ("It is our ignorance of things that causes all our admiration, and chiefly excites our passions"), and the "artificial infinity" produced by repetition (57–58, 61, 73–76, 139–43). The very sensation of personal littleness that these phenomena create is a stimulus to awe. Readers themselves are intended to experience, through the encounter with vagueness and vastness and danger, the terror that elevates and expands the soul.

That the theme of the boundaries of the self is an interface between the two varieties of Romanticism can be illustrated from the other side as well. If the light of the Gothic gloom is most obvious at this point, so is the gloom of the Transcendental light. The issue of the epistemological prison of the self-reflecting mind is an example. Hawthorne's epistemological prisons sometimes offer the possibility of paradoxical self-transcendence through confinement in self. Conversely, Emerson's exuberant idealism is sometimes perilously close to "solipsistic fear." The beginning of "Experience" illustrates this fact, in a passage in which Emerson seems to be suffering from a phenomenon that Maturin described in *Melmoth*: "At night his *creed retaliates on him*":

> Where do we find ourselves? In a series of which we do not know the extremes, and believe that it has none. We wake and find ourselves on a stair; there are stairs below us, which we seem to have ascended; there are stairs above us, many a one, which go upward and out of sight. . . . Sleep lingers all our lifetime about our eyes. . . . All things swim and glitter. . . . Dream delivers us to dream, and there is no end to illusion. . . . Temperament . . . shuts us in a prison of glass which we cannot see. (254–55, 257, 258)

Here is a vision close to Gothic nightmare: the man on Piranesi's[8] endless stairs, unbounded by any extremes, lost in infinity, but trapped all the same. He is unable to know; things dazzle before him; half-images only are "flung . . . on the straining eye." His life resembles a dream. He is locked in the prison of temperament, a glass prison he cannot even see: the prison of himself. In *Nature*, the idealist's credo—"What we are, that only can we see" (56)—led to the triumphant conclusion, "Build therefore your own world" (56). Here that credo is transposed to quite another mode, as if, for all the first-person plurals, Emerson were speaking alone from the prison of his solitary mind. Indeed, a personal grief surfaces early in the discussion: "In the death of my son, now more than two years ago, I seem to have lost a beautiful estate,—no more. I cannot get it nearer to me" (256). And the conclusion of the idealist's meditation in "Experience" is correspondingly different from the earlier one: "Nothing is left us now but death. We look to that with a grim satisfaction, saying, There at least is reality that will not dodge us" (256–57).

Characteristically, Emerson moves out of this despair toward a renewed faith that we are not locked into self.

> Into every intelligence there is a door which is never closed, through which the creator passes. The intellect, seeker of absolute truth, or the heart, lover of absolute good, intervenes for our succor, and at one whisper of these high powers we awake from ineffectual struggles with this nightmare. We hurl it into its own hell, and cannot again contract ourselves to so base a state. (259)

"A door which is never closed," through which the Other has continual access to the self: Emerson's final article of faith is the Gothicist's source of terror. For although Gothicism participates in "the myth of the infinite self," its intuition of the soul's immensities is often a shocked and fearful one, and where it sees the possibilities of transcendence it is often most afraid. "Each generation has something different at which they are all looking," as Gertrude Stein said. The issue of the boundaries of the self was that "something" for the Romantics of both "parties." But if those Romantics who used the Gothic legacy and those who, like Emerson, refused to "grope among the dry bones of the past" (*Nature,* in *Selections* 21) were looking at the same thing, they were nonetheless looking from radically different perspectives. For Emerson "the only sin is limitation"; the only contract with the base "state" of Hell is the soul's contraction to the base state of not knowing its divinity. The Other is immanent; it is within as well as without. For the positive Romantic, that discovery is an awakening from nightmare; for the negative Romantic, it may *be* the nightmare.

> The Body—borrows a Revolver—
> He bolts the Door—
> O'erlooking a superior spectre—
> Or More—

Emily Dickinson knew her Emerson as well as Gothic melodrama. The "superior spectre" is the self behind the self concealed, but it is, at the same time, More.

Pierre is in many ways a negative Romantic meditation on the ambiguous interface between Gothic nightmare and Transcendental epiphany, as evidenced by Melville's choice of a Transcendental religious establishment for the setting of Pierre's Gothic horrors. It is Pierre's discovery of a "divine unidentifiableness" (125) that effectively makes him an orphan, brings him to this place, and isolates him in a private hell of self. This "unidentifiableness" is in Emerson's philosophy precisely the means of escape from the potential prison of self: the point at which the supposedly finite self finds itself connected to the Infinite. But Melville presents Transcendental revelation itself as a kind of Gothic nightmare:

> Now, that vague, fearful feeling stole into him, that, rail as all atheists will, there is a mysterious, inscrutable divineness in the world—a God—a Being positively present everywhere;—nay, he is now in this room; the air did part when I here sat down. I displaced the Spirit then—condensed it a little off from this spot. He looked apprehensively around him; he felt overjoyed at the sight of the humanness of Delly. (441)

God here is a kind of ghost, an inhuman apparition to be "fearful" of. This points to an essential difference between the positive and negative Romantic approaches to the problem of the boundaries of the self. Emerson rejoices in self-reliance because the self is God; he rejoices to discover the "door which is never closed," because he has no doubt that the creator who passes through it is beneficent. The "party of memory" has a different view. Gothicists, and their Romantic descendants who used Gothic conventions, see the possibility of transcendence through self-reliance, but they fear the nature of the self; they see the potential for self-transcendence through unity with something Other, but they fear the nature of the Other. This is not to say that Radcliffe or even Maturin fail to strive, at least, for a philosophy reconciled to the ways of Providence, mysterious as those ways may be. But Gothic romances are nothing if not long, tormented, hallucinatory meditations on the problem of evil.[9] The Gothicists who, like Maturin or Lewis, flirt most dangerously with blasphemy present a picture of the world that makes it difficult to reconcile the ways of God to man, and even the most pious Gothicists do not always quite manage to reconcile the ways of God to woman. The cosmic problem of evil as Gothicists present it raises questions about the goodness of the supernatural Other. The social problem of evil—of public, institutional tyranny as well as what Godwin called "domestic and unrecorded despotism" (*Caleb Williams* 1)—raises the same questions about human society and the human heart. What the party of memory is always remembering is the Fall.[10]

Thus while Gothicism aspires toward transcendence, at the same time it regards the possibilities of transcendence with ambivalence and fear. *Wuthering Heights* illustrates how Gothic gloom tends to shade into transcendental light where the "myth of the infinite self" is concerned.[11] At the same time it illustrates the ambivalence inherent in the Gothic version of that myth: an ambivalence that reveals from what radically different perspectives, after all, the two Romantic "parties" look at the boundaries of the self.

III

Wuthering Heights begins with an encounter at a threshold, as Lockwood seeks entrance to Heathcliff's domain. Heathcliff leans over the gate and, making no motion to open it, invites Lockwood in. He finally admits the unwanted guest when he sees Lockwood's horse "fairly pushing the barrier" (45). Despite this unpleasant reception, Lockwood repeats the "intrusion" (50) the next day, jumping over the gate when he cannot remove the chain, knocking "vainly" at the door until his knuckles tingle, and resolving, "At least, I would not keep my doors barred in the day time— I don't care—I will get in!" (51). He rattles the latch to no avail and, being refused admittance by Joseph, is finally let in by Hareton. Having thus deliberately and rashly crossed the threshold between his own world and Heathcliff's, Lockwood, not understanding the consequences, fastens his bedroom door that night, slides back the "panelled sides" of the bed, pulls them together again, and naïvely feels "secure against the vigilance of Heathcliff, and everyone else" (61). Ominously, however, this inmost place has a window on the heath, and Lockwood will find himself unable to remain secure from either the storm or Heathcliff.

Indeed, Lockwood has unwittingly shut himself "securely" into the center of Heathcliff's haunted mind. Immediately he is assailed by repetition— writing all over the ledge: "a name repeated in all kinds of characters, large and small. . . . In vapid listlessness I leant my head against the window, and continued spelling over Catherine Earnshaw—Heathcliff— Linton, till my eyes closed; but they had not rested five minutes when a glare of white letters started from the dark, as vivid as spectres—the air swarmed with Catherines . . ." (61). The recess where Lockwood tries to secure himself for the night is the repository of Catherine's diary and so the center of her private world. Filled as it is with repetitions of her name, it is also the center of Heathcliff's private world, emblem of the obsession he later describes so vividly:

> I cannot look down to this floor, but her features are shaped on the flags! In every cloud, in every tree—filling the air at night, and caught by glimpses in every object by day, I am surrounded with her image! The most ordinary faces of men, and women—my own features mock me with a resemblance. The entire world is a dreadful collection of memoranda that she did exist, and that I have lost her! (353)

To relieve himself of this obsession in which he has unwittingly become trapped, Lockwood examines Catherine's books and, discovering that they contain her diary, begins trying "to decypher her faded hieroglyphics" (62). Beneath a caricature of Joseph begins the account of a childhood Sunday marred by Joseph's pious notions about the proper relations between the "sowl" and its God. In the midst of this attempt—by way of a diary written in a book of sermons—to gain access to another person's inner self, Lockwood dozes off and dreams that Joseph is berating him for lacking the proper "pilgrim's staff" to gain access to "the house" (65). It strikes him as strange that he should "need such a weapon to gain admittance into [his] own residence" (65), but then he realizes that the house referred to is a chapel. Thus in this opening dream sequence, Lockwood's earlier difficulties gaining admission to Heathcliff's Gothic world become confused with difficulties gaining readmission to his own world and finally with difficulties gaining admission to God—or at least to God as Joseph defines him.

Joseph's God, as Catherine's book of sermons reveals him, is not a particularly approachable Deity, although he intrudes insistently on human life. (Catherine's own religion seems to be the "religion of the self" that is Romanticism and not Joseph's church-bound variety). On the Sunday recorded in the diary, this God, through his self-appointed earthly vicar Joseph, trapped Cathy and Heathcliff in a cold garret for a three-hour-long service and later intruded on their retreat "in the arch of the dresser" (63) by tearing down the curtain they had put up for privacy. In the dream, this God is difficult to reach: one must have the proper pilgrim's staff, "a heavy-headed cudgel" (65), to get into his place of worship. And the point of getting in is, absurdly, to hear a sermon preached for the purpose of throwing someone out. The Reverend Jabes Branderham is to preach a sermon of excommunication against that sinner who has committed the four hundred and ninety-first sin no Christian is obliged to forgive.

The sermon is divided into four hundred and ninety parts, about four hundred and ninety sins—"They were of the most curious character—odd transgressions that I never imagined previously" (65). After enduring through the Seventy Times Seven, Lockwood leaps up and accuses Branderham of himself having committed the four hundred and ninety-first, unforgivable sin: preaching this sermon. The preacher responds with the counteraccusation that it is Lockwood who has committed the sin by listening impatiently. The identity of the unforgivable sinner is finally revealed. *"Thou art the Man!"* the preacher cries, and the congregation sets on Lockwood with their pilgrim's staves. Branderham participates by rapping loudly on the pulpit, and the din finally wakes the dreamer, who discovers that this sound was the branch of a fir tree rattling against his window in the storm (66).

Lockwood sleeps again and dreams that in trying to stop the branch, he breaks the window and grabs the "little, ice-cold hand" of the child Catherine, who sobs, "Let me in—let me in!" (67). The pilgrimage of the first dream sequence—a pilgrimage toward both the self and God as Joseph defines him—reappears in the second dream as an effort, on the part of something supernatural beyond the self, to intrude on the self in its inmost "secure" retreat. In his terror, Lockwood rubs the little arm against the broken pane until the blood runs down and soaks the bedclothes. He piles books up against the hole in the pane, but there is "a feeble scratching outside, and the pile of books move[s] as if thrust forward" (67). Lockwood wakes screaming "in a frenzy of fright" (67); footsteps approach his door; an "intruder" pushes it open; and the "intruder" (Heathcliff) hears to his horror the panels of Catherine's bed creaking open. Lockwood reveals that it is only he, and Heathcliff, nearly maddened by Lockwood's behavior and his account of the ghost, finally sends him out of the room. From outside the chamber, Lockwood sees Heathcliff wrench open the lattice and call desperately after the ghost, who will not come back.

After so many Gothic heroines' miserable nights in so many insecure rooms, Brontë's innovations here have a startling force and intensity. The extraordinary power and psychological realism of the scene in the haunted chamber are a measure of her genius. Into a relatively short narrative space she compresses a range of Gothic conventions that might have served Radcliffe well for a hundred pages. This compression has the effect of charging with multiple significance the boundaries and barriers in the narrative and thereby ultimately confusing them with one another. Access to the inner self becomes identified with access both to other selves and to something "wholly Other."[12] These identities make the initial Gothic episode an appropriate prelude to the central narrative: an account of a tormented relationship in which an inaccessible beloved is identified with the lover's own inaccessible soul, and the lovers' passion for each other is identified with Romantic aspiration toward something "beyond and above" (197) this world.

In a metaphysical sense there are two boundaries at issue in this episode. First is the boundary that sets Lockwood off as a separate person from other people, specifically Heathcliff and Catherine, and distinguishes his world from the world of Wuthering Heights. Corresponding to this metaphysical boundary are several physical boundaries: the entrance to Heathcliff's house, the entrance to Lockwood's house in the dream, the door to Catherine's room, and the panels of her bed. Second is the boundary dividing the human from the superhuman, the supernatural, the "wholly Other." Corresponding to this metaphysical boundary are several physical boundaries: the entrance to the chapel (Joseph's version of access to the supernatural), the window on the heath (the Romantics' alternative version of access to the supernatural), and the bed panels that Heathcliff thinks are opening to reveal a ghost.

In Lockwood's visit to Heathcliff, all of these physical boundaries, and thus the metaphysical boundaries they represent, become confused with one another. Roudaut refers to the haunted castle as a place of tension between an inside and an outside (729). The confusion of inside and outside in Brontë's version of the haunted house is first manifested in the fact that the house itself takes its name from what is outside it. By crossing the threshold of Heathcliff's world, Lockwood finds himself at the same time deeply inside the secret life of the house and perilously close to an outside that threatens to intrude on him in his retreat. One of the first things we learn about Lockwood is that he tends to withdraw into himself "like a snail" (48). By entering Heathcliff's house and Catherine's bedchamber, he jeopardizes his shell, as it were: one of the first effects of his encounter with the world of Wuthering Heights is a confusion over his own identity.[13] In the dream this confusion manifests itself in the suggestion that Lockwood may have trouble getting back into his own house. For a moment he feels alienated from himself in the same way that he initially found himself shut out of Heathcliff's world. The Sunday experience of two people he knows almost nothing of, recorded in the manuscript, becomes in an altered form his own dream experience. In Heathcliff's house he beings to suffer from Heathcliff's obsession: Catherine. In Catherine's room he becomes Catherine herself for a moment, as Heathcliff hears with horror the sound of her bed panels creaking open. And as Kiely points out, so great is the confusion of identities here that Heathcliff "rushes to the window and addresses the specter of *Lockwood's* dream" (236, emphasis added).

The world of Gothic terror is always a world in which the boundaries one relied on prove undependable, shifting, nonexistent. Such is the case at Wuthering Heights. Indeed, in this Gothic world even the distinctions among the boundaries themselves tend to "shift and blur." The manuscript/book containing both Catherine's diary and Branderham's sermon, like the bedchamber opening on the "natural supernaturalism"[14] of the heath, is an emblem of the way access to the self, other selves, and the Other are confused throughout the whole episode. Lockwood's attempts to get into Heathcliff's house reappear in the dream as Joseph's warning that he will not be able to get into his own house. The pilgrimage into his own house in turn is revealed as a religious pilgrimage into a church. The events inside the church are revealed as events outside the window in nature. The natural phenomenon of the branch tapping on the window is revealed as the supernatural phenomenon of a ghost trying to get in.[15] And the ghost beyond the window is perhaps only a dream: a projection outward of Lockwood's inner self. Strangely, this inner self takes the outer form of Catherine, who is in turn Heathcliff's inner self, his "soul" (204). Lockwood, who intrudes on Heathcliff, is in turn intruded on by Heathcliff, who in turn perceives the supernatural intruding on him in the form of Lockwood as the ghost of Catherine. Heathcliff's own stormy intrusion into Lockwood's room corresponds to the intrusion, by way of the window, of the storm in the outside world of heaths and cliffs.

Thus in the haunted world of Wuthering Heights, the barriers between Lockwood and Heathcliff, between him and his inner self, between him and Joseph's God, between him and nature, and between him and some supernatural spiritual world revealed in nature all become confused with one another. The result of this confusion is that the frustrated desire for access to something beyond the self becomes strangely identified both with self-alienation and the fear of intrusion on the self by something beyond it. This identity derives most fundamentally from the blurring of distinctions between two radically different characters: the man of heaths and cliffs who opens the window and summons the ghost to come in and the man of interiors and closed places who would lock the ghost out if he could. Lockwood's perils of the night are the object of Heathcliff's soul's desire. Yet in the confusion of identity between the two men, their fear and desire are revealed as two aspects of the same dilemma. In their two responses to the ghost, the window becomes a symbol both of the terrible proximity of something Other and its terrible inaccessibility. Perversely, Lockwood is unable to maintain a defense against the ghost, and Heathcliff is unable to unite himself with it. Even barricading the window will not keep it out; even wrenching open the lattice will not bring it in. Together Lockwood and Heathcliff represent the double terror of unity and separateness. Lockwood discovers that the boundary between the inmost retreat of the self and the outermost Other is a precarious one; yet in Heathcliff's torment we see how hard it is to bridge the chasm between them. Lockwood is haunted by fear of what is beyond the window, and Heathcliff is haunted by longing for it—for this Other that impinges so terrifyingly on human life but recedes as humans reach out for it.

In her use of the Gothic tradition to portray this double fear and longing, Brontë takes as her subject a double frustration that permeates all of Gothic romance and contributes to its tone of desperation and extremity. On the one hand Gothic romance envisions some Other as always and threateningly impinging on this world. But at the same time it conveys a sense that contact with this Other is nearly impossible. Sometimes Gothicists present this frustration overtly as a subject of the narrative. More often they convey it, perhaps unconsciously, through their ambivalent attitude toward the supernatural, an attitude revealed in their narrative procedures.

It has never been fully recognized that the sense of disappointment, even of being cheated, that most readers experience at the end of many Gothic works is shared by the characters themselves and is actually a subject of many Gothic narratives. Coleridge objected that *The Mysteries of Udolpho* raises our curiosity to such a pitch that it cannot possibly be satisfied. That kind of curiosity, or of aspiration, is in fact a primary subject of the book. The romance is about those impulses of the soul that can never, it seems, be satisfied. Emily St. Aubert would have liked to believe that contact with her father's departed spirit was possible, but the "ghost" is only a man. *Montorio,* similarly, is on one level a Protestant allegory of the disappointments in store for anyone who thinks to find access to spiritual realities through what Maturin regards as the hocus-pocus of the Catholic church. The supposed priest who promises his victim this access turns out to be a fraud, a trickster, an "Archimage."[16] In such works as these, the romancer holds out the hope for hundreds of pages that there is something out there, scares us out of our wits with its always imminent approach, then snatches it out of reach with the final explanations. And so in the next romance and the next and the next, the "Gothic Quest"[17] goes on in both terror and hope and is continually brought to nothing.

Montague Summers was contemptuous of and impatient with the explained supernatural because he perceived it as a symptom of failure in the Gothic quest. Yet the failure of this quest seems to be an essential aspect of Gothic romance, which often deals, and often deals overtly, with the frustrations attendant on spiritual aspiration in a universe governed by the laws of reason. Even the authors of those works frequently cited as exemplifying the unabashed use of the unexplained supernatural, *The Castle of Otranto* and *The Monk,* betray a much more ambivalent attitude toward their irrational and supernatural materials than is commonly recognized.[18] Walpole prefaced his romance with an account of his relation to the story: as the enlightened translator of an old tale. The tale itself, he speculates, was written by "an artful priest" attempting to turn literature—the reformers' own weapon against superstition—into a means of "confirm[ing] the populace in their ancient errors . . ." (39). The unexplained supernatural in *Otranto* is thus set in a frame deploring superstition, rejoicing in it, calling for a willing suspension of educated disbelief on the part of modern readers, and asserting the "translator's" own rationality as a modern man.

In *The Monk,* Lewis's presentation of the "real," unexplained supernatural is part of a total narrative context in which rational skepticism, real ghosts, and burlesques of ghost stories all operate together to qualify one another in complicated ways. Raymond is punished for his skeptical and humorous account of the Bleeding Nun by a terrifying encounter with the ghost herself. But in contrast, Antonia's encounter with her mother's ghost is framed by two other accounts of the supernatural that suggest the author's own skepticism. The appearance of Elvira's ghost is preceded by Antonia's perusal of a ghost story. Antonia was overly susceptible to such tales, Lewis says:

> She had naturally a strong inclination to the marvellous; and her nurse, who believed firmly in apparitions, had related to her, when an infant, so many horrible adventures of this kind, that all Elvira's attempts had failed to eradicate their impressions from her daughter's mind. Antonia still nourished a

superstitious prejudice in her bosom. . . . With such a turn of mind, the adventure which she had just been reading sufficed to give her apprehensions the alarm. (244–45)

After this preparation, it is not even clear whether the ghost of Elvira is really there or merely imagined. And shortly after the (genuinely frightening) appearance of the ghost, we are treated to quite a different version of it. The superstitious nurse tells how the apparition appeared from Hell, rattling its chains "piteously," breathing clouds of fire, and bewailing a sin committed on the Friday before she died: "Oh! that chicken's wing! my poor soul suffers for it!" (251).

If such works as *Otranto* and *The Monk* embody, in many ways, an aspiration toward something reason cannot approach, in other ways they mock and qualify that aspiration. The authors feel the lure of the Gothic quest, but they are not quite able to leave their skepticism behind as they embark on the journey. Thus in much Gothic romance—even some that makes boldest use of the supernatural—a frustration with the apparently simultaneous immanence and inaccessibility of the Other is either an overt subject of the narrative or inherent in its procedures. Furthermore, Porte's perception that the Gothic quest for God is also a desperate flight away from him ("In the Hands") points to another source of ambivalence. The Gothic focus on evil balances the impulse toward transcendence with an element of suspicion. Perhaps unity with the Other is not something to seek but something to shrink from. Gothic works and Romantic works that use the Gothic tradition are filled with symbols of this ambivalent and frustrated impulse toward transcendent unity. The principal such symbol is the pursuit/chase between two characters both fleeing and seeking each other. Thus Moby-Dick is both the ever-receding object of desire and, as the prison wall "shoved near" (220–21), the ever-impinging source of terror. Another emblem of this frustration is the unity in separateness of Pierre's pseudomarriage. Another is the double reaction of Lockwood and Heathcliff to the ghost at the window.

This double reaction introduces the theme of the haunted soul, shut into itself but at the same time separate from itself, tormented by a constantly intruding Other. This Other is perhaps identical with the soul's own deepest source of life and yet, like that source itself, is somehow never accessible. This theme is worked out most fully in the account of Catherine and Heathcliff's relationship, the central metaphor in the novel for the soul's simultaneous struggle in toward its own depths and out toward transcendence.

Brontë's own ambivalent view of this journey is inherent in the elaborate framing device, which operates simultaneously to qualify and intensify the passions it contains.[19] On the one hand, the frame encloses the love story within the limits of what Lockwood, with the equally limited Nelly as his primary source, is able to imagine. On the other hand, their restrained rendering of the story, and their outsiders' wariness of contact with its depths, make the passions they describe seem all the more explosive. One of the most electrifying scenes in the novel is that in which Nelly, having closed the window next to Heathcliff's deathbed, vainly attempts to close the dead man's eyes—to shut out from her own sight that "life-like gaze of exultation" (365). Like Lockwood, she tries to shut out the Other beyond what is human and shut in the Other at the depths of what is human; thus her role in this scene represents something typical of Lockwood as well: a deeply ambivalent relation to the subject of the narrative.

On Lockwood's part, this ambivalence is inherent from the beginning in his account of his events in the haunted chamber. His urbane account of the first dream is quite amusing on one level, with the humor turning on an impatient churchgoer's mildly wicked fantasy of rising from his pew and denouncing the preacher as an intolerable bore. The dream is a humorous version of religious terror. It jokes about one of Brontë's most serious themes, much as the story of the ghost and the chicken wing jokes about one of Lewis's most serious preoccupations, the damnation of the soul. Lockwood's next dream is reported in a different tone, reflecting his deeper submersion in his psyche and in the sadistic impulses that are in a sense the psyche of the house. As Kinkead-Weekes says, "[T]he most terrible and inhuman moment in the novel is not Heathcliff's but Lockwood's—that nightmare moment no reader ever forgets, when the civilized city man rubs the ghost-child's arm against the broken glass of the window . . ." ("Place of Love" 90).[20] Waking, however, Lockwood recovers his usual demeanor, at least to the extent of managing the tone of fussy peevishness characteristic of urbanity caught a little off guard. "And that minx, Catherine Linton, or Earnshaw, or however she was called—she must have been a changeling—wicked little soul!" he exclaims to Heathcliff (69). The impulse behind this thoughtless outburst is clearly one with the more deeply submerged impulse that made him rub Cathy's arm against the glass. Nevertheless, the tone of the exclamation succeeds in again setting Lockwood outside Heathcliff's world, a world in whose overt physical cruelties Lockwood participates only in dreams.

The reestablishment of Lockwood's separation from his host is reflected physically in their actions. Heathcliff himself retreats behind the bed panels; Lockwood is completely outside the room when he witnesses, in secret, the final explosion of passion at the window. Nevertheless, Lockwood has at that very window just engaged, at least in imagination, in an act of cruelty reminiscent of Heathcliff in his worst moments. Thus Lockwood's observation of Heathcliff from outside the room—emblematic of his narrative stance in general—points to his alienation, in his waking moments, from his own psychic depths.[21] Freud described repression as the construction of a wall; we see Lockwood in the act of repression as he barricades himself against the ghost. This dream act represents Lockwood's self-alienation, but his waking actions reveal how unconscious that alienation is.

Heathcliff's self-alienation, in contrast, is conscious; indeed, Heathcliff seems conscious of little else: "I cannot live without my soul!" (204). The scene in the haunted chamber symbolically identifies Heathcliff's passion for Catherine with both an aspiration toward the Beyond and the Gothic journey into the "recesses of blind human hearts." Heathcliff refers to Catherine as "my soul." Ironically, although he is shut into himself at Wuthering Heights, his own soul is beyond his reach. That the self may be inaccessible to the self is revealed in Lockwood's dream of needing a cudgel to get into his own house and in the ghost's desperate, unsuccessful attempt to get into her own room. Catherine's chamber is filled with her name in obsessive repetition, yet her ghost is outside the window and cannot get in to this repository of her own identity. Heathcliff sees Catherine everywhere, even in his own features, and yet cannot reach her. Even in his own features—he could hardly be closer to the object of desire. Yet the very resemblance is only an image of loss. If Joseph's God was terrible, intrusive, and inaccessible, the God of the "religion of the self" seems even worse. Lockwood's experience in Heathcliff's house reveals that the inmost retreat of the self is exactly the point of access to what is most other. But the word *other* identifies the problem.[22] As Daiches says, there is in *Wuthering Heights* "the recurrent and disturbing suggestion that the depths of man's nature are in some way alien to him" (27). The great irony of Catherine's and Heathcliff's passion is that although they each see the other as identical with their own inner life, they find each other unattainable. The Other is immanent; it is within as well as without. Yet in neither sense is it accessible. Heathcliff is locked into himself at Wuthering Heights, but he has no contact with his soul. His name establishes him as—literally—an outsider, yet in the scene at the window he fails miserably to establish contact with what is outside.

In *Wuthering Heights* as in Gothic romance, the ultimate source of all this frustration is simply the boundary that stops short the Gothic protagonist again and again: the limitations of mortality. Catherine gives voice to this frustration in her passionate rejection of the real Heathcliff, whose personal littleness she suddenly recognizes but will not accept. Her outburst is a perfect expression of the Romantic longing that created "the myth of the infinite self":

> ". . . Well, never mind! That is not *my* Heathcliff. I shall love mine yet;
> and take him with me—he's in my soul. And," added she, musingly, "the
> thing that irks me most is this shattered prison, after all. I'm tired, tired of
> being enclosed here. I'm wearying to escape into that glorious world, and to
> be always there; not seeing it dimly through tears, and yearning for it through
> the walls of an aching heart; but really with it, and in it. . . . I shall be
> sorry for *you*. I shall be incomparably beyond and above you all." (196–97)

Catherine cannot accept Heathcliff's limitations; she would rather reject the real person entirely and cherish her idea of him. This impatience with each other's limitations is characteristic of both Catherine and Heathcliff, and in both cases it amounts to an impatience with those things that define the otherness of the other: the boundaries of the other's distinct and separate self. The immensely destructive nature of their relationship derives from this impatience; they would destroy each other as individuals to achieve the narcissistic union they desire.[23] Catherine's expression of infinite desire is, in its impatience with her own personal littleness as well as Heathcliff's, also self-destructive, because it is a rejection of life itself. Only in death can the walls of the aching heart be broken through, the shattered prison of the body be transcended. Not surprisingly, the one image of this love's consumation is an image of death: Heathcliff's body, locked in his room beside an open window, the bedclothes drenched with rain, on his face a "life-like gaze of exultation" (364–65).

The tableau of Heathcliff's death is ambiguous in the same way the tableau of Pierre's death is ambiguous. In Melville's book, the comparison of the shattered vial to a shattered hourglass, together with a final reference to the prison wall, suggests that the heart, "prisoner impatient of his iron bars" (127), has finally transcended time and space. Yet the tableau itself is an image of enclosure: Pierre in prison, arbored in the ebon vines of Isabel's hair. In Brontë's tableau, the open window and Heathcliff's look of exultation suggest that Heathcliff, like Catherine, is finally "beyond and above." Yet the image is one of mortality; Heathcliff's "life-like gaze of exultation" is also, to borrow a phrase from Emily Dickinson, "the look of Death." And the parallel with the earlier scene in the haunted chamber recalls two things that render this later scene ambiguous: Lockwood's terror of such union as Heathcliff may have attained and the desperate attempt of Catherine's ghost, finally "beyond and above," to come back inside.

Furthermore, there is the question of what kind of transcendence this scene may represent. Joseph's interpretation of the wild look on Heathcliff's face is that Heathcliff looks wicked, "girnning at death!" "Th' divil's harried off his soul," he says (365). What kind of egress has Heathcliff, locked into the haunted chamber of his own soul, finally found? What kind of transcendence is represented in the wild relationship of Catherine and Heathcliff? What is it, out beyond the window, toward which the soul aspires? If the outermost Other is indeed somehow identical with the inmost life of Wuthering Heights, a world of human cruelty at its most perverse, perhaps Nelly is right to try to shut it out. Whatever transcendence Cathy and Heathcliff have achieved, they have achieved it by destroying themselves and each other. The destructive nature of their love, ultimate source of all the sadism and masochism that run in an undercurrent through the novel, was a necessary result of their struggle to realize "immortal longings" in a mortal relationship.

Whose responsibilty is the destruction? It seems that the relationship is mortal, in both senses, because the lovers are themselves mortal, and that is not their fault. It is perhaps their fault that they rebelled with such ferocity against their mortal condition. "[W]ell may my heart knock at my ribs,—prisoner impatient of his iron bars," says Pierre (127). The heart is in its prison because that is the nature of the human condition. To escape the boundaries of the self in the way Catherine, Heathcliff, and Pierre desire is to rebel against the human condition itself. "Ah, muskets the gods have made to carry infinite combustions, and yet made them of clay!" cries the narrator of *Pierre* (150). Such images suggest a demonic religion of the self that asserts the soul's immensities in defiance of God, deliberately transgressing the limits of mortality, even though, by definition, to do so is to die. Those who thus baptize themselves *in nomine diaboli* are thereby compelled to "strike through the mask"; the first article of their creed is that "the only sin is limitation." But in their view, the sin is God's.

IV

Radcliffe's biographer Talfourd said that the soul holds its "obstinate questionings with the sepulchre" precisely because it senses something on the other side of the grave:

> The tremblings of the spirit, which are base when prompted by anything earthly, become sublime when inspired by a sense of the visionary and immortal. They are the secret witnesses of our alliance with power, which is not of this world. We feel both our fleshly infirmity and our high destiny, as we shrink on the borders of spiritual existence. Whilst we listen for echoes from beyond the grave, and search with tremulous eagerness for indications of the unearthly, our Curiosity and Fear assume the grandeur of passions. We might well doubt our own immortality, if we felt no restless desire to forestall the knowledge of its great secret, and held no obstinate questionings with the sepulchre. We were not of heavenly origin, if we did not struggle after a communion with the invisible; nor of human flesh, if we did not shudder at our own daring. . . . (108)

The soul insists on looking mortality in the face, because it longs for immortality. Maturin uses a similar argument in defending the passion of terror as a subject worthy of romance: "It is absurd to depreciate [*sic*] this passion, and deride its influence. It is *not* the weak and trivial impulse of the nursery, to be forgotten and scorned by manhood. It is the aspiration of a spirit; 'it is the passion of immortals,' that dread and desire of their final habitation" (*Montorio* 1: v). According to this view, the self insists on confronting its personal littleness because it hopes thereby to discover its immensities. As Talfourd puts it, "on the borders of spiritual existence" we feel "both our fleshly infirmity and our high destiny."

Maturin's equation of terror with aspiration, that is, with the soul's motion outwards, is characteristic of late eighteenth- and early nineteenth-century defenses of Gothic romance. The key word *sublime* in the excerpt from Talfourd derives from the same theoretical context: the Gothic aesthetic, with its obsession with confinement, was often justified by reference to the sublime aesthetic, with its promise of expansion, dilation, "egress." The classic example is Radcliffe's defense of Emily's curiosity about the black veil: "[A] terror of this nature, as it occupies and expands the mind, and elevates it to high expectation, is purely sublime, and leads us, by a kind of fascination, to seek even the object, from which we appear to shrink" (*Mysteries of Udolpho* 248).

Nothing is more suggestive of the role of the sublime in the Gothic search for transcendence than Schiller's essay "On the Sublime." Schiller takes as his starting point the issue of human "freedom" in the face of "forces" that threaten "violence": "This is the position in which man finds himself. Surrounded by countless forces, all of which are superior to his own and wield mastery over him, he lays claim by his nature to suffer violence from none of them" (193). The key to our freedom in the face of these forces, Schiller explains, is "the feeling for the sublime," whereby "we discover that the state of our minds is not necessarily determined by the state of our sensations, that the laws of nature are not necessarily our own, and that we possess a principle proper to ourselves that is independent of all sensuous affects" (198). The "sublime object," he says, gives us "a painful awareness of our limitations" (198), but we are drawn irresistibly to it, realizing that "nature in her entire boundlessness cannot impinge upon the absolute greatness within ourselves" (199). Schiller describes the feeling of the sublime as a form of self-defense against what would otherwise be a crushing external power reminding us of both our incapacity for knowing and our physical weakness. "So long as man was merely a slave of physical necessity, had not yet found an egress from the narrow sphere of his wants, and still did not suspect the lofty *daemonic* freedom in his breast, he was reminded by *inscrutable* nature only of the inadequacy of his conceptual faculties and by *destructive* nature only of his physical incapacity" (203). What sets us free is the recognition that this grand external force is a "mirror" of something in ourselves:

> But no sooner has free contemplation set [man] at a distance from the blind assault of natural forces—no sooner does he discover in the flood of appearances something abiding in his own being—then [*sic*] the savage bulk of nature about him begins to speak quite another language to his heart; and the relative grandeur outside him is the mirror in which he perceives the absolute grandeur within himself. (203)

Although Schiller's argument would have been more congenial to Emerson than to Radcliffe, its dominant images and metaphors suggest nonetheless the whole world of Gothic romance. The opening focus on the individual "surrounded" by forces of violence; the recurrent images of boundaries and limitation; the picture of the painfully limited individual in the "boundlessness" of nature, discovering himself larger inside than the infinity that would otherwise "impinge" on him; the concern with "egress"—all suggest the intimate relation between Gothic terror and sublime transcendence. The key word in this connection is *egress*. For Schiller the sublime "afford[ed] an egress from the sensuous world" (201). The emphasis is Schiller's, but the image of escape is in some form central to every theory of the sublime.

By associating Gothic terrors with such egress, writers like Talfourd, Maturin, and Radcliffe attempt to show that Gothic terrors are themselves a mode of transcendence. Yet it is not without significance that Gothicists seek their transcendence in such paradoxical ways, locking themselves in to get out, looking for a way up by going down, searching for immortality in the charnel house. The black veil of Udolpho is a disturbing emblem of the Gothic quest, despite Radcliffe's evident faith in a benevolent Deity approachable through the sublime. Before the veil, sublime curiosity elevates the soul, but in the reader's case, the elevation is only preparation for a letdown. Behind the veil was the waxwork image of a corpse crawling with worms, made to be contemplated as an act of penance. To approach the black veil is to approach transcendence through the "purely sublime," but behind the veil is only another image of sin and death. That fact points to the central dilemma of Gothic romancers: their images of transcendence have a disconcerting way of reverting to images of mortality even as one contemplates them. What looked like an immortal spirit turns out to be a man wandering about in the night. What seemed "the secrets and communion of another world" is a murderous hoax. Everywhere Gothic romancers look, they see sin and death. Their Romantic heirs had the same tendency. Those writers who, in Emerson's phrase, "grope among the dry bones of the past" (*Nature* in *Selections* 21) ally themselves only intermittently and skeptically with "the party of hope" because they cannot stop remembering the Fall. Even Pierre's sublime egress from his prison at the Apostles' culminates only in a vision of the fallen Titan hurling himself in vain against "the invulnerable steep" (482).

Pierre's own "boundless expansion" led out of his mother's house to imprisonment inside his "four blank walls" in the city (482). His escape back to nature and up into the sublime mountains led only to "the precipice's unresounding wall" (482). That pattern is one Melville inherited from Gothic romance, in which the repetitious plots tend to emphasize the tentative nature of the authors' faith in egress of any sort. Confinement succeeds escape succeeds confinement succeeds escape; the reader's experience of such predictable sequences contributes to a sense that the happy endings are somewhat arbitrary. One suspects sometimes that the author's last desperate attempts to put bounds to these infinitely repetitious torments was simply to bind them between the covers of a book.

The essentially tentative nature of the Gothicists' ambivalent faith in transcendence is well expressed in a passage from *Pierre:* "It is the not impartially bestowed privilege of the more final insights, that at the same moment they reveal the depths, they do, sometimes, also reveal—though by no means so distinctly—some answering heights. But when only mid-way down the gulf, its crags wholly conceal the upper vaults, and the wanderer thinks it all one gulf of downward dark" (237). Here is an expression of the Gothic faith that the way down is the way up, but the expression itself is tentative, full of qualifications. The insights at issue are not absolutely final but only comparatively so. These "more final insights" "sometimes" reveal "some" heights, though the heights are re-vealed "by no means so distinctly" as the depths are. The passage comes from the chapter entitled "More Light, and the Gloom of that Light; More Gloom, and the Light of that Gloom." The title suggests that whatever illumination Pierre found through his Gothic experience may only have been what Spenser called "A little glooming light, much like a shade" (*The Faerie Queene* 1.1.14.5). The hint that Pierre's metaphysical spec-ulations may be merely a shadowy light in the Den of Errour is typical of Melville's sly ambiguities and also of the ambivalence with which Gothicists in general regard their own images of transcendence. The one thing Melville is certain of in his discussion of the heights and depths is that to be in darkness, cut off from all extremes and believing there are none, is a nightmare.

Gothic romance conveys an almost visceral sense of this terrible tran-sitional state, the state of being "only midway down." As Thompson says, "Romantic Gothic deals with the tormented condition of a creature suspended between the extremes of faith and skepticism, beatitude and horror, being and nothingness, love and hate . . ." (3). In one sense Gothic tries to get to beatitude by way of horror, but all it finally manages to be convinced of is the reality of this state of being "suspended be-tween." It is in an effort to end or transcend the angst this state produces that Gothic romance itself is so extreme and extravagant. The fascination with pain and death in Gothic works manifests the authors' own impulse to push things to their limits, to violate taboos and decorum, and so perhaps finally to get across some ultimate barrier. Almost from its in-ception, the genre has itself been described metaphorically as engaged in resisting confinement and constriction, destroying barriers, going too far. Talfourd criticized Maturin for approaching "the borders of the forbidden in speculation, and the paradoxical in morals" (131). Maturin defended his use of terror as the central passion in *Montorio* by saying that this subject was "calculated to unlock every store of fancy and of feeling" (1: iii–iv). Walpole's second preface to *The Castle of Otranto* defended his experiment on the similar ground that "[T]he great resources of fancy have been dammed up, by a strict adherence to common life" (43). He was "desirous," he said, "of leaving the powers of fancy at liberty to expatiate through the boundless realms of invention" (43). Radcliffe's fictions, Talfourd said, may be favorably contrasted with the Greek fables, which "rather tended to inclose the sphere of mortal vision . . . with more definite boundaries, than to intimate the obscure and eternal" (109). More recently, Fiedler has seen Gothic romance as a symptom of a general "Break-through" (*Love and Death* 129); Kiely refers to the way Gothicists "opened the doors of fiction and let in everything—or so it seemed" (8); Lévy refers to the brutal eruption of the irrational "dans la banalité romanesque" (139).

The recurrence of such metaphors in descriptions of the enterprise in which Gothic fiction itself engages is not mere coincidence. The Gothicists' obsessive use of boundaries and barriers as conventions and stage properties betrays an impatience with limits, an impulse away from what can be circumscribed and defined by human reason, a desire to move out toward "the obscure and eternal." The very language of Gothic romance—its hysterical breathlessness, its straining after the sublime style—bespeaks a longing for something "incomparably beyond and above." The Gothicists' extravagance was quite different from Thoreau's, but it originated in an impulse he shared: the desire "to speak somewhere *without* bounds."

Epilogue

For Thoreau, "to speak somewhere *without* bounds" was to speak "like a man in a waking moment, to men in their waking moments . . ." (*Walden* 289). Gothic romancers choose instead to speak in the language of dreams—those moments when, in their view, the mind is most free "to expatiate through the boundless realms of invention." Pierre's sublime journey into the mountains takes place not in a waking moment but in a sightless state of "torpor—some horrible foretaste of death itself," "a state of semi-unconsciousness" (476). Melville's picture of Pierre attaining escape through confinement, knowledge through unconsciousness, and sight through blindness typifies the Gothicist's usual paradoxical approach to the possibilities of transcendence. The vision itself only intensifies the paradox. What Pierre sees in the mountains is that struggle as he may, he will never be free. But there is a further paradox. However terrible the truth may be, the experience of ascending toward it is, in Melville's view, sublime. Whatever terrors the vision itself represents, the act of vision is an act of freedom. And significantly, this act takes place as Pierre, "states-prisoner of letters," sits at his writer's desk.

Henry James once dreamed that he was "defending himself, in terror, against the attempt of someone to break into his room."

He is pressing his shoulder against a door and someone is bearing down on the lock and bolt on the other side. Suddenly the tables are turned. Terror is defied. Nightmare is routed. It is Henry who forces the door open in a burst of aggression—and of triumph. Now he is no longer afraid. Now he is triumphant. He experiences an extraordinary sense of elation. The figure had tried to appall him. But now it is appalled. The pursuer, the attacker, becomes the pursued. (Edel, *Life* 1: 61).

Far down the "long perspective" of a "tremendous, glorious hall," James sees his "visitant" as a mere "diminished spot," fleeing "for *his* life while a great storm of thunder and lightning [plays] through the deep embrasures of high windows at the right."[1] The lightning reveals that the "great line of priceless *vitrines*," the "deep embrasures and the polished floor" are the Galerie d'Apollon at the Luxembourg Palace, scene of a great moment in James's childhood education. "The lightning that revealed the retreat revealed also the wondrous place and, by the same amazing play, my young imaginative life in it of long before, the sense of which, deep within me, had kept it whole, preserved it to this thrilling use . . ." (74).

James's boyhood experience of the Galerie d'Apollon was an exhilarating moment of education; thus the escape into that art gallery, in the dream, is an apt symbol of "the growth of the mind," the "boundless expansion" of an inner life. For James the gallery represented the knowledge he had gained, as a boy, through art. But perhaps in the dream it also represents the art into which as a man, he managed to transmute his knowledge. That knowledge, as the dream represents it, is not, in its initial form, public: it is the mind's consciousness, in "awful privacy," of its secret terrors. The dream records a triumph, in a public place, over these private fears: the triumph of art over the perils of the night. It records the victim's sudden realization that the castle is his; the strength is his; the key is his; because he and not the villain knows the secret of this door.

Lockwood's dream revealed in the blind recesses of the human heart a window on the sublimities of nature. The discovery of that window accounts, at least in part, for the light of the Gothic gloom. But that light finally has another source, represented symbolically in James's dream. Whatever its terrors and despair, Gothic fiction is based on at least one faith: the confidence that there is a door always open from the haunted mind into yet another region of sublimity, the palace of art.

II

BOUNDARIES OF THE SELF
IN WOMEN'S GOTHIC

On the day when it will be possible for woman to love not in her weakness but in her strength . . . love will become for her, as for man, a source of life and not of mortal danger.

Lock the doors and close the shutters as she will . . . woman fails to find complete security in her home. It is surrounded by that masculine universe which she respects from afar, without daring to venture into it. And precisely because she is incapable of grasping it, through technical skill, sound logic, and definite knowledge, she feels, like the child and the savage, that she is surrounded by dangerous mysteries.

It is [woman's] duty to assure the monotonous repetition of life in all its mindless factuality. It is natural for woman to repeat, to begin again without ever inventing, for time to seem to her to go round and round without ever leading anywhere.

The male is called upon . . . to transcend himself toward the totality of the universe and the infinity of the future; but traditional marriage does not invite woman to transcend herself with him; it confines her in immanence, shuts her up within the circle of herself.

SIMONE DE BEAUVOIR, *The Second Sex*

5

Speaking "I" and the Gothic Nightmare: Boundaries of the Self as a Woman's Theme

Alas! you knew not the wretched fate of your mother, who then gazed upon you! Although you were at too great distance for my weak voice to reach you, with the utmost difficulty I avoided throwing open the window, and endeavouring to discover myself. The remembrance of my solemn promise, and that the life of Vincent would be sacrificed by the act, alone restrained me.

RADCLIFFE, *Sicilian Romance* (2: 170)

. . . Miss d'Allenberg behaved like a heroine; she said little, but that little was extremely proper.

ELIZA PARSONS, *Mysterious Warning* (358)

I might have cleared myself on the spot, but would not. I did not speak.

LUCY SNOWE

At a crucial moment in *Northanger Abbey* it seems that Catherine's friendship with the Tilneys and her prospects of living happily ever after are about to be destroyed. Her friends mistakenly think she has rebuffed them, and it is a heroine's duty at such times to remain proudly silent, secure in her "conscious innocence," willing to suffer the consequences of refusing to exonerate herself. Fortunately, such standards are inimical to Catherine's personality, and she rushes impulsively to explain her behavior. "Feelings rather natural than heroic possessed her; instead of considering her own dignity injured by this ready condemnation—instead of proudly resolving, in conscious innocence, to shew her resentment towards him who could harbour a doubt of it, to leave to him all the trouble of

seeking an explanation . . . she took to herself all the shame of miscon-
duct, or at least of its appearance, and was only eager for an opportunity
of explaining its cause" (73). Although Catherine sacrifices some coherence as well as heroic dignity in her haste to get the explanation out all
at once, the result is most satisfactory. Henry Tilney believes her, and
his good opinion is happily restored.

The convention Jane Austen mocks in this scene was a staple of Gothic
romance, which, despite its own rhetorical extravagance, took as one of
its favorite subjects the restraint proper to female discourse. When they
choose to speak, Gothic heroines can soar to rhetorical heights far beyond
their enemies' range, but again and again they also choose to remain
silent, even if it means remaining persecuted and misunderstood. In a
genre requiring plot complications for three to five volumes, the formal
reason for this convention is obvious, but the high moral and emotional
charge so often associated with it suggests that it had a significance beyond that of convenience. That significance is a function of the fact that
most writers and readers of the genre, like most of its protagonists, were
women.

Feminist critical theory suggests that the problem of "saying 'I' " is
important both thematically and formally in literature by women, for whom
finding and using a voice has been fraught with special difficulties rang-
ing from unequal educational opportunities to social strictures against ap-
pearing before the public as an author and moral strictures against the
egotism implied in literary self-expression.[1] In this light it is especially
interesting that the moments when Gothic heroines speak and those when
they remain silent should be so important in Gothic romances. By the
same token, one of the most important questions about the genre is why
so many women writers from the 1780s to 1820 and after found their
voice by speaking the Gothic nightmare.

The answer to this question is implicit in the Gothic theme of the
boundaries of the self, because for women in the late eighteenth and
nineteenth centuries the question of "the possible reconcilement of this
world with our own souls" had a special relevance and meaning. The
heyday of Gothic romance was also a time during which woman's place
in society was becoming a matter of increasing debate, and a number of
writers sought to clarify the issue. With some notable exceptions, including Wollstonecraft's *A Vindication of the Rights of Woman* (1792), most
of these attempts to define woman were also attempts to confine her to a
separate "sphere" bounded by the duties of home and to ensure her participation in an ideology that limited the exercise of her physical, intel-

lectual, and emotional faculties. Most Gothic romance by women sub-
scribes both to this ideology and the related set of restraints, articulated
or assumed by literary critics, that limited women's discourse in terms of
subject matter, taste, and diction.[2] Like the heroines of Gothic romance,
women writers knew when it was proper not to speak. The "nameless
dread" that suffuses their works is often simply a dread of naming. And
yet, at a symbolic level, they give voice to all sorts of unnameable—and
perhaps unthinkable—discontents with the very ideology they overtly espouse. Those discontents, in their relation to the issues of self-defense,
knowledge, repetition, and transcendence, circle continuously around the
theme of the boundaries of the self. That theme had a particular significance for women, who were in a variety of ways—socially, psychologically, even epistemologically—set apart, circumscribed, and subject to
intrusion.

I

The Gothic preoccupation most obviously relevant to women's social reality
is that of self-defense. The kinds of anxiety states Radcliffe explores, for
example, "are identifiably feminine and closely associated with isolation,
dependence, and sexual fears" (Howells 49). Doody relates women's Gothic
to the women's nightmares presented in earlier novels, in which they
represent "the sense of individuality under attack" (532). Women's Gothic
in general speaks for women's feelings of vulnerability in a world where
their only power was the power of "influence." For it is only half the
story to say, as so many critics have said in various ways, that the maiden
lost in oneiric space is the mind beset with its own internal dangers, lost
to the order and reason of the daylight world. The other half of the story,
for women writers and readers, is that in symbolic form Gothic interiors
were the daylight world, apprehended as nightmare.[3] Their disorder and
illogic was the logic of the social order as women experienced it. Woman
in these nocturnal spaces is really woman in her everyday relations, "surrounded by [the] vice and violence" of the social and political institutions
that dominate her life. As Doody says, "It is in the Gothic novel that
women writers could first accuse the 'real world' of falsehood and deep
disorder" (560).[4]

This identity of the oneiric Gothic world and women's diurnal world
is masked by displacements and disguises. The contemporaneity of the
suffering described in women's Gothic, for example, is most often dis-

guised by the portrayal of the institutions that oppress the Gothic heroine as outdated,[5] foreign, or illegal even in their own relatively barbaric contexts—profoundly alien, in other words, to the lives of eighteenth-century readers. But the disguise itself makes the point: women's Gothic shows women suffering from institutions they feel to be profoundly alien to them and their concerns. And those institutions were all too contemporaneous with the lives of the women who wrote and read Gothic romance in the 1790s and early 1800s: the patriarchal family, the patriarchal marriage, and a patriarchal class, legal, educational, and economic system.

Wollstonecraft protested the virtual enslavement of daughters to parents, who she said thus prepared them for "the slavery of marriage" (*Rights of Woman* 232), and the greater subjection of girls than boys to "the irregular exercise of parental authority" (234). She attacked as well the civil and political inequality that kept women "immured in their families groping in the dark" (*Rights of Woman* 26)—a plight that assumes a literal form in most Gothic fiction by women. The heroine of *A Sicilian Romance,* for example, must escape her tyrannical father's castle by fleeing through its dark underground passageways. At the climax of the story, another flight leads her unwittingly back into this hidden world, where she discovers, alive, her long "dead" mother, for years imprisoned secretly by her husband in her own house. The mysterious noises that frightened Julia's brother in the deserted wing at the beginning of her adventure were the sounds of their mother's grief.

Julia's elopement from her father's house has somehow led back to this same domestic prison, and the door through which she entered it turns out now to be locked behind her. Thus the discovery of her mother's secret is identical to her own entrapment in the same situation, and the story becomes a literal account of how a daughter, crossing the threshold of adult knowledge, enters into her mother's suffering. Louisa May Alcott tells a similar story, in which a young woman is sent to a madhouse after a fit of rage ("Did they never see anyone angry before?" [284]). There she is "haunted" by the thought of a "mysterious," closed room above her own. Once she even wakes to find herself standing, at midnight, "opposite the door whose threshold I had never crossed" (293). Through the keyhole she hears "A Whisper in the Dark"—the voice of her long "dead" mother, for years imprisoned in this same place. Such scenes describe a daughter's coming of age: the discovery, through her own experience, of her mother's unsuspected life.

"When she considered the long and dreadful sufferings of her mother, and that she had for many years lived so near her ignorant of her misery, and even of her existence—she was lost in astonishment and pity" (*Sicilian Romance* 2: 167). Gothic romances tell again and again this story of the woman hidden from the world as if she were dead, her long suffering unknown to those outside—or sometimes even inside—the ruined castle,[6] crumbling abbey,[7] deserted wing,[8] madhouse,[9] convent,[10] cave,[11] priory,[12] subterranean prison,[13] or secret apartments.[14] The final revelation of Louisa's imprisonment at the hands of her husband in *A Sicilian Romance* merely retells in literal form the earlier, supposedly false story of the cause of her "death": "[T]hough the mildness of her position made her submit to the unfeeling authority of her husband, his behavior sunk deep in her heart, and she pined in secret" (1: 75).

"Ah, how easy it is to be unknown!—to be entombed alive!" Ellinor says in *The Recess* (3: 103). "Unknown": the story of burial alive is not just about domestic entrapment but also about women's forced conceal-ment of the suffering it occasioned. And it is also about the unknown woman inside the female writer or reader, who perhaps concealed her suffering even from herself. For Julia's confrontation with her lost mother, the unsuspected sufferer, is only one version of the discovery of the Hid-den Woman,[15] a staple of women's Gothic that takes two different but related forms. One is the discovery (in person, through another charac-ter's narrative, or in a first-person manuscript), of a Good Other Woman, long-suffering and angelic, whose imprisonment and/or death was un-merited. The other is the discovery of an Evil Other Woman, who got no more than she deserved and is now either dead or sorry for her sins and about to die. The revelation of these sins usually implicates her as a bad (selfish) mother, a bad (undutiful) daughter, and/or a bad (sexual) woman. The wicked Lady Dunreath of Roche's popular *The Children of the Abbey* is a perfect example of all three. Guilty of filial ingratitude to the "be-nevolent" woman who raised her when she was an orphan (a circum-stance, by the way, that establishes her as not morally related to the heroine), she married that fine lady's widower and turned her stepsister/ daughter "from her paternal home" (4: 114) on a dark and stormy night, thus establishing herself as a wicked mother as well as a bad daughter. She then wrested the heroine's ancestral house from its rightful heirs by means of a sexual liaison with her husband's lawyer (4: 116).

Like the Good Other Woman, the Evil Other Woman often spends much of her life hidden away in the castle, secret room, or whatever,[16] a fact suggesting that even a virtuous woman's lot is the same she would have merited had she been the worst of criminals. The heroine's discov-ery of such Other Women is in the one case an encounter with women's oppression—their confinement as wives, mothers, and daughters—and in the other with a related repression: the confinement of a Hidden Woman inside those genteel writers and readers who, in the idealization of the heroine's virtues, displace their own rebellious feelings with filial piety, their anger with fortitude, and their sexuality with sensibility.[17] Both discoveries reveal complementary aspects of women's subordination: their immurement in domestic spaces as sisters, wives, and daughters and the immurement inside themselves of an angry, rebellious, sexual Other Woman that conventional morality taught them to reject.

The Good Other Woman is likely to be related to the heroine,[18] who has much in common with her, including a sweet, uncomplaining disposition in the face of unprecedented wrongs. In Gothic comedy, when this lady's true life is made fully known and her wrongs—emblems of domestic oppression—are acknowledged, the heroine herself can go home and live happily ever after in perfect domestic bliss. The role of the Evil Other Woman is less clear. That the heroine has some intimate relation to her is often obvious. In Musgrave's *The Solemn Injunction,* for example, Alicia must, upon her coming of age at sixteen, go to a secret room where the narrative of a stupendously wicked woman is hidden away. Beneath that room, in a vault hung with black cloth on which is embroidered the prologue and moral of this narrative, she must lift the pall of a coffin and, beneath that, discover a sinister clue to her own identity: "Alicia trembled as she thought of raising the mysterious veil, which, as it were, concealed her even from herself" (2: 151). Ostensibly the hidden identity in Alicia's metaphor involves only the question of her true family relationships. But what is beneath this black "veil" is the key to the chest containing a "wretched penitent's" story of her passion, pride, and ambition. The result of Alicia's journey to this room is the revelation that the emotion she perceived as pure love is in fact the most guilty passion: her beloved is her brother. In the incidents surrounding her discovery, she is also revealed as guilty of the worst filial impiety, the murder of her own father. But the *éclaircissement* at the end does away with all these dark truths. The man she killed was not her father, but only his evil look-alike brother, and her real father justifies her violent action as self-defense anyway. Furthermore, the man she loves is not her brother, so her chaste love is just what it appeared to be and not some other, guilty passion. The suggestion that a Bad Woman's life could somehow be the secret truth about a Good Woman's life is made and then as quickly effaced.

The intimate relation of the heroine and the Evil Other Woman in *The*

Mysteries of Udolpho is treated with similar timidity. The existence of such a relation is strongly suggested by a number of factors. First, as critics like Howells (e.g., 52), Butler, and Wolff have pointed out, Emily's own "latent sexual feelings" (Butler 141) are at issue in the Udolpho scenes. "In spite of her conviction that she is in sexual danger on all sides, Emily repeatedly puts herself in the way of the fierce men who surround her and seems endlessly fascinated by the picturesqueness of their appearance . . ." (Butler 141). In the passage Butler cites, Emily, watching the banditti, finds herself "hoping, she scarcely knew why, that Montoni would accompany the party . . ." (*Mysteries of Udolpho* 302). Wolff suggests that the dangerous sexuality of the banditti is itself a projection and dramatization of a *woman's* sexual feelings (208–10), and that the Gothic typically pictures a woman "trapped between the demands of two sorts of men—a 'chaste' lover and a 'demon' lover—each of whom is really a reflection of one portion of her own longing" (213). In this way "the sexual inclinations that rightly belong to women are projected onto men," who can thus play the active roles while the women characters remain "relatively passive" (218).

As Wolff points out, Radcliffe and other women Gothicists equate danger "with a specialized form of 'inner space'; and if the heroine can manage to stay away from the treacherous cave—tunnel, basement, secret room—she will usually be safe" (209).[19] Implicit in this portrayal of inner space is the Gothicist's own fear of her subject matter, which comes to the surface in the scenes most explicitly linking the heroine and Evil Other Woman. Emily St. Aubert is haunted by the strange music of the mad nun Agnes, who has, like her, lived at Udolpho and who accuses herself wildly of passion, anger, and murder, in encounters with Emily that disturb the heroine deeply. The cause of Emily's disquiet, interestingly, is twofold: Agnes's story seems to attack the securely patriarchal moral center of the novel, St. Aubert, by implicating him in a sexual liaison with someone other than Emily's mother, and her story also hints that the heroine herself is morally akin to the passionate and sexual villainess. In fact, the nun even goes so far as to accuse Emily, whom she repeatedly addresses as *Sister,* of her own sins: "You are young—you are innocent! I mean you are yet innocent of any great crime!—But you have passions in your heart,—scorpions; they sleep now—beware how you awaken them!—they will sting you, even unto death!" Emily weeps at these words, and Agnes responds, "Ah . . . so young, and so unfortunate! We are sisters, then indeed. Yet, there is no bond of kindness among the guilty . . ." (574). But, dear reader, this nun is mad; she thinks

Emily is someone else. In these sequences of Radcliffe's narrative is the covert suggestion of a more realistic, less romanticized Emily who actually is someone else, a person far different from the young lady so lovingly fashioned and idealized by the benign patriarchy whose purity is also questioned in these scenes. But what the narrative says explicitly is that seeing sexual depths in a genuinely good woman, or unsuspected evil in a good patriarch, is simply insane.[20]

Nonetheless, this Other Woman's sin, like the Other Woman's suffering, must be discovered in order for the heroine to be happily married. If the author were Maturin, we might see this as the necessary discovery of one's own propensity for evil; when the author is Radcliffe or Musgrave or Roche, the camouflage by which apparent revelations are qualified or "corrected" makes the meaning of the discovery less clear. It may be that in some way the happy endings of Gothic romances that use the Evil Other Woman depend on the punishment and exorcism of the rebellious feelings the narrative itself expresses through its portrayal of women's silent suffering. The heroine, in other words, can live happily ever after in a perfect marriage because (1) the sources of women's long grievance at domestic confinement have been duly punished,[21] but (2) anger, rebellion, passion, and filial ingratitude—which one might have thought the logical concomitants to such grievance—are shown emphatically not to belong to the wronged heroine and/or her wronged female relative, but to somebody else, who was ultimately sorry for them, anyway, and furthermore is dying or dead. The death of this vengeful and passionate Other Woman means that "she" is no more able to trouble the heroine's prospects of domestic felicity.

The villains who hide their women away in Gothic confinements are often in violation of the law and will be brought to justice in the end, as is the case with the outlaw Montoni. Sometimes, on the other hand, they actually represent the law—but outdated, benighted law. Thus the eighteenth-century reader can see that the days of tyranny have been rightly superseded by more enlightened times. But in fact the real tyranny at issue in Gothic romance had not been superseded; it still existed in the patriarchal family of the eighteenth century, in which fathers could legally, if they wished, be virtual tyrants. Similarly, the behavior of Gothic outlaws was often no more than a picture of women's lawful subjection under the judicial system of the Gothicists' own society. A husband's right to imprison a wife in his house was not challenged legally until 1891 (Strachey 15 n. 3), and the Gothic villain's concealment of a wife simply enacted in literal form the laws regarding married women's status as Blackstone described them: "By marriage the very being or legal existence of a woman is suspended, or at least it is incorporated or consolidated into that of the husband, under whose wing, protection and cover she performs everything, and she is therefore called in our law a feme covert [*sic*]." [22] As *femmes couvertes*, married women *were* hidden away; for legal purposes their state of being "covered" was a burial alive. Gothic pictures of women victimized by barbaric law or by outlaws show the writers' sense of subjection to the legal power that they nonetheless experienced as illegitimate.

Women's experience of the illegitimate exercise of male authority as Gothic romance portrays it is often read as an expression of masochistic desire,[23] especially sexual desire. Such interpretations depend on a reading of the villain as secretly the hero, to whom the heroine (or, more accurately, the writer), is secretly attracted and for whose domination she longs. The glaring inadequacies of most such readings are obvious—not only that they blame the victims of sexual oppression but also that in their haste to do so they ignore the most basic fact about Gothic plots: Gothic romances tell, again and again, the story of woman trapped in domestic space. The basic function of the Gothic pursuit in women's romances should be all too obvious: the threatening male portrays "a woman's projected fears and sense of actual victimization; the pursuit justifies adventure and escape, which contrast dramatically with her . . . everyday domestic experience; and the moral victory of the heroine over the pursuer reflects a desired, but repressed emancipation from actual oppressors" (Roberts 47). Whatever masochistic desire speaks through women's Gothic narratives must be understood in the context of the desperate unhappiness they express at the same time. Indeed, the two are intimately related. Russ's comment on modern Gothics is true of their ancestors as well: "[T]he Heroine's suffering is the principal action of the story *because it is the only action she can perform.* The Modern Gothic as a genre, is a means of enabling a conventionally feminine heroine to have adventures at all" (50).

The delight that women readers experienced identifying with these "adventures," the heroine's excruciating sufferings, allowed at the same time for a release of anger and a masochistic reveling in the cathartic acknowledgment of its existence and its sources. Masochism is a form of pseudopower, which gives the victim the illusion of willing circumstances she cannot control. It allows for an honest attribution of the physical source of those sufferings to someone else, but it mystifies their cause by deluding the victim into experiencing her passive victimization as active, self-generated desire. In Gothic romance, this dynamic operates not at the level of the plot, in which heroines are portrayed as victims rather than masochists, but at the level of writing and reading, themselves acts of pseudopower in which the writer or reader, by willing the heroine's suffering as the source of a pleasurable literary experience, gains the illusion of being in control of it. The deepest masochism of women's Gothic is here, in the false sense of empowerment with which it infuses its readers' and writers' identification with women's suffering.

A further inadequacy of the readings of Gothic villain as secret hero is that they omit the actual hero from consideration as a significant character. This is a serious omission, because whatever suspicion there may be in women's Gothic that the villain is really the hero is balanced by an important complementary suspicion: the hero is really the villain. At least twice this equation is made overtly in the form of a heroine's "mistake": when Charlotte Smith's Emmeline flees Godolphin through the dark woods, not realizing it is her beloved who pursues her (*Emmeline* 377–78), and when Roche's Madeleine, hearing the approaching step of her beloved, whom she first apprehends as an enemy, collapses "in an agony of fear" (*Clermont* 2: 6–8). Most often, however, the suspicion that the hero is really the villain surfaces in the juxtapositions of the narrative sequence, in which the temporal conjunction *and then*—"at once the most unrevealing and the most suggestive of narrative links" (MacCaffrey 48)— stands in for causal or logical connections: "because," "and so," "therefore," "that is to say." This is a common procedure in allegorical romance especially, as critics of allegory have shown (e.g., Hough 135– 36, MacCaffrey 47–48). More important to the oneiric atmosphere of Gothic narrative, it is the procedure of dreams,[24] which "reproduce *logical connection by simultaneity in time*" and represent "causation . . . by temporal sequence" (Freud, *Interpretation of Dreams* 349, 351).[25]

The way that Emily comes to be in the power of Montoni at Udolpho exemplifies perfectly the narrative sequence in which temporal contiguity, standing in for logical connection, identifies the hero as the villain. Emily is engaged to a man of sensibility and benevolence with whom it is obvious she will live happily ever after. The preparations are made for her wedding; the plans are set, the decorations procured. But at the last minute a surprising substitution is made. Emily's deluded aunt uses the decorations for her own marriage to Montoni and insists that Emily wear to the celebration the clothes intended for her wedding to Valancourt. Emily, her sensibilities shocked by this wedding so different from the one she was anticipating, is whisked away to the scene of a brutal, unhappy

marriage in which the husband is a tyrant. This "scene" becomes pro-
gressively more sinister. At first, in Venice, it seems delightful but is
then is revealed in its full horror as Emily is imprisoned at Udolpho.
Here, trapped in the new husband's house, Emily is subject to the omnipresent threat of sexual and economic domination. The good husband
she expected vanishes for a long stretch of narrative. Later we learn that
during this same period, the antipated good husband was away at Paris,
indulging in the bad husband's sins: gambling, the motivation for Montoni's attempts to steal Emily's money; association with "a set of men, a
disgrace to their species, who live by plunder and pass their lives in
continual debauchery" like the banditti at Udolpho; and sexual impro-
priety, source of the attempts on Emily's virtue by Montoni's cohorts.
(Even later, of course, the dangerous significance of this conjunction is
blurred when it turns out that the hero did not really indulge in these sins;
it only looked that way.)[26]

This sequence of events bears a remarkable similarity to that in *The
Faerie Queene* in which Amoret, on the night of her wedding to the
adoring Scudamour, is whisked away to the House of Busirane and subjected to confinement and torture. As readers of Spenser's allegory have
seen, the "and–then" connection here stands in for a logical connection:
"because" or "that is to say." Amoret is married to Scudamour, and then
she finds herself in the House of Busirane. Amoret is married to Scudamour; that is to say, certain aspects of their relationship and their views
of love deliver her into the power of a sorcerer whose idolatrous "religion
of love" subjects her to pain instead of bliss (Hough 136, MacCaffrey
112–13). Similarly, Emily is planning to marry the hero, and then a
marriage places her in a situation of terrible sexual and economic[27] domination. That is to say, the hero who rescues the young woman and takes
her away to live happily ever after may really be the villain who captures
her and takes her away to live unhappily in a situation of confinement,
sexual domination, and economic exploitation.[28]

Emily's harassment by Montoni and his men, in other words, is the
nightmare version of the valiant court paid her by the hero. This is the
same theme Joanna Russ finds in modern Gothics: "Somebody's Trying
to Kill Me and I Think It's My Husband." Although Russ dissociates
these modern Gothics from the earlier ones (31), their central theme as
she interprets it seems merely to be a more overt version of the phenomenon I am discussing here.[29] According to Russ, a characteristic twist in
modern Gothics is that the man who at first appears to be kind, gentle,
and sensitive is really the person who most endangers the heroine's life,

while the "dark, magnetic, powerful brooding, sardonic," more sinister male is really the hero (32, 44). The second equation, only vaguely hinted at in earlier Gothic, suggests a dissatisfaction with the asexuality of the hero and with the asexuality of the image of womanhood to which he corresponds[30] in the schizophrenic separation of both the hero and heroine from their own passions. The first equation (the identification of apparent hero as secret villain), as earlier Gothic works it out, is more thoroughly disguised than the other precisely because it more deeply challenges the schizophrenic view in its most comprehensive form. The suspicion that the hero is the villain, in other words, embodies the writers' suspicion that the whole ideology of womanly purity and domestic bliss is a lie.

An interesting substantiation of this relation between villain and hero is found in Doody's analysis of female dreams in eighteenth-century fiction. In the "occasionally-glimpsed landscape" of these dreams she sees a prototype for "the entire setting" of the Gothic novel (552). In this context she sees it as hardly surprising that the first Gothicists were women. She reads two of the examples as "dreams of fear . . . before marriage, . . . quite separate from fear . . . of sex" (539). In them such images as deserts, troubled waters, and ruined buildings bespeak "an apprehension of the self under attack" (538), "a panic about identity and about the future" (540). Thus, "In an apparently placid situation the heroine's relationship . . . to marriage may be fraught with anxiety amounting to dread" (532). In the context of Doody's argument, it is suggestive that Radcliffe's own dream of the ruined building that is Montoni's Udolpho occurs as the sequel of Emily's engagement to Valancourt.

There is another sense in which Gothic romances give voice to women's discontent with their role in eighteenth-century English society. The plot of many Gothic romances represents married middle-class women's experience of "status incongruence" in a patriarchal class system. Charlotte Smith's Emmeline grows up in a castle that, as it turns out, belongs by right to her but in which her status is that of a social inferior. Roche's Amanda returns penniless to the seat of her ancestors, to work as a subordinate in a place that rightfully belongs to her brother. In such cases, the heroine experiences, in her own home, a deprivation of the status and freedom to which her class ought to entitle her. M. Jeanne Peterson discusses "status incongruence" as an aspect of Victorian governesses' lives: employed for their theoretical social status as gentlewomen, they found disturbingly ambiguous their actual position in the families in which they were in some sense servants, in another sense the social equals of their employers, and in still another sense neither. But as feminist economists have pointed out, this kind of status incongruence can be characteristic of middle-class women in general, in their own families.[31] The middle-class woman theoretically may share her husband's privileged social position, but in practice her vicarious privileges mean little, as she has none of her husband's freedom or authority.

In the sinister family dwellings of Gothic romance, women writers expressed their sense of entrapment by and subjection to patriarchal familial, legal, and class structures. But a patriarchal economic system meant that the alternative to depending on a father or husband for sustenance was grim. As Wollstonecraft pointed out, few occupations were open to women in her day (*Rights of Woman* 222). She herself in fact exhausted all those considered appropriate to her class: schoolteacher, governess, companion (Flexner 32). The life of her friend Caroline Blood illustrated two other options for a single woman of no means: destitute and unable to support herself, she finally chose the workhouse as a last alternative to prostitution (Flexner 150).[32] The prospect of being without the economic protection of a husband or father must have been terrifying; thus it is not surprising that the other architectural space into which women Gothicists projected their fears was that symbol of the single life, the convent. In the Castle of Udolpho, Emily was trapped in a claustrophobic marriage (not hers, of course—someone else's!). Cloistered at the convent of San Stefano, Ellena is in the opposite plight, separated from her beloved by the walls and veils that set the nuns apart from men. But for all practical purposes, the situations are not much different; in both the woman is trapped.

Heroines' experiences in convents represent a number of conflicting emotions about the prospects of being shut out of the security of the married state. At the most basic level, the convent represents the terrors of poverty, chastity, and obedience: the difficulty single women had in supporting themselves, the emotional and sexual deprivations of the single life, and the subjections it entailed. After all, the convent is in one sense simply an alien household where the heroine must obey a stranger's orders. Many a single woman found herself in a similar situation, subject to the domestic rule of an unsympathetic employer or the petty tyrannies of an in-law, to whom she stood in the relation of supernumerary dependant. Wollstonecraft describes both situations in *The Rights of Woman* (111). A terror of spinsterhood manifests itself not only in these pictures of alienation and subservient dependence but also in the portraits of the nuns themselves. The nuns of San Stefano are a parody of the moral evils supposed to be the special property of women: cattiness, petty jealousy, obsession with trivialities. Such portraits show a striking absence of a feeling of female solidarity: a horror of being sex segregated, cooped up forever up with no company but that of other women.

In addition, the rules of the convent are an extreme version of the decorum expected of women. Wollstonecraft protested the unreasonable subjection of women to "blind propriety" (*Rights of Woman* 217), insisting that the genuinely moral life must be based on experience. More freedom in being "permitted to overleap the boundary that secures content" enabled men, in her view, to "enlarge their minds" and attain stable principles (*Rights of Woman* 170). She attacked Rousseau for advising that girls be subject to more restraint than boys are, to prepare them for that confinement expected of women—"the most constant and severe restraint, which is that of decorum" (*Émile,* quoted in *Rights of Woman* 134). Convents were a perfect symbol of this "most constant and severe restraint." The Lady Abbess in *The Romance of the Forest,* for example, is "a woman of rigid decorum and severe devotion; exact in the observance of every detail of form . . ." (1: 79). That the convent of San Stefano in *The Italian* likewise stands for decorum is clear in the fact that leaving it will be a violation of both its rules and the propriety of which Ellena's mind is "so tremblingly jealous" (122).

On the other hand, the convent is often portrayed as an object of desire, sometimes at the same time that it is being shown as an object of terror. To some, the convent must have seemed an attractive, and sadly lost, alternative for single Protestant women in eighteenth-century England.[33] It was a place of refuge, where women with no means of financial support could at least have been assured of not falling prey to prostitution or the workhouse. The heroine of *The Children of the Abbey* is at various times a schoolteacher, governess, and companion (like Wollstonecraft, exhausting all the possibilities); but at one point, she simply lives safely in a convent,[34] where she receives three offers of alternative living arrangements: she can be a "tutoress," a mistress, or the wife of a man she hardly knows. Without the convent, Roche seems to be demonstrating, these would have been her *only* options (*Children of the Abbey* vol. 3). In addition, there are almost always in women Gothicists' pictures of convents touching portraits of women's friendships and often in portraits of the Good Abbess examples of the good works that women in positions of authority could accomplish. In these pictures, the convent is a safe refuge, a place of female solidarity, and an opportunity for the full exercise of those moral qualities that in the 1790s were so often portrayed as a special province of women—benevolence, humanity—but for which they often had no meaningful sphere of action.[35]

These representations of women as aliens in relation to the dominant familial, social, and economic institutions of their society shed some interesting light on the question of the extent to which self-defense in women's Gothic is defense against the self. Rictor Norton sees Gothic horror as an expression of ambivalence in which the ego is "simultaneously and equally attracted to and repelled by a desire of the id which the superego finds particularly abhorrent" (31). Porte sees as an essential element of Gothic romance the moment when "[g]uilt and innocence have changed places; the evil 'other' is oneself" (54). In some senses these are accurate descriptions, even of such decorous romance as those of Radcliffe and Roche. Women's Gothic does indeed struggle to acknowledge—albeit in the process of denying—a violent, sexual, desiring, and angry dimension of even good women. The fact that the heroine's restoration to happiness may require the discovery of an Evil Other Woman is as close as the decorous Gothicists come to admitting that the encounter with the oneiric world is an encounter with the heroine's own possibilities for evil. The reasons writers like Radcliffe and Roche would have shied away from exploiting the implications of this plot device of the encounter with another woman's sin are obvious: indoctrinated with the moral schizophrenia that segregated women into angels and demons, they could not afford to present a whole woman's psyche except in two distinct halves. But there is another reason these women writers shy away from revealing that the evils with which the heroine struggles are her own inner evils: to an overwhelming extent, they are not. In an important sense, the evil Other cannot be fully acknowledged by women writers as the self behind the self concealed, simply because it is not the self at all; it is Other. And this Other in women's Gothic is almost always male.

The ease with which criticism ignored for so long the social dimension of women's Gothic is related not only to sexual politics but also to the question of genre. Are these novels or romances? Romance, it is often assumed, turns away from social reality to look inward.[36] Thus those who read Godwin's *Caleb Williams* as romance see it as a theological allegory of guilt and redemption; those who read it as a novel see its subject as social and political institutions. Godwin, however, entitled this work *Things as They Are; or The Adventures of Caleb Williams*. Those who read it as a novel are reading the social document *Things as They Are;* romance readers are looking at the psychological study, *Caleb Williams*. But the work itself is both; it describes "the modes of domestic and unrecorded forms of despotism" ("Preface" 1) in both their social and psychological dimension and looks at the relations between those dimensions. Gothic "romances" by women are engaged in a similar enterprise. As Roberts points out, what Walpole conceived was really a "gothic romance-novel"; the preface to *The Castle of Otranto* emphasizes his attempt to combine the virtues of the ancient and modern romance—that is, what would now be called medieval or renaissance romance and the modern realistic novel. Roberts associates the "romance" side of women's Gothic with the projection of women's fears, wishes, and fantasies, and the "novel" side with "a rational and moral frame that appeals to its audience's ideal of delicacy and reinforces the feminine acceptance of patriarchal ideals" (35). Gothic fiction in her view thus provides "both a glorification of and escape from actuality" (57). The double status of women's Gothic as novel and romance is indeed central to its representation of women's lives, but it is more accurate to see the division between novel and romance in these works as essentially structural rather than thematic. The moral framework of Gothic romance-novels like *The Mysteries of Udolpho* is implicit in both the novel and romance sections. Furthermore, the projection of women's fears is often associated not just with oneiric events but also with narrative sequences in which a novelistic section (e.g., Emily's preparations for her wedding) is re-presented as romance (confinement at Udolpho).

An obscure work by Anne Fuller that qualifies as a Gothic romance-novel provides an intriguing example of this location of women's anxieties in the interface between realistic sequences and romance sequences. The title—*The Convent; or The History of Sophia Nelson*—is a clue to the shape and concerns of the work. The heroine, Sophia, an admirer of Fielding, writes witty and elegant letters presenting a novelistic world of domestic realism in which she engages in the ordinary social activities of women in her class: visiting and receiving visits, evaluating the relative merits of her suitors, discussing literature, and the like. Her sister Cassandra, an admirer of romance, is a figure of the novelist's satire. However, in the middle of the novel, Sophia herself becomes trapped, as it were, in a Gothic romance: imprisoned in a convent, she must find some means of escape. In various ways this incident is a romance version of the earlier novelistic plot. In the "novel" her guardian insists she marry a man she does not want; in the "romance" the danger to which she is thereby subjected is re-presented as entrapment in a convent, where the nuns attempt to convert her from Protestant rationalism to superstitious Catholicism. This is a version of her uncle's attempt to intrude not only on her life but on her mind, by pressuring her to make a radical change in her preferences and thereby give up the Wisdom that, as her name indicates, is her essential identity. Because the husband her uncle has selected for her is characterized primarily by his extreme ignorance and lack of education, the nuns' attempt to replace Sophia's independent reason with dependent and obedient superstition retells the story of her uncle's attempt to undermine her identity as an intellectual woman. There is another twist, however, for the convent itself represents a truth of which, up to this time, Sophia's rationalism has taken no account. Nothing in her excellent education has prepared her for the experience of suddenly discovering that as a woman, she has "no prospect, but confinement for life!" (Fuller, *Convent* 2: 114). While she is in the convent, Sophia remains true to her name, fending off Gothic nightmare with daylight reason, and her romantic sister, Cassandra, continues to be an object of satire. The sister's name is a joke on the fancy names of romance heroines, but the real joke may be even more sly. In the context of Sophia's danger of "confinement for life," it suggests the possibility that the Gothic romancer, however absurd she may seem, speaks truth, though it is doomed to be heard as foolishness by the literary realists.

The Convent is a rather extreme example of the way domestic social reality and nightmarish Gothic irreality coexist in Gothic romance and an intriguing example of those interrelations between them implied in the "and then's" of the romancer's characteristic "paratactic" narrative form.[37] However, it is not just that women's social reality is present in certain novelistic sequences of women's Gothic romance; the "romance" aspect of these works is their most significant presentation of social reality. Gothic romance by women represents the hidden, unspeakable reality of women's lives: not just their lives in the private inner world of the psyche, but also their social and economic lives in a real world of patriarchal institutions. The oneiric settings of Gothic romance are superficially removed from that world in space and often in time, but they nonetheless represent it symbolically. The oneiric world, set apart from diurnal reality, *is* that reality: not simply in the sense that it expresses the heroine's psychological state but also in that it represents her social situation, with its dominant power relations stripped of their civilized disguise. The conflicts and terrors that reign in that world reveal her place in society, her relationships, her special vulnerability.

II

A major part of that vulnerability is a woman's difficulty knowing and being known in a position that isolates her by locking her into herself but at the same time renders her susceptible to perpetual intrusion. Gothic romance is especially a woman's genre because, in all sorts of ways, it is about the nightmare of trying to "speak 'I' " in a world in which the "I" in question is uncomprehending of and incomprehensible to the dominant power structure. The difficulty of knowing and being known arises in several contexts in women's Gothic, all linked to this problem of alienation: the relationships of women to men, the restriction of women's education, and the need for and impossibility of self-defense through self-explanation.

For not only are men the Other in Gothic romances by women; a deep sense that men are *unknowably* Other manifests itself continually in characterizations of the villain as inscrutable ("O could I know," thinks Emily of Montoni, "what passes in that mind; could I know the thoughts, that are known there . . ." [*Mysteries of Udolpho* 243]) and in the frequent appearance of the man "enveloped in a cloud of mysteries" (Barrett 1: 107), who may be the villain but may also be the hero, as in *Clermont,* and/or even the father, as in *Clermont, The Mysteries of Udolpho, The Solemn Injunction,* and to some degree *Manfroné.* This mysteriousness means that much of the heroine's time is spent in subtle analyses of the people, especially the men, around her. Russ points to this phenomenon in modern Gothics as a glorification of "what most real women spend their time doing" (45). In real life, she says, this task is "usually necessary, but boring" (45); in Gothics the glamour of "Over-Subtle Emotions" (46) exalts the heroine, engaged perpetually in deciphering other people, as an expert at "this sacred version of everyday gossip" (47). The object of the wish fulfillment thereby expressed on behalf of the reader is a sense of significance: "I am a virtuosa at interpreting faces and feelings. This ability is not 'wasted' on the everyday drudgery of infants' needs or husbands' grumpiness—it is vital in saving my life and the happiness of all about me" (51).

Wollstonecraft saw male–female relationships in her society as based mainly on mutual exploitation and self-concealment. That is, men's purported homage to women is really a reinforcement of their own superior status—"It is not condescension to bow to an inferior" (*Rights of Woman* 100)—and women, placed in the position of slaves, are forced to the "sinister methods" of "govern[ing] by obeying" (*Rights of Woman* 50).

In opposition to these relationships, based on the relations of power, Wollstonecraft portrayed an ideal of mutual companionship and intellectual friendship. A similar ideal manifests itself in the wish fulfillment dreams of women's Gothic romance, which relegate power struggles to the heroine's relationship with the villain and portray her relationship with the hero as an exchange of sentiments, in all the senses that word had accrued by the 1790s.

The heroines who participate in such relationships are products of an idealized educational system—a special, private arrangement resulting from the enlightened supervision of a governess or father. This ideal is presented as a pastoral idyll in "Radcliffe-Romance."[38] The realities of women's education, far from this idealized picture, would be more accurately portrayed, if we were to accept Wollstonecraft's picture of them, in the Gothic villainesses whose petty tyrannies, insusceptibility to nature, and trivial preoccupations are linked to their narrowness of mind. Wollstonecraft deplores the lack of equal education as the basis for all of these deficiencies in women, who "at present are by ignorance rendered foolish or vicious . . ." (*Rights of Woman* 284). As if to illustrate Wollstonecraft's point, the villainess of *The Children of the Abbey* learns to repent of her evil doings because during her imprisonment she is supplied with excellent religious and moral books: "[T]hey enlarged my heart, they enlightened its ideas concerning the Supreme Being . . ." (4: 127). The fact that when the idealized educator is female she seems almost never to be the heroine's mother but is instead some kind of substitute mother (e.g., the governesses in *The Recess* and *A Sicilian Romance*) perhaps suggests the writers' sense that real mothers simply were not well enough educated themselves to give their daughters the extensive learning about which women Gothicists fantasized.

The portrayals in Gothic romances of the heroine's pastoral childhood seclusion that idealize it as a time of education and "sentimental conversation" (*Sicilian Romance* 125) under the care of a special parent or tutor were perhaps romanticized versions of the writers' own experience or wishful fantasies of what their education should have been. On the other hand, there is also a frequent sense in these pictures that something important has been excluded from the world of learning in which the heroine delights. St. Aubert shares the treasures of knowledge with Emily but conceals from her a mystery about his own past; the father of the heroine in *Clermont* imparts a refined education to his daughter in the delightful setting of "a deep, romantic, and verdant valley" (8), but he suffers from some mysterious melancholy he does not explain to her. The sisters in *A*

Sicilian Romance have the benefit of an excellent governess, but "Beneath [her] gentle guidance . . . they were ignorant alike of the sorrows and pleasures of the world" (1: 31). Indeed, "though Emilia was now twenty, and her sister eighteen, they had never passed the boundaries of their father's domains" (1: 13). In the "happy tranquillity" (1: 31) of this seclusion Julia sometimes experiences a "painful curiosity . . . concerning the busy scenes from which she [is] excluded" (1: 14), but the "books, music, and painting" of idealized summer evenings in a pavillion among pastoral surroundings always restore "her usual happy complacency" (1: 15). The ambivalence in this portrait of women's education as a consolation for lack of some other, forbidden knowledge beyond the boundaries of the pastoral world is intensified by the revelation later that the sisters are ignorant of a terrible secret walled up within this world itself. On one of these very evenings of educational bliss, the girls' imprisoned mother watched them longingly from a grated window, too far away to be heard even if she cried out to make her existence known to them and restrained by a "solemn promise" from attempting such a communication anyway. Appropriately, after a time the girls' father moves the site of their genteel education itself to the dark and crumbling deserted wing of the castle, beneath which he hides this mother of whose life and suffering he wishes them ignorant.

Similarly, the sisters in *The Recess* are privileged to have an excellent teacher, but part of her job is to keep them from knowing who they really are. The opening scenes of *The Recess* picture the bounded world of the heroines' "educational idyll"[39] in all its most resonant ambiguity. "As soon as capable of reflection," the heroines, two sisters, find themselves in a strange, dim, enclosed place rather hard to define: it "could not be called a cave, because it was composed of various rooms; and the stones were obviously united by labor . . ." (1: 3). In the narrator's initial rejection of the impulse to compare this dim place with a cave, there is perhaps an allusion to Plato, for much of what the girls seem to learn here is, as they later realize, an incomplete and distorted representation of the world above them. In addition, this first description of the sisters' original darkness as not natural but artificial points to the arbitrary quality of an environment that they must nonetheless accept as simply the state of Things as They Are. In this place the light comes through "small casements of painted glass, so infinitely above our reach that we could never seek a world beyond; and so dim, that the beams of the sun were almost a novelty to us when we quitted this retirement" (1: 3). In this darkness cut off from any "world beyond," the girls are safe and loved, cared for by a woman they know as "mamma," "whose only employ-ment," Matilda explains, "was that of forming our minds . . . the world we were taught to dread.— *She* was our world, and all the tender affec-tions, of which I have since proved my heart so full, centred in her, and my sister" (1: 5).

This mother/teacher has "a most extensive knowledge, to which she was every day adding by perpetual study" (1: 6), but she also exhibits that "feminine helplessness which is, when unaffected, the most interest-ing of all charms" (1: 5). Her care to make the dim seclusion of the Recess attractive to her charges is reinforced by the sterner figure of Father Anthony, the patriarch and true authority of this little domestic world. He begins each day with mass, concluding "with a discourse cal-culated to endear retirement. From him we learnt that there was a terrible large place called the world . . . [from which] Providence had graciously rescued us . . . nor could we ever be sufficiently grateful" (1: 4). Well into the nineteenth century (and indeed beyond), young women were in-structed similarly about their lot. Although the heroines' subsequent ex-periences in the outside world seem fully to justify Father Anthony's view of it and although Matilda later expresses sorrow that she ever longed to leave her childhood seclusion, nonetheless this indoctrination is de-scribed as dangerous:

> Young hearts teem with unformed ideas, and are but too susceptible of ele-vated and enthusiastic impressions. Time gave this man insensibly an influ-ence over us, as a superior being; to which his appearance greatly con-tributed. Imagine a tall and robust figure habited in black, and marked by a commanding austerity of manners. . . . The fire and nobility of his eye, the gracefulness of his decay, and the heart-affecting solemnity of his voice . . . gave an authority almost irresistible to Father Anthony. . . . (1: 5)

That Father Anthony is a frightening figure of authority whose influence takes hold "insensibly" but irresistibly lends a sinister air to his indoctri-nation of young girls in the virtues of a retirement that they experience not as choice but as fate. His sermons are, after all, simply the doctrine of what would later be called "woman's sphere." This Father Anthony is the mamma's brother, but his name and function make the "Recess" a symbol of the world of the patriarchal family where women are "immured groping in the dark."

Not that Sophia Lee has set up this scene as a feminist protest against women's position in the patriarchal family; on the contrary, it is her narrative, not she, that presents this image, and her ambivalence toward it pervades the early scenes of the novel. About "our origin, and our imprisonment," for example, the sisters have two opposing theories. Ellinor "conjectured that we were in the power of some giant; nay, such was her disgust to Father Anthony, that she sometimes apprehended he was a magician, and would one day or other devour us" (1: 6). Father Anthony, in other words, is the devouring Bad Father represented in the ogres and monsters of fairy tales. Indeed, Ellinor's theory comes from her association with the servant Alice, who tells "marvellous tales" and has helped develop the girl's "lively imagination," always receptive to "the romantic and extravagant." Matilda, more in the company of the scholarly mother-educator, has "a very different idea; [fancying] our retreat a hallowed circle to seclude us from the wicked, while Father Anthony appeared to me our guardian genius" (1: 6–7). In the sisters' opposing theories lies the secret relationship between childhood idyll and Gothic horror: they are one and the same. Women's domestic space is either nightmare or hallowed retreat, depending on one's vision of the patriarchal authority there as presiding genius or devouring monster.

Lee's portrayal of the Recess is infused with this kind of ambivalence. The mother-educator, ideal of retiring femininity, provides a delightful education, but it tends to be described in the context of the ignorance she imparts at the same time: "[S]he carefully avoided our enquiries [about the Recess], endeavouring to diversify our hours by music, drawing, poetry, geography, and every ornamental branch of education" (1: 10). Here the girls' education is both valued as extensive and excellent and devalued as a diversionary tactic to keep them from too much curiosity about their lot in life. Father Anthony preaches the value of retirement every morning but also complains "against our being shut up in a place which bounded our ideas so much that he despaired of making us comprehend half of what he taught us" (1: 11)—an old dilemma of educators who try at the same time to make girls wise and keep them ignorant. The description of the girls' first egress from seclusion is prepared by Mrs. Marlow's warning of the bitterness of knowledge and by Matilda's lament that she ever left this place of innocence. Having portrayed herself as "entombed alive in such a narrow boundary" (1: 9), she nonetheless tells the reader these were her happiest days: "Pardon me if I linger over these scenes; alas . . . they are all of my life upon which my heart dares to pause. How are we born to invent our own miseries! . . . How have I wept the moment I quitted the Recess. . . ." (1: 11).

This is a lament for a paradise lost through knowledge, but the escape from the Recess is also described as an escape into Paradise: "We flew into the garden . . . and how strong was the impression of the scene before us! from the mansion, which stood on a hill, spread a rich and fertile valley, mingled with thickets, half seen or clustered hamlets, while through the living landscape flowed a clear river . . ." (1: 15). What comes next confirms that this emergence from "entombment" into the "living landscape" is, however, a fall: "flowed a clear river,—*and to the main / The liquid serpent drew his silver train.*" The serpent already inhabits this Eden, and the sun, which the two young women now see with enthusiasm for the first time, is sinking. Even so, the rich beauty of this outside world, which is to be the world of pain and experience, glows with its revelation of the heroines' loss: "The sun was sinking, involved in swelling waves of gold and purple, upon whom we almost gazed ourselves blind . . ." (1: 15). The glorious new illumination could be blindness; the beauty of the "liquid serpent" in its "silver train" recalls the seductive beauty of Milton's tempter as he approaches Eve; the sun is setting. But the sense of release and freedom is immense. In the opening scenes of *The Recess,* the consciousness that Eden was lost through desire for knowledge is juxtaposed with the sisters' impatience at the ignorance imposed on them against their will. Although this impatience is on the one hand the inevitable temptation to the Fall, there is on the other a strong sense that in what is already a fallen world, the arbitrary bounding of knowledge is a grotesque, even sinister, lie. This is made even more evident by the true relation of mamma and Father Anthony, who, on the eve of the sisters' first emergence from their childhood Eden/ prison, are revealed to have a strange secret: they married each other long ago without knowing they were brother and sister. Lee delicately makes sure the reader understands that the revelation came before the marriage was consummated and that now all sexual passion has been purged. Nonetheless, the fact remains that the sexuality of the parent figures is the mystery of this seeming childhood paradise; its discovery marks both the sad end of Eden and a welcome escape from immurement in the dark.

The ambivalence associated on the one hand with womanly retirement—warm, safe, and maternal but dark; innocent but imprisoning—and with emergence into the world (full of danger and suffering but exhilarating, too) is reproduced in the characterizations of Mary and Elizabeth as alternative models of womanhood. Mary is characterized by "sweetness," "affability," "softness . . . of character" (1: 122), "patient sufferance" (1: 196). In addition, because she is in need of rescue when we first hear of her, she is characterized by that lovely "feminine helplessness" deemed so attractive in Mrs. Marlow. (Indeed, in her daughters' only sight of her she walks in a "small" garden supported by two attendants [1: 195]). In a passage that reverberates with the hidden meanings of women's Gothic, she is described as "an exile from her own country, a prisoner in another . . . a stranger to her children . . ." (1: 75). Helpless and confined, Mary is engaged in that feminine activity of waiting passively for something to change, an activity to which her daughters are also urged. Elizabeth, in contrast, is bold, masculine, aggressive, fickle, cruel, and—most importantly—active. Her court is the "world" of corrupt experience from which the seclusion of Mary's children protects them. Nonetheless the very vigor of Elizabeth's evildoings, source of energy throughout the book, is enviably attractive in contrast with the helpless vulnerability of the heroines, whose lives are never once in their own power and are consequently nightmares of passive suffering. Furthermore, Mary's inactivity is a consequence of her wrongs, as is the necessity for her patient fortitude: like the dispossessed Gothic heroines immured in the very castle they should own, Mary is rightful ruler of the realm in which she has been deprived of all her status. She is the lost, imprisoned mother of whose life the girls learn as an inevitable part of their preparation for their own emergence into womanhood, and her daughters' "entombment" is itself a direct consequence of her own unjust persecution: another hint that some deep injustice informs the "educational idyll" of her children.

Thus in *The Recess* the bounded pastoral world of the heroines' education is identical to the claustrophobic space of their Gothic confinement. In most women's Gothic, the bounded world of home in the sense of a glorious pastoral childhood is emphatically separate from the bounded world of the dark Gothic space into which the heroine's coming of age (i.e., her encounter with the opposite sex as an adult) introduces her. But this case, in which the two are the same, and the case of *A Sicilian Romance*, in which the first is transformed into the second, signal a hidden identity of pastoral and Gothic enclosures in Gothic romance—a suggestion that somehow the genteel enlightenment of one may be the same thing as the darkness of the other. *The Recess* makes the point most explicitly by portraying "entombment" not as a condition into which the heroines fall by accident but as their original condition. At first they enjoy it, "content, through habit and ignorance" (1: 3) but then feel a restlessness, discovering an outward impulse that must be thwarted. This is a picture of something Simone de Beauvoir describes:

It is a strange experience for an individual who feels himself to be an autonomous and transcendent subject, an absolute, to discover inferiority in himself as a fixed and preordained essence. . . . This is what happens to the little girl when, doing her apprenticeship for life in the world, she grasps what it means to be a woman therein. The sphere to which she belongs is everywhere enclosed, limited, dominated, by the male universe: high as she may raise herself, far as she may venture, there will always be a ceiling over her head, walls that will block her way. (334–35)

Matilda and her sister Ellinor should grow up, but to do so they must struggle to get out of the womb/tomb in which they are confined.[40] The struggle to escape this condition—to succeed in what Roberts calls "the female quest for experience" (105)—is difficult not only because it is hard for such women to know more of the world but also because it is so hard for them to make themselves known to it. "Ah, how easy it is to be unknown!—to be entombed alive!" (*Recess* 3: 103).

Ballin's *The Statue Room,* the story of another heroine deprived, as are Ellinor and Matilda, of the kingdom to which her true status should entitle her, ends with a fantasy of self-revelation, as Romelia removes her mask and reproves the guards who have seized her: "Off, off, ye base-born plebeians . . . behold who I am!" (2: 135). In women's Gothic, this old story of the noblewoman whose true identity is unknown acquires a special resonance, for the difficulty of being known is the real subject of Gothic paranoia, and the heroine's impulse to cry out, "behold who I am!" is the strongest and most stifled impulse women Gothicists portray. Women's Gothic is infused with the atmosphere of persecution, produced not only by an obsessive narrative focus on attempts to lock the heroine up, separate her from the hero, take her money and property, violate her, kill her, but often by a pervasive sense that the heroine is being falsely charged with feelings and intentions she does not have. This is part of a larger motif of the misknowing of the heroine: the false categorizing and misnaming of her essential innocence. Thus Montoni suspects Emily of being a vascillating coquette, and Mme. Cheron sees her as indecorous, perhaps unchaste.[41] Even as Ellena di Rosalba stands at the altar to be married, she is torn from her lover by those (supposedly the Inquisition) who accuse her of breaking her nun's vows (*The Italian* 188–89). Barrett's heroine complains about "us poor heroines" in general, "No, never can we get through an innocent adventure in peace and quietness, without having our virtue called in question" (1: 187).

One of the most remarkable examples of such misprizing occurs in *The Children of the Abbey,* in which the whole plot turns (with numerous digressions, of course) on misinterpretations of the heroine. Some of these misjudgments are the work of the libertine ("one of the completest villains upon earth" [5: 89]) who stalks her throughout the book. Others result from prohibitions against her speaking up to explain or defend her strange (but innocent!) conduct. The source of both Amanda's suspicious behavior and these prohibitions is parental: Amanda's father, out of "scrupulous delicacy" (2: 73) in financial matters, forces her to desert her lover without explanation, thus causing her to appear unfaithful. This involves her both in concealing her real motives (filial piety) from her lover and trying, at least briefly, to conceal her grief from her father, who is a Good Father[42] and whom she loves.

As is often the case in Gothic romance, this same story is then retold, but in a way that allows for the expression of the feelings that the first version has served to repress—another instance of the "and then" that means "that is to say." The Good Father, whose prohibition against the heroine's making her true feelings known is hard to accept but understandable and just, dies. And then the Evil Father of Amanda's lover steps in with what amounts to exactly the same prohibition, forcing her, for financial considerations of his own, to leave the hero without a word of explanation and thus causing her to appear unfaithful.[43] This time the fatherly prohibition is based on the most odiously selfish of motivations, and Amanda is justified in responding with righteous indignation at the man who has wantonly destroyed her happiness. Nonetheless, as in the case of the first paternal prohibition, Amanda must obey and keep silence, whatever her feelings: alas, if she does not, the bad father will be forced to commit suicide.

The result of this remarkable patriarchal coercion is that Amanda is almost constantly throughout the book suspected of sexual perfidy by her beloved and his relatives. "Ah! if your mind resembled your person, what a perfect creature had you been!" exclaims Lady Martha (4: 181). Such outbursts sorely tempt Amanda to speak up and defend herself:

> Now, now was the test, the shining test of Amanda's virtue . . . she knew by a few words she could explain the appearances which had deprived her of his good opinion, and fully regain it; regain, by a few words, the love, the esteem of her valued, her inestimable Mortimer, the affection, the protection of his amiable aunt and sister. She leaned her head upon her hand,

the weight on her bosom became less oppressive: she raised her head—"Of my innocence I can give such proofs," cried she. Her lips closed, a mortal paleness overspread her face . . . she trembled; the solemn, the dreadful declaration Lord Cherbury had made of not surviving the disclosure of his secret, her promise of inviolably keeping it, both rushed upon her mind; she beheld herself on the very verge of a tremendous precipice. . . . (4: 181–82)

Here the Fall is equated not with the act of knowledge but with the act of making oneself known, and the heroine resists, with noble fortitude, the temptation of speaking "I."

So it goes on. Amanda obeys her vow of silence. As the misconstructions of her highly suspicious conduct multiply, she can only reply to her accusers with refusals to explain herself: "I cannot help . . . the misconstructions which may be put on my actions; I can only support myself under the pain they inflict by conscious rectitude" (4: 185). The "pride of injured innocence" (4: 185) is hers, but it cannot clear her name in the world's eyes; it can only enable her to endure her unjust trial. And that, in the end, is the most consistent function of "conscious innocence" for the Gothic heroine: not as a defense against forces beyond her, who are always more powerful than she, but as a means whereby the heroine can preserve a coherent vision of herself in an environment in which everything works to make her seem, even in her own eyes, other than what she is.

In one sense, these Gothic heroines accused of not being what they are supposed to be—and this almost always amounts to the accusation that they are sexual beings—seem after a time to be protesting (or, rather, refusing to protest) too much. The recurrent, obsessive dream of having to defend one's innocence suggests that the dreamer suspects a buried dimension in the self for which there is, in fact, no defense. Ellena at the altar with the hero *is* about to give up her chastity; the "Inquisition" bursts in to announce, in essence, that her desire for the hero is sexual. The accusation that she is a nun about to violate her vow stands in for the real accusation, which is that the heroine, model of purity, has a passionate side her society—and her author—regard as a betrayal of the feminine ideal.

But there is another side to this motif of perpetual accusation. As de Beauvoir points out, women traditionally lack the opportunity of justifying their own value in the world; they must wait for justification from a source beyond them. "In a sense [woman's] whole existence is waiting, since she is confined in the limbo of immanence and contingence, and since her justification is always in the hands of others. She awaits the homage, the approval of men, she awaits love, she awaits the gratitude and praise of her husband or her lover" (679). Even the woman mystic who seems independent of these concerns "feels the need for a witness from on high to reveal and consecrate her worth" (773). Or as Amanda would say, "To heaven I leave the vindication of my innocence" (*Children of the Abbey* 3: 20). The pervasive emphasis on conscious innocence as an aid to fortitude, together with the forces (decorum, promises, concern for the welfare of others) working to inhibit the heroine's communication of the facts that would vindicate her, is suggestive in the context of de Beauvoir's observation. Gothic romances show women trying resolutely to build up an inner sense of worth but in fact suffering from a continual sense that the real determination of their value—their real "justification"—is not within their own power.

The threats of accusation or even Inquisition, coupled with the horror of not being able to be known, suggest as well another dimension of women's experience as de Beauvoir describes it. Women, she says, are the Second Sex, the Other, assigned definitions as objects in accordance with men's needs rather than invited to achieve self-definition as subjects in accordance with their own nature. The Gothic heroine's characteristic experience of being taken for other than herself is in one sense simply this experience of being Other. Not only can Amanda not speak "I"; by the terms in which she and the world define female virtue, her status as a good woman depends on her willingness to refrain from disabusing the world of its false definition of her. This dilemma is a ridiculous double bind, but it makes perfect sense in a society in which woman plays the role of Other: feminine virtue in such a world consists of submitting to definition by an alien patriarchy, even in the extreme case, the reductio ad absurdum, when that definition labels the woman as devoid of feminine virtue. Roche's idealization of the heroine who glories in her "conscious rectitude" in such circumstances is the locus of the novel's conservative ideology of womanhood, but Roche's own sense of the double bind this ideology entails comes through in the subplots, whose moral is that duplicity is always wrong and always self-defeating. The incompatibility of this moral with the heroine's achievement of virtue through her submission to a duplicity forced on her by the fathers is the central contradiction of the book—one that the author cannot, within the framework of her own ideology, resolve.

III

To be assigned the role of Other, of object rather than subject, is in de Beauvoir's view to be deprived of the possibility of transcendence, relegated to the self-enclosed life of "immanence" which is its opposite. This is a life of repetition, and women are confined to repetition in special ways—because their one major role is to continue the species (480) and because the "work" they do in their enclosed "circle of self" (500) is itself circular. "Few tasks are more like the torture of Sisyphus than housework, with its endless repetition . . ." (504).

Repetition in women's Gothic serves a double and self-contradictory function. It mimes the claustrophobic circularity of women's real lives in that it shows the heroine, who must confront the same terrors repeatedly, doing the same thing over and over. In its presentation of multiple female victims, Gothic romance also shows the same thing being done to women over and over: it suggests the inescapable victimization of women in general. Emily escapes but then Blanche is trapped; Julia escapes but then she finds that her mother is trapped; and so on. In the final closure of each book, the repetition from which these women have suffered ends once and for all. But as with many other aspects of women's Gothic, this device operates in two opposite ways. It provides a wish fulfillment conclusion in which the repetitive horror of a woman's life is ended and she can live happily ever after. On the other hand, the fact of the seemingly endless, random repetition of the episodic plot gives the final closure an arbitrary quality that undercuts its message that the repetition is over.[44] The Gothic narrative goes on and on, not only from volume to volume but from book to book; for if Alicia is rescued in one novel, the reader knows that Matilda or Adelfrida or Elvina or Emilia, who looks exactly like her and plays the lute equally well, will soon be captured in another.

This very repetition, while giving voice to women's discontent with the monotony of their domestic lives by imitating its claustrophobia, makes the books themselves an escape from that monotony. Jane Eyre describes her method of egress from the deadly sameness of her woman's work:

> Then my sole relief was to walk along the corridor of the third story, backwards and forwards . . . and allow my mind's eye to dwell on whatever bright visions rose before it . . . to let my heart be heaved by the exultant movement, which, while it swelled it in trouble, expanded it with life; and, best of all, to open my inward ear to a tale that was never ended—a tale my imagination created, and narrated continuously; quickened with all of inci-

dent, life, fire, feeling, that I desired and had not in my actual existence. (141)

In the final closure of the happy ending, women's Gothic bounds the Gothic horrors of repetition, but the sense of a "tale . . . never ended" always suggests that no woman's escape is final—and, paradoxically, that the escape of reading the tale is therefore a permanent possibility. The arbitrariness of endings and the repetitious quality of the romances themselves individually and collectively are integral to the role these books play for women readers. Through its continuous pictures of imprisonment and escape, Gothic romance offers an illusion of liberty—the heart "expanded . . . with life"; the sense of endless adventure, excitement, "a door always open" to some other, more exciting world. But at the same time the claustrophobic repetition itself describes the claustrophobia of female readers' real lives, giving voice to their experience of the immanence of everyday deadly iteration even as it provides the illusion of transcendence.

IV

Women's impulse toward transcendence is itself the chief subject of women's Gothic romance, but in ways that implicate the genre in its deepest contradictions. At the most basic level, the desire for transcendence as Gothic plots portray it manifests itself simply as a desire for escape from the house, the prison, the convent, the secret room, the outlaw's retreat—escape, in other words, from the extraordinary confinements of romantic heroines that signify the ordinary confinements of women's lives. Such escape is fraught with difficulty: the heroine is isolated and weak; she knows too little; she has no place to go if she gets out. But there are other constraints on the heroine's ability to escape that have nothing to do with the physical circumstances of her imprisonment: the constraints of that ladylike decorum to which female writers pay such devout homage even as they express their indignation at the heroine's physical constraint.

The relation between these two kinds of constraint is suggestive, especially in those cases in which Gothic romance shows women either abstaining from self-rescue because of decorum or saving themselves only through a violation of decorum. Both situations were the subject of satire. In *The Convent,* the flighty romance reader has such refined scruples that

they almost prevent her from saving her sister: having sent for help, she
has too much delicacy to reveal all the details the rescuers will need:
"[K]now then . . . that this person is immured in the recesses of a Convent, somewhere within the Kingdom of Gaul—haply I would be more
explicit, but that duty forbids me" (Fuller 2: 18). (The "duty" is all in
her imagination and thus obscure, but it seems to involve filial piety.)
The heroine's opposite tendency—to contravene decorum—is a subject
of Barrett's satire: "[T]he Heroine often acts, to all appearance, indis-
creetly; but then, 'tis just as true, that her most unpromising enterprises
always terminate best; and therefore, what appears rashness, is only the
refinement of discretion." And so, supposedly possessed of the nicest
scruples and finest delicacy, Barrett's heroine is nonetheless constantly
involved in ludicrous violations of the most fundamental social conventions. Far from observing refinements of propriety to which ordinary mortals
are not even attuned, the delightful Cherubina blows up a house; stays
alone at the home of a man she scarcely knows; and refuses to pay for a
bonnet she has "bought" (heroines do not buy things with vulgar money),
stamping her feet at the shop owner in the ensuing scuffle. In addition,
she lies a great deal: "At first, I hesitated at deviating from veracity; but
soon consented, on recollecting, that though heroines begin with praising
truth, necessity makes them end with being the greatest story-tellers in
the world" (1: 108).

The aptness of the joke is instructive. Cherubina is engaged, with high
spirits, in the pursuit of independent projects in the world outside her
home, a fact that in itself is enough to establish her as a "Female Quixote" figure. The hero is the man her father wants her to marry ("Large
estates, you know,—handsome, fashionable . . ."); Cherubina's view of
him as "my bitter enemy, the wily, the wicked" (1: 37) shows that Barrett
recognized the secret equation of hero and villain in the Gothic and considered it perverse. The happy resolution of the book comes when the
natural order is reestablished by Cherubina's submission to the better
judgments of her father and suitor and to the convention of happy marriage. The real butt of the satire here is the independence of mind implied
in what Roberts describes as that "recurrent situation" of Gothic romance,
"the female quest for experience" (105).[45] As Moers says in her analysis
of "traveling heroinism" in women's Gothic, "For Mrs. Radcliffe, the
Gothic novel was a device to send maidens on distant and exciting journeys without offending the proprieties" (126). But Barrett's real message
is perceptive: whatever its pretenses, Gothic heroinism *is* a violation of
the female proprieties, precisely because it violates the patriarchal order.

The tension between the adventure implied in "the female quest for experience" and the female decorum supposedly exalted in the Gothicist's portrayal of that quest means that definitions of the Gothic as quest romance must take gender issues into account. To define Gothic as quest romance, without qualification, almost necessitates the masculinization of the canon, as a female quest in the old romance traditions of Spenser and Ariosto was, by the eighteenth century, something only a *Female Quixote* would undertake. When women in that period are portrayed seriously as questers, the quest must be qualified in various ways. If the woman is good, (1) the journey is confined primarily to a proper female space—a house or similar interior, and/or (2) the search is not an act of autonomy and self-definition or a response to the call of adventure per se but an attempt to establish the woman in her proper relationships. It may well be an act of filial piety resulting from some kind of *Solemn Injunction,* or it may be a search for a lost relative. Beatrice looks for her father in *A Northumbrian Tale.* In Ballin's *The Statue Room,* Romelia's dramatic asassination attempt on Queen Elizabeth is prompted by a vision of her mother, who charges her (and thereby authorizes her in terms of the most sacred virtue of Gothic heroines, filial piety), to avenge her death. Even Victoria's "quest" in Dacre's *Zofloya,* if one could call it that, boils down to an attempt to steal another woman's husband. The only genuine female questers in Gothic are precisely the Female Quixotes of the parodies,[46] who are in quest of a Gothic quest. And the joke is precisely that: just as questing itself violates female propriety, so does the impulse behind the whole female genre of Gothic romance.

Thus the morally problematic status of a heroine's relation to the act of questing translates itself in Gothic romance either directly into parody or into the most serious contradictions and formal problems of the narrative. Into this category fall both the preceeding qualifications of female quest mentioned and such phenomena as the necessity of providing a working-class, female detective figure, the heroine's servant, so that the heroine can learn things without implicating herself in too sordid a search for knowledge. In medieval and Renaissance quest romance, the hero or heroine is sometimes defeated and sometimes wins but is always setting out on adventures. That act, repeated again and again, provides the central impetus of the narrative. In Gothic, in contrast, the focus is on the heroine's repeatedly being trapped, brought back after the escape, and locked in once more. That is one reason *The Mysteries of Udolpho* is a nightmare while *Yvain and Gawain* is not. Both narratives proceed in circles,[47] but the central drama of *Yvain* comes from the hero's various departures on adventure, and that of *Udolpho* comes from the heroine's various entrapments. Thus, once again, even the portrayal of the heroine's activity centers on a portrayal of her feminine passivity.

Despite the passivity, delicacy, and filial piety to which it pays homage, women's Gothic shows women's attempts at self-preservation frustrated or made difficult by the constraints of feminine decorum. Even the impulse to escape physically may conflict with propriety—not surprising, considering the subversive impulse disguised in the heroine's desire to get out of the house. Thus Ellena di Rosalba must violate decorum in order to escape the convent : "It was true that Vivaldi had discovered her prison, but, if it were possible, that he could release her, she must consent to quit it with him; a step from which a mind so tremblingly jealous of propriety as hers, recoiled with alarm, though it would deliver her from captivity" (*The Italian* 122). This moral dilemma is partly resolved by the revelation that the issue is not simply whether to leave in the company of a suitor or remain to be imprisoned but whether to leave in his company or be murdered. Even so, the heroine's decision must be validated by the authorization of an older woman. This woman's authority is itself further authenticated by the subsequent revelation that she is the heroine's mother; thus the heroine's violation of decorum was really the higher decorum of filial respect.[48] Similarly, in *A Sicilian Romance,* Julia worries about the propriety of escaping her father's castle in the company of Hippolytus. Here the necessary violation of decorum is authorized by her brother, in an admonition that shows Radcliffe to have been conscious of the issues with which she was dealing in such scenes: "Do not suffer the prejudices of education to render you miserable. Believe that a choice which involves the happiness or misery of your whole life, ought to be decided only by yourself" (1: 129).

Other escape routes, too, are blocked by decorum. Roche's Amanda could save herself from isolation and unhappiness by telling her lover the real truth, but the fathers have forbidden it. Finally her name is cleared by the evil father ("[D]id he then at last justify me?" Amanda cries in relief), and the hero declares his love: "Yes . . . he proved you were indeed the most excellent . . . of human beings" (*Children of the Abbey* 5: 123). But Amanda's assumption that the hero is married to another woman creates yet another obstacle, and once again she must refrain from making her feelings known. "Oh! With what difficulty at this moment did she confine herself within the cold, the rigid rules of propriety . . ." (5: 122).[49]

The one escape route of which the Gothic heroine may always avail herself while still confined within "the cold, the rigid rules of propriety" is transcendence through an appreciation of the sublime. As she looks from her room with a view, the heroine's experience of the sublime affords a psychological escape, placing the villain in a perspective that reveals his powerlessness in the larger scheme of things.

> Hither she could come, and her soul, refreshed by the views [the turret] afforded, would acquire strength to bear her, with equanimity, thro' the persecutions that might await her. Here, gazing upon the stupendous imagery around her, looking, as it were, beyond the awful veil which obscures the features of the Deity, and conceals Him from the eyes of his creatures, dwelling as with a present God in the midst of his sublime works; with a mind thus elevated, how insignificant would appear to her the transactions, and the sufferings of this world! How poor the boasted power of man. . . . Thus man, the giant who now held her in captivity, would shrink to the diminutiveness of a fairy; and she would experience, that his utmost force was unable to enchain her soul, or compel her to fear him, while he was destitute of virtue. (Radcliffe, *The Italian* 90–91)

This kind of transcendence has its limits. It is merely a substitute for the physical escape the heroine is powerless to achieve; in addition, it reinforces the heroine's ability to "bear" her suffering "with equanimity" rather than giving her strength or inspiration to end it. Here, as elsewhere in women's Gothic, the escape through the sublime remains, in essence, the heroine's secret—an inner flight of which the villain is not aware and of which he himself is not capable. Such silent and secret escapes change nothing but the heroine's own mind, the only realm over which women could attain power. Even that power, as romancers like Radcliffe knew, was vulnerable to external pressures, which is why they made such a point of insisting that women work to control their reactions to oppression and why madness—the loss of power over one's inner realm—is one of the ultimate Gothic horrors. The "giant" villain will "shrink to . . . diminutiveness" only in proportion as the heroine's mind is "elevated"; if she loses that faculty of elevation, she herself is lost.

The inwardness of women's escape through the sublime in Gothic romance points to another aspect of their relation to the transcendence that the sublime represented generally in late eighteenth-century thought. Wollstonecraft berated Burke for his treatment of women's relation to the sublime. As she perceived, he associated women with beauty (they are little, smooth, symmetrical, and weak), and men (larger, rougher, more angular, and stronger) with the sublime. In addition, she ridiculed the way Burke defined women out of participation in the moral sublime.

> You may have convinced them that *littleness* and *weakness* are the very essence of beauty; and that the Supreme Being, in giving women beauty in the most supereminent degree, seemed to command them, by the powerful voice of Nature, not to cultivate the moral virtues that might chance to excite respect, and interfere with the pleasing sensations they were created to inspire. . . . [I]f virtue has any other foundation than worldly utility, you have clearly proved that one half of the human species, at least, have not souls; and that Nature, by making women *little, smooth, delicate, fair* creatures, never designed that they should exercise their reason to acquire the virtues that produce opposite, if not contradictory, feelings. The affection they excite, to be uniform and perfect, should not be tinctured with the respect which moral virtues inspire, lest pain should be blended with pleasure, and admiration disturb the soft intimacy of love. (*Rights of Men* 112–14)

As Wollstonecraft perceived, Burke's theory of the sublime has to do not just with the inner exercise of the faculties but also with action in the world: lofty behavior, heroic deeds. Her reading of Burke casts an important light on Gothic heroines' relation to the sublime, which is based solely on contemplation and leads not to action but to endurance, fortitude, resignation. "If I am condemned to misery," says Ellena, "surely I could endure it with more fortitude in scenes like these, than amidst the tamer landscapes of nature!" (*The Italian* 63).

Furthermore, even Radcliffe associates the heroine herself primarily with the beautiful when a discrimination between her sensibility and the hero's is at issue. The following passage puts Ellena, despite her much-described capacity for appreciating the sublime, in her proper place: above the servant, whose interest in a landscape has nothing to do with aesthetics, but below the hero, whose sympathies are drawn first to the sublime.

> "See" said Vivaldi, "where Monte-Corno stands like a ruffian, huge, scared, threatening, and horrid! . . . mark how other overtopping ridges of the mighty Appennines [*sic*] darken the horizon far along the east. . . ."
> "Mark too," said Ellena, "how sweetly the banks and undulating plains repose at the feet of the mountains; what an image of beauty and elegance they oppose to the awful grandeur that overlooks and guards them! Observe, too, how many a delightful valley . . . spreads its rice and corn fields. . . ."
> "Ay, Signora!" exclaimed Paulo, "and have the goodness to observe how

like are the fishing boats . . . to those one sees upon the bay of Naples."
(*The Italian* 158–59)

When women in the Gothic are actually associated with a combination of
the sublime and action—when, as de Beauvoir would say, they seek to
transcend themselves in projects, the sublime of which they partake is
the grand, amoral sublime: they are wicked women, and their projects
are horrifying schemes. Such a one is Dacre's Victoria, her vivacity like
"the brilliant glare of the terrible volcano, pregnant even in its beauty
with destruction!" (*Zofloya* 2: 133). Resolved "to overstep common
boundaries, and that which is termed female delicacy, by openly declar-
ing [her] passion" (2: 169), she pursues her dire schemes of lust and
murder amidst "beautifully terrific" scenery: "the immeasurable waste of
endless solitude" (2: 200), "steep rocks . . . inaccessible mountains, with
here and there a blasted oak . . . huge precipices . . . the torrent . . .
foaming in the viewless abyss with mighty rage" (2: 237). Her own "mighty
rage" is directed against the ostensible heroine of the novel, "delicate,
symmetrical, and of fairy-like beauty . . . small . . . sweet . . ." (1:
104). Victoria hatches her final plans against Lilla in a violent storm (3:
68–73), then pursues and destroys her in an astounding fantasy of ferocious hatred for the archetypal Gothic heroine:

> Victoria pursued her flying victim. At the uttermost edge of the mountain
> she gained upon her, when . . . Lilla . . . caught frantic . . . at the scathed
> branches of a blasted oak, that, bowed by repeated storms, hung almost
> perpendicularly over the yawning depth beneath. Round these, she twisted
> her slender arms, while, waving to and fro with her gentle weight over the
> immeasurable abyss, they seemed to promise but precarious support.
>   Victoria advanced with furious looks—she shook the branches of the
> tree. . . . Enhorrored [*sic*] at this terrible menace, the miserable girl quitted
> suddenly her hold, and on the brink of the mountain sought despairingly to
> grapple with the superior force of her adversary!—Her powers were soon
> exhausted. . . . (3: 101–2)

Victoria stabs her victim repeatedly and throws her over the cliff, watching as the body bounces down the mountain: "Her fairy form bounded as
it fell against the projecting crags of the mountain, diminishing to the
sight of her cruel enemy, who followed it far as her eye could reach" (3:
104). Having indulged in this wild fantasy of anger against the feminine
ideal of sentimental Gothic, Dacre waits until the idealized "fairy form"

finishes its long plunge to earth and then loads her villainess with terrified guilt.

Not surprisingly, the woman who engaged in these actions is described as having a "masculine spirit" (2: 275) and even "bold masculine features" (3: 65), and her capacity for the amoral sublime is embodied literally in the masculine spirit Zofloya, who is summoned by her evil desires and who, in his grand darkness, stalks sublimely across the spectacular landscape of Victoria's evil deeds (3: 74).[50] Female characters like Victoria are unusual as protagonists in women's Gothic, but the mode in which she is associated with sublimity is only a logical extension of the ideology implicit in the more usual manner of linking the sentimental heroine with the sublime. Heroines contemplate grandeur and learn from it grand fortitude; grand action is possible only for the woman who, like Victoria, is willing to "overstep common boundaries" of "female delicacy."

But the deepest contradiction of women's Gothic with relation to the sublime is that the heroine's impulse toward transcendence is always translated in happy Gothic into an impulse toward marriage. (This is true even in Victoria's case: she wants to break up an idyllic marriage, but in order to get the man for herself.) Thus, although at one level marriage is the immanence against which heroines struggle symbolically—a life of repetition, confinement, sexual domination, economic powerlessness, seclusion, ignorance—the protest implicit in this symbolic struggle is undercut by the final identification of escape with domestic enclosure, itself the very source of the suffering the escape is supposed to alleviate.

Behind this contradiction is the fact that, as de Beauvoir points out, repetition and immanence are not only dangers for women; they are temptations. Gothic romance by women portrays women's unhappiness and confinement, their horror at finding themselves "immured in their families groping in the dark," their profound alienation from the patriarchal institutions that dominate their lives, their sense of claustrophobic repetition, the transcendent impulses that express their longing to escape. But it also—and continuously—portrays a longing for security, enclosure, the bounded world of childhood safety. "Woman [longs] . . . to reconstruct a situation: that which she experienced as a little girl under adult protection. . . . What she wants to recover is a roof over her head, walls that prevent her from feeling her abandonment in the wide world, authority that protects her against her liberty" (de Beauvoir 716). Emily begins as a child in the pastoral security of La Vallée, its boundedness implicit in its name. The reward of her trials is to go back there, this time with her husband. Howells identifies *asylum* as a key image in *The Children of the Abbey:* "What is so obviously appealing here is the common romantic yearning to recapture the childish illusion of perfect security. . . . Where Mrs Roche comes close to the sentimental novelists is in her reluctance to show her heroine coming to terms with adult experience; Amanda sees the world purely as a threat and what is emphasised is her need for protection. . . . the many refuges described usually turn out to be illusory till finally the heroine finds her true asylum in marriage . . . " (87). (Indeed, like that of Emily, Amanda's marriage is set in the very scene of her childhood bliss.) There is, after all, no self-defense in women's Gothic; the final escape is escape into a marriage that "recaptures[s] the childish illusion of perfect security"; the final protection is seclusion in domestic space.

"The ideal of happiness has always taken material form in the house, whether cottage or castle; it stands for permanence and separation from the world" (de Beauvoir 501). Gothic romance presents this kind of separation as a nightmare in the stories of the heroine's confinement (Udolpho) but as wish fulfilment in the final enclosure (La Vallée). The fantasy of happy Gothic by women—and Gothic by women is almost always happy—is that somehow these two forms of enclosure and separation are radically different: that the subject of all those excruciating episodes was really something other than domestic claustrophobia. The real protection the final domestic enclosure affords is asylum from all the previous revelations of its true meaning.

Such endings reveal women's Gothic to be deeply conservative,[51] in a sense importantly different from that described by critics who discuss it from a nonfeminist perspective. Durant, for example, gives a very different reading of the conservative function of final pastorals in Radcliffe's Gothic. He reads the "death" of the ideal childhood parents, followed by their replacement by jealous mothers and competitive fathers, as a representation of the inevitable familial conflict of adolescent psychodrama. This drama he sees as ending unsatisfactorily: the novels defeat our expectations of a predictable end in which "the heroine will win her new love and then, perhaps, be able to accept her parents in their new role as equals" (528). Instead, "[t]he heroines persist in their adolescent view and are proven correct. Those selfish adults were not her real parents, but vile impostors. She will never achieve equal status with her parents; instead, she will rediscover them as distant arbiters and absolute authorities. The adolescent will have to sacrifice any hope of adult status, ignore the real world, and live docilely as a child for all of her life. But it is worth it: the outside world is too fraught with perils to be endured" (528). What is missing here is a sense of what "adult status" meant for women in Radcliffe's time. Wollstonecraft called for reforms that would enable women, like men, fully to "unfold their faculties" as rational beings (*Rights of Woman* 33), an ideal she saw as far distant from the real condition of women. She would have recognized the penultimate sentence in this quotation from Durant as quite an accurate description of the kind of adult "maturity" that women in her day were expected to attain. And the last two sentences could almost come straight from Simone de Beauvoir—as descriptions of how traditional gender roles truncate a woman's psychological development so that she will remain dependent and childlike all her life, and of the compensations she must make in order to believe that the substitution of protection for adult autonomy is "worth it."

Durant discusses the juxtaposition in Radcliffe's works of an initial "familial pastoral" (521) with "a fallen world where a father-villain betrays and persecutes the heroine" (520) but does not recognize those two worlds as different pictures of the same place. Thus, for example, he says that Radcliffe's "heroines discover a nightmare world beneath the pastoral" (523) and describes the way that Julia, once she has fled her home, "finds that the world consists of an interconnected series of underground sites . . ." (524). Radcliffe's pastorals are, indeed, a retreat in bad faith from the vision of a fallen world, but it is important to see exactly what this vision is. Durant's reading of Radcliffe's fallen world as "the world outside the family" (525) essentially ignores the meaning of the fact that the first and last of these "underground sites" Julia discovers is quite literally "beneath" the pastoral world of her childhood home and that the revelation of her mother as a prisoner in that world seriously undercuts the earlier idyllic representation of it. There can be no question of the conservative and escapist nature of the final retreat to "familial pastoral" at the end of Radcliffe's books. Radcliffe does, as Durant argues, look back nostalgically to a premodern past, and her endings do retreat from the possibility that the heroine might achieve autonomy. But something important is lacking in this account, too. What the final pastorals retreat from is the insight that women, whatever their own impulses toward transcendent autonomy, are neither permitted to grow up to be autonomous individuals in an adult world nor acknowledged, at any point in their lives, to be the equals of the patriarchs who rule it. This final evasion of the women Gothicists is a blindness to their own insight that the happy bounded world of home, the heroine's compensation for the loss of full selfhood, is the same prison from which she sought escape.

This evasion is in keeping with the many others that characterize women's Gothic. As Radway demonstrates, Gothic, like all popular literature, initiates in readers a "complex process of expression and eventual recontainment of dissatisfaction" (141):

> [P]opular novels can freely prompt their readers to construct situations which will arouse in them, through identification and response, latent discontent and a previously suppressed desire for change, precisely because the ordered narrative will later prompt the same readers to demonstrate through new constructions the needlessness of their earlier reaction. The narrative resolutions reconcile them, then, to the social order which originally gave rise to the disaffection expressed through their construction of the early stages of the narrative. Popular literature can be said to legitimate the social order only because it also embodies the materials of a historical protest. (141)[52]

Howells, Holland and Sherman, Kahane (52), Mussell, Poovey (328–29), Radway, Roberts, and Russ all discuss, from different perspectives, the ways women's Gothic undercuts its most subversive themes. Roberts, for example, sees Gothic devices as simultaneously "appeal[ing] to the repressed fantasies and fears" of the woman reader and "support[ing] her temporary status quo" ("Abstract," n.p.): "What is needed for these women is an artistic outlet that both reinforces their limited cultural and social positions upon which they are emotionally and economically so dependent and offers them escape at the same time, a flight from the 'pains' resultant from subordination in a patriarchal society" (27–28). Mussell ("But Why Do they Read those Things?") discusses the "fantasy of significance" (61) in contemporary Gothic, which assures the woman reader "not merely of the essential *rightness* of social mythology but also of the *meaning-ness* of that belief system for her" (65). Gothics offer escape from the "powerlessness . . . meaninglessness . . . lack of identity" associated with women's activities, but they also offer escape to a world in which what amount to the same activities have deep and crucial meaning. Thus in the end, Gothic "provides a reconciliation with the roles and situations from which the reader is initially trying to escape" (67). Mussell is talking about contemporary Gothics, which differ significantly in many ways from the original women's Gothic, but in this respect the descendants seem remarkably similar to their ancestors. In both cases, the ending provides an overt reinforcement of the same domestic ideology that, at another level, their narratives show to be the cause of terrible suffering. This recanting is a profound necessity of the narratives, because, as Kahane says, the true Gothic fear is "a fear of femaleness itself"—a fear that the very fact of womanhood is "threatening to one's wholeness, obliterating the . . . boundaries of self" (59).

Women's Gothic is a deeply subversive genre, but often only to the extent that it subverts itself.[53] For like dreams, women's Gothic offers its insights together with protection from their meaning. The heroine kills her father, but it wasn't her real father; the real father arrives to explain that the act was justifiable self-defense; anyway, the victim isn't dead after all, so she didn't kill him (Musgrave, *Solemn Injunction*). The heroine violates decorum, but the woman who urged her to do so is really her mother, so she conformed to decorum anyway *(The Italian)*. The heroine renounces her ties to her father and declares that she will "struggle for liberty and life" *(Romance of the Forest* I: 81), but that wasn't her father, after all, and her struggle for liberty is vindicated when it turns out that her real father was murdered by the false one against whom she rebelled. The heroine's lover acts like the villain, but for the most part it only seemed so, and he undoes the one sin that connected them—gambling—by turning his final act of gaming into the most exquisitely benevolent act of generosity *(Mysteries of Udolpho)*. The heroine's father is trying to kill her, but no—he is not her father; it was all a mistake *(The Italian)*.

The Houses of Osma and Almeria contains an even more contorted example. When the heroine's father, "the most arrogant of mankind" (I: 34), opposes her marriage, her lover kills him. She is torn between love for and revulsion toward the murderer, but the conflict is resolved when it turns out that the man the lover killed was not her father after all. Unfortunately, her real parents are even worse than he was: the father "gaunt and ferocious," the mother "loaded with tawdry ornaments" (3: 91). (This last may seem a minor failing, but it is presented in dire terms, presumably an adolescent fantasy of embarrassment at one's parents' bad taste.) Their "mouldering" house, with its shattered windows (3: 82), "withering grass and weeds" (3: 121) and "mutilated statues" (3: 103) is now revealed to be both her true family dwelling and her prison. But hidden away there, it turns out, is her real father—the first one, after all—who is not only alive but now completely sympathetic to her plight. No wonder the subject of Gothic romance is fear: women Gothicists are desperately afraid of their real subject, which is anger.

V

From this perspective on women's Gothic, Mary Shelley and Emily Brontë can be seen as belonging to that tradition despite their ostensible focus on male protagonists. Another look at the "educational idyll" in *Franken-stein,* for example, reveals to what an extent Shelley, although ostensibly writing a male Faustean tragedy in the Gothic mode, belongs to the tradition of women's Gothic in her treatment of the problem of knowledge. Safie's education at the heart of the De Lacey family is presented as an alternative to her prospects as a woman in the Moslem world, where the creative and intellectual potential connoted by her name (which suggests both Sophia and Sappho) would be, literally, walled up: Safie's mother taught her "to aspire to higher powers of intellect and an independence of spirit forbidden to the female followers of Muhammad. This lady died, but her lessons were indelibly impressed on the mind of Safie, who sickened at the prospect of again returning to Asia and being immured within the walls of a harem, allowed only to occupy herself with infantile amusements . . . "(390). This picture of the woman shut in from a knowledge outside her is another version of the picture of Frankenstein shutting a woman, his fiancée, out of his search for knowledge, which can take place only in an enclosed "cell" from which she is excluded. The utopian vision of Safie's escape from the prospect of life in a harem to a more enlightened enclosure, the charmed circle of her adopted family (for this, too, is a woman's version of the family romance), would appear to offer a model for women's proper invitation to "unfold their faculties." But this vision of a female educational paradise is undercut in two important ways. First, at its center, as Gilbert and Gubar remark, is a blind patriarch (243)—a variation on the characteristic women Gothicists' theme of the darkness of the heroine's enlightened education. Second, this circle is haunted by what has been left out of it: a monster who suffers from an anxiety about "discovering" himself and who has no name to reveal anyway. "Sometimes I wished to express my sensations in my own mode," he says of his earlier mental gropings, "but the uncouth and inarticulate sounds which broke from me frightened me into silence again" (368). Gilbert and Gubar show that this monster is "a female in disguise" (237), one of Shelley's versions of "the fall into gender" (225). If that is true, then in this "educational idyll" the old Gothic fantasy of the lovingly educated heroine comes together, as it so often did before Shelley, with the sense of women's exclusion from the mysteries of knowledge and with an image of women's fear that to seek knowledge, and to make oneself known by speaking, may themselves be monstrous.

In Brontë, the female impulse to transcendence is presented in all its ambiguity, as a counterpart to the pull toward immanence that draws Cathy into the closed world of domestic peace at Thrushcross Grange. In Cathy's passage from the wild, lawless, Gothic childhood paradise of Wuthering Heights to the peaceful domestic asylum of the Grange, Emily Brontë reverses the conventions of sentimental women's Gothic. For it is at the Grange that Cathy has the experience Adeline fears in the haunted chamber of Radcliffe's *The Romance of the Forest,* the experience of looking into the mirror and seeing a face other than her own. This face, in Brontë's version of the Gothic, is an image of the hideous transformation wrought in Cathy by domestic confinement.[54] Against this confinement of marriage to Edgar, Cathy has only the defense of further self-enclosure, shutting her husband out of the private nightmare in which she ends her life in a fever of transcendent longing, begging that the windows be opened.

Finally, this perspective on women's Gothic reveals some interesting aspects of Gilman's "The Yellow Wallpaper," published almost exactly a century after the romances that made Radcliffe famous and clearly a commentary on the hidden meanings of the long female literary tradition that followed them. In fact, "The Yellow Wallpaper" could almost be an allegory of the way the female Gothicist uses mystery to mediate between her anger at domestic ideology and her need to believe in it. For the narrator, a woman excluded from the mysteries of masculine knowledge ("I am a doctor dear," her husband says, "and I know" [23]), compensates by making her own wallpaper, symbol of her domestic confinement, into a mystery that she must then decipher. Her obsessive concentration on the wallpaper is both a desperate attempt to validate the ideology that limits women's proper sphere of knowledge to the mysteries of interior decorating and a way for her to inscribe her own mystery—the angry, Hidden Other Woman inside her—on the walls of her domestic prison.[55] Ironically, what her husband thinks he "knows" is his wife; her increasing sense that she is the guardian of a deep secret that "nobody knows but me" (22)—a treasure of self-knowledge she must hoard with the greatest care—marks her increasing awareness that her husband's so-called knowledge of her has mystified her even in her own eyes. It is her final triumph to force this supposed expert on feminine psychology to confront directly, and literally, the fact that her life is really a locked room to him:

a room to which only the imprisoned woman herself can provide the key. At the end she assaults the male rationalist with the revelation that this house is haunted by a mystery—an idea he scoffed at earlier—and that this mystery is his own wife. The husband's response to the Gothic vision with which the woman writer has confronted him, however, is to become unconscious—as unconscious as male readers in Gilman's day seem to have been of the real secret she was revealing.[56] And the narrator, crawling triumphantly over his inert form, is still defeated by that unconsciousness: still trapped in repetition, as she goes around and around the "circle of herself."

6

Gothic Romance and Women's Reality in *Jane Eyre*

"If I were to marry you, you would kill me. You are killing me now."

His lips and cheeks turned white—quite white.

"I should kill you—I am killing you?" Your words are such as ought not to be used: violent, unfeminine, and untrue. They betray an unfortunate state of mind: they merit severe reproof. . . .

JANE EYRE AND ST. JOHN RIVERS (438)

The nineteenth-century writer who gave most audacious expression to the latent, subversive message of women's Gothic, and to the anger it implied, was Charlotte Brontë. Because *Jane Eyre* itself became a prototype for so much later women's Gothic and perhaps because *Villette* did not, the subtlety of Brontë's transformation of the genre in those two works has never received the attention it deserves. This extraordinary transformation develops the submerged meanings of the genre through an interlocking treatment of the themes of self-defense, knowledge, repetition, and transcendence. By this means, *Jane Eyre* and *Villette* become both readings and reworkings of women's Gothic, using the genre to consider the problems of the boundaries of the self as an aspect of women's special psychological, social, and moral dilemmas. The result is a conflation of realism and romance that asserts the identity of ordinary women's lives and the Gothic nightmare and explores the problem of the self and its boundaries specifically in the context of the modes of transcendence available to women.

When we first meet Jane Eyre, she is an alien in a world determined both to set her apart and to intrude on her. The result is the double obsession that Yeazell describes as a key to Jane's psychic development throughout the novel: "two central longings—to be independent and to be loved" (129). The Reeds perceive her as perversely inaccessible: a little girl with too much "cover" (44), whose true nature ought to be found out. In response to their prying, she retreats behind barriers and longs for escape, but she also suffers, ironically, from a desire to make herself known: to end her radical separation from a world incapable of understanding her. Thus the book opens with the heroine "shrined in double retirement" (39) behind a curtain, protecting herself from her "young master" (44) John and meditating, with longing and horror, on pictures of extreme isolation: Bewick's images of solitude, persecution, melancholy, and death.

> "[T]he solitary rocks and promontories" . . . "the vast sweep of the Arctic Zone, and those forlorn regions of dreary space—that reservoir of frost and snow, where firm fields of ice . . . concentre the multiplied rigours of extreme cold". . . . death-white realms. . . . the rock standing up alone in a sea of billow and spray . . . the broken boat stranded on a desolate coast; . . . the cold and ghastly moon glancing through bars of cloud at a wreck just sinking . . . the quite solitary churchyard . . . girdled by a broken wall. . . . two ships becalmed on a torpid sea, I believed . . . marine phantoms. The fiend pinning down the thief's pack behind him . . . an object of terror . . . the black, horned thing seated aloof on a rock, surveying a distant crowd surrounding a gallows. (40)

This symbolic catalogue is Brontë's version of an old Gothic convention: the series of prophetic images that, in the form of a dream, sometimes prefigure the horrors in store for the Gothic protagonist. These images set forth the perils to which Jane is already subject and will be subject throughout the book. But paradoxically, they also offer release from her restricted world—escape, through seclusion, into wide spaces, distant lands. Jane's enthusiasm for such pictures reveals her imagination to be energetic, with an outward impulse toward the wild and distant and sublime. But the pictures themselves reveal the dangers to which such an imagination is peculiarly subject in the everyday world Jane inhabits. They evoke the perils of being alone and cut off ("solitary . . . alone . . . stranded on a desolate coast . . . quite solitary"); imprisoned ("the cold and ghastly moon glancing through bars"); pursued ("the fiend behind him"); haunted ("marine phantoms"). In the image of the gallows is the peril of being isolated and misjudged—"always accused, forever condemned" (46), as she describes herself later. And there is another peril, too: the danger of being "becalmed" like the ships "on a torpid sea."

This inclusion of terrible calm in the catalogue of horrors to which the heroine may fall prey—as a horror equal to those of isolation, haunting, pursuit, imprisonment, condemnation, death—represents the insight central to Brontë's reading of the Gothic: that Gothic romance paints, in extraordinary forms, the deadliest but most ordinary peril of a woman's life. Opposed to that peril always is the activity, energy, "exercise" of human faculties that expand the heart "with life" (141) and, throughout the book, form the center of Jane Eyre's dream of transcendence. Emerson's chief article of faith could serve as the motto for all of Brontë's novels: "The one thing in the world, of value, is the active soul" ("American Scholar" 68).

The paradoxical exercise of Jane's "active soul" in the contemplation of the perils to which it is subject leads inevitably to disaster: John's intrusion on her painful and desirable isolation, his suspicion of her private self ("What were you doing behind the curtain?"), her violent physical self-defense against this "tyrant" and "murderer" (43), and Mrs. Reed's attempt to calm Jane forcibly by confining her to the Red Room. This confinement is a more extreme version of being shut away behind the curtain: in a family where the mother attempts to draw a "line of separation" (59) between Jane and the other children, Jane both desires self-enclosure for protection and suffers from the terrors of being "force[d] deeply into herself" (Gilbert and Gubar 340), confined in her own nightmarish interior.

The place of her confinement is the deserted suite, complete with secret drawer, old parchments, and miniature. In Gothic romance such places are secret repositories of identity, where the truth about the heroine, her family history, and her rightful place in the social hierarchy is hidden away. Brontë uses this convention to establish, ironically, Jane's lack of a family, her lack of place in the social hierarchy, and the resulting paradox that her identity is at once alien to her world and shaped by that world into a form alien to her. For the Red Room is, in two senses, an external image of Jane's own passionate interior. Imprisoned there alone, she encounters a strange spiritlike creature, "gazing at me with a white face and arms specking the gloom, and glittering eyes of fear moving where all else was still. . . ." (46). This fearfully alien thing is her own fearful self, a self in great part created by Mrs. Reed's tyranny: "What a miserable little poltroon had fear, engendered of unjust punishment, made of me in those days!" (63). Showalter identifies the Red Room, "with its deadly and bloody connotations, its Freudian wealth of secret compartments, wardrobes, drawers, and jewel chest," as "a paradigm of female inner space" (114–15)—Jane's true self, in other words. But it also resembles the exterior world as Jane perceives it: "[T]he red-room, stately, chilly, swathed in rich crimson, with a great white bed and an easy chair 'like a pale throne' looming out of the scarlet darkness, perfectly represents [Jane's] vision of the society in which she is trapped . . ." (Gilbert and Gubar 340). In fact, this place is an image both of the external world that oppresses Jane with its alien rule (the stately room, the throne) and her most private inner life as that world has colored it. As Kinkead-Weekes says of the red-and-white color scheme, "The life of the heart in this prison seems to present only a choice between frozen wintriness and red passion" ("Place of Love" 81). Gateshead both takes the heart prisoner and makes it a prison by defining its only realities as extremes of ice and fire. Here the self is unrecognizably Other not just because Jane has yet to come to terms with her own depths but because something genuinely Other than the self—a force of external tyranny—has helped to define it and indeed to constitute it.

Thus from the beginning, Jane's perils of the night are neither exclusively internal nor external but identified doubly with a repressed self and an external oppressive Other. The "self behind the self concealed" is a threat, but its alien aspect is in part created by another, external threat. Jane must defend herself against interior perils, but also against an exterior force of oppression that makes her particularly susceptible to those perils and in important ways determines their form. The psychological insight here is developed more fully later, in the complexities of Bertha's relation to the hidden selves of both Rochester and Jane and still later in more refined form in *Villette,* in which a conflation of novel and romance identifies the inhabitants of the public world outside Lucy with the allegorical figures of her private psychomachia as that public world has shaped it.

Against Mrs. Reed, responsible for her confinement, Jane defends herself in the first of several incidents that associate saying "I" with self-defense and egress: "Ere I had finished this reply, my soul began to expand, to exult, with the strangest sense of freedom, of triumph, I ever felt. It seemed as if an invisible bond had burst, and that I had struggled out into unhoped-for liberty" (69). It is not surprising that Jane should have such a sensation of liberty through speaking—through the act of forcing her world for once to know her as she is—for Mrs. Reed is particularly concerned with regulating her self-expression: "[U]ntil you can speak pleasantly, remain silent" (39); "Silence! this violence is almost repulsive" (49). Jane's defiant verbal act in the face of the compulsion to remain silent is described in images of power, energy, expansion, escape, and bursting bounds: all connected throughout the novel with acts of self-defense. But this transcendence through "fierce speaking" (70) turns out to be only an illusion: "A ridge of lighted heath . . . would have been a great emblem of my mind when I accused and menaced Mrs. Reed; the same ridge, black and blasted after the flames are dead, would have represented as meetly my subsequent condition, when half an hour's silence and reflection had shown me the madness of my conduct . . . " (69–70).

At Lowood Jane encounters another attitude toward both speaking and self-defense. To Helen Burns she explains her ideas on the proper response to oppression: "When we are struck at without a reason, we should strike back again very hard . . . so hard as to teach the person who struck us never to do it again" (90). Helen replies that this is the view of "a little untaught girl" (90). Her own philosophy links the complete rejection of self-defense to a vision of complete transcendence—beyond the grave. "If we were dying in pain and shame, if scorn smote us on all sides, and hatred crushed us, angels see our tortures, recognize our innocence . . . and God waits only a separation of spirit from flesh to crown us with a full reward" (101). Helen herself is characterized by a capacity not to speak fiercely against unjust accusation, indeed not to speak at all: "Burns made no answer: I wondered at her silence. 'Why,' thought I, 'does she not explain . . . ?' " (86). In Helen's philosophy what matters is not whether one is rightly known on earth; that the angels "recognize our innocence" is enough. For her, self-vindication is not necessary in the face of mere earthly tyranny. Her mentor Miss Temple is similarly associated with verbal restraint, responding to Brocklehurst's accusations by becoming colder and harder in deathly silence. "Miss Temple had always something . . . of refined propriety in her language, which precluded deviation into the ardent, the excited, the eager . . ." (104).

At Gateshead, Jane discovered that the transcendence associated with fiery speech was illusion; at Lowood she is drawn to a view of transcendence associated with restraint rather than passion, ice rather than fire, self-containment rather than self-justification. Helen and Miss Temple are clearly admirable figures, and yet the version of escape they offer proves, for Jane, to be one with unbearable confinement. She comes to see the place where she learned this philosophy as "prison grounds, exile limits" and finds herself at a window looking out, longing for escape beyond the "boundary of rock and heath," for "liberty . . . liberty . . . liberty" (117). Miss Temple has played the role of the special mentor who educates the Gothic heroine in a bounded world; the limitations of that education are implied in Jane's sudden realization as she looks out her window "that the real world was wide, and that a varied field of hopes and fears, of sensations and excitements, awaited those who had courage to go forth into its expanse, to seek real knowledge of life amidst its perils" (116). "School rules, school duties, school habits and notions, and voices, and faces, and phrases, and costumes, and preferences, and antipathies: such was what I knew of existence," she says. "And now I felt that it was not enough" (117).

Both the feeling that the heroine's limited sphere of knowledge is "not enough" and even the suspicion that the beloved educator's system of education was somehow bound up with a system of ignorance infuse women's Gothic, but never, before *Jane Eyre,* were they expressed so bluntly. Even the picture of the heroine longing for "real knowledge of the world" is a departure from women's Gothic: not a departure from what their narratives actually represent—"the female quest for experience" (Roberts 105), the lure of "traveling heroinism" (Moers Chap. 7)— but a departure from their overt ideology, which portrays heroines propelled by external forces into a confrontation with experience but rarely choosing it deliberately over the innocence of their first bounded world.[1] Characteristically, Charlotte Brontë reworks Gothic romance to bring to the surface its representation of reality. Jane is harassed not by repeated encroachments on her person, but by the deadly, mundane iteration of "school rules, school duties, school habits." Accordingly, Brontë's version here of the room with a view and the heroine's flight of imagination ends not with rapturous romantic expansion into spiritual ecstasy but with a plunge to earth and common sense. Liberty, perhaps, is too much to hope for. Jane opts for "a new servitude," and where the Gothic heroine's longings for egress would have found expression in an improvised ode to nature or to melancholy, hers find expression in a newspaper advertisement: "A young lady accustomed to tuition is desirous of meeting with a situation in a private family where the children are under fourteen" (118–19).

This act of self-expression, at once mundane and bold, brings Jane to Thornfield. Here the heart of the Gothic plot is discovered to the reader through a sequence of related scenes, all reworkings of Gothic set pieces: the pause at the threshold, the meeting with the housekeeper, the tour of the deserted wing, the panoramic view from confinement, the encounters with the man of mystery and the Evil Other Woman, the intrusion in the heroine's room by night, the narrow escape from the villain's domain, the expulsion from Eden. The key to Brontë's changes in all of these set pieces is the way her rendering of the Gothic conflates realism and romance to suggest the true meaning of women's Gothic. The technique is best illustrated in the most original of these scenes, in which Jane, returning from the walk on which she has met Rochester (but without knowing it was he), hesitates before entering the gloomy house from which her outing was a temporary escape.

> I did not like re-entering Thornfield. To pass its threshold was to return to stagnation; to cross the silent hall, to ascend the darksome staircase, to seek my lonely little room, and then to meet tranquil Mrs Fairfax, and spend the long winter evening with her, and her only, was to quell wholly the faint excitement wakened by my walk—to slip again over my faculties the viewless fetters of a uniform and too still existence; of an existence whose very privileges of security and ease I was becoming incapable of appreciating. . . . I lingered at the gates; I lingered on the lawn; I paced backwards and forwards on the pavement: the shutters of the glass door were closed; I could not see into the interior; and both my eyes and spirit seemed drawn from the gloomy house—from the gray hollow filled with rayless cells, as it appeared to me—to that sky expanded before me—a blue sea absolved from taint of cloud; the moon ascending it in solemn march, her orb seeming to look up as she left the hilltops, from behind which she had come, far and farther below her, and aspired to the zenith, midnight dark in its fathomless depth and measureless distance; and for those trembling stars that followed her course, they made my heart tremble, my veins glow when I viewed them. Little things recall us to earth: the clock struck in the hall; that sufficed. I turned from moon and stars, opened a side-door, and went in. (147–48)

This unusual reworking of the heroine's pause at the threshold reveals much, both in itself and in connection with other such scenes, about how Charlotte Brontë read the latent content, and the latent potential, of Gothic romance. There is, first, the double status of the house as exotic Gothic mansion and ordinary, boring domestic space—and the fact that the Gothic imagery functions as a description of the boredom rather than a contrast to it. This double view of the house goes back to Jane's arrival at Thornfield when she was given the usual tours of the Gothic mansion, beginning on the first night with the "eerie impression" created by a "dark and spacious" staircase, a "high latticed" window, and a "long, cold gallery" suggestive of "a church rather than a house." Through the "chill and vault-like air" of the stairs and gallery, "suggesting cheerless ideas of space and solitude," Jane passed to her room—not, however, a vast, gloomy room full of dimly-perceived dangers but a room "of small dimensions, and furnished in ordinary modern style," a welcome "safe haven" from the outside world of her journey (129).

The mixture of everyday realism and Gothic atmosphere here means that from the beginning of Jane's stay at Thornfield the usual boundary in Gothic romance between the everyday world and the oneiric world—a boundary ordinarily equated with the Gothic threshold itself—is blurred. And this blurring applies both to the house and to the events that occur there. Jane begins her stay at Thornfield, for example, by confusing Mrs. Fairfax, who is merely the keeper of the house, with its owner. The novelty of this confusion is particularly striking in view of the iconography of class distinctions in the romance of Radcliffe and most of her imitators. For all the misinterpretations to which Gothic heroines are prey, they are not subject to the delusion that the aged retainer is the mistress of the house. In a sense, however, this first misreading is correct: in terms of both Jane's own initial experience of Thornfield and the perils it represents for her, Thornfield is the domain of a housekeeper and of housekeeping. In Gothic romance, housekeepers are often the only people looking after an old deserted mansion, but the mansion itself is never described preeminently as a housekeeper's domain. Thornfield as Jane first experiences it, however, is such a place. The inmates on whom the narrative focuses are women, and the primary activities of this female world are, as far as Jane can see, raising a child and running an ordinary household.

Such a world has its own horrors, as de Beauvoir points out in her comparison of "housework, with its endless repetition," with the torture of Sisyphus (504). For de Beauvoir, repetition is an aspect of *immanence,* her term for the state of self-enclosure and stagnation that is the opposite of self-transcendence through outward-directed "projects." That Jane herself associates her work at Thornfield with exactly this kind of repetition and stagnation is evident in Charlotte Brontë's version of another Gothic set piece: the scene in which the heroine looks out of her prison castle toward the possibility of transcendence. In earlier Gothic romance, that transcendence is represented, or even attained, in the heroine's exalted apprehension of sublime Nature. Thus Ellena di Rosalba climbed to her tower room and looked out over the mountains, feeling the greatness of God and the smallness of her oppressors (*The Italian* 90–91). In *Jane Eyre,* the heroine climbs to the battlements of Thornfield and looks out, longing for a "power of vision which might overpass" the limits of her narrow life (140). The object of Jane's transcendent longings here, however, is touchingly ordinary, just as it was in the similar scene at Lowood. There she wished for more "real knowledge of life" (116); at Thornfield she yearns for "the busy world, towns, regions full of life I had heard of but never seen . . . more of practical experience than I possessed; more of intercourse with my kind, of acquaintance with variety of character . . ." (140–41). In retrospect, Jane the narrator comments on these longings:

> Who blames me? Many, no doubt; and I shall be called discontented. I could not help it; restlessness was in my nature; it agitated me to pain sometimes. . . . It is in vain to say human beings ought to be satisfied with tranquility: they must have action; and they will make it if they cannot find it. Millions are condemned to a stiller doom than mine, and millions are in silent revolt against their lot. Nobody knows how many rebellions besides political rebellions ferment in the masses of life which people earth. Women are supposed to be very calm generally: but women feel just as men feel; they need exercise for their faculties, and a field for their efforts as much as their brothers do; they suffer from too rigid a restraint, too absolute a stagnation, precisely as men would suffer; and it is narrow-minded in their more privileged fellow-creatures to say that they ought to confine themselves to making puddings and knitting stockings, to playing on the piano and embroidering bags. (141)

These meditations on the lot of women are especially interesting in the context of Gothic romance, because they defend Jane's longing for transcendence by suggesting the banal truths hidden in women's Gothic all along: that most women are "confined"—not to a dungeon but to "making puddings and knitting stockings"—and that they are victims of repetition—not because specters haunt them night after night but because they do the same things day after day. The passage suggests also that women suffer silently and in secret—not because no one knows in what castle or convent or dungeon they have been hidden away, but because no one knows the restlessness hidden beneath their apparent calm. Indeed, as Jane looks out from the battlements, there rages just beneath her a hidden life even she herself does not know, the as-yet unsuspected life of the madwoman.

Jane encountered hints of this life on her tour of the deserted wing, a place where "no one ever sleeps" (137) anymore, complete with "hush" and "gloom"; the "imperfect light" of "narrow casements"; old tapestries that "would have looked strange, indeed, by the pallid gleam of moonlight"; decaying embroideries wrought by those whose fingers now are "coffin dust." The tour led up to the sunlit battlements. Coming down again into this darker world, Jane had to "grope" her way into the passage "narrow, low, and dim," lined with "small black doors all shut" like the doors "in Bluebeard's castle." From one of these identical doors a strange laugh emanated, repeated horribly in an echo seeming to come from all of them (138). But again the Gothic realm became "ordinary" and "modern" (129) with the emergence of the apparent source of the laugh: Grace Poole. "[A]ny apparition less romantic or less ghostly could scarcely be conceived" (138).

This scene marks the beginning of Grace Poole's role as interface between the routine and the romantic, the boredom of repetition in women's ordinary lives and the Gothic nightmare of the Bluebeard's doors and reiterated laugh. In her association with the madwoman, the taciturn Grace Poole is the very type of the duality of outer calm and inner restlessness. Her name suggests a smaller, bounded version of the "torpid sea" on which Jane feared being "becalmed" and the ironic assumptions that such calm is both the chief grace of women and a chief sign of God's grace to them. (One thinks of Father Anthony's doctrine that Providence has "graciously rescued" the young women from "a terrible large place called the world.") Her job consists of endless solitary sewing, "as companionless as a prisoner in his dungeon" (194), while she keeps stolid watch over the madwoman whose restlessness may erupt into violence at any moment. Once a day she comes out to "glide along the gallery": a romantic activity associated with ghosts, but one that Grace performs in a most unghostly way, stopping in the "topsy-turvy" rooms to comment on "the proper way to polish a grate, or clean a marble mantlepiece, or take stains from papered walls" (194). That this boring woman is for a long time perceived by Jane Eyre to be the madwoman she guards, to be a "living enigma . . . mystery of mysteries" (232), hints at their essential identity. As Gilbert and Gubar say, it is "almost as if, with her pint of porter, her 'staid and taciturn' demeanor, she were the madwoman's public representative" (350). Although Jane is wrong literally, symbolically she is right. Grace is an emblem of those ordinary women who do, in fact, guard silently a mystery "nobody knows": their true feelings. Herself "a person of few words" (142), with "miraculous self-possession" (185), Grace is the supposedly calm and uncomplaining woman "confined" to sewing, and Bertha is the carefully guarded inner nature of such women, locked away but still violently and angrily alive. Appropriately, one of Grace's chief duties is to keep Bertha from speaking "I" in her distorted way: "Too much noise, Grace," calls Mrs. Fairfax after the laugh: "Remember directions!" (139).

Thus it is natural that at the end of the passage describing Jane's visits to look out from the battlements in secret discontent with her domestic routine, Grace Poole—in her double aspect as both the Hidden Woman and the woman who hides her—should put in an appearance: "When thus alone, I not unfrequently heard Grace Poole's laugh: the same peal, the same low, slow ha! ha! which, when first heard, had thrilled me: I heard, too, her eccentric murmurs; stranger than her laugh. . . . Sometimes I saw her: she would come out of her room with a basin, or a plate, or a tray in her hand, go down to the kitchen, and shortly return generally (oh, romantic reader, forgive me for telling the plain truth!) bearing a pot of porter" (141–42). Heilman reads such intrusions of realism on romance in Charlotte Brontë's work as "infusion[s] of the 'anti-Gothic' " functioning to achieve a "partial sterilization of banal Gothic by dry factuality and humor" (123). The function of these "infusions," however, is more complex. First, the question of the relation of romance and realism in *Jane Eyre* is bound up with the question of their relation in Gothic fiction in general. When the copresence of realism and romance in the Gothic is discussed, one or the other, or the copresence itself, tends to be regarded as some kind of failing or incongruence. Thus Haggerty sees "a confusion of intention" in the clash of realism and romance in Gothic writers: "We find ourselves laughing again and again at the Gothic novel. Whether Walpole's ghost marches 'sedately,' Radcliffe's greatest horror turns out to be a waxen image, Lewis muses over the social implications of the Inquisition, or Maturin preaches fiscal responsibility, we experience a confusion of intention which results in a sacrifice of Gothic intensity for the sake of more 'realistic' narrative concerns" (381). In Maturin and Lewis, Haggerty sees a move toward a way of

overcoming the dichotomy which Walpole first recognized as inevitable in Gothic fiction. Objective and subjective states blend in the depths of a perceiving consciousness in tales such as theirs, and, as a result, the limits of the real can be extended to include detail of a kind that is inadmissible in objective narrative. Moreover, subjective reality begins to achieve a kind of objective force in these works: metaphorical language attains the representational power of the metonymical, and the metonymical becomes understood as metaphor. (391)

The final effect of such discussions is to valorize the way Gothicists, and later writers in the Gothic tradition, extended the territory of the "real" to include the "psychological realism" that Ewbank praises as Charlotte Brontë's most successful fusion of "her two kinds of truth, realism and poetry" (178). While the most successful aspect of the Gothic romance may well have been its insistence on the reality of the irrational, nonetheless it is disturbing that the social reality Maturin and Godwin were presenting in their Gothic novel-romances (or, in Brontë's case, a novel-romance that made use of the Gothic) somehow vanishes in these final summings up of the writers' achievements, just as, conversely, the ghostly nun is all too shadowy a presence in Eagleton's very "social" reading of *Villette*. Maturin's lectures on "fiscal responsibility" may be ineptly funny, but it is important to acknowledge that poverty, in all its brutal reality, is a central subject of his Gothic tale. The same is true of *Pierre,* a romance in which Lucy Tartan is the hero's "good angel" (437) and a novel in which, desperate to stave off poverty, she sells portraits for $1.75 (461). The conjunction of sordid financial detail with meta- physics reveals that the psychological realism of these writers, achieved through symbol and dream, is inextricably woven into a social context and that the social content is set in the context of private nightmare.

Both contexts are interrelated and inseparable parts of a whole.[2] It was Brontë's special achievement to recognize the true meaning of that whole in women's Gothic, in which the social context of the private nightmares had traditionally been displaced or disguised. Whereas in one sense the "infusions" Heilman refers to do "undercut" the Gothic (Heilman 120), in another they bring to the surface its true, and "real," subjects, the mundane details of women's ordinary lives. These details are themselves, in all their "dry factuality," responsible for the kind of "feeling that is without status in the ordinary world of the novel" (121) and that Heilman identifies with Brontë's "new Gothic." Similarly, when Hook says, "There is much in *Jane Eyre* that is Gothic, romantic, extravagant. . . . But there is an equally strong awareness of the 'plain and homely,' of the realities of pain and suffering in the most ordinary contexts of life" (142), the two phenomena he is describing are in fact the same; Charlotte Brontë's romantic, extravagant Gothic is bound up with, and indeed expresses, her awareness of the "realities of pain and suffering" in their "most ordinary contexts."[3]

"Oh, romantic reader, forgive me for telling the plain truth!" In retro- spect the narrator's apology is ironic, since the real mystery behind Grace Poole turns out to be anything but prosaic. And on the other hand, the passage just before this—the description of ordinary women's hidden an- ger at being "confined" to domestic tasks—asserts that Gothic romance *is* the "plain truth": just as the stolid seamstress is the madwoman and, at one level, the exotic Bertha is plain Jane.[4] This overt identification of the oneiric world of Gothic inner space with the everyday world of women's domestic interiors reveals Brontë's perception of the hidden life buried in all female Gothic romance: an insight central to every aspect of her Gothic vision.

At the core of that vision is the perception, introduced in the images from Bewick, that being "becalmed" is a source of Gothic horror. At the threshold of the Gothic domain, most heroines tremble in fear of they know not what, feel unaccountable dread, go cold with a sense of unimaginable doom. It is characteristic of Charlotte Brontë's rendering of Gothic terrors that her heroine should be overcome, not by nameless sensations of fear and trembling, but by a sharp, specific sense of her peril: the prospect of boredom. Jane's pause at the threshold after her outing has to do not with any gloomy forebodings of "vice and violence" but with a fear of the "viewless fetters of a uniform and too still existence" (147). For her the "gloomy house" with its "rayless cells" (148) is not the realm of a tyrant-outlaw but of "tranquil Mrs. Fairfax," and Jane knows that by crossing the threshold she will be subject to the darkness, repetition, and confinement not of a terrible villain but of women's work. The "rayless cells" and the "viewless fetters" are sources of dread because they represent the lack of a "power of vision" that would connect Jane with wider knowledge, more varied activity, a larger world.

This "gloomy" place of "confinement" to making puddings and knitting stockings has also been presented as a Gothic mansion complete with battlements, decaying embroideries, a row of doors reminiscent of Bluebeard's castle, and mysterious sounds echoing through the dim, deserted wing. But the mysterious sounds occurred at high noon; at the end of the vaultlike hall the heroine's room was small and modern; although the tapestries would have been "strange, indeed, by the pallid gleam of moonlight" (137), that is not when the heroine saw them. The constant superimposition of realism on Gothic romance equates the darkest, eeriest Gothic mystery with the dullest version of an ordinary woman's life. That life is what Jane seeks to evade by lingering at Rochester's door. Her pause there, significantly, itself marks a repetition she would like to evade: "I did not like re-entering Thornfield." Like many Gothic heroines, she has effected a temporary escape from her prison only to find herself brought back to it again. "Brought," however, is not quite right; Jane approaches the house herself, alone, and the compulsion to reenter it—to commit the act of repetition that will again subject her to the horrors of repetition the house embodies—is a compulsion produced by external circumstances, but internalized as a sense of duty. Jane must earn a living, and Thornfield is her place of employment. "Little things recall us to earth" (148): the heroine hears not the sonorous tolling of the castle bell but a clock in the hall, announcing no ghostly adventure but the necessity for being realistic. Like every Gothic heroine on the threshold, she finds she has no choice but to enter. She enters, however, not because a Montoni compels her into his strange oneiric realm set apart from all the reality she knows but because this Gothic interior is her workaday world.

Ironically, Jane's conception of the perils she faces proves, as does her assumption that Thornfield belongs to Mrs. Fairfax and that Grace Poole is Bertha, to be both completely mistaken and exactly right. Jane hesitates to go in, because her adventure outside with the mysterious rider on the bridge offered an excitement she would be loath to end by closing herself up again in a "rayless" cell. However, the man she associates with escape to the world outside is now inside, master of the "gloomy" mansion she so dreads. As they become acquainted, he will "open" to Jane the world beyond her, "glimpses of its scenes and ways" (177). Her meditations on the boredom Thornfield represents are thus in one sense dramatic irony: it is not confinement and stagnation Jane is about to encounter, but exercise for her faculties; the prospect of a "heart . . . expanded . . . with life" (141). Her impending friendship with Rochester will offer an escape from the humdrum life she hates, because Rochester knows, and will share with her, the outside world she so longs to know. In another sense, however, that encounter will subject her more fully than before to the Gothic perils of fetters, darkness, and confinement in exactly the form in which she has already discerned them: the form of domestic immanence. For the angry woman hidden away at the heart of this boring domestic world is Rochester's wife, and there are strong suggestions in the sequences that follow that his attempt to commit the repetition that is bigamy may indeed make Jane his wife—condemn her to repeat Bertha's experience. Association with Rochester makes Jane susceptible to confinement in the same realm Bertha inhabits. A point has been made in Jane's tour of the house that there is more than one little door in the upper story, as if Thornfield were "some Bluebeard's castle" (138) and Bertha's echoing laugh sounded from these rooms, too.

The allusion to Bluebeard suggests that marriage may be mortal. The passages on the restlessness hidden away behind women's calm suggest that the kind of death most fearful to Jane would be the burial, in a too-limited domestic world, of her considerable energies. Thus it is significant that the image of transcendence that tempts Jane as she paces outside the door of Thornfield, on the eve of her relationship with Rochester, is a traditional image of virginity, the moon. Jane watches the moon, personified as a woman, rise "to the zenith, midnight dark in its fathomless depth and measureless distance" (148)—a symbolic alternative to reentering the claustrophobic dark of Thornfield. Her exultant sympathetic response shows that like Emily Brontë's Catherine, she has longings to be "incomparably beyond and above," free of all earthly ties, drawn outward into infinity. But despite her powerful imagery of solitary escape, Charlotte Brontë, unlike her sister, always ends by defining the highest metaphysical longings in deeply social terms. That is why, as her heroine looks out beyond the Gothic mansion, she longs for, instead of expansion into the infinity of nature or God, a little more knowledge of the "busy world, towns, regions full of life I had heard of but never seen . . . more of intercourse with my kind, of acquaintance with variety of character" (140). When Rochester proves himself capable of "open[ing]" this wider world to her, providing the longed-for "power of vision" (140) through the "new pictures he portray[s]" (177), Jane responds with passion. Her language reveals how profoundly transcendence for her involves human ties: "I love Thornfield: I love it, because I have lived in it a full and delightful life—momentarily at least. I have not been trampled on. I have not been petrified. I have not been buried with inferior minds, and excluded from every glimpse of communion with what is bright and energetic and high. I have talked, face to face, with what I reverence, with what I delight in—with an original, a vigorous, an expanded mind. I have known you, Mr Rochester . . . " (281).

"Communion" with Rochester's "expanded mind," in other words, is Jane's hope of rescue from the Gothic perils of ordinary life as she experienced it in Rochester's house before meeting him: calm and stagnation ("I have not been petrified . . . excluded from . . . what is energetic"), burial alive ("I have not been buried with inferior minds"), darkness ("I have not been . . . excluded from every glimpse of communion with what is bright . . ."), lack of knowledge in the sense of intellectual stimulation ("I have talked, face to face, with an original . . . mind"), lack of knowledge in the sense of social relations ("I have known you, Mr Rochester . . .").

The implicit view of Rochester as Jane's means of transcendence here is made explicit in the climax to which the passage builds up:

"Do you think, because I am poor, obscure, plain, and little, I am soulless and heartless? You think wrong!—I have as much soul as you—and full as much heart! And if God had gifted me with some beauty and much wealth,

I should have made it as hard for you to leave me, as it is now for me to leave you. I am not talking to you now through the medium of custom, conventionalities, nor even of mortal flesh: it is my spirit that addresses your spirit; just as if both had passed through the grave, and we stood at God's feet, equal—as we are!" (281)

Helen Burns had imagined perfect transcendence in another world, after death. Here Jane envisions, and enacts, another kind of overpassing of limits: perfect communication in this human world, without any medium, as if in the perfect equality of the communion of saints before God. Unlike Helen's version of transcendence, linked to a rejection of the necessity for speaking "I," this mode of transcendence is one with Jane's ability fully to make herself known, without the barriers of "custom, conventionalities, even mortal flesh"—as if she and Rochester had indeed attained that final revelation alluded to in the reference to 1 Cor. 13: "For now we see through a glass, darkly; but then face to face: now I know in part; but then I shall know even as I am also known."

But it is in this world, and for a human relationship, that Jane makes such lofty claims. And although she speaks at this one moment with remarkable freedom, the relationship in general does not yet justify the religious imagery she uses to describe her speech. For Jane does not in fact know Rochester even as she is also known;[5] he is a version of the Gothic man of mystery, who speaks in riddles and alludes obscurely to some secret source of grief. Rochester indulges in what Jane calls "discourse which [is] all darkness to me" (169), forcing her to say, "I don't understand you at all" (168). He values her as a "confidante" (174); yet he also values and promotes her ignorance: her innocence of the "mysteries" beyond the "porch of life" she has not yet "passed" (167).

Once again a Gothic heroine finds herself in an "educational idyll" in which the supposed education is somehow part of an effort to keep her in the dark. Brontë reveals her understanding of earlier Gothic by perceiving that the bounded, sunlit pastoral of which Thornfield is the "centre" (138) is somehow the same as the Gothic prison. Indeed, the symbolic connection is made in the description of Jane's first visit to the leads. Having looked out over the "bright and velvet lawn . . . the field, wide as a park . . . the tranquil hills, all reposing in the autumn day's sun; the horizon bounded by a propitious sky, azure, marbled with pearly white. . . . that sunlit scene of grove, pasture, and green hill" (137–38)—a scene that establishes Thornfield as a vantage point for sight—Jane is temporarily blinded by the sunshine (appropriately, the false illumination is blinding) as she gropes her way back down into the darkness of the real Thornfield: the attic, "black as a vault," and below it the third floor where Bertha is hidden in a windowless dungeon.

Rochester delights both in confiding in and mystifying Jane, and it is his attempt to have it both ways—to know her as her husband without confiding his secret—that ends, temporarily, in disaster. The "web of mystification" (228) in which, disguised as a gypsy, Rochester "involve[s]" her is typical. Throughout the whole scene of their conference in the library—and the whole of their relationship from the first meeting, in which Rochester learns Jane's identity but conceals his, until the final revelation of Bertha's existence—Rochester tries to know more of Jane than he is willing to reveal about himself. Jane, too, can be secretive. The mutual game that she and Rochester are playing is revealed in her retort to the "gypsy": "I came here to inquire, not to confess" (229). Jane unwittingly describes their situation perfectly when, to Rochester's impassioned acknowledgment that they are equal, she responds, with her customary discretion, "Yes, so, sir . . . and yet not so: for you are a married man . . ." (281). Rochester denies that he is "as good as" married to Blanche Ingram, and Jane is overwhelmed: "roused from the nightmare of parting—called to the paradise of union" (284). But the truth is that she was right. Rochester is married, in secret, and he wishes to know Jane without fully acknowledging part of himself—either to himself or to her.

His attitude toward this secret is summed up in his final revelation of it: "[A] nature the most gross, impure, depraved I ever saw, was associated with mine, and called by the law and by society a part of me" (334). And yet the disavowal that this "gross" and lustful being could be "part of me" is belied by his descriptions of his attraction to Bertha in the first place: "I was dazzled, stimulated: my senses were excited" (332); "I married her: gross, grovelling, mole-eyed blockhead that I was!" (333). The syntax itself implies an identity: the direct object, *her,* is followed by a colon and a list of adjectives, the first of which Rochester subsequently uses to describe Bertha and the second of which has previously been used of the beastlike creature that "grovelled, seemingly, on all fours" (321). Only at the end of the sentence are these adjectives established as describing Rochester and not Bertha. Rochester's proposal to Jane is based on the same "mole-eyed" blindness at work in this later self-justification. Thus the scene in which Jane declares her passion for "communion" with Rochester is inevitably followed by a revelation of separation and self-division: the orchard chestnut, riven in two by lightning.

The blasted tree is a characteristic image of the sublime, but in the setting of the orchard ("No nook in the grounds more sheltered and more Eden-like . . ." [276]), it is also an emblem of the Fall. One thinks of Thomas Cole's painting *The Expulsion from Eden,* in which Paradise glows behind Adam and Eve with the golden light of Beauty, and the rugged, stupendous world of the Sublime lies "all before them." As in that painting, Brontë's picture has a certain ambiguity; the shelter of Eden is attractive, but the wild, pent-up forces unleashed by Jane's self-revelation are more compelling in their power. It is as if, once again, Jane had spoken "I" in fire. The effect is desolation, but the act reveals a human energy commensurate with that of the wildest natural forces. Rochester's own association with such energy, and with the transcendence it promises, was expressed in the imagery associated with his first arrival in Jane's world, when his advent transformed what would have been the beautiful into the sublime: "A rude noise broke out . . . which effaced the soft wave-wanderings; as, in a picture, the solid mass of a crag, or the rough boles of a great oak, drawn in dark and strong in the foreground, efface the aerial distance of azure hill, sunny horizon, and blended clouds, where tint melts into tint" (143).

But the sublime in itself is dangerous; furthermore, Charlotte Brontë suggests constantly that what looks like sublime transcendence for the heroine may instead be Gothic nightmare. Rochester's sublime approach, effacing the calm evening scene, is also described in Gothic mode: the sound gets closer and closer; Jane imagines the arrival of a terrible supernatural creature. And only a few paragraphs after the description of Rochester's sharing with Jane his knowledge of realms beyond her ken, "open[ing]" glimpses of the world as she "follow[s] him in thought through the new regions he disclose[s]" (177), the knowledge he will not disclose—the mystery of his own Gothic interior—is "groping" along the gallery outside Jane's door in the dead of night. "The clock, far down in the hall, struck two. Just then it seemed my chamber door was touched. . . . a demonic laugh—low, suppressed, and deep—uttered, as it seemed, at the very keyhole . . ." (178–79). Rochester imparts only the purest treasures of knowledge to Jane: "[H]e liked to open to a mind unacquainted with the world, glimpses of its scenes and ways (I do not mean its corrupt scenes and wicked ways . . .)" (177). But he is also the guardian of a threatening, demonic knowledge he hopes to conceal: "[D]on't turn out a downright Eve on my hands!" he warns Jane at one point (290). Rochester seems to offer transcendence through union with him, but in trying to gain it, Jane risks union with the Gothic perils he also represents.

If women's Gothic romance before Charlotte Brontë suspected that the hero who offered rescue and marriage was in some way the same villain who threatened to trap the heroine in his house forever, Charlotte Brontë's representation of Rochester as both hero and villain, egress and entrapment, brings that hidden identity to the surface. There had been hero-villains before, but in a significantly different sense. Walpole's Manfred draws attention from the real hero, because through his guilt-ridden projects he generates most of the energy in the book. Radcliffe's Schedoni, although the villain, comes almost to seem the hero in the sense of being the male character who compels most attention from the reader, but he is not the hero in the sense of offering the heroine marriage happily ever after; another character fills that role. Frankenstein is a Faustean hero-villain whose ambition represents the highest and basest human capacities. Heathcliff is hero-villain in his double role of sadistic monster and sublime object of desire. Rochester belongs to the same line of descent, but he differs from all these predecessors. He is Gothic hero in that he represents the possibility of the kind of transcendence Charlotte Brontë valued most, a marriage of equals speaking "face to face," sharing their experience of what is "bright and energetic and high" (281). That is, he is a hero in the same sense as Radcliffe's Valancourt is. At the same time, like a Gothic villain, he represents the perils of "immanence," which *Jane Eyre* also associates with marriage. He offers rescue from solitude through domestic communion between a husband and wife; he offers Jane "power of vision," an opportunity to be alive instead of buried, active instead of paralyzed. Jane meets him outside; he knows the "busy worlds, towns" she wants to know; her relationship with him is described in metaphors of vision, openness, expansion, travel, adventure in a sublime landscape. But as "master" of an inside world of "rayless cells" and Bluebeard's doors, he also represents the danger of blindness, confinement, stagnation; the possibility that domestic interiors are places where, as Wollstonecraft protested, women are "immured in their families groping in the dark."

The double role Rochester plays as villain who menaces the heroine with Gothic perils and hero who offers her release from them is part of a complex relationship, throughout the novel, between threats that Jane will be destroyed by being confined and hopes that she will be rescued by enclosure in a "safe haven"; threats that her selfhood will be destroyed by violation of the barriers that define it and hopes that her true self will be fulfilled in the "paradise of union" with someone else. Hence one of the central themes of the book is the necessity for self-defense against the Gothic nightmare masquerading as transcendence: darkness as vision, separateness as unity, violation as communion, repetition as escape, restraint as release.

At Thornfield, the possibility of self-transcendence is confusingly one with threats to the self. The reason for this confusion lies both in the frank equation of the Gothic hero with the Gothic villain and in Brontë's bold approach to the convention of the Gothic heroine's discovery of an Evil Other Woman. Instead of being, like the Other Woman of Radcliffe's Gothic, a consequence of the schizophrenic view that women are either good or bad but not both, Bertha actually represents the dangers of such schizophrenia—the dangers of relationships based on lack of self-knowledge and full mutual knowledge. This woman plays multiple roles in Jane's struggle to defend herself against the perils of the night, for there is more than one way in which she is the "impediment" to the perfect union Jane dreams of with Rochester: a communion of equal—and equally active—souls, knowing fully and being fully known.[6] Bertha's existence makes Rochester a man-of-mystery figure and is thus an impediment to perfect knowledge between him and Jane. A woman whom Rochester married for money and lust rather than love, she is the nightside of Rochester, a thing of darkness he refuses to recognize as "a part of me" but must acknowledge his before his relationship with Jane can be based on the perfect union he pretends to offer. As the hidden meaning of Grace Poole's becalmed and isolated life, Bertha represents the possibility that marriage will not deliver Jane from restlessness but, rather, confine her to it; as the victim of Rochester as Bluebeard, she is the emblem of what Rochester's bigamy would make of Jane. Entering Jane's room in the dead of night to rend her bridal veil, Bertha represents Rochester's potential for violating Jane,[7] but in the same scene she is also the unknown nightside of Jane herself,[8] the figure in the mirror who wears Jane's dress but whose face, distorted with passion, cannot be recognized. Like the little girl whose mind was a burning heath, she speaks "I" in fire: she represents the consequences of having no outlet but violence, a false means of transcendence that Jane has rejected on principle but still endangers her.

Thus, Bertha plays a significantly fuller role than does the Evil Other Woman of most Gothic romance before Charlotte Brontë. As the nightside of both Rochester and Jane, she is both the evil Other as threatening male and the evil Other as self. She is the alien "self behind the self concealed," threatening always to burst out of confinement in a destructive act of self expression. But she stands also for the external alien force that threatens women with confinement (two little rows of black doors . . .), silence ("Too much noise, Grace!"), and violence (intrusion on the bride, the rending of her veil). This double function means that Bertha's nocturnal visit to Jane is a threat to the boundaries of her self from within—a forcing of the barriers of repression—as well as from without.

The complexity is intensified by the identification of the romantic Gothic interior of Thornfield with the all-too-realistic world of domestic stagnation. Symbolically this identification associates Bertha's restlessness with longings that Jane Eyre has identified as normal and legitimate rebellion against enforced calm. Thus Bertha's tendency toward the destructive exercise of her pent-up faculties is strangely linked with those longings for transcendence that express Jane's highest potential. But this link means also that Jane's own longings for "other and more vivid kinds of goodness" beyond the "limit" of her "sequestered" woman's life (141) are dangerously close to Bertha's anger: a fact represented in their literal proximity in the roof scene of Chapter 12. In this scene the conventional picture of the confined Gothic heroine looking out of her casement is broken into two parts: Jane's experience of exalted longings as she looks out beyond her confinement at Thornfield, and Bertha's experience—as yet unknown to Jane, but going on just below her—of animal rage at what is surely her "stiller doom." These two forms of desire are clearly connected—Bertha's "eccentric murmurs . . . uncannily echo the murmurs of *Jane's* imagination" (Gilbert and Gubar 349)—and in their connection is the Gothicist's old suspicion that the way up and the way down are the same. But the relative moral status of these types of desire is carefully distinguished in the physical positions of the two women: Jane's longings are higher; Bertha's are lower.

It is in self-defense against these baser longings and against the external forces that help give them their most monstrous shape that Jane must finally separate herself from Rochester and Thornfield. Before her wedding day, she dreams that Thornfield is "a dreary ruin, the retreat of bats and owls. . . . that of all the stately front nothing remained but a shell-like wall . . . I wandered, on a moonlight night, through the grass-grown enclosure within . . ." (310). She dreams, in other words, the same "dream" presented indirectly through the narrative sequence surrounding Emily's marriage plans in *The Mysteries of Udolpho*—the dream that her bridal home is a Gothic ruin. So it is; and so it would be, were the repetition that Rochester desires allowed to take place.

When the "impediment" to Jane's marriage is announced, Rochester tempts Jane to accept his version of outlawry: "Is it better to drive a fellow-creature to despair than to transgress a mere human law . . . ?" (343). That Jane is clearly tempted is another daring departure from the schizophrenic decorum of earlier women's Gothic romance, in which if the female protagonist actually is tempted sexually, her fall is already assured. The landscape in which Gothic heroines find themselves may suggest the danger of a fall, and they are often in danger from outlaws. But they themselves are not overtly portrayed as in danger of being outlaws or of being fallen. The outrage some critics expressed at the supposed "coarse" vulgarity of *Jane Eyre* shows how daring it was to represent another alternative. Brontë allows her heroine to experience the full force of sexual temptation. Jane's attempt to know Rochester earlier has been associated with the enticing danger of an "abyss" in a sublime landscape of "volcanic-looking hills" (217); her own desire has been associated, through the imagery of fire, with Bertha's lusts. Her passion for Rochester has been described as a barrier between her and God, eclipsing him (302) (another image revealing that Rochester, though apparently offering knowledge, really is offering "viewless fetters"). Even before the revelation of Rochester's secret, Jane found it necessary to protect both herself and him from dangerous emotional excess, using the one weapon she wields so successfully throughout the book: "Soft scene, daring demonstration, I would not have; and I stood in peril of both; a weapon of defence must be prepared—I whetted my tongue . . ." (301).

At the greatest moment of crisis, Rochester tempts Jane to act on her passions by allowing him to shut Bertha away at Thornfield and joining him in a sequestered retreat, where she would live as his wife. ". . . I'll shut up Thornfield Hall: I'll nail up the front door, and board the lower windows" (328); "I have a place to repair to, which will be a secure sanctuary from hateful reminiscences, from unwelcome intrusion—even from falsehood and slander" (329). But Charlotte Brontë implies that this version of escape by means of boundaries—locking up the madwoman and then shutting themselves away from the world as well—would not be a separation from Bertha at all; it would really be union with her, for both Rochester and Jane. Rochester has said of Bertha that he avoided the indulgence of passions that seemed to "approach me to her and her vices" (338), but during his pleading with Jane, he himself looks like a man "who is just about to burst an insufferable bond and plunge headlong into wild licence" (330). Jane perceives that what Rochester offers is only to make her his mistress, and by her standards of sexual morality that would make her an indulger in wild license too, no better than the lustful Bertha.

Furthermore, it is important that Rochester is offering, in essence, not only to lock his wife Bertha away but to shut Jane away from the world as well. She would resemble Bertha for yielding to the temptation of the kind of self-indulgence Bertha represents and also, as in Bertha's case, because her "marriage" would really be a confinement. Earlier Jane had thought with pleasure, during Rochester's temporary absence, of her impending union with him: "I thought of the life that lay before me—*your* life, sir—an existence more expansive and stirring than my own . . ." (308). Now this "expansive" existence is revealed as something else: enclosure, seclusion.

Jane escapes the temptation Rochester offers her by leaving Thornfield secretly, at once escaping the Gothic mansion and casting herself out of the apparent Eden whose fallen nature has finally been revealed. In doing so, she deliberately subjects herself to that situation she has always feared: the state of the "most desolate wanderer in most dread and dangerous regions" (53). It is significant that having evaded the perils of Gothic horror masquerading as transcendence, and the temptation of allowing Rochester to become an idol eclipsing God, Jane recovers her own mode of religious transcendence by escaping into sublime nature and the religious awe it evokes. Alone on the heath at night, she looks up:

> We know that God is everywhere; but certainly we feel His presence most when His works are on the grandest scale spread before us; and it is in the unclouded night-sky, where His worlds wheel their silent course, that we read clearest His infinitude, his omnipotence, His omnipresence. I had risen to my knees to pray for Mr Rochester. Looking up, I, with tear-dimmed eyes, saw the mighty Milky Way. Remembering what it was—what countless systems there swept space like a soft trace of light—I felt the might and strength of God. (350–51)

This scene is reminiscent of Jane's awed contemplation of the night sky at the threshold of her Gothic adventure, when she was drawn to the transcendence represented by the moon's ascent. By evading the false transcendence Rochester offered, she has recovered her earlier outward impulses, which for a while had been confined to her relationship with him. This recovery resulted from the exercise of her own faculties, inspired by yet another vision of the moon that, in the dream shape of her mother, urged her to leave Thornfield (346). But having defended herself through separation and isolation and having chosen the transcendence of solitude, Jane must encounter the special perils they entail. She has chosen the moon and virginity; therefore the next phase of her life will be spent in the pleasant company of Diana and Mary—and in fierce struggle with an appalling danger related to them: their brother St. John. At Gateshead Jane closed herself off in her search for outward expansion and so became subject to death by freezing in the wintry solitude illustrated by Bewick. The "tyrant" and "murderer" of that world was John, who should have acted to her as an equal and a brother but instead posed as her "young master." At Moorhead, St. John, as his name suggests, is another version of the same oppression. And once again, as at Thornfield, Jane must perceive that the supposed transcendence a man offers her is really Gothic horror before she can defend herself and escape.

The version of transcendence that St. John offers Jane—participation in his own vocation—is particularly dangerous, because his own longings for egress and expansion have a strong affinity to Jane's own and spring from a deep restlessness and horror of repetition reminiscent of her own emotions on the battlements of Thornfield and at its threshold. He perceives and plays on her own need for escape: "I am sure you cannot long be content to pass your leisure in solitude, and to devote your working hours to a monotonous labour wholly void of stimulus: any more than I can be content . . . to live here buried in morass pent in with mountain—my nature, that God gave me, contravened, my faculties, Heaven-bestowed, paralysed—made useless . . . I . . . almost rave in my restlessness" (382). He tells her of his own release from the torment of repetition and inaction: "A year ago I was myself intensely miserable, because I thought I had made a mistake in entering the ministry: its uniform duties wearied me to death. I burned for the more active life of the world. . . . After a season of darkness and struggling, light broke and relief fell: my cramped existence all at once spread out to a plain without bounds; my powers heard a call from Heaven to rise, gather their full strength, spread their wings, and mount beyond ken" (388).

St. John's description of his own restlessness before finding his mission is filled with images recalling Jane's discontent with a life of enforced calm: the references to monotonous labor, paralysis, darkness, dissatisfaction, and burial alive recall the view of women's lot presented in the image of Thornfield as a domain of housekeeping and in the impassioned account of the secret rebellion of apparently calm women. Likewise, the reference to being "pent in with mountain" (382) recalls Jane's earlier suffering from a bounded horizon: at Lowood where the high mountains seemed "barriers of separation from the living world" (131) and again at Thornfield where the hills were "not so lofty . . . but yet quiet and lonely hills enough, and seeming to embrace Thornfield with a seclusion I had not expected . . ." (131). And in St. John's ecstatic description of his release from such torment is the very language associated throughout the book with Jane's own longings for transcendence: images of expansion, freedom, action, energy, boundlessness.

The ice-cold St. John tempts Jane to share this transcendence with him, just as the fiery Rochester seemed to promise contact with "what is bright and energetic and high" (281). Indeed St. John expands Jane's knowledge and horizons with a vengeance, forcing her to learn Hindu, pressing her to leave England forever and go out to India. But St. John's version of transcendence, like that of Helen Burns, has its end in death. And just as the Eden of Thornfield was revealed as a Gothic ruin, its treasures of knowledge mere ignorance of the Fall, so the egress St. John offers Jane is revealed as a Gothic nightmare. St. John offers Jane religious ecstasy, enlightenment, release. But in the imagery associated with their relationship, Jane suffers torture, darkness, and imprisonment instead. Like his earthly prototype John, the spiritual St. John turns out to be a tyrant; like Bluebeard he turns out to be a wife murderer. Far from liberating Jane from the self-enclosure of egotism, he in fact is proposing an intrusion, a violation of her psychic privacy. Against these perils Jane defends herself in a long and desperate struggle that culminates in a scene of speaking "I" which, like so much else in *Jane Eyre,* is an audacious revision of Gothic romance.

The most desperate phase of this long struggle begins with St. John's proposal of marriage, the climax of an increasingly sinister intimacy in which Jane has felt herself "in thrall" (424), in "fetters" (424), in "servitude" (423), "under a freezing spell" (423); scrutinized so thoroughly and coldly by her friend's attempts to know her that she experienced his presence in the room as "something uncanny" (422). Increasingly she has felt powerless to resist his influence. Now, as he speaks of how strange it is that everyone has not chosen the same vocation as he, Jane feels "as if an awful charm was framing round and gathering over me: I trembled to hear some fatal word spoken which would at once declare and rivet the spell" (427). St. John demands to know what her heart says, and she claims it is "mute." "Then I must speak for it," St. John replies: "Jane, come with me to India . . ." (427). It is characteristic of their relationship at this point—and of the danger it poses to Jane's integrity of self—that St. John, asserting his colossal will, purports to speak for Jane's own "mute" heart, attempting to make his voice her own.

In the debate that follows, Jane tries to give her opponent some glimpse of her real state of mind, by describing it in Gothic imagery: "Oh, I wish I could make you see how much my mind is at this moment like a rayless dungeon, with one shrinking fear fettered in its depths—the fear of being persuaded by you to attempt what I cannot accomplish" (428). St. John counters by claiming to know her intimately—"I have made you my study for ten months" (428)—and to recognize in her "a soul that revel[s] in the flame and excitement of sacrifice" (429). He offers her, that is, an opportunity to be consumed by fire, not Bertha's fire of lust and self-indulgence that was the false transcendence of Thornfield, but the fire of martyrdom through self-abnegation. And Jane is tempted. St. John's "persuasion" "contract[s]" around her like an "iron shroud"—an image of torture and burial alive; it "advance[s] with slow, sure step" (429) like a Gothic intruder. Like Rochester, St. John offers Jane a marriage that is not a marriage at all. Having earlier rejected being made a mistress, and hence a monster like Bertha herself (the type of lust), Jane now rejects St. John's loveless proposal as an offer of "monstrous" "martyrdom" and insists she will go as his sister, not his wife. But St. John refuses: "I want a wife: the sole helpmeet I can influence efficiently in life, and retain absolutely till death" (431). This is a chilling view of marriage, to say the least, and indeed Jane shudders in response: "I felt his influence in my marrow—his hold on my limbs" (431).

Jane escapes, however. Instead of asserting her moral superiority like a sentimental Gothic heroine (as St. John himself already claims to be speaking for God as well as for Jane's own mute heart, she can hardly attain more consciousness of virtue than he), she suddenly recognizes her equality with her adversary: "The veil fell from his hardness and despotism. . . . I felt his imperfection, and took courage. I was with an equal—one with whom I might argue—one whom, if I saw good, I might resist" (432). As his curate, his comrade, she would be "free." "I should still have my unblighted self to turn to. . . . There would be recesses in my mind which would be only mine, to which he never came, and sentiments growing there, fresh and sheltered, which his austerity could never blight, nor his measured warrior-march trample down. But as his wife . . . forced to keep the fire of my nature continually low, to compel it to burn inwardly and never utter a cry, though the imprisoned flame consumed vital after vital—*this* would be unendurable" (432–33). With St. John, that is, Jane would suffer the perpetual threat of intrusion, and her inner self—compelled to silence like the confined Bertha whose passions finally do consume her prison with fire—would become a force of destruction.

In the period that follows, Jane experiences St. John's cold rejection of her as "refined, lingering torture. . . . I felt how, if I were his wife, this good man, pure as the deep sunless source, could soon kill me, without drawing from my veins a single drop of blood . . ." (436). This is the same act of violence Montoni perpetrated, wife murder without actual bloodshed. Jane finally accuses St. John of it directly: "If I were to marry you, you would kill me. You are killing me now" (438). Once again, as when she tried to explain to St. John that his effect on her was to make her soul a dungeon, Jane speaks "I" in the same way so many women authors had already done, by speaking the Gothic nightmare. The difference is that her fiction is no disguise; she uses the Gothic imagery overtly as a metaphor for her relationship with St. John and in a direct exposition to him of the way he makes her feel. To this remarkable violation of decorum, St. John responds, not surprisingly, with the same horror some critics expressed at *Jane Eyre* itself: "Your words are such as ought not to be used: violent, unfeminine, and untrue. They betray an unfortunate state of mind: they merit severe reproof. . . ." (438). But the very act of speaking such "unfeminine" words in defiance of the compulsion not to "utter a cry" (433) means that, at least for a while, Jane has won.

St. John regains ascendency when Jane, admiring one of his "sublime moments," is "tempted to cease struggling with him—to rush down the torrent of his will into the gulf of his existence and there lose [her] own" (443). The image is reminiscent of an image from the contest of wills that ended with Jane's departure from Thornfield: "I saw that in another moment, and with one impetus of frenzy more, I should be able to do nothing with him. . . . But I was not afraid: not in the least. I felt an inward power; a sense of influence, which supported me. The crisis was perilous; but not without its charm: such as the Indian, perhaps, feels when he slips over the rapid in his canoe" (330). In both passages Jane contends with a sublime force outside her, but there is a crucial difference between them. The thrill of confronting Rochester evoked a sense of "inner power," and the image of the Indian negotiating the rapids is one of active, energetic skill at the art of self-preservation. The image associated with St. John suggests passivity rather than action; the temptation of merely yielding to the force of the cataract, a loss of self.

By the time Jane's final, definitive act of self-defense takes place, St. John has come to represent all the Gothic threats: dungeon (428), fetters (428), imprisonment (447), torture (436), confinement (429), wife murder, violation, and an erasing of the boundaries of the self. He has come to play the role of the villain-priest of Gothic romance: the apparently pious and ascetic cleric, like Schedoni with his fame for self-discipline and almost inhuman piety, who is nonetheless revealed in his supposed self-abnegation to be a colossal egotist.

As was the case with Thornfield, what makes this Gothic threat so dangerous is its false aspect as transcendence. St. John has admitted that his "ambition is unlimited" (401), and the sheer force of his desire to soar into the heavenly empyrean is in danger of sweeping Jane away. Helen Burns proffered a version of Christian transcendence associated with a patience and longsuffering ultimately uncongenial to Jane's fiery temperament. St. John's version of Christian transcendence is more tempting because although it begins also with Helen's assumption that this world is nothing compared with the "kingdom of spirits" (101), it is associated, as her vision was not, with intense energetic activity. Jane's own longings for transcendence have been constantly linked to a desire for the exercise of mental, spiritual, and emotional energy. St. John offers her a vast field for strenuous endeavor: so strenuous, indeed, that Jane perceives it would kill her.

But this appeal to Jane's "active soul" is deceptive, as the temptation to passivity, the sublime rush down the torrent, suggests. The Gothic heroine here is not being offered sublimity as power and action; she is being offered an opportunity for the same passive appreciation that was the only relation the sentimental Gothic heroine ever had to the sublime and that Charlotte Brontë rightly perceives as merely another version of self-loss. Furthermore, the imagery associated with St. John, whose soul is apparently so energetic, suggests that his energy is really a form of paralysis. He is "cold" (400), hard, "frozen" (421) and at various times compared to stone (418), glass (421), "a cold cumbrous column" (419). He too, like Rochester, seems to offer activity of mind that is really terrible stagnation, access to a vast world that is really narrow confinement, and a possibility for self-fulfillment that is really self-loss. Instead of escaping the bounds of self through the energetic activity of the soul, Jane is in danger of having the boundaries of her self obliterated by St. John's intrusion on her "liberty of mind" (423).

Jane's preservation of self-respect by leaving Thornfield depended on the ability to recognize, at the crucial moment, that what Rochester offered her was only the illusion of freedom. Now, just as she is in the greatest peril of losing her liberty to a similar illusion, alone with St. John in a room full of moonlight, her heart stops: "[A]n inexpressible feeling . . . thrilled it through, and passed at once to my head and extremities." This feeling rouses her senses from dangerous passivity and inspires them to action, "as if their utmost activity hitherto had been but torpor, from which they were now summoned and forced to wake. They rose expectant: eye and ear waited while the flesh quivered on my bones" (444). The language recalls that of Gothic romance when an intervention of the supernatural, or the apparently supernatural, is about to occur. What follows is a simultaneous presentation both of the supernatural and its explication. Jane hears a voice calling her name—not a supernatural voice, but "the voice of a human being—a known, loved, well-remembered voice—that of Edward Fairfax Rochester; and it spoke in pain and woe, wildly, eerily, urgently. 'I am coming!' I cried. 'Wait for me!' " The "spectre" of superstition rises "black by the black yew at the gate," but Jane quells it by recognizing immediately that the apparently supernatural is natural after all: ". . . It is the work of nature. She was roused, and did—no miracle—but her best" (445). Thus Charlotte Brontë claims the moment of telepathic communication for "nature"—a clever version of the *surnaturel expliqué.* The explanation, instead of producing a sense of anticlimax (it was only natural, after all), adds intensity to the claims Charlotte Brontë makes for a relationship in the natural world: this moment of perfect communion, as energizing as any moment of Gothic frisson, is possible in real life—no miracle, but nature at its best.

The "mysterious summons" (472) is Jane's rescue:

> I broke from St. John, who had followed, and would have detained me. It was *my* time to assume ascendancy. *My* powers were in play and in force. I told him to forbear question or remark; I desired him to leave me: I must and would be alone. He obeyed at once. Where there is energy to command well enough, obedience never fails. I mounted to my chamber; locked myself in; fell on my knees; and prayed in my way—a different way to St John's, but effective in its own fashion. I seemed to penetrate very near a Mighty Spirit; and my soul rushed out in gratitude at His feet. I rose from the thanksgiving—took a resolve—and lay down, unscared, enlightened— eager but for the daylight. (445)

Gothic heroines are remarkably active and resourceful: they travel, they explore, they debate, but in the end the ideology of Gothic romance idealizes female passivity and dependence. At the crucial moment Gothic heroines are rescued, almost always by a man. Jane is also rescued by a man—but not by his careful arrangements for escape or his sudden arrival just in the nick of time. She is rescued by his cry, out of his own "pain and woe," for her help. Her determination to answer this "urgent" cry enables her to resist St. John by commanding him to silence and ordering him to leave her alone. She locks herself in her own chamber, reestablishing the barrier between herself and him, and reasserts her spiritual individuality by communicating with God in her own way, "a different way to St John's" (445).

Like many Gothic rescues, this one is associated with providential intervention:

> The wondrous shock of feeling had come like the earthquake which shook the foundations of Paul and Silas's prison; it had opened the doors of the soul's cell and loosed its bands—it had wakened it out of its sleep, whence it sprang trembling, listening, aghast; then vibrated thrice a cry on my startled ear, and in my quaking heart and through my spirit, which neither feared nor shook, but exulted as if in joy over the success of one effort it had been privileged to make, independent of the cumbrous body. (446–47)

Thus Jane describes her deliverance from St. John in the imagery of divine intervention, and yet this exhilarating escape is fully an act of self-defense as well, both a divine visitation and an achieved freedom associated with Jane's own spiritual energies— *"My* powers were in play and in force." These powers free her and enable her to speak *I* imperiously— "Where there is energy to command well enough, obedience never fails." And instead of leaving her mind like a blasted heath, as in the first scene of self-defense by speaking, they provide genuine transcendence, giving her access to something "beyond and above": "I seemed to penetrate very near a Mighty Spirit. . . . my soul rushed out. . . ."

Thus Jane's escape from St. John is both physical and metaphysical, an exalted moment of self-defense that is also sublime transcendence. It is, as well, a supreme act of knowledge, for the act of communication that initiates the rescue is an exalted version of the transcendence idealized earlier in Jane's impassioned address of Rochester "face to face," as an "equal," without the impediment of custom, conventionalities, or even mortal flesh.[9] The allusion to 1 Cor. 13 in that earlier scene associated the potential for human relationships with the final transcendence of knowing even as one is also known, with no impediment to vision. Jane's claim of the right and ability to see Rochester face to face, without the dark glass, had its truth at the moment but in another sense was belied by his insistence on locking his darkest secret away from her. And the religious imagery of perfect vision in that scene was rescinded in the image of Rochester as an eclipse, an impediment to Jane's view of God. But now Jane's knowledge of Rochester's need for her is linked to the divine intervention that liberated Paul and Silas from their prison. This time there is no contradiction or qualification of the religious imagery, and Jane's religious transcendence itself is promoted by her earthly communion, not inhibited by it.

Perhaps at this moment, Rochester tells Jane later, her "soul wandered from its cell to comfort" his (472). Jane's self-defense here is associated both with maintaining the boundaries of her self and escaping them. Self-defense interposes a barrier between herself and St. John, the man who would violate her psychic privacy in a communion of unequals; but the barriers between her and Rochester vanish as she is now truly "roused from the nightmare of parting—called to the paradise of union." Thus from a perilous communion based on loss of identity and associated with imprisonment, torture, and intrusion, she is rescued by another kind of communion based on perfect communication, knowledge, and equality.[10]

The relationship thus reestablished, from having once been associated with the mere illusion of egress through "power of vision," now becomes redemptive, as in a quiet but remarkable reversal of conventions, the heroine returns to rescue the hero from the Gothic perils that once menaced *her* in his house: self-enclosure, burial, "viewless fetters." The place where she finds him is an ordinary house, of "moderate size, and no architectural pretensions," but nonetheless a version of the Gothic ruin: a building "of considerable antiquity," "deep buried" in a "gloomy wood," approached "just ere dark" by way of "Iron gates" and "a grass-grown track." The walls are "decaying," the windows "latticed and narrow"; "the front door was narrow too" (455). The narrowness of the door and windows stands in for the usual difficulty of access across the Gothic threshold; one suspects the quester[11] will have trouble getting in, as is so often the case. The quester, however, does not at first try to go in; instead, in keeping with the mutuality of which this double rescue is a picture, the inmate comes forth. " 'Can there be life here?' I asked. Yes, life of some kind there was, for I heard a movement—that narrow front door was unclosing, and some shape was about to issue from the grange. It opened slowly: a figure came out into the twilight and stood on the step . . ." (456). Jane has arrived at Ferndean, "deep buried in a wood," to assist at Rochester's resurrection, to help redeem him from "narrow" isolation and restore *his* "power of vision." The result is a marriage in which "We talk, I believe, all day long" (476), a redemptive human communion that does not impede communion with God but facilitates it, as Rochester himself acknowledges a "Master" greater than he.

"All my confidence is bestowed on him, all his confidence is devoted to me" (476), Jane says. Earlier she said she could not "rest in communication with strong, discreet, and refined minds . . . till I had . . . crossed the threshold of confidence, and won a place by their heart's very hearthstone" (400). That is a good description of the end of *Jane Eyre*. The heroine has found a true "safe haven" and can "rest in communication" with one other person. Rochester's earlier invitation, "Here, come in, bonny wanderer!" (168) can finally be accepted; Jane can "stay [her] weary little wandering feet at a friend's threshold" (273).

The peace and rest of this ending are a disappointment to many modern readers, dissatisfied that Jane's tremendous passions should at last find a calm and ordinary outlet in the secluded domestic world of Ferndean, with a husband whose sexual energies have been distinctly tamed. There is an interesting anticipation of this dissatisfaction in St. John's reaction to Jane's role of happy housekeeper. Soon after Jane comes into her inheritance, St. John finds her, to his disgust, delighted with the prospect of being "as busy as I can" in the tasks of baking and cleaning at Moorhouse all day long:

> "It is all very well for the present," said he; "but seriously, I trust when the first flush of vivacity is over, you will look a little higher than domestic endearments and household joys."
>
> "The best thing the world has!" I interrupted.
>
> "No, Jane, no; this world is not the scene of fruition; do not attempt to make it so: nor of rest; do not turn slothful." (416)

St. John's own escape into the "wide field" (394) and boundless plain (388) of his mission work depends upon a rejection of the domestic joys Jane loves: "He could not—he would not—renounce his wide field of mission warfare for the parlours and the peace of Vale Hall" (394). The "peace of Vale Hall" is the "safe haven," the "asylum" longed for throughout happy Gothic romance and finally attained at the end. The allusion, in "Vale," to the state of being "pent in with mountain" (382), recalls not only St. John's dissatisfactions but Jane's as well. In St. John, Charlotte Brontë represents, with some sympathy, the evasion of asylum, the rejection of the bounded Eden as a place of repetition, confinement, immanence. But this rejection is achieved at a price. St. John's "large views" (441), "wide field," and expansion into a "plain without bounds" require the imposition of another set of barriers, as Jane sees when he rejects Rosamond Oliver: "His chest heaved once, as if his heart, weary of despotic constriction, had expanded, despite the will, and made a vigorous bound for the attainment of liberty. But he curbed it . . ." (390).

St. John's escape from bounds necessitates another kind of boundary: a deliberate and "despotic constriction" of those feelings that constitute human ties. This "constriction" of the heart is necessary for St. John because his temperament is unsuited to domestic enclosure or the "calm [a loaded word for Jane, as well] of domestic life" (419). His version of transcendence requires solitary exile; Jane's is the opposite: the communion of domestic love in the kind of bounded world her cousin hopes to escape. Transcendence for Jane is not merely consistent with human ties; it consists of them. Although her fascination with Bewick suggested an affinity with remote, cold solitudes as well as revulsion at the thought of them, her longing for something beyond the limits of her daily life is deeply social, directed toward companionship: a knowledge of "worlds, towns" (140), a desire for "more of intercourse with my kind" (141). Jane is drawn in imagination to vast solitary arctic regions, dark fathomless depths of space, but in the end the kind of escape from self she most longs for and cares about is simply knowing and being known in human relationships; and it is for this kind of transcendence that Charlotte Brontë reserves her most powerful religious imagery.

From this perspective, the reason that St. John is wrong to condemn Jane's exultation in "commonplace home pleasures" lies in the social context of the housework Jane contemplates with such joy. She has discovered that she is not alone in the world but has a family. Diana and Mary are her cousins; it is for them she is renovating the house and baking Christmas treats. Housework here is not the deadly, repetitive enforced calm that foments secret rebellions, not the solitary isolation of the seamstress Grace Poole in her "dungeon," but an act of belonging and fellowship.

In the sympathetic portrait of Helen Burns and in the final tribute to St. John with which the novel ends, Brontë pays homage to the aspirations of souls that can find transcendence only through the search for a "world elsewhere." But Jane must find her fulfillment in the world, in fellowship with her "kind." Just as the Gothic perils at Thornfield are eerily oneiric and at the same time one with the oppression and repetition of dull everyday immanence, Jane's final transcendence is both miraculous, supernatural release—communion face to face beyond the restraints of convention, custom, even "mortal flesh"—[12] and the attainment of a social goal: equality between a woman and man that consists of perfect knowledge through a full, and fully realizable, ability to speak "I": "[T]o talk to each other is but a more animated and an audible thinking" (476).

Even so, Jane's fulfillment at Ferndean continues, rightly, to create a sense of disappointment in most of the book's readers. That sense derives from the deepest contradictions in Brontë's special subversion of Gothic romance. One of her innovations was to unveil what women's Gothic before her had known only in disguise: the fact that the rescue men seem to offer women is often one with the Gothic perils those women hope to escape. Again and again Brontë casts doubt on the efficacy of a woman's attempts to find transcendence vicariously through a man's broader sphere of activity. Twice Jane must reject marriage for exactly this reason. Having looked forward to sharing Rochester's life—"an existence more expansive and stirring than my own" (308)—she is forced to reject that hope as a delusion. St. John promises her a wide field for her endeavors, but she sees that he is making her soul like a rayless dungeon and that, far from offering her what he claims, he proposes to murder her. What these sequences make clear is that one man's transcendence may be another woman's Gothic nightmare. Implicit in Charlotte Brontë's version of Gothic romance is the barely submerged perception that the Gothic imprisonment by the villain and the Gothic rescue by the hero may be identical in the end, that La Vallée may be Udolpho, that the expulsion from Eden and the flight from the Gothic stronghold may be one and the same. But in the end, Brontë was unable to break away from the association of a woman's transcendence with a relationship to a man. In the final chapter of *Jane Eyre,* the restlessness of Jane's spirit loses its metaphysical connotations as Jane finds peace in a marriage of constant and perfect communication. For Charlotte Brontë, the difference between domesticity as Gothic nightmare and domesticity as perfect bliss turns on the self-knowledge and mutual knowledge the male–female relationship at its center is capable of accommodating. The force of this insight should not be minimized. One need only read a few of the strictures on marriage in advice books contemporaneous with *Jane Eyre* to realize that a vision of such radical equality of communication at the center of a marriage was not common. But the final and deep contradiction of *Jane Eyre* remains: while portraying, in a shockingly specific and overt way, the perils of ordinary domesticity and equating them with the worst Gothic nightmare of confinement, Charlotte Brontë nonetheless ultimately defines woman's transcendence as domestic enclosure.

Women's Gothic romance always involves the contradictory longings for an "asylum" (Howells) or "safe haven" and for "transport" (Kroeber 116)[13] beyond the "limit" of the bounded world. The contradiction that so disturbs readers at the end of *Jane Eyre* is simply this same contradiction at the heart of all women's Gothic, but intensified by the degree to which Charlotte Brontë has brought the discontent with domestic confinement, a discontent latent in all women's Gothic, to the surface of her narrative. As Gilbert and Gubar say, "In all her books, writing . . . in a sort of trance, [Brontë] was able to act out that passionate drive toward freedom which offended agents of the status quo, but in none was she able consciously to define the full meaning of achieved freedom . . ." (369).

The contrast with *Wuthering Heights* is instructive. There the happy marriage is not a resolution for the central characters; marital bliss belongs to the next generation, but not to Catherine and Heathcliff. In *Wuthering Heights,* the search by a man and a woman for perfect transcendence through union with each other is really another search, for transcendence in an ultimate, and ultimately solitary, sense in which knowledge of the other person as Other does not matter at all: "That is not *my* Heathcliff!" At the end of *Jane Eyre,* it turns out that the search for transcendence in an ultimate, solitary sense was really, after all, a search for domestic love. In Emily Brontë, to reach a certain intensity of transcendence one must shut oneself in. The delightful openness of Wuthering Heights after Heathcliff's death, an openness associated with love and marriage, is balanced by the exalted image of Heathcliff alone, shut up in his inmost chamber but open to all those wild forces "beyond and above" social unities. For Jane Eyre, seclusion with "my Edward" at Ferndean is enough. The dissatisfying nature of this final retreat is due in great measure to a phenomenon Eagleton describes: "Where Charlotte Brontë differs most from Emily is precisely in [her] impulse to negotiate passionate self-fulfilment on terms which preserve the social and moral conventions intact, and so preserve intact the submissive, enduring, everyday self which adheres to them" (16).

The final seclusion is not quite the ending of the book, of course; the description of it is followed by an account of what became of the Rivers family. And once again, like the happy marriage at Ferndean, the final reference to St. John in *Jane Eyre* often leaves modern readers disappointed and puzzled. Why should St. John, the villain associated with torture, violation, and wife murder, receive such a glowing eulogy in the final paragraphs? This eulogy, however, is simply the other side of the asylum/flight dichotomy. Jane ends in domestic bliss in a house "buried" in a secluded wood, but the "safe haven" of this closure is brought into question as the vision of another possibility opens up once more in the final paragraph. Far from ironic, the ending is a sincere and admiring vision of one man's transcendence: a kind that Jane Eyre rejected, but one that has clearly been pictured as the response to an excruciating restlessness and sense of confinement that Jane has experienced herself and that, according to her, many women experience every day as a matter of course. One *man's* transcendence: that is the key to the many contradictions of the ending.

7

Villette: Demystifying Women's Gothic

I tore her up—the incubus! I held her on high—the goblin! I shook her
loose—the mystery! And down she fell—down all round me—down in
shreds and fragments—and I trode upon her.

Villette

I

With the air of an optimistic parable, *Jane Eyre* ends, if not in unquali-
fied fairy-tale wish fulfillment,[1] in an idealized marriage and "safe haven."
Villette presents a more pessimistic and claustrophobic version of the "fear-
spent, spectre-ridden life" and a grimmer view of the possibilities of transcendence for those whom society, for whatever reason, consigns to
personal littleness. Both more grotesquely surrealistic and more bitterly
realistic, *Villette*'s images of suffering are more extreme than are those
in *Jane Eyre.* Restraint is more recurrent and pervasive; release rare and
impermanent. Like the oneiric and everyday worlds of *Jane Eyre,* the
eerier nightmare and intenser realism of *Villette* are shown to be one and
the same, but in *Villette* their identity is more consistent and therefore
more bizarre. An ordinary boat ride to a channel ferry is a journey across
the Styx; the examiners at Lucy's viva voce are the lechers who pursued
her through the night maze of Villette; a family picnic centers on something resembling "a head severed from its trunk" (558). In *Villette,* Gothic
conventions operate at the same time in a psychological and a social
context, as a novel and a romance unfold concurrently, with something
like the effect of Bruegel painted over Bosch. The eerie distortions that
result are pictures of social ills and their psychological counterparts. Thus,
for example, in a "splendid assemblage" of the elite of Labassecour in
"grand toilette" (286), Lucy perceives the king to be a victim of the
"spectre, Hypochondria" (290). This picture of "the low court" whose

king is secretly ill is an image both of disorder in Lucy's deepest psychic realm and the social order that disorder reflects. The king of Labassecour is a hypochondriac, because the sickness of Lucy's mind is the sickness of her world.

In such a world, self-defense and defense against the self are both the same and not the same: once again, but with more consistency than in *Jane Eyre,* the forces of violence outside the heroine are also inner perils, so that her most intimate psychic dramas are dangerously one with the social dramas of the world outside her—a world she is powerless to change. In such a world, too, mystery is not a single secret confined to a gloomy mansion but a disturbing quality of everyday reality, which may at any moment become opaque to the inquiring eye—or "I," which is always losing its capacity for naming things and so constantly in danger of losing itself in the act of losing them. Because of this epistemological uncertainty, perils eluded once are likely to reappear in different forms. The horror of repetition in *Villette* is that the same mysteries must be solved over and over; the same relations of social knowledge between people must be constantly reestablished. In this context, the problem of transcendence, bound up with all these other problems, seems almost insoluble.

The greater pessimism of *Villette* is expressed in several formal differences that distinguish the use of Gothic conventions here from that in *Jane Eyre:*[2] a different approach to the device of the lost Eden, the choice of convent instead of family mansion as setting for the Gothic plot, a different and more intense focus on the mystery of knowledge, a bizarre and original version of deadly iteration, the addition of the Gothic device of the secret conspiratorial organization, and a change in the nature of the Other Woman[3] who haunts the heroine. The combined effect of these changes is to place in a more insistently social context the perils, including the psychological perils, the heroine must face. As a result, the question of the "reconcilement of this world with our own souls" (*Pierre* 290) takes on a greater urgency than it had in *Jane Eyre,* even as the possibility of such reconcilement comes to seem much more bleak.

II

Lucy's special vulnerability comes from a conjunction of external and internal "forces of violence" that derive their existence and strength from her lack of a tenable social position. This placelessness is apparent from the beginning, in her situation at Bretton. Gothic romances often begin with an evocation of home: primal version of the "asylum" for which, as Howells points out, so many heroines search until the dénouement of a happy marriage. *Villette* begins with a bizarre version of this convention, in which the peace and calm of Lucy's asylum at Bretton are threatened by the arrival of a little girl who desperately misses her father, Mr. Home. The displacements point to the extremity of the pain *Villette* explores. The heroine's own experience of missing home is too agonizing even to be expressed directly: instead of calling attention to the fact that at Bretton she is away from home, she pictures the distress of another child at Bretton, Paulina, whose Home is away. Alone in a room with this sad little girl, she feels as if the room were "haunted" (69).[4] To fill up the blank caused by Home's absence, Paulina transfers her affections to Graham. And in that relationship too she experiences loss: when she is about to leave, he feels no particular grief. In her sorrow at this experience of not being missed, she seeks warmth from Lucy Snowe, approaching "like a small ghost gliding over the carpet" to be taken into Lucy's bed (92). Against these pictures of Lucy's haunting sense of loss is set an idealized image of happy security: the life of Graham and his mother, with its steady, consistent exchange of affection.

The security of this family unit is expressed in an important indication of the concerns of the novel: in contrast with Lucy, Graham and Louisa are so much at home in their world that it bears their name. They are the Brettons of Bretton and have been so "for generations" (61). This perfect state of reconcilement with one's world, the opposite of alienation, is the Eden evoked at the beginning of Lucy's Gothic romance. But it is someone else's Eden, and the heroine herself is already an alien there, with a strong sense of the need to protect herself: not, like Jane Eyre, against some overt external cruelty but against her own feelings, and against the possibility of laying herself open to rejection by a world to which she cannot fully belong. This defensiveness is evident in her response to Paulina's lavishing of affection on Graham, an action that strikes her "as strangely rash," like the heedless fondling of a half-wild animal (87).

Paulina's experience at Bretton centers on missing Home; Lucy's, on a hope that this emotion will be kept—like the scene of grief she rises to "check"—"within bounds" (67). So strong is Lucy's internal system of restraints that even when her own emotions seek an outlet, she experiences their pressure as a desire for someone else to cry out, "so that I might get relief and be at ease" (71). This impulse toward internal restriction and restraint is reinforced by Lucy's subsequent experiences, as a final loss of her own kindred, who themselves stood in for an earlier, lost home, leads her first to make Miss Marchmont's "two close, hot rooms . . . [her] world" (97) and then, when that asylum is lost, to seclude herself in a "demi-convent" (163) in a foreign land. The way Brontë uses this "convent" as the primary setting of Lucy's Gothic adventures is at the center of what makes *Villette* so much more bleak than *Jane Eyre*.

III

In *Jane Eyre* the primary focus of the Gothic plot is on the perils, and possibilities for transcendence, associated with love and marriage. Although much of the novel takes place in settings other than Thornfield, the heart of Jane's conflict concerns her relationship to one particular man, and the heart of the Gothic plot is set in his "gloomy house" (148). In *Villette,* the setting in a convent and in a city means that throughout the major part of the book, Lucy's difficulties pertain to her place in society at large as well as to her most intimate relationships. The influence of social status on women's lives is also a major concern of *Jane Eyre,* whose heroine, like Lucy, is a single woman faced with the necessity of supporting herself in a society in which marriage is women's almost only source of financial security. Thornfield is her workplace and Rochester her employer; the first impediment to their relationship is the class difference between them. In *Villette,* however, the setting intensifies the focus on the heroine's social status by keeping in constant view the perils associated with her work relations, friendships, and place in society. In addition, the suggestion, implicit in the Red Room scene and in Bertha's multiple roles, that the form of the perils "shrouded within the recesses of blind human hearts" is in part determined by external oppression is here elaborated as the explicit center of the Gothic plot. The convent is both Lucy's inner psychic space— "the house of her own self" (Gilbert and Gubar 408)—and an alien society outside her. In the drama that takes place there, the chief figures play novelistic roles as members of the social sphere in which Lucy must establish a place; at the same time they play allegorical, romance roles in her psychomachia. By means of this double function Brontë explores the complex identity of outer social perils and inner psychological perils.

Discussions of Charlotte Brontë's use of realism and the Gothic, or realism and Romanticism, have tended to see them as "discordant" (Johnson 325), contradictory, incompatible (e.g., Eagleton 78, 86–88; Heilman 119; Jacobus 228; Moers 81). Even Crosby, who begins by saying that in *Villette* Brontë "integrated Gothic and romantic elements with the conventions of realism" (1), refers to the nun as an "intrusion . . . into a realistic text" (4), and reads the personifications not as traditional elements of an allegorical romance but as disruptions, "as troublesome to a realist text as the nun itself," that "work to decenter the coherent self which Brontë tries to guarantee her heroine . . ." (5). Hook sees *Villette* as abandoning "the disguise of romance . . . in favor of a basic realism. . . . The trappings of the world of romance persist in the later novel in the legend of the nun. . . . But the point is the sham/deceitful quality of such romantic stuff . . ." (152–53).

On the contrary, the double function of Gothic setting in *Villette* shows Brontë using both romance and realism to render at the same time two facets of one reality that is simultaneously psychological and social. There is indeed a dissonance, throughout the text, between the realistic discourse of "Reason" and the romantic discourse of "necromantic" fancy, but that discord at the level of Lucy's style is part of a larger harmony at the level of narrative structure. The coherence of this structure derives from the double, mutually illuminating meanings that result when in Brontë's simultaneous novel and romance, characters function as counters in both a representation of psychic reality and a representation of social reality. This reading has the advantage of acknowledging the denser social texture of *Villette* in comparison with *Jane Eyre* while nonetheless avoiding the assumption that the Gothicism of *Villette* is somehow misplaced or merely incidental—an assumption implicit not only in a "social" reader of the text like Eagleton, but even in Jacobus, who insists on the importance of the nun but sees "supernatural haunting and satanic revolt, delusion and dream" as "disrupt[ing] a text which can give no formal recognition to either Romantic or Gothic modes" (228). Similarly, Heilman says of Charlotte Brontë that "formally she is for 'reason' and 'real life'; but her characters keep escaping to glorify 'feeling' and 'Imagination' " (119). He identifies this "feeling" as Charlotte Brontë's "version of the Gothic" (119). The Gothic, however, is as much formally integral to Brontë's work as is the "real." In both *Jane Eyre* and *Villette* it is their formal copresence that makes her reading of the Gothic so perceptive.[5]

The picture of the convent and its inmates is a perfect example. In both its concurrent meanings, as a social space and a psychological space, the convent stands for the experience of being hidden away.[6] Inside the social world of the convent itself, Lucy's means of employment places her in a position of such inferiority that she hardly exists. She is "a mere shadowy spot on a field of light" (200). Such is her nonentity that Gine-vra can ask her at one point, "But *are* you anybody?" (394). Dr. John, who should know her personally, fails for a long time even to recognize her as his countrywoman, addressing her in French (170) and according her the significance of an uninteresting carpet or ordinary chair (162). Within the microcosmic social world of the convent Lucy is hidden; in the social world outside it she is equally obscure, a fact that her seclusion in the convent itself represents. Lucy is immured there because she needs money, and in that position she risks being forgotten by those on whom money confers freedom of movement in a wider sphere: "Those who live in retirement, whose lives have fallen amid the seclusion of schools or of other walled-in and guarded dwellings, are liable to be suddenly and for a long while dropped out of the memory of their friends, the denizens of a freer world. Unaccountably, perhaps . . . there falls a stilly pause, a wordless silence, a long blank of oblivion" (348).

But the convent, a novelistic picture of Lucy's social and economic relations, is also an allegorical picture of the psychology those relations engender.

> The hermit—if he be a sensible hermit—will swallow his own thoughts, and lock up his own emotions during these weeks of inward winter. He will know that Destiny designed him to imitate, on occasion, the dormouse, and he will be conformable: make a tidy ball of himself, creep into a hole of life's wall, and submit decently to the drift which blows in and soon blocks him up, preserving him in ice for the season.
>
> Let him say, 'It is quite right: it ought to be so, since so it is.' And, perhaps, one day his snow-sepulchre will open, spring's softness will return, the sun and south-wind will reach him; the budding of hedges, and carolling of birds and singing of liberated streams will call him to kindly resurrection. *Perhaps* this may be the case, perhaps not: the frost may get into his heart and never thaw more; when spring comes, a crow or a pie may pick out of the wall only his dormouse-bones. (348–49)

In this passage, being walled up is a state imposed by external forces, but it is also a horrible form of self-defense. Those already walled in from the world, Lucy implies, will suffer less if by building internal barriers, they "submit decently" to the force that "blocks [them] up." "La Décence" (200) is one of Mme. Beck's watchwords, appropriate to the director of a convent, that old Gothic symbol of decorum. With her al-legorical name, Modeste, and her love of "la Convenance et la Décence" (200), Mme. Beck guards Lucy from the outside world rather like the medieval romance figure of Daunger, personification of a quality necessary for virtue but also inimical to love. The possibility that Lucy will fall prey to the "decency" of submitting to burial alive results from her extreme decorum in the relations of love and friendship. "Going beyond [her]self" (222) voluntarily is a rare occurrence; most often, she waits to be summoned forth.

The danger that Lucy will submit to burial alive in the Snowe sepulcher of herself is the danger of self-enclosure from her willingness to remain unknown or unacknowledged, a "blank of oblivion" to the rest of the world. For Charlotte Brontë, the psychological danger of this extreme self-abnegation is one with the moral danger of self-absorbed egotism: a paradoxical identity manifest in Lucy's relationship with another inmate of the convent, Ginevra. Ginevra as a novelistic character interacts with Lucy in a social world where she has a marketable commodity, her beauty, and Lucy has none. In this world Ginevra espouses the views of a social class that regards Lucy as "nobody's daughter" (215), and therefore "nobody" (393). It is this view of Lucy's social status that makes her in turn susceptible to the moral and psychological danger Ginevra represents as an allegorical figure—the danger of self-immurement that subjects one, by definition, to the insatiable demands of a hungry ego. Lucy's self-abnegation is bound to Ginevra's self-absorption from the beginning of their acquaintance, on the voyage during which Ginevra, Lucy says, "tormented me with an unsparing selfishness" (118). From one angle this is a picture of Lucy tormented by a social superior who fails to perceive her as an independent subject. From another, it is a picture of Lucy tormented by selfishness—by the self-absorption that results from her own self-erasure, her collusion in the fiction that she is nobody. The image of this collusion is reinforced by the fact that Ginevra herself is in much the same plight as Lucy: although she has wealthy relatives, her financial future depends on her success in the marriage market. Thus her superior airs mask the fact that the woman she treats as her inferior is, when it comes to their real economic value, her double.

The inevitable link between self-abnegation and selfishness is revealed again at the convent, where Lucy and Ginevra, apparent opposites, are nonetheless inevitably paired together. Thus, for example, Lucy does not eat very much—a measure of her tendency to self-erasure—but as a consequence she must feed Ginevra, who devours her unwanted pistolets with a hearty appetite. Standing before the mirror with Ginevra, Lucy gazes in fascination at her insatiable counterpart: ". . . I stood and let [Ginevra's] self-love have its feast and triumph: curious to see how much

it could swallow—whether it was possible it could feed to satiety . . ."
(215). Lucy deems herself capable of being satisfied with "calm comfort
and modest hope" (304), but in fact she is often possessed by the most
desperate emotional hunger, and her obsession with not being obsessed
with her appearance is absurdly self-defeating. Thus, standing together
before the mirror, Ginevra and Lucy are merely two faces of the same
problem. Lucy has no vanity, wheras Ginevra, feeding her self-love, is
entirely consumed with it. Nonetheless in the mirror scene, Ginevra's
criticism of Lucy's appearance, so reminiscent of Lucy's own masochistic self-inventories, reveals vanity and self-deprecation as two faces of
the same image.[7] Similarly, on the picnic, Lucy seems so determinedly
self-effacing as to have no self at all, but this apparent selflessness is
belied by the fact that Ginevra insists on walking beside her and encum-
bering her with the "burden" of her considerable weight (470). Ginevra
here embodies literally what Lucy elsewhere, referring to her isolation as
a single woman, calls "the whole burden of human egotism" (450). And
the spectacle of Lucy shifting about so as to keep Ginevra always between herself and M. Paul (470) suggests something more: that egotism
is an impediment to human relationships and that Lucy's hiding from
Paul's friendship in self-effacement is exactly the same as allowing egotism to come between them. Lucy cannot say "I," and Ginevra can only
say "I." Brontë's indications that these two dilemmas are the same is a
sharp commentary on the Victorian canonization of the selfless woman.
In *Villette,* as will become clear, that canonization is a source of Gothic
horror.

The contradictions at the heart of this canonization are at issue as well
in Lucy's relation to another inmate of the convent, the cretin. In his
strictures on Lucy for not being able to give herself fully to the care of
this creature, M. Paul says, " 'Ah! you are an egotist. . . . Women who
are worthy the name ought infinitely to surpass our coarse, fallible, self-
indulgent sex . . ." (279–80). Ironically, the image of Lucy immured in
the convent with the cretin, so clearly "a last nightmarish version of herself" (Gilbert and Gubar 414), is yet another image of her self-obsession.
Like her, the cretin is there because no one outside the convent loves her
enough to desire her company, and it is one expression of the horrors of
Lucy's own isolation that being left to care for herself is the same as
being left to care for a being who exists only as a needy and demanding
ego and does not speak. In the allegorical "romance" of *Villette* the description of this servitude is another picture of Lucy "tormented . . .
with an unsparing selfishness" (118). In the realistic "novel," Paul equates

this servitude with virtuous, womanly self-sacrifice. The conjunction points once again to the dangerous identity, asserted in so many ways throughout the novel, of self-renunciation and self-obsession.

IV

The shift in architectural setting from the Gothic family mansion of *Jane Eyre* to the Gothic convent in *Villette* thus produces a more intense focus on the heroine's social ills as they relate to her psychological ills: a focus implicit in *Jane Eyre* in the conflation of realism and romance but not so consistently present before the reader as in *Villette*. Related to this change is another. The intersection of realism and romance in the representation of the particular way the Gothic terrors center on the issue of knowledge in *Villette* contributes to an even more intense focus on the problem of self-transcendence as it relates to the difficulties and dangers of knowing and being known. Crossing "the threshold of confidence" (*Jane Eyre* 400) is problematic for Lucy in ways that it was not for Jane Eyre, because of the special form of her social and psychological problems and the special relationship between them.

M. Paul refers to Lucy's "high insular presence" (455), a term that points both to her tendency to set bounds between herself and others and to the related fact of her effort to retain her national identity in a foreign place. The inhabitants of this place she persists in referring to as "foreigners," but it is clearly they who are at home and she who is "foreign." In their world her identity is imperiled partly because she is poor and homeless: she must earn a living,[8] and earning a living at Mme. Beck's means subjection to the endless intrusions of a "Jesuit inquisitress" (378) who copies keys, opens drawers, and reads letters. The Brettons, who belong to Lucy's hereditary social class (245), nearly lost their own economic independence at one time, but they escaped Lucy's difficulties because Graham, as a man, could become a doctor and so recoup their losses to a comfortable degree. The social status thus maintained enables the Brettons, as their name suggests, to maintain their own "insular" dignity—to continue being themselves, Britons—wherever they go. In contrast, the sequence in which Lucy blacks out during her efforts to find her way through Villette suggests both the fierceness of her struggle to maintain her identity in this foreign world and the central danger she faces: that already defined as "nobody," she will become nobody even to herself,[9] losing self-knowledge altogether.

Lucy's internal and external struggle to defend herself against the loss of identity is presented in an extraordinarily subtle examination of the Gothic terrors of unity and separateness. These terrors are produced by Lucy's special dilemma: to establish a "fruitful" relationship with the foreign world outside her, she must overcome what divides her from it, while at the same time maintaining the special individuality that accounts in great part for her separateness.[10] Moving outside herself in order to be known entails the danger of self-dissolution. Paradoxically, however, the effort to protect a distinct selfhood imperils it as well. For defense of the "insular" self entails the danger of becoming too self-absorbed and so "tormented" by "unsparing selfishness," overcome by "the whole burden of human egotism": the danger of becoming walled up, buried alive, and so ironically erased as a separate being, after all.

The difficulties inherent in Lucy's effort to be connected while remaining separate—to be known as a distinct individual—make the act of knowledge itself problematic for her. The relationship between her difficulties knowing and being known is illuminated by that type of self-absorption, Ginevra, with whom Lucy's seclusion in a convent—that is, her immurement inside herself—brings her inevitably into intimate and oppressive contact. Ginevra is inordinately proud of not knowing anything: ". . . I am quite an ignoramus. I know nothing—nothing in the world—I assure you . . ." (115). Both this incapacity and her pride in it are a consequence of egotistical self-enclosure. In her discourse, places and people suddenly go blank, as she gives them the wrong names or even the non-name of *chose*. The world for her is Ginevra; her incapacity for knowledge, revealed in what Tanner calls her "linguistic oblivion" (17), signals her inability to confront honestly the otherness of the people around her.[11] Graham's own experience of her flirtation with him does not obtrude itself on her self-centered consciousness. Even his name has no reality to her, as she discards it for the romance of "Isidore." She imagines Mrs. Bretton adoring "my son John," unconscious of the fact that his mother calls him "Graham" (352).

Once again the self-effacing Lucy is the inverse and therefore the double of the self-aggrandizing Ginevra. An inability to acknowledge the Otherness of others is, in effect, the same as an inability to assert oneself as a distinct individual. Thus Ginevra's tendency to lose the names of things and people is one of Lucy's own great perils. Indeed, it is the primary form in which mystery threatens the Gothic heroine of *Villette*.

In Gothic romance, mothers are lost, fathers are lost, ancestral homes are lost, the pastoral bliss of childhood is lost, civilizations fall to dust and decay. Although the tone of loss infects even the endings of Gothic romance, the solution of the central mystery always redeems to some significant degree at least one of the central losses. Because a mystery is solved, Julia recovers her mother (Radcliffe, *Sicilian Romance*); Emily recovers La Vallée, Amanda recovers Lord Mortimer (Roche, *Children of the Abbey*), and so on. Thus in an important sense Gothic romance sees mystery as loss, and the solution of mystery as the recovery of what was lost. The fact that mystery signifies deprivation[12] in the Gothic (if one does not know one's mother is hidden in the castle, one has no mother; without reading the lost manuscript, one cannot know that the inheritance is one's own . . .) helps explain why in works like *The Recess*, the motif of the loss of Eden through knowledge coexists in such unreconciled tension with an almost excessive valuing of knowledge. The source of this tension becomes even clearer when one considers the kind of deprivation the whole atmosphere of mystery might have signified for women writers: a meaning suggested in de Beauvoir's picture of women cut off from the knowledge of the world that would give them competence in it and therefore victimized by a sense that they are "surrounded by dangerous mysteries" (673). Such exclusion must always be painful, however Edenic the seclusion it involves. The loss of this seclusion—the expulsion from Eden because of knowledge—is also painful; hence the ambivalence of *The Recess* toward exactly this question of which loss is worse, the loss that is mystery or the loss that is knowledge.

One of the most bizarre aspects of *Villette* is the particular form in which it makes the connection between mystery and loss: through a cluster of narrative techniques whose subject, goal, or consequence is a blanking out whereby what ought to be known becomes unknown instead. These techniques tend to fall into three categories: the blanking out created when Lucy's dread of naming creates a gap in the reader's knowledge; retractions whereby Lucy describes an experience, then strikes it from the record; and the blanking out created for Lucy and/or the reader when the known returns as the unknown.

All of these techniques of creating mystery describe and enact emotional loss, making us undergo Lucy's own experience of emotional privation through the only experience of privation into which she can force her readers—a loss of knowledge. But as Lucy's own blankings out show, the narrator of *Villette* finds emotional loss so intolerable that for her, too, it often manifests itself through displacement, as epistemological loss. Hence the disturbing form mystery takes in this Gothic romance-novel: a sense of disorientation among the recurring and ordinary objects, experiences, and social relations of everyday life. The chief subject of blanking out shifts with the progression of Lucy's tale, reflecting a sequence of loss, replacement, and new loss, from Home to Graham to Paul. Throughout this progression, Lucy's losses of knowledge are another version of the danger that at any moment she may herself be lost in a more dire sense than any heroine of Roche or Radcliffe: forgotten, blanked out. In the blankings out that she experiences, what ought to be the Same is rendered Other—a phenomenon in which Lucy's experience of the world is an emblem of her own relation to it, as almost everyone thinks she is other than what she is. At its most extreme this is the same as being perceived as no one at all, a danger that is one with her central Gothic peril of being immured in a convent. For, as Gilbert and Gubar point out, Lucy is in danger of "feeling that she is a nun (none) as a single woman" (428).

The first type of mysterious blanking out results when Lucy's dread of naming withholds information from the reader, as when she explains Louisa's coming to fetch her to Bretton: "[S]he then plainly saw events coming, whose very shadow I scarce guessed; yet of which the faint suspicion sufficed to impart unsettled sadness, and made me glad to change scene and society" (62). These events are throughout the book the subject of narrative blanking out, representing a loss too terrible to relate except by silence, periphrasis, or metaphor. Lucy refers once explicitly to her uncles, but she never speaks directly of her parents except in two references that are themselves a blanking out. One is Ginevra's description of Lucy as "nobody's daughter"— doubly appropriate because she has no hereditary place in society and because her parents no longer exist. The phrase evokes the radical nature of Lucy's orphanhood as we experience it. She seems to be "nobody's daughter" in the most fundamental sense, because even the essential facts about her loss are lost to the reader through her silences.

Lucy also speaks of this loss—or, rather, does not speak of it—in a second form of blanking out: the retraction whereby she describes an event, then ("Cancel the whole of that, if you please, reader" [117]) strikes it from the record and forces us to re-know it as something different from what we first imagined. Most characteristically these retractions offer pictures of hope or happiness and then erase them, forcing the reader to experience, as epistemological loss, Lucy's emotional loss. Such is Lucy's description of whatever event it was that deprived her of family:

> It will be conjectured that I was of course glad to return to the bosom of my kindred. Well! the amiable conjecture does no harm, and may therefore be

safely left uncontradicted. Far from saying nay, indeed, I will permit the reader to picture me, for the next eight years, as a bark slumbering through halcyon weather, in a harbour still as glass—the steersman stretched on the little deck, his face up to heaven, his eyes closed: buried, if you will, in a long prayer. A great many women and girls are supposed to pass their lives something in that fashion; why not I with the rest?

Picture me then idle, basking, plump, and happy, stretched on a cushioned deck, warmed with constant sunshine, rocked by breezes indolently soft. However, it cannot be concealed that, in that case, I must somehow have fallen over-board, or that there must have been wreck at last. I too well remember a time—a long time, of cold, of danger, of contention. To this hour, when I have the nightmare, it repeats the rush and saltness of briny waves in my throat, and their icy pressure on my lungs. I even know there was a storm, and that not of one hour nor one day. For many days and nights neither sun nor stars appeared . . . a heavy tempest lay on us. . . . In fine, the ship was lost, the crew perished. (94)

The intensity of Lucy's grief at this loss is manifest in her dread of naming it to the reader, and its effect seems to be that she hesitates later to possess, by naming, people or things that will, if she claims them as hers, subject her again to the terrible danger of losing them. Lucy's temptation not to confirm her knowledge by assigning a name is the temptation of choosing privation: if she has nothing, at least she cannot lose it. Thus, for example, a letter she has longed for appears first as "a white object on my black desk, a white, flat object. . . . That shining thing on the desk" (354). Lucy's tendency to blank things out is a version of her fear of being blanked out to others. The letter may not be what she hoped—an assurance that the long silence preceding it, making her weeks like "blank paper" (349), did not really mean that she herself had become a blank to her friends. And so she dares not fully acknowledge its presence as if the very act of naming "a letter," instead of affirming the letter's reality, might dispel the illusion that there is anything there to correspond to such a potent word.

The connection between blanking out and being blanked out is clearest in the chapter entitled "The Long Vacation." Possessed of neither family nor social importance, unlike the other inmates of the convent, who go away to join their relatives and friends, Lucy is herself erased in the hiatus of the long vacation, forgotten by those outside. In this hiatus she has a dream of her family—the most specific reference to them in her narrative. But the specificity, such as it is, is canceled out by the context, in which Lucy herself is a blank to them: "Amidst the horrors of that dream I think the worst lay here. Methought the well-loved dead, who had loved *me* well in life, met me elsewhere, alienated . . ." (231). This terrible nightmare of not being known finally sends Lucy out of her convent to seek relief from isolation. Symbolically, she plans not only to leave the convent but also to get far beyond the city walls (235): escaping the psychological condition of self-confinement implies escape from the social limits on which it depends.

Lucy's subsequent wanderings in Villette recall those of Jane Eyre after leaving Thornfield. As Gilbert and Gubar point out, Jane's "journey across the moors suggests the essential homelessness—the nameless, placeless, and contingent status—of women in a patriarchal society" (364). Appropriately, at the climax of this narrative sequence, Lucy blacks out, losing consciousness totally, in the absolute form of not knowing the world which is also the absolute form of not being known. By losing her sense of her own existence, she enacts literally her metaphorical blankness in the dream of meaning nothing to those she loves.

Lucy recovers self-consciousness and consciousness of the world in the same process, waking in a strange room that is nonetheless oddly familiar. Things she knew intimately as a child, returned as the unknown, have the quality of "ghosts": "These articles of furniture could not be real, solid arm-chairs, looking-glasses, and wash-stands—they must be the ghosts of such articles. . . ." (241). They are "phantoms of chairs . . . wraiths of looking glasses, tea urns, and tea cups" (251). It is as if Lucy's strenuous efforts to repress her sense of loss had backfired and the past had returned in a strange, redeemed version of the dream of meeting "elsewhere, alienated" (231). This scene reveals Brontë's perception that ghosts represent the problem of relations between past and present. By definition they are repetition: they are what has been lost but will not go away; what can neither be retrieved from the past nor exorcised from the present. In this context it is especially apt that Lucy's disorientation among these ghosts of Bretton is both an act of returning to her childhood asylum and a reenactment of its loss. This is Bretton, but with a foreign name, La Terrasse; and Bretton was never more than a substitute for her true home, anyway. Thus there is more than one meaning to the fact that in this scene "the lost home *(heimlich)* and the uncanny *(unheimlich)* coincide" (Jacobus 235).[13] Even this "home" was and is alien to Lucy, just as there is the vaguest hint that her original home itself—never fully possessed and validated by that name—was early a place where she did not belong.[14] The uncanny nature of the objects in the scene at La Terrasse serves not only to reveal Lucy an alien there (opposed, as Jacobus points out, to Paulina, the "true inmate" of this paradise [235]) but to establish her as an alien in what is for her the unknowable world of other peoples' most homely reality: teacups, urns, chairs.

In the scene of Lucy's waking at La Terrasse, the known returns first as the unknown, then takes its proper shape as the known again. This return of the familiar as the alien is the third technique of blanking out, which usually has one of two sources. When it represents Lucy's own failure to recognize what should be familiar, the blanking out is a mimesis of her own epistemological experience. In other cases it functions to force readers into the position of having to re-know what they have already known before. The former puts Lucy in the role of Gothic heroine trying to solve the mystery and so imitates her difficulties knowing. The latter puts her in the role of Gothic mystery writer who hides important clues from the reader and so represents her reluctance to make herself known.

For a great part of the book the most salient object of this kind of blanking out is Graham, who appears and reappears in a variety of personae. He is the "stranger" (123) who guides Lucy through the dripping trees on her first night in Villette, the "Dr John" of the pensionnat, and the "Isidore" of Ginevra's perverse romance. Twice he is an anonymous "gentleman" (286, 325); once "a young and handsome man" (459). These blankings out whereby Graham reappears as someone Lucy does not recognize, or does not allow the reader to recognize, portray the frustration of friendship with a man who is "never quite within the compass of [her] penetration" (167), and they force the reader to participate fully in Lucy's recurrent experience of finding that someone she thought she knew is in fact a perfect stranger. This series of blankings out, the most mundane but most painful version of the mystery of knowledge, symbolizes Lucy's repeated loss of Graham. In each case Lucy fails at first to recognize him—a surprising phenomenon, as throughout the book he is clearly an object of intense desire. And yet the desire and blankness are related, for Graham's elusiveness as an object of knowledge as information stands in for his elusiveness as an object of social, perhaps sexual "knowledge," or knowledge as communion.

When Lucy loses Graham entirely as an object of passion, M. Paul begins to replace him as the object of this type of blanking out: he is an anonymous "professor by whom the 'discours' [will be] delivered" at a public function (395); "a head, chest and arms . . . above the crimson desk" (396); "a severe, dark professorial outline . . . seen only in vista" (400); "some former pupil" of Père Silas (485); "a face" (557); "the third member" of a company; a "master carpenter" (579). Most of these blankings out associated with Paul, however, are of the variety that occur when Lucy is afraid to name the object of desire rather than the variety that result from the kind of elusiveness that characterizes Graham, who never makes himself fully open to Lucy's knowledge and who has a way of rescinding his few gestures of communion. These blanking outs of M. Paul, however, do have one important quality in common with those of Graham: they are often related to the discrepancy between Lucy's social status and his. Like Graham's world, Paul's world is a mystery to Lucy partly because she does not have the status to belong to it. Thus at times Graham is an anonymous "gentleman," sitting, for example, with his back to the door as she enters, conversing in a social circle from which she is decidedly excluded (325). Similarly, M. Paul is an important lecturer in a gathering of Villette's elite, or an honored guest at the Hotel Crécy, where Lucy's place is on the periphery. When Graham and Paul are with their social peers, among whom Lucy herself is a blank, they also are blanks to her. Once again, Charlotte Brontë makes explicit the implicit social meaning of a Gothic convention: a woman's sense of being surrounded by mysteries, as de Beauvoir points out, is an aspect of her social exclusion (673), which is the same thing as her seclusion "within the circle of herself" (500).

Thus the process whereby what Lucy knows as familiar becomes "other" has its counterpart in the process whereby Lucy herself is made "other" by those who cannot interpret her correctly. Ginevra, in her double role that asserts the identity between the social perils without and psychological perils within, is a key to the connection. In her novelistic role Ginevra embodies the set of social assumptions that define Lucy as *chose*— a piece of furniture (162) or a "thing" (169)—and so trap her "within the circle of herself," forcing her into the form of egotism Ginevra embodies in her romance role as an allegorical figure of self-absorption. Charlotte Brontë sees that not to be allowed to speak "I"—to make oneself known— is the same as being allowed *only* to speak "I"—the same as being immured in one's private self. And this in turn is the same as an inability to know the world. If Ginevra represents in one sense the self-absorption in Lucy that drains the outside world of its identity, transforming it to *chose,* a blank, she nonetheless also represents the social order that, by blanking Lucy out, subjects her to these dangers of solipsism. And she represents as well the bad faith that makes Lucy assume the role of *chose* for herself. This bad faith is revealed again and again, as when Lucy elects not to tell Graham who she is and thereby challenge his manner of regarding her as a "neutral, passive thing" (169).[15]

However, it is not mere perversity that keeps Lucy from speaking "I," or completely her own responsibility that she is not known.[16] At a crucial moment she recognizes, "with . . . welcome force," Graham's "entire misapprehension of [her] character and nature": "He did not at all guess what I felt: he did not read my eyes, or face, or gestures; though, I doubt not, all spoke" (404). Like Radcliffe's Emily or Roche's Amanda, Lucy is a victim of the misprizing of the heroine which makes it impossible for her to be known even when she speaks. In Radcliffe and Roche, such misknowing is identified with the failure to recognize the heroine's essential innocence. Thus Amanda insists that she is innocent, and her auditor's reaction is to exclaim, "Depend upon it . . . she has been an actress" (*Children of the Abbey* 5: 41). The context of the misknowing in *Villette,* however, is much broader. Like Jane Eyre, whose misfortune it is to be regarded as having the most "cover" precisely when she is being most forthright in revealing her true nature, Lucy Snowe suffers from a radical disjunction between her own experience of herself and the world's assumptions as to what inner states are possible for a woman like her. Thus when Dr. John responds to her "inquiring gaze" with an accusatory look and Lucy decides not to "[clear her]self on the spot" (163) by explaining that she has just recognized him as an old friend, the issue is not that her innocence could not thereby be established but that her selfhood could not thereby be established—that "clearing" herself by announcing her name would not actually make her known. "Suffering him, then, to . . . accuse me of what he would, I resumed some work. . . . There is a perverse mood of the mind which is rather soothed than irritated by misconstruction; and in quarters where we can never be rightly known, we take pleasure, I think, in being consummately ignored" (163–64).

"There is much that is right about Dr. John's infatuation with the empty-headed, unfeeling Ginevra Fanshawe" (Hook 149). Like Ginevra, and for a version of the same reason, Graham is a nonknower, and his incapacities in this regard make him a representative of most of the world in its relation to Lucy. His "perfect knowledge of Villette" gives him the "Open! Sesame" to many closed doors (273), but he admits to being shut out from Lucy's central experience: "My art halts at the threshold of Hypochondria . . ." (257). The reason for this exclusion is that Graham has "dry, materialist views" (338) and is therefore incapable of acknowledging the reality of the ghost that haunts Lucy. His knowledge, though great, is circumscribed. Because he lacks the Gothic imagination that sees specters, there are thresholds he cannot cross, mysteries that cannot haunt him. On her first night in Villette, Lucy felt the impulse to follow him "through continual night, to the world's end" (125), but a later incident shows how ironically misplaced was this passionate trust. The Brettons and Lucy are driven far from home by a drunken coachman who seems to be taking them to "the world's end" (304). Graham takes over and drives them home; as on Lucy's first night in Villette, he keeps her from being lost. Unlike Lucy, Graham always knows where he is. But that knowledge is related to his deeper ignorance: Lucy could never follow him to the world's end because he would never imagine going so far. Graham is associated with "rest and refuge" (Eagleton 71), home and safety; his very name identifies his appeal with that of Lucy's childhood asylum. But like the limited pastorals of Gothic romance, the Bretton of Lucy's childhood was a place where much went unknown and unacknowledged. There Paulina hid her true nature from the Brettons "[w]hile lavishing her eccentricities regardlessly before" Lucy (90), who also kept her feelings to herself.

Like Ginevra, the Brettons see themselves in the world and are therefore unable to know much of what is there. After her agonizing loneliness during a seven-week break in their acknowledgment of her existence, Lucy receives a letter from Louisa: "I daresay you have been just as busy and happy as ourselves at La Terrasse" (354). Lucy's response is to see the wisdom, once again, of remaining a mystery "in quarters where we can never be rightly known" (164):

[H]ow very wise it is in people placed in an exceptional position to hold their tongues and not rashly declare how such position galls them! The world can understand well enough the process of perishing for want of food: perhaps few persons can enter into or follow out that of going mad from solitary confinement. They see the long-buried prisoner disinterred, a maniac or an idiot!—how his sense left him—how his nerves, first inflamed, underwent nameless agony, and then sunk to palsy—is a subject too intricate for examination, too abstract for popular comprehension. Speak of it! you might almost as well stand up in an European market-place, and propound dark sayings in that language and mood wherein Nebuchadnezzar, the imperial hypochondriac, communed with his baffled Chaldeans. (356)

Here is the irony of Lucy's need for self-expression: in a world of Brettons, there is no language in which she could say "I" and be understood.

Graham's incapacity for understanding Lucy is complemented by a related carelessness about sharing himself with her. He sends her letters, but after a while they lose their "sap and significance" (350): his communications have so little substance that their meaning easily drains away. When his first letter arrives, in fact, the imagery associated with it subtly blanks out the overt associations it has with gift giving and the provision of spiritual sustenance. Here, Lucy says, was "the wild savoury mess of the hunter, nourishing . . . and life sustaining . . . what the old dying patriarch demanded of his son Esau, promising him in requital the blessing of his last breath" (318). The man to whom this "life-sustaining" gift was brought, however, was, in Brontë's version of the story, "dying" anyway. Furthermore, the manner in which the feast was presented was a trick: the son who brought it was not the one the father had thought to bless; the recipient of his urgent communication was not the person he imagined. The "Cyclops eye" of the letter's seal recalls an even worse trick, by the monster so wanting in hospitality that instead of feeding his guests, he tried to eat them. The disappointed expectations alluded to in this imagery of feast and ceremony gone awry or perverted are confirmed when Graham, in the "dim garret," actually steals back the letter he has sent (326).

The feast Graham offers is not what it appears, and the Graham who offers it is never the person Lucy keeps wanting him to be. He rescinds his communication; the gold he offers withers to leaves (350). The images typify Lucy's failure in general to attain communion with a frustratingly elusive world beyond her. The incident in which Graham sends her a letter but then reappropriates it recalls an earlier one in which Lucy receives a love letter in a setting full of the imagery of sensuality and marriage: a place to "keep tryste with the rising moon, or taste one kiss of the evening breeze," with vines that "hung their clusters in loving profusion about the favoured spot where jasmine and ivy met, and married them" (173). But the letter was not for her; in fact, it included an insensitive description of her.

Lucy's narrative is infused with the sense that what knowledge people have of one another, what communication they exchange, is subject at any moment to cancellation. There is a strong sense, too, that Lucy's susceptibility to such cancellation is related to her low social status. This connection is illustrated in her conversation with de Bassompierre and Paulina, which is broken by a hiatus of two minutes (368) when Lucy says she is a teacher. The blank following this announcement of her true position reflects the fact that in the society in which Lucy finds herself, she is fundamentally something others are not accustomed to seeing. As "nobody's daughter" she is nobody; as an outsider she has feelings that cannot be imagined by people like Mme. Beck and so are a blank to them; and as the "heretic"[17] hidden in supposedly calm but in fact rebellious women, she is something her society represses—the secret that society has buried, as Lucy buries the letters, in order to hide it from consciousness.

The status that makes Lucy a mystery to others is defined not only by her economic position but also by the way she falls outside the conventional categories of womanhood. Silver points out that Lucy's intelligence, for example, has no "value in the context of cultural expectations for women." Thus when she meets a former schoolmate less intelligent than she but now a blooming wife and mother, "Intelligence, she perceives, does not lead to social visibility or acceptance: she recognizes the older woman but is not in turn recognized by her" (97). There are, however, two characters more capable of recognizing Lucy's real self than is most of the world: Paulina and Paul.

"If anyone knew me," Lucy says at one point, "it was little Paulina Mary" (386). Paulina's capacities as a knower are portrayed in the significant scene in which Lucy observes her reading a book she read with Graham as a child: "Her eyes were the eyes of one who can remember . . . she would not take life, loosely and incoherently, in parts, and let one season slip as she entered on another . . ." (359). Lucy praises Paulina's ability to experience life whole, without gaps: to escape the mystery of knowledge that confronts Lucy at every turn. Between 1849 and 1850, Brontë, according to Carlisle, had been reading autobiographies that treat memory as "the source and proof of personal identity" ("Face" 264).[18] One of these autobiographies was Wordsworth's *Prelude;*[19] and Carlisle identifies Paulina's "sense of the past" as Wordsworthian, pointing out that for both Wordsworth and Paulina "[m]emory . . . is literally a source of integrity, that sense of a self that is 'consistent,' 'harmonious,' and 'unwavering' " ("Face" 286).

Paulina has the secure and graceful ability to know; Lucy is constantly in danger of not knowing. The reference to "a stilly pause, a wordless silence, a long blank of oblivion" (348) from her description of others' relations with her is a good definition as well of the kind of blanking out that characterizes Lucy's narrative and her experience. The source of the difference between Paulina and Lucy in this respect is that throughout the whole sequence at La Terrasse after the reunion of Graham and Paulina, Paulina's ability to remember is contrasted with Lucy's tendency to be forgotten. The prologue to the sequence begins with the description of the "stilly pause" and the "snow-sepulchre"; even after Lucy is supposedly "disinterred" (356) and rescued to La Terrasse, the image of being snowed in persists in the descriptions of the snowstorm, "that passion of January" (373) that keeps the women shut in at home, waiting for their men to return. The real "passion of January" that is locking Lucy once more in her Snowe sepulcher is Paulina and Graham's revival of love for each other. Even as she describes its bloom, Lucy fills her narrative with cold, snow, winter, ice. The truth is that as Paulina increasingly knows and is known, Lucy is increasingly forgotten and must try to forget; that is why the next chapter describes "A Burial."

Lucy and Polly are much alike as children: they are distinguished by extraordinary self-control, lose their Home, love Graham and lose him, find him again, receive his first letter, and respond with a letter carefully rewritten to conceal its passion. But Paulina is the heroine of Gothic comedy who is restored to Home, gains a fortune, and is reunited with the beloved she lost at first. Lucy's experience is the opposite. The difference between them is that Paulina is attractive and wealthy, while Lucy is neither. As Tanner says, Paulina's "lucency in a world tending increasingly to opacity" is linked to her "protected position and good fortune." The novel asks how such "lucency" is possible in Lucy's different position (23).

Paulina's own similarity to Lucy gives her insight into Lucy's strange character, but in the end she allies herself with the non-knower Graham, to whose views of Lucy she assimilates her own. " 'Graham says you are the most peculiar, capricious little woman he knows; but yet you are excellent; we both think so,' " says Paulina (520). "You both think you know not what," Lucy retorts, relegating Paulina also to the category of non-knower and shutting herself out of the couple's happy life: "I have my sort of life apart from yours" (520).

Lucy's "life apart," her separateness, is the source of her most excruciating suffering, but she is afraid of the unity that comes from being known. The most dangerous threat in this respect is M. Paul, who makes the most insistent and perceptive attempts to know Lucy, and who has considerable "inquisitorial curiosity" (311) as well as inquisitorial powers. These powers, and Lucy's reactions to them, recall the strange resemblance of rescuing hero and threatening villain in women's Gothic. M. Paul is jesuitical and inquisitorial; it is he who arranges for her to be "put to the torture" of the "show trial" (492–93) in which his eminent colleagues repeat, *mutatis mutandis,* their lecherous pursuit of the Gothic heroine on her first night in Villette. At his very first encounter with Lucy, M. Paul puts on his glasses in order to "read" her face—the same glasses Lucy later breaks, in an action symbolic of her resistance to the kind of reading of which he is capable. Lucy describes M. Paul's remarkable powers of knowledge with horrified awe: "[I]n some cases, he had the terrible unerring penetration of instinct, and pierced in its hiding-place the last lurking thought of the heart, and discerned under florid veilings the bare, barren places of the spirit: yes, and its perverted tendencies, and its hidden false curves—all that men and women would not have known . . ." (423–24). So thorough is his research into "female human nature" (453) that he uses a glass to "read" Mme. Beck's garden, "banquet[ing] secretly and sacreligiously on Eve's apples" (456).

Again and again Paul figures as an intruder on Lucy's private space. He inaugurates their friendship by marching into her closed "sanctuary": "The closed door of the first classe—my sanctuary—offered no obstacle; it burst open, and . . . two eyes . . . hungrily dived into me" (201). Later, weeping over her loneliness, Lucy looks up to find his face at the window before her (310). As their relationship progresses, he makes a practice of rifling through her desk. Not only does M. Paul intrude on Lucy; he also confines her, at one point shutting her in the garret and at another insisting that she remain in an overheated room.

These activities of intrusion and confinement suggest Gothic villainy, and it is a measure of Brontë's subtlety that she presents Lucy's fear of Paul the knower both as justified (he is threatening, intrusive, confiningly sexist)[20] and as something to be overcome, a symptom of her pathological reserve. His efforts to know Lucy resemble Jane Eyre's determination to " 'burst' with boldness and good will into 'the silent sea' " of St. John's soul (398). Not only are Paul's intrusions an evidence of friendship; his storming of Lucy's reserve comes to resemble the siege of the soul by Christ. The comparison is by no means exaggerated. Paul is described as a shepherd with his sheep (475) and is implicitly compared with the master in the biblical parable of the talents (593). His surname Emanuel associates his presence with incarnation, and his many arrivals have the nature of advents.[21] This is most evident when he appears before Lucy's eyes in the park with his godchild Sauveur and when Lucy in her convent interprets his approaching footsteps as those of a master carpenter (579). His first name links him to Paulina, with her ability to receive experience whole, unmarred by the blanks of not knowing. And it links him as well to the saint who hoped someday to know fully, even as he would be fully known.

Paul's willingness to know fully is important. Unlike Mme. Beck, who pries in order to confirm her suspicions and is merely baffled by discrep-

ancies that suggest an interpretation of Lucy she has not already anticipated, Paul is able, to a significant extent, to learn Lucy's nature—which
is, after all, radically Other than his in many ways. As Platt points out,
Paul's agreement that Lucy should keep her religion, and his provisions
for her independence while he is away, show that he "even comes to
realize Lucy's need for a character and an identity of her own, a realization which few heroes in Victorian novels ever approach" (23). The
"junta" expend much effort in an attempt both to make Lucy the same as
themselves, Catholic, and to make Paul regard her as fearfully Other. It
is a measure of Paul's triumph over this sinister conspiracy that both
these endeavors fail: he can give up his attempt to convert Lucy to Catholicism, because he overcomes his fear of her as what de Beauvoir
would call an independent "subject" (xviii–xxiii).

Paul's willingness to be known as well as to know is also important,
for unlike the inquisitorial research of the guarded Mme. Beck (to whom
he is, however, related), his prying is associated with generosity and
gifts. He dives "hungrily" into Lucy but feeds her royally later; he rifles
through her desk but leaves presents there; he arranges the "show trial"
to make her display her knowledge, but he also imparts to her his own.
Indeed, like the good father or hero of Gothic romance, he shares with
the heroine the treasures of knowledge: "[H]is mind was . . . my library,
and whenever it was opened to me, I entered bliss" (472). Nevertheless,
Lucy is afraid: not only of being known by Paul, but even of knowing
him. In an extraordinary scene, her impulse to console Paul, whom she
sees standing sadly outside, turns to terror with his impulse toward her,
and she flees through her convent like any hapless Gothic heroine. "Nor
did I pause till I had taken sanctuary in the oratory, now empty. Listening
there with beating pulses, and an unaccountable, undefined apprehension,
I heard him pass through all the schoolrooms, clashing the doors impatiently as he went; I heard him invade the refectory . . ." (476). Lucy's
escape is successful; she hears Mme. Beck sending her pursuer away.
"As that street-door closed, a sudden amazement at my own perverse
proceeding struck like a blow upon me. I felt from the first it was me he
wanted—me he was seeking—and had not I wanted him too? What, then,
had carried me away? What had rapt me beyond his reach? He had something to tell: he was going to tell me that something: my ear strained its
nerve to hear it, and I had made the confidence impossible" (477). As a
logical consequence of this flight from confidence, Lucy is left in a horrible state of not knowing: "[H]ere was dead blank . . . and drear suspense" (477).

The heroine's flight from the hero as if he were a villain recalls the flights of Emmeline from Godolphin (Smith, *Emmeline* 377–78) and Madeleine from de Sevignie (Roche, *Clermont* 2: 6–8). Charlotte Brontë, however, makes more obvious the psychological meaning of such accidental or mistaken flights by having Lucy know she is fleeing in terror from precisely the man she wants most to see. And her subtlety is revealed in the fact that there are both good and bad reasons for Lucy's retreat.

Lucy's desire to know and be known is hemmed in by fears, but it asserts itself nonetheless—for example, in the feverish romance she makes of Ginevra's life, imagining her far from Graham but linked by "a fine chain of mutual understanding . . . carrying, across mound and hollow, communication by prayer and wish" (230). She romanticizes Ginevra and Graham, in other words, into Jane Eyre and Rochester—a fantasy grotesquely inappropriate, as their egotism makes them incapable, both singly and mutually, of such an act of knowledge. The desire revealed in this fantasy—Lucy's desperate longing for a communion of which her selfish double Ginevra is incapable—shows that M. Paul is right to see her own egotism, which no one else perceives, as his true enemy. Lucy is locked up; M. Paul intrudes on her both to offer his communion and to liberate her from the prison of self. The latter motive is revealed not only in his insistence that Lucy communicate with him but also in his decision to help her become "known" in Villette: "After all, you are solitary and a stranger, and have your way to make and your bread to earn . . ." (227).

Lucy does finally become "known" outside Mme. Beck's walls, in an extraordinary version of the Gothic heroine's escape from the convent. This escape is the climax of a Gothic drama of confinement and release, in which the heroine exorcises a ghost, overcomes a secret conspiracy, and finds the power to say "I." Brontë's treatments of the Gothic device of the conspiracy and the ghost operate, like the shift from family dwelling to convent, both to establish a social context for this drama and to identify that context fully with the psychological one that it in great measure creates.

V

The social forces that work against Lucy's self-transcendence are strong with the sinister, omnipresent energy of the old Gothic secret conspiratorial organization. The choice of a conspiracy as Lucy's Gothic enemy is especially significant in the light of Caroline Helstone's musings, in the earlier novel *Shirley,* on the question of who is responsible for single women's fate: "[N]obody in particular is to blame, that I can see, for the state in which things are; and I cannot tell, however much I puzzle over it, how they are to be altered for the better; but I feel there is something wrong somewhere. I believe single women should have more to do . . ." (376–77). In *Villette,* somebody "in particular" is to blame. The use of the Gothic conspiracy represents an attempt to assign responsibility for, among other things, the social pressure on women to resign themselves to something else Caroline believed was not "enough": "abnegation of self" (*Shirley* 190).[22] Lucy's struggle against the "junta" raises the moral question of the relation of women's self-transcendence to self-indulgence on the one hand and self-abnegation on the other. This question was at issue as Jane Eyre struggled first with the temptation to indulge her fiery nature as Rochester's mistress and then with St. John's equally dangerous lure, "the flame and excitement of sacrifice" (429). It becomes an even more urgent issue for Lucy, as the junta works to usurp what Wollstonecraft would have called her "power over her self."

The junta is an especially sinister conspiracy, because it works both outside its victim and in her mind. Lucy says once that she seems to have "two lives—the life of thought, and that of reality," the latter being concerned with "daily bread, hourly work, and a roof of shelter" and the former with "the strange necromantic joys of fancy" (140). In *Villette* the forces of violence that imperil the heroine, threatening on the one hand to isolate her from the world and on the other to break down the barriers and distinctions that define her "insular" selfhood, are both internal and external, psychological and social. As aspects of "the life . . . of reality," the junta represents the foreign institutions that constitute the establishment of Villette: schools, church, money interests. The choice of the political term *junta* calls attention to the public context in which Lucy's private drama is set: it suggests a concerted effort by forces in the outer world to usurp the rule of her inner life. The members of this junta play roles as figures in the social world with which Lucy is forced to interact and in which she must try to find a place despite her placelessness and alienation. At the same time they play allegorical roles in the psychomachia of her inner world. Their double novelistic and romance roles signify the shaping of psychic reality by social pressures, and indeed the internalization[23] of social pressures as psychological forces.

The name of the prime mover of the junta, Modeste, is the first indication of her significance as an allegorical figure in Lucy's psychomachia: the director of a convent, Mme. Beck is a representation of Lucy's tendency to wall herself up, shut herself away, remain unknown. As an embodiment of Lucy's modesty, Mme. Beck represents an internal force that works against self-expression. But she is also an external force that renders Lucy unable to speak "I." Lucy's confinement to Mme. Beck's pensionnat, the only place she could get a position in Villette, is an emblem of her nonexistence in the eyes of a world in which her social status is nil. From this world she is hidden away, invisible. Even to think of self-expression in such a case seems ludicrous; thus Lucy's speech, like her life, is marred by "pain, privation, penury" (307).

Mme. Beck also represents a force of inhibition on Lucy's self-expression because she is the embodiment of cold reason divorced from emotion and imagination. In Lucy's inner world it is Imagination who longs for self-expression and Reason who says no. "But if I feel may I *never* express?" Lucy asks in her inner debate. " '*Never!*' declared Reason" (307). It is Reason who rewrites and revises Lucy's letter to Graham, forcing her to say less than she would like; Reason who constricts and constrains and sets up the "bounds" Lucy feels compelled to "break . . . at intervals" (308). Imagination is different: "Divine, compassionate, succourable influence! . . . To thee neither hands build, nor lips consecrate; but hearts, through ages, are faithful to thy worship. A dwelling thou hast, too wide for walls, too high for dome—a temple whose floors are space . . ." (308). The implication is that Lucy has such a faculty—this infinite space—inside her: the temple of Imagination is in one sense an image of the immensities of her own soul. But to these immensities her environment is inevitably hostile. Throughout the novel she is continually finding herself in places too small for her: the "two hot, close rooms" at Miss Marchmont's that economic necessity constrains her to make her "world" (97); the little "closet" (120) assigned her at the hotel in London by those who perceive her financial value as small; her "tiny chamber" (241) at La Terrasse, which, "though pretty, was small . . . confining" (245); and the "little closet" Graham keeps for her in his heart, with "Lucy's Room" written over the door (555). These narrow spaces are Lucy's because of her economic status; Graham himself judges her by her appearance (162) (her value in the marriage market), and her modest means: "Ah, Graham! . . . Had Lucy been intrinsically the same, but possessing the additional advantages of wealth and station, would your manner to her, your value for her have been quite what they actually were?" (401).

These modest means are the reason for the "extreme modesty of [the] appointments" in Lucy's hotel "closet" (120) and indeed are the reason she finds Modeste herself in charge of her life. Mme. Beck is the inner tyranny born of Lucy's consciousness of her economic insignificance; she is constrained to shy withdrawal because her lack of place in society warrants no other relation to the people around her. But Mme. Beck is also the corresponding external tyranny that encloses Lucy in this all-too-narrow self-definition. In social terms, her subjection to Mme. Beck expresses the relations natural between a person of no social standing and an employer of reputation and authority in her world. Commanding deference and respect, Mme. Beck moves in elite circles, has important relatives, and displays her name on a building in the city where she lives. Lucy is small, Mme. Beck is robust; Lucy speaks haltingly, Mme. Beck never falters in her smooth manipulation of the people around her. Lucy needs money and Mme. Beck pays her; in exchange Lucy submits to the rules of an alien institution—a "convent" in a foreign country—that significantly curtails her freedom.

This institution is an economic system in which Lucy finds herself near the bottom of the ladder, first as a governess and then as a teacher receiving half the salary of her male counterpart for "thrice the work" (144); a social system in which Lucy is "nobody"; and a system for the education of girls that is really a system of "slavery" (195). Once again, that is, a Gothic heroine's relation to alien institutions shows an ordinary woman's experience of contemporary social, economic, and educational institutions as alien and oppressive forces.

Mme. Beck's role as an educator is especially interesting, because she defines it solely in terms of maintaining order. The qualities Mme. Beck requires in a teacher are revealed in her approval of Lucy's first classroom victory, locking a "mutinous" girl in the closet (144)—[24] an ominous triumph at best, considering Lucy's own tendency to be confined in small rooms. In this identification of education with restraint Mme. Beck represents once again both external and internal threats to Lucy: the alien institutions that regulate her life by locking it up; her own attempts to form her character by a system of restraint and calm.

Mme. Beck's full name, suggesting "modest beak," points to the viciousness of her quiet and unassuming methods of control: one thinks of the crows and pies that will come to pick the bones of the dormouse out of his wall. In order to maintain calm she indulges in perpetual vigilance, surveillance, espionage. Mme. Beck has little interest in imparting to others the legitimate knowledge that should be the business of an educational establishment, but much in gaining illicit knowledge about them for her own use. Sneaking around with her duplicate keys, opening drawers, entering other people's rooms, and going through their pockets, she is an "inquisitress" (378): one of the many terms that paint her pensionnat as a place where Lucy is subject to perpetual judgment, including the "torture" of the "show-trial" (492–93). The book is filled with these explicit and implicit images of judgment that express Lucy's sense of alienation in a world where—like all misprized Gothic heroines and all the real women whose pain theirs represents—she is powerless to establish her own worth.

In this world Lucy is haunted by other people's attempts to know her, a desperate shyness represented in the association of Mme. Beck's inquisitorial activity with ghostliness. Lucy awaits her first appearance with a pounding heart and "eyes fixed" in terror on a door that remains closed as Mme. Beck simply appears in the room, having come in by another entrance (126–27). Lucy realizes this is "No ghost" (127), but the incident is of course the beginning of Lucy's haunting by the suspicions of Mme. Beck, who appears in her room as "a white figure" "in the dead of night" to analyze her countenance and who is wont to "glide ghost-like through the house watching and spying everywhere, peering through every key-hole, listening behind every door" (136). Like Jane Eyre, Lucy lives as an alien in a world both determined to find her out and absolutely impermeable to any knowledge of her real nature.

The ruthless, dispassionate inquisition that haunts Lucy is again both external and internal. Her vulnerability to Mme. Beck's careful espionage represents her perpetual subjection to the judgments of a foreign society, but also to the paralyzing calm of her own "self-surveillance."[25] For her inner world, like the convent, is haunted by cold Reason, forever on the lookout for passion, determined to keep every scene "within bounds," insistent on submitting the most delicate feelings to torturous scrutiny. Like Mme. Beck, in whose house no "key [is] a safe-guard" or "padlock a barrier" (379), "Reason" is always intruding into Lucy's affairs: "the doors of my heart would shake, bolt and bar would yield, Reason would leap in . . ." (335). Mme. Beck's inquisitorial methods as an educator represent the violence of Lucy's own attempts to know herself and, having rooted out her passions in their hiding places, to school herself brutally in restraint and control. The logic of Mme. Beck's simultaneous status as an internal force of repression and an external spy for an alien society is illuminated by Eagleton's comment:

> To allow passionate imagination premature rein is to be exposed, vulnerable and ultimately self-defeating: it is to be locked in the red room, enticed into

bigamous marriage, ensnared like Caroline Helstone in a hopelessly self-consuming love. Passion springs from the very core of the self and yet is hostile, alien, invasive; the world of internal fantasy must therefore be locked away, as the mad Mrs Rochester stays locked up on an upper floor of Thornfield, slipping out to infiltrate the 'real' world only in a few unaware moments of terrible destructiveness. The inner world must yield of necessity to the practical virtues of caution, tact, and observation . . . the wary, vigilant virtues by which the self's lonely integrity can be defended in a spying, predatory society, a society on the watch for the weak spot which will surrender you into its hands. (17)[26]

The endless conflict between Lucy's natural emotions and the "wary, vigilant virtues" that judge them makes its way even into her narrative style, in which the rhetoric of self-justification bursts out at surprising moments: "Of an artistic temperament, I deny that I am" (122); "I, Lucy Snowe, plead guiltless of that curse, an overheated and discursive imagination . . ." (69); "I, Lucy Snowe, was calm" (79); "[I]t was no yearning to attain, no hunger to taste; only the calm desire to look on a new thing" (175); ". . . (once, for all, in this parenthesis, I disclaim, with the utmost scorn, every sneaking suspicion of what are called 'warmer feelings' . . .)" (335). Lucy protests that she is not passionate and imaginative and artistic, that she did not desire too much, that she was not in love with Graham. But because there is no one to accuse Lucy of such crimes but herself, the very act of self-defense, as in the Gothic dream of perpetual unjust accusation, is an admission of guilt. Speaking in these passages is the voice of one part of Lucy trying not to be known by the other—the Imagination saying that it is not overheated. And above it speaks the voice of another faculty that, although suspicious, wants the defense to be true, prefers not to know: Reason insisting that she, not some more unruly power, is in control.

Against Mme. Beck's prying, Lucy is finally reduced to sealing her letters in a glass jar and burying them beneath the tree where the grave of the ghostly nun is reported to lie. The act reveals her own repressive tendencies as a form of self-defense. What better way to keep from being known than to bury one's passions so that they are inaccessible even to oneself? And what better way to escape one's own self-scrutiny?

Lucy's self-enclosure at Mme. Beck's is in great measure a consequence of being too different from, too radically Other than, her world. In Père Silas, the second member of the junta, she encounters the temptation of making herself the same as her world, by giving up the "strange, self-reliant, invulnerable creed" (512) that sets her apart as a Protestant in Catholic Villette. This conversion would be for Lucy a dissolution of the boundaries of the self in two ways: by depriving her of something that distinguishes her as inimitably herself in a foreign land and by making her vulnerable to monkish prying. In Lucy's anti-Catholic view, this prying is the inevitable relationship between the priesthood and the devotee, on whom the church intrudes with a wicked disregard for the integrity of the individual soul. Lucy sees as sinful Paul's "Jesuit-system" of research into female human nature in Mme. Beck's garden—"I wish you were a Protestant"— and implies that "Eve's apples" are standard fare for Catholics (455–56).

In this context the way Lucy meets Père Silas is significant: she comes upon him in the aftermath of the terrible nightmare that "the well-loved dead, who had loved *me* well in life, met me elsewhere, alienated" (231). This nightmare of not being known even by those who should know her best helps explain her arrival at the temptation Père Silas represents: the confessional booth.

Lucy's self-burial at Mme. Beck's is a response to the fear of being known. Père Silas, on the other hand, presents the temptation of putting herself in a position in which complete strangers, routinely, would know her completely. "These Romanists are strange beings. Such a one among them—whom you know no more than the last Inca of Peru, or the first Emperor of China—knows you and all your concerns . . ." (486). As is so often the case in Gothic romance, however, there turns out to be little difference between fearful unity and fearful separateness. The confessional booth is itself the smallest room into which Lucy has yet been tempted: Gilbert and Gubar discuss its role as "an even more limiting" space than the "confining" convent and point out that, ironically, Lucy can only "confess" here "that she does not belong in this narrow space which cannot contain her: 'mon père, je suis Protestante' " (414–15). Père Silas tempts her to renounce her status as Other by making this space her own and, indeed, by shutting herself inside a real, not merely a figurative, convent.

In his appeal he gives voice to one of Lucy's worst fears: that, for the "class of natures" to which she belongs, "[t]he world . . . has no satisfaction" (234). Lucy's own preference for repression speaks in Père Silas: "[A] mind so tossed can find repose but in the bosom of retreat . . ." (234). Better to shut oneself up and renounce the desire for transcendence entirely than to be continually disappointed. If becoming a nun is not literally a temptation for Lucy, it nonetheless represents something that is: the temptation of privacy and privation, of "retreat" from the desire that is Lucy's spiritual energy and therefore, however painful, her life.

As Rose Yorke says in *Shirley,* defending the way *The Italian* evokes her desire to travel, "Better to try all things and find all empty, than to try nothing and leave your life a blank" (385).

In essence, Père Silas tempts Lucy with the view St. John presented to Jane, that "this world is not the scene of fruition" (*Jane Eyre* 416). In her visit to the withered crone who refuses her offer of fruit, Lucy encounters a different aspect of the same temptation: the most bizarre member of the junta. This strange figure, Magloire Walravens, resides at Numero 3, Rue des Mages. The magic implied in the address suggests the extraordinary strength of the uncanny power Malevola represents, the power not only of ill will toward Lucy from the alien society outside her but of Lucy's own capacity for shutting herself in and shutting other people out. Because this is an inner capacity created by the malevolence directed toward her from outside, it is aptly represented by the same figure who embodies that external force.

Malevola's surname suggests a wall, and much of her significance as an internal and external threat to Lucy is revealed in her association with barriers. The difficulty of crossing her "inhospitable threshold" (480), old convention of Gothic romance, is here used not only to call attention to the dividing line between diurnal and oneiric spaces but also to suggest one of Lucy's greatest perils: her own tendency to keep other people out of her private world. Even inside her well-secured house, Mme. Walravens secludes herself in a hidden apartment behind a secret door. In her ungenerous self-enclosure she is the opposite of M. Paul, who is revealed in this episode to be the very type of "charity unbounded" (489). Malevola refuses to extend hospitality; she refuses also to accept it, turning away Lucy's gift with an assertion of self-reliance: she can buy what she needs (482). In a book in which food so often stands for the spiritual sustenance of friendship, this proud refusal of fruit (and by implication, fruitfulness) makes Mme. Walravens the symbol of a force inimical to the free and generous exchanges of love. Indeed, before Lucy can discern her shape she perceives her first as a vague "obstruction" (481).

What this obstruction is in social terms is suggested by Malevola's representation of money interests. She prevented the union of Justine Marie and M. Paul because the latter was not rich enough, just as she will try to prevent Lucy's union with M. Paul in order to keep his money for herself. Her grotesque figure with its fabulous jewels "blazing" in the "deep gloom" (481) makes her house a Cave of Mammon—later she is associated with Mammon directly (559)—but in an appropriate paradox, she is destitute. The jewels are only mementos of her splendid lost youth

("ma gloire," presumably). In this context they point to the spiritual penury of the fanatical materialism that assesses people's value by their economic status. By this standard of value Lucy is nobody; thus Mme.
Walravens represents the social forces that threaten, on the basis of material considerations, to blank Lucy out. The result, to use Gilbert and
Gubar's phrase, would be to make her "nun(none)."

What Mme. Walravens represents in psychological terms is Lucy's
tendency to collaborate with these social forces by accepting her role as
"a mere shadowy spot on a field of light" (200), hiding herself away in
perverse self-reliance, erasing herself by refusing even to make an old
friend aware of her identity, and burying herself alive. As an aspect of
Lucy, Malevola represents Lucy's own difficulty giving people admission
to her inner world. She too is inhospitable, placing Ginevra between herself and M. Paul, moving away from him on the bench, fleeing when she
knows he is seeking her. But just as Ginevra stands for the egotism of
Lucy's self-effacement in her dealings with Paul, Magloire's name suggests that the tendency to self-abnegation is merely a version of vanity.
In Magloire's dwarfed and haughty form, the identity of self-aggrandize-
ment and self-belittlement is revealed: an equivalence reinforced in the
relation of this crabbed egotist to the mild and obedient nun, Justine
Marie.

This relation is presented symbolically in the fact that the nun's picture
opens like a door to reveal Malevola:[27] a brilliant version both of the
moving portrait of Gothic romance and the Gothic heroine's discovery
of an "unsuspected door" (Brown, *Ormond* 232). When a Gothic heroine
discovers an intriguing portrait, she is sooner or later bound to discover
in it a relation to herself, perhaps even a clue to her own identity: the
portrait is that of her mother, her father, her aunt, and so on. Here the
secret significance of the mysterious portrait is indicated by the fact that
it is the unsuspected door, hiding the real nature of the conventual life
into which Justine Marie was forced by Mme. Walravens and into which
the junta would like to tempt Lucy. The picture of what at first seemed a
Madonna (483), and then a young nun, rolls back to reveal the deformed
and stunted life of fruitlessness, relationships refused, impoverished egotism blazing in a childish display of vanity. In this last quality Magloire
resembles that other admirer of baubles, Ginevra, who, incapable of generosity herself, lives ungratefully off that of other people. Magloire represents the hideous deformity of that seclusion deep in self which is, in
Brontë's resolutely Protestant view, the conventual life. Together Malevola and the nun, like the twin mirror image of Lucy and Ginevra, show

that passionate egotism and total self-abnegation are two faces of the same self-enclosure.

In the portrait of the nun Lucy recognizes "inactive passions, acquiescent habits" (484). Thus like the other members of the junta, Malevola is the lure of restraining or stupefying one's "active soul." One of the subtleties of this lure is that the nun, as Blom points out, represents the temptation, to Paul, of idealized, sexless feminine passivity: ". . . Justine's power is real, for Paul . . . who . . . demands of himself and his mate a purity which equates with sexual abstinence—may allow 'the picture of a pale dead nun to rise, an eternal barrier' because she alone can satisfy 'his heart, sworn to virginity' " (99).[28]

Père Silas calls the dead nun Paul's "beloved saint" (488), but in the *lectures pieuses*— "tales of moral martyrdom inflicted by Rome"—the reader has seen what saints' lives are: "nightmares of oppression, privation, and agony" (184). Père Silas has tried already to tempt Lucy to escape her longings through privation instead of fruition; in the figure of Malevola, the woman concealed behind the placid face of the "saint" with her "inactive passions," the dangers of repression as a remedy for desire are made plain. That Lucy's adventure in Malevola's house is an encounter with the repressed is evident in the aged, decaying aspect of the house, hidden away in the oldest, deepest part of town, the "Basse Ville." This, together with its difficulty of access, suggests that in her visit here Lucy is finding the past, confronting what has been locked away and surrounded with walls. To enter here, as it turns out, is to cross what Jane Eyre would term Paul's "threshold of confidence" (*Jane Eyre* 400), for the House of Malevola belongs to him. The walls are his; it is his past that is buried here.

This burial is in one sense an image of dangerous repression, but the portrait in its dark "shrine of memory" (a phrase from Jane's initial impression of Thornfield that is interestingly appropriate here [*Jane Eyre* 137]) is also a clue to something else: the danger of not being able to forget. "[H]e disclosed what seemed more like an oratory than a boudoir . . . looking as if it were a place rather dedicated to relics and remembrance, than designed for present use and comfort" (483). The moving portrait of Gothic romance suggests the power of the dead, especially ancestors, to come to life at any moment. Thus Alfonso, for example, steps out of his frame in *The Castle of Otranto* to intervene in the lives of the present generation.[29] As the movement of the portrait indicates, Justine Marie, who should be dead, is still alive in this old house. As that fact in turn reveals, Paul, like Lucy, is tempted to retreat from the possibility of fruition in the world. This "pale dead nun" (491) is the ghost that haunts him, attaching him to the past and threatening to deprive him of "present . . . comfort" for the sake of a passion that should have been buried long ago. Instead of burying this one passion, he has tried to bury all passion, insisting that the very feeling is "alien" to him: "It died in the past—in the present it lies buried—its grave is deep-dug, well-heaped, and many winters old . . ." (433). But he, like Lucy, is visited by the ghost, and on one occasion they see it together (458). After Lucy visits Malevola, Paul cautions against the "morbid fanc[y]" of thinking the ghostly nun is the ghost of Justine Marie. "Yet I should have liked to ask M. Paul," says Lucy, "whether the 'morbid fancies,' against which he warned me, wrought in his own brain" (502). As in *Jane Eyre,* the hidden Other Woman belongs to the heroine, the hero, and the interaction between them.

For Lucy, too, has a passion to bury before she can be free to love Paul. She has put Graham's letters in the ghostly nun's grave beneath the pear tree, but sometimes she dreams "strangely of disturbed earth, and of hair, still golden and living, obtruded through coffin-chinks" (451). The reference to Graham's golden hair recalls other references to gold, including the unattainable fruit of the Hesperides (281) and the "golden fruitage of Paradise" to which Lucy angrily compares happiness when Graham blithely exorts her to "cultivate" it (330). These images evoke a lost, inaccessible Eden that both is and never was the past: a past elusive, longed-for, unable to be retrieved, but also (as in the grotesque image of golden hair), haunting, unable to be exorcised. Both Lucy and Paul must give up the image of a lost paradise in order to exorcise the past and be fruitful in the present.[30] The junta tries to promote the sanctification of the past at the expense of the present. As Lucy notices, it is a strange "shrine" indeed at which Mme. Beck chooses to offer up her fruit and an "uncouth thing she worship[s]" (482).

This is the same strange shrine at which M. Paul himself offers up his life, and in the story of his worship in the "oratory" (483) there, Lucy recognizes the perils that threaten her own relationship with him. "Was I, then, to be frightened by Justine Marie? Was the picture of a pale dead nun to rise, an eternal barrier? And what of the charities which absorbed his worldly goods? What of his heart, sworn to virginity?" (491). These are the dangers of poverty (what would she and Paul live on if they married?), chastity (what of Paul's vow of virginity?), and obedience (the "acquiescent habits" of the nun, which the junta wants Lucy to accept by yielding her will to it and the Catholic church).

All the members of the junta tempt Lucy to acquiescence, confinement, repression; to a hiding away of self that is one with the vain delusions of egotism. All represent, in different ways, the danger of "inactive passions," the loss of the vital energy that is desire. Mme. Beck, reason divorced from emotion, is the danger of too much calm—"You envenom and you paralyze" (544), Lucy tells her later. Père Silas tempts Lucy to choose privation instead of risking desire, to renounce the active for the contemplative life. Malevola is the true shape of that life, the twisted woman hidden behind the placid face of the "saint" Justine Marie.

Such are the forces Lucy must resist if she is to escape burial alive. The extent of her collusion with these forces is manifest in her most characteristic response to her own longings for transcendence. In a startling instance of this response, Lucy describes her wild reaction to the sublime:

> One night a thunderstorm broke; a sort of hurricane shook us in our beds. . . . the tempest took hold of me with tyranny: I was roughly roused and obliged to live. I got up and dressed myself, and creeping outside the casement close by my bed, sat on its ledge, with my feet on the roof of a lower adjoining building. It was wet, it was wild, it was pitch-dark. . . . I could not go in: too resistless was the delight of staying with the wild hour, black and full of thunder, pealing out such an ode as language never delivered to man—too terribly glorious, the spectacle of clouds, split and pierced by white and blinding bolts. (176)

Here the heroine is quite literally drawn out of her convent room, through her casement window, into an impassioned communion with a sublime nature that speaks, in a language beyond words, for her inmost self. She longs, "achingly, then and for four-and-twenty hours afterwards, for something to fetch me out of my present existence, and lead me upwards and onwards" (176). Her response is to muster a force of inner repression strong enough to quell such a passionate transcendent impulse: "This longing, and all of a similar kind, it was necessary to knock on the head; which I did, figuratively, after the manner of Jael to Sisera, driving a nail through their temples. Unlike Sisera, they did not die: they were but transiently stunned, and at intervals would turn on the nail with a rebellious wrench; then did the temples bleed, and the brain thrill to its core." (176) The image is a shocking reminder of Lucy's collaboration with the powers that would torture her, wall her up, bury her alive. She has described her fear of stimuli that might wake "the being I was always lulling": "About the present, it was better to be stoical: about the future—such a future as mine—to be dead. And in catalepsy and a dead trance, I studiously held the quick of my nature" (175). The shocking word here is *studiously;* like the matter-of-fact tone of "This longing . . . it was necessary to knock on the head," it implies a dangerous, desperate self-division in which one part of Lucy, with calm reason and meticulous care, does wrenching violence to the other.

With such a psychological makeup, external enemies hardly seem necessary; Lucy does enough violence on herself. Similarly, if other people consign Lucy to rooms too small for her, she is nonetheless easily persuaded to choose such spaces as her own. After only a week with Miss Marchmont, for example, she is ready to make the invalid's small "world" her own (97). But this internal impulse to self-confinement and self-violence itself derives from the external forces of violence:[31] the fact that, formally, Modeste and Magloire play at the same time novelistic roles as members of a social hierarchy and romance roles as figures in Lucy's psychomachia asserts the identity of the external and internal perils that threaten her. The junta represents internal perils because it symbolizes forces in Lucy that work against her self-expression in the world, but it also represents external perils—threats from the established powers of wealth, institutionalized religion, and social prestige that rule a society in which she is powerless. And it represents the connection between—indeed, in a sense the identity of—the perils within and without. If the public forces that threaten Lucy socially have a frightening reality in her inner, psychic space as well, it is because she has internalized the oppression they represent. Her social position as a single woman lacking both the personal attractions necessary for success in the marriage market and a source of income apart from poorly paying work has created the internal figures of tyrannical reason and pathological modesty, self-abnegation that is the extreme egotism of inhospitable self-enclosure, and an inner prohibition against even the mildest attempts to bring her desires to fruition in the world.

The conflation of novel and romance in the portrayal of Lucy's external-internal enemies reveals Brontë's special insight into the question of the extent to which the evil Other that the Gothic heroine must confront is really herself. Conventional women's Gothic backs away from identifying the evil Other as the heroine's self, for two reasons: a schizophrenic moral view that forbade the recognition of evil depths in a good woman and a perception that, in fact, for women the evil Other genuinely is other—radically different from and external to the heroine it oppresses.

In her portrayal of the junta as an allegory of Lucy's psychology, Brontë acknowledges that the evil Other is the heroine's self. But she shows too that for a member of an oppressed group[32] the most threatening inner peril *is* other, external, alien—a conspiracy from the outside, internalized—and that it is precisely the internalized forces of violence that, as Mary Daly would say, have alienated women from their authentic selves.[33]

The individual members of the conspiracy represent dangers that threaten Lucy generally. As a combination they work, in particular, to inhibit Lucy's relationship with one man, M. Paul. This fact in itself distinguishes the treatment here of the interrelationship of the social and psychological forces of violence from that in *Jane Eyre.* Whereas Jane's drama is essentially focused on her relation with one man, Lucy's relation with M. Paul, which occurs comparatively late in the book, is described as problematic because of the psychological difficulties her social status has created. Her trouble getting to know and be known by M. Paul is partly the consequence of his temperament but also results from the neurosis created by Lucy's consciousness of her social alienation. The ways in which the constitution of society interferes with her capacity to love and be loved are evident in the fact that the junta's conspiracy is precisely to separate her from M. Paul. To say this is not to minimize, by contrast, the social dimension of *Jane Eyre.* The impediments in Jane and Rochester's relationship include the class and gender difference between them. The constitution of society endangers Jane's relationship with Rochester to the extent that marriage in general presents the dangers of being "becalmed" and to the extent that Rochester is implicated personally in the confinement of women to domestic spaces too small for them. But at the end, hard-won spiritual and psychological freedom enables Jane and Edward to live happily ever after in seclusion from the world, whereas Lucy can attain such freedom only by finding a way to live successfully in interaction with the world. The shift in primary focus from personal psychological problems to those problems as they are shaped by social position is reflected in the shift in titles from *Jane Eyre,* the name of the heroine, to *Villette,* the name of the alien world where the heroine must try to make a home.

Ironically, it is the Malevolence of the junta's specific focus on Lucy's hopes of love that finally liberates her own will. The "decoy[ing]" of Lucy "into the enchanted castle" (482) to see the picture of Justine Marie is part of the attempt to separate her from M. Paul, but the recognition of the conspiracy against her causes Lucy to rebel. "Was the picture of a pale dead nun to rise, an eternal barrier?" (491). The questions raised for

Lucy by this visit are an "obstruction" but also "the keenest stimulus, I had ever felt" (491). The visit to Malevola's house marks the beginning of the end of Lucy's internal collusion with the external forces that would bury her; by their very violence, like that of the storm earlier, she has finally been "roused and obliged to live" (176).

VI

Lucy's impulse to live is realized in her escape from the convent: an old Gothic plot device that Brontë "makes new" in some remarkable ways. The full meaning of her escape is announced in what precedes it: a series of events that emphasize Lucy's vulnerability to blanking out, her inability to speak "I," the outer and inner tyrannies that prevent her from breaking out of self-enclosure. M. Paul's imminent departure is announced, followed by a "week of suspense, with its blank yet burning days" (538). On the last day of this week, Lucy's inability to assert her desire makes the atmosphere of the convent "stagnant . . . smothering," and her longing takes shape as a desperate urge to self-expression: "Would no one lend me a voice? Had no one a wish, no one a word, no one a prayer to which I could say—Amen?" (539). M. Paul's relationship with Lucy began when he imposed on her by giving her, against her will, a part to speak in a play—by lending her a (masculine) voice she did not want. Now she has progressed so far as to long for a voice to be lent her—not so far as to think of speaking herself, but so far as to wish that someone else would voice her own emotions. On the night Paul lent her a voice, Lucy was twice stimulated into "going beyond [her]self" (222), but Paul's absence so long after that incident finds her still waiting, characteristically, to be "summoned": "I knew where he lived: I knew where he was to be heard of, or communicated with; the distance was scarce a stone's-throw; had it been in the next room—unsummoned, I could make no use of my knowledge" (539). Lucy knows, but because she cannot make herself known, the knowledge is useless. "To follow, to seek out, to remind, to recall—for these things I had no faculty" (539).

This oppressive modesty comes into full play when M. Paul is about to arrive, as Mme. Beck tries to shut Lucy away from him, insisting that she help with some work in her chamber, where she closes both doors and locks the window. This procedure is a literal enactment of the self-enclosure that keeps Lucy, psychologically, from "going beyond [her]self" to meet Paul. She makes an effort to escape her Modesty, but it is not enough: ". . . I . . . left her. Left her? No: she would not be left . . ." (540). Mme. Beck follows Lucy to the room where Paul is taking leave of the students and, at the crucial moment, blanks her out: "He was approaching. . . . But Madame was before me; she had stepped out suddenly; she seemed to magnify her proportions and amplify her drapery; she eclipsed me; I was hid. She knew my weakness and deficiency; she could calculate the degree of moral paralysis—the total default of self-assertion—with which, in a crisis, I could be struck" (541). Here Mme. Beck is the barrier that keeps Lucy from being known—appropriately so, because she is Lucy's modesty—her tendency to submit with "decency" to being walled up and forgotten, her tendency to "catalepsy" instead of action. The result, Lucy thinks, is that Paul perceives her as "absent."

In its quiet way this is perhaps the most nightmarish scene of the book, one in which Lucy's sense of personal littleness almost overcomes her as the proportions of her enemy magnify themselves in her imagination. It is the opposite of those scenes in which the Gothic heroine, inspired by the sublime, finds that her enemy has shrunk to "the diminutiveness of a fairy" (Radcliffe, *The Italian* 91). Here Lucy's sense of her own littleness is itself the gigantic enemy that blanks her out. The desperate impetus in Lucy to make herself known recalls the extremity of her feeling when Home took leave of Polly, and Lucy longed for her to "utter some hysterical cry, so that I might get relief and be at ease" (71). The whole scene, she thought then, "was . . . of feeling too brimful, and which, because the cup did not foam up high or furiously overflow, only oppressed one the more" (71). This is a good description of the reader's experience of Lucy throughout the whole book. Here, as Lucy's own hope of "Home" seems destined to be lost, it seems almost impossible that the cup should not finally overflow.

Paul sends Lucy a letter telling her to "be ready" for an interview at an unappointed time. "All that evening I waited . . ." (542). Here as in other similar scenes, Brontë captures the real meaning of suspense in a woman's day-to-day life—"that long wait," de Beauvoir calls it (679). Because they are not empowered to act, de Beauvoir says, women are at the mercy of anxious suspense:

> [F]or woman condemned to passivity, the inscrutable future is haunted by phantoms . . . being unable to act, she worries. Her husband, her son, when undertaking an enterprise or facing an emergency, run their own risks. . . . But woman flounders in confusion and darkness; she gets used to it because she does nothing; in her imagination all possibilities have equal

reality: the train may be derailed, the operation may go wrong, the business may fail. What she is endeavoring to exorcize in her gloomy ruminations is the specter of her own powerlessness. (673)

In such a manner have Lucy and other women waited throughout the book. But this period of waiting is different from those that precede it, for this time even waiting is an act of defiance. Lucy is violating "rules I had never forgotten or disregarded before" (543) and so is renouncing the "acquiescent habits" of the ghostly nun, who represents in so many ways "the specter of her own powerlessness." She is defying, that is, the social, institutional, economic, and psychological force that is Mme. Beck, who arrives to announce that "the rule of the house has . . . been transgressed too long" (543). Mme. Beck offers a sedative: she offers, in other words, to reduce the "quick" of Lucy's nature to "catalepsy and a dead trance" (175). Before, Lucy was wont to perform this act of violence on herself; Mme. Beck here represents the inner forces of calm, order, decency, and reason that made it possible. Now Lucy vanquishes that inner force, refusing her customary collusion with the outer force that Mme. Beck also represents. "Let me alone. . . . Oh, Madame! in *your* hand there is both chill and poison. You envenom and you paralyze" (544). When Mme. Beck persists, Lucy bursts out with a startling verbal attack on her: "Dog in the manger!" (544).

In this brief encounter Lucy's refusal to paralyze herself translates itself naturally into a self-assertion through speech that is at the same time an access of knowledge and an act of self-defense: "Two minutes I stood over Madame, feeling that the whole woman was in my power, because in some moods, such as the present—in some stimulated states of perception, like that of this instant—her habitual disguise, her mask and her domino, were to me a mere network reticulated with holes; and I saw underneath a being heartless, self-indulgent, and ignoble" (544). The passage is reminiscent of that in which the "veil" falls from St. John's despotism (*Jane Eyre* 432) and so reduces him in Jane's imagination to his proper, human proportions. Both scenes reveal again Charlotte Brontë's interest in the factors that reinforce the heroine's collusion with illicit power, giving her inner perils of the night the shape of those "forces of violence" outside her. For Lucy to see through the mask and domino of the inquisitress is thus to see through one of her own disguises as well as to identify clearly an external enemy. Unlike most such revelations in women's Gothic, the heroine's full vision of the enemy here is both a moment of self- recognition and the rejection of an alien Other heretofore internalized as an aspect of the self. These connections explain why Lucy's defense against the calm, paralyzing Mme. Beck is associated with energy: a "stimulated" state of perception resulting from the rejection of emotional paralysis as a remedy for desire and from the consequent liberation of Lucy's own "active soul."

Lucy wins an inner victory over Modeste, but Mme. Beck as an external threat retains her power, managing to administer the opiate even though Lucy no longer cooperates in the paralysis of her inner self. The extent of her inner rebellion becomes clear when her system responds to the drug with energy instead of catalepsy. Imagination, old foe of Reason in Lucy's psychomachia, is "roused" and set free, to urge Lucy out of the convent: " 'Look forth and view the night!' was her cry . . ." (547). In response Lucy lifts the blind from the window and recognizes "the narrow limits, the oppressive heat of the dormitory . . ." (547). But here the heroine in her room with a view does not merely gain fortitude to endure her imprisonment; she resolves to break out of it.

Because it represents an end to self-alienation, this impulse to break out is, logically, identical with an impulse to break in: Lucy imagines leaving the convent and stealing into the summer park of Villette, "shut up, locked, sentinelled" (547). The image of her goal there is an image of her own female sexuality: a "mirror of crystal" (551), a basin "deep set in the tree-shadows, brimming with cool water, clear, with a green, leafy, rushy bed" (547). Lucy's fantasy is both of escaping the boundaries of the self—the walls that Modeste and social insignificance have constructed around her—and of finding a passage through the inner boundaries that lock her away from her own passionate nature.[34] Her desperate thirst for the water in the park is a measure of the suffering produced by separation from her own desire. The image of the sentinels guarding the fenced-in park of Villette emphasizes the identity of the inner barriers with official, external barriers imposed by an alien social order. If Lucy can violate these barriers, she will, paradoxically, be completely private, in complete possession of a public place: "the whole park would be mine . . ." (547).

This version of the room with a view is revealingly different from an earlier one: "In summer it was never quite dark, and then I went up stairs to my own quarter of the long dormitory, opened my own casement (that chamber was lit by five casements large as great doors), and leaning out, looked forth upon the city beyond the garden, and listened to band-music from the park or the palace-square, thinking meantime my own thoughts, living my own life in my own still, shadow-world" (185). There is pleasure as well as loneliness in this picture of Lucy's "insular" self. It is an interesting version of the Gothic room with a view, because instead of being a picture of the soul led "upwards and onwards," it is a picture of the self securely, if a little sadly, enclosed in its private space. The woman who looks out on this scene does not expand outwards into it and so achieve a sense of power; rather, she seems content to be separate from it, living her "own" inner life in the only world to which she fully belongs—the one place that, in this all-too-public room, is hers. The sense of pleasure mixed with the sadness comes from the iteration of "own": the sense it gives of secure possession, especially self-possession, and belonging. It is touching that the heroine at the casement here has, in her shared and public bedroom, only this one window that is truly hers to look out of. She looks out of her own part of the communal room not to the solitude of nature but to another public place: the city of Villette, with its band music, square, and all the communal life they imply. Between both public spaces she stands in the one world that is hers. Its insularity is precious as well as lonely.

Lucy's delight at the idea of having the park all to herself recalls that earlier comfort in having her "own" place in the dormitory room: both are images of secure enclosure. But the difference is immense. In the earlier passage Lucy was passive, finding comfort in her imprisonment despite her outward longings—falling prey, in other words, to the temptation of immanence despite her transcendent impulses. In the latter passage she is active rather than passive, not rejoicing in the enclosure in which she already finds herself and so accepting the boundaries that external factors have constructed around her, but actively seeking, both inside and outside herself, a space that can be hers alone. This search is a transgression of the bounds imposed on her from without: the walls of the convent, the sentineled fence of the park. The fact that the journey through them is at once a journey out of the boundaries of her self and in through the boundaries that keep her from herself is a consequence and reflection of the identity of the outer and inner threats that menace her.

Envisioning the park as hers alone, Lucy takes possession of her own hitherto alien inner space: a psychological act of possession identical with the social act of "going beyond [her]self" into a public domain. It forecasts her final establishment, outside the convent of her walled self, in a secure pensionnat of her own that, although private because it is her own house secure from Mme. Beck's intrusion, is also a public institution representing her new place in the society and economy of Villette.

To violate the boundaries dividing her from the inner and outer world,

Lucy must acknowledge the full force of her thirst; having done so, she escapes the convent. With the delicate touch so characteristic of her imagination, Brontë starts the heroine on her journey by having her leave her room not in a grand passion for transcendence but from a very ordinary impulse. "What was the time? I felt restless to know. There stood a clock in the classe below; what hindered me from venturing down to consult it?" (548) The most mundane quest for knowledge—and yet the question "what hindered me?" bespeaks the desperate state of timidity from which the heroine is beginning to free herself. Gothic heroines venture into the darkness through strange secret doors; Lucy dares more by simply walking downstairs to consult a clock.

Barrett satirized Gothicists for the way their clocks never strike anything but "the frightful hour of ONE!" Brontë once again makes a delicate adjustment of the conventions. "Hush!—the clock strikes. Ghostly deep as is the stillness of this convent, it is only eleven" (548). Again, the ordinariness of this ghostly scene, this desperate adventure, is brought home to the reader, and that is part of its force. It is a desperate adventure, but it is only eleven o'clock; outside the "ghostly" convent with its "spectral . . . memories," as Lucy now begins to realize, are the sounds of city life. And so she comes to the door.

> There is no lock on the huge, heavy, porte-cochère; there is no key to seek: it fastens with a sort of spring-bolt, not to be opened from the outside, but which, from within, may be noiselessly withdrawn. Can I manage it? It yields to my hand, yields with propitious facility. I wonder as that portal seems almost spontaneously to unclose; I wonder as I cross the threshold and step on the paved street, wonder at the strange ease with which this prison has been forced. (548)

In *A Sicilian Romance,* Radcliffe's heroine opens doors freely that then lock behind her with a spring bolt, shutting her in. Brontë's spring bolt works the other way. Here is a convent and a tyrannical abbess and a "huge, heavy" door. But all the prisoner ever had to do to escape was simply walk out. "There is no key to seek"; the lock is on the prisoner's side. Brontë's innovation in her description of this escape from the convent is surely a measure of her subtlety in reading Ellena's escape from San Stefano in *The Italian.*[35] Ellena's dilemma is one of decorum—of "la Convenance et la Décence" (*Villette* 200), in fact. After she finally resolves it, she is then rescued by her lover in an ordeal fraught with difficulty. He sends her a note, but the light goes out before she can read it (132); the time appointed for meeting has already passed when she finally learns of it (133); she must elude the notice of the nuns as she hastens toward the gate (133); the gate seems "to retreat before her" (134); she loses strength and must rest before proceeding (134); after the gate, she must pass through a "subterraneous labyrinth" (137); her guide appears to have betrayed her and so forth. Charlotte Brontë works out with more subtlety the implications of the heroine's decision to leave the convent. Once Lucy has overcome her own repressive tendency—the restraints of decorum on her behavior—there is no other impediment to her escape: she can simply walk out the door. This is a climactic moment in the allegorical romance of *Villette*—the revelation that the heroine's freedom was in her power the whole time. But the reader of the novel *Villette* remembers something else: the reason Lucy could not have left before of her own free will is that she cannot afford to lose her job.

Entering the park, too, is easy. There are no sentinels; the gate is not locked. And the anticipated dark, quiet inmost self, the park "shadowy and calm" (549)—words Lucy has used repeatedly to describe herself—is not at all calm and shadowy but brilliantly lit and stirring with life. Lucy's surprise is an appropriate emblem of the dissolution of her earlier mask of cool and calm, a self-deception evident from her first reactions to the child Paulina,[36] but one that has broken down periodically throughout the book—increasingly so since her admission to Paul, "Oui, j'ai la flamme à l'âme, et je dois l'avoir!" (404).

Lucy's journey inward to the center of herself—the circular mirror of the cool basin—is now revealed as a journey into the most public space of *Villette*. In the park are the figures of Lucy's psychomachia arranged in allegorical tableau: that fierce educator of girls, Modeste, holding by the hand her restless daughter Désirée (for, of course, the daughter of Modesty is Desire); the old priest, Père Silas, the tempter who would lure Lucy to "inactive" "retreat" and so render her "nun(none)"; and before them on a sort of throne, Malevola—center of their "reverent circle" (556), object of their homage. Malevolence strikes out at Desire with her "gold-knobbed cane" (558) (scepter of the reign of Mammon); she resembles "a head severed from its trunk" (the rule of reason without passion) "and flung at random on a pile of rich merchandize" (the jewels that symbolize both her self-aggrandizing vanity and the money interests that, by making women into commodities, belittle and mutilate them). The extent of the danger the junta poses is reflected in the presence, among the votaries of Malevola, of Paul's brother Josef Emanuel, who resembles Paul except that he lacks his brother's "fire" and ardor. That is, Paul deprived of his energy of soul would be a worshiper at this same shrine; and so the paralysis of the "active soul," the agent of transcendence, is exactly the junta's project.

Thus Lucy's romance-journey inward through the barriers that separate her from herself ends logically in a confrontation with her own private demons, the junta. But this is also a journey outward through the barriers that cut her off from other people; the park has a novelistic dimension as well as an allegorical one. It is a picture of a social world, which includes the Brettons chatting in their usual way, the Labassecouriens in their family groups, and M. Miret the bookseller. Lucy's emergence into this social world is only partial, for she is obsessed with not being known: she has gone so far as to enter, alone, a public space, but she does not want to be recognized there. This fear manifests itself in her shrinking from Graham, accompanied by a paranoid desperation that recalls her earlier flight for "sanctuary" from Paul: "[T]here were thousands to meet his eye and divide its scrutiny—why then did he concentrate all on me— oppressing me with the whole force of that full, blue, steadfast orb? . . . He could not see my face, I held it down; surely, he *could* not recognize me; I stooped, I turned, I *would* not be known. He rose, by some means he contrived to approach, in two minutes he would have had my secret; my identity would have been grasped between his, never tyrannous, but always powerful hands" (554). With a "supplicatory gesture" she convinces him to leave her alone. Part of the tyranny implied in Graham's impending assault on Lucy's "secret"—her "identity"—consists in his real incapacity for knowing Lucy in the sense she had longed for earlier. She alludes to this incapacity in her comment on the success of her silent supplication: had it not worked, she says, Graham might have seen a Lucy he would not have recognized—a being "incensed," not "absolutely inoffensive and shadowlike" (555).

M. Miret, however, has also seen and known Lucy—in a much less highly charged, more ordinary sense of the word—and engaged her in a normal social exchange. He made way through the crowd to give her a "better situation" and thus secure her "a place and a seat" (553). Although at first Lucy herself perceived this man as a stranger, she then recognized him as a tradesman who had in the past reminded her of M. Paul. The polite attention paid her by this M. Miret—who, we learn later, knows her not merely as a customer but as the director of the school to which he will be sending his daughters—signals that Paul himself will soon find Lucy a "better situation" by "secur[ing her] a place" and that the citizens of Villette in general will now make room for her, "know" her as a person in her own right, with an ordinary and legitimate place in their world.

The meeting with M. Miret is an omen of Lucy's real liberation, for although she later misinterprets the junta as having attained its goal of marrying Paul to someone else, the truth is that the festival celebrates the triumph of Labassecour over some "peril to the rights and liberties" of its citizens (550). And unbeknownst to Lucy, M. Miret's acknowledgment of her is the signal of her new freedom and her triumph over the peril of the junta: she has not been blanked out but has been given a "place" in Villette. The last line of the chapter in which she recognizes "the whole conjuration, the secret junta" for what it is reveals why she will be able to occupy this place: the junta is powerful, but she is free forever of her collusion with the external forces of violence its members represent, and so has ended their role as psychological forces inside her. The chapter ends with her defiance: "I was worsted and under their feet; but, as yet, I was not dead" (558).

In the scene that follows, however, the junta's victory seems complete. Lucy has explained a priest's attendance at the fête by saying that to the church "[t]his was not considered a show of Vanity Fair, but a commemoration of patriotic sacrifice . . ." (558). Now the sacrifice being celebrated at the throne of Malevola is revealed as the one exactly appropriate at a Vanity Fair: a sacrifice to "Mammon" and "Interest" of "one unselfish" man by "three self-seekers" (559–60). Mme. Beck and Père Silas stand in the "reverent circle" around Magloire, Vanity, to celebrate the sacrifice of M. Paul; they wait expectantly for Justine Marie.

" 'Justine Marie!' What name was this? Justine Marie—the dead nun— where was she? Why in her grave, Madame Walravens . . ." (561). Mme. Walravens's confidence that this "pale dead nun" (491) will appear is congruent with the junta's happy confidence that its goal, early identified with keeping M. Paul's lost love alive in his memory as a force to inhibit the desire for "present . . . comfort" (483)—as a means, paradoxically, of keeping his passion "buried" (433)—has been realized. Justine Marie is the "barrier" (491) between Lucy and Paul; Lucy seems to see the junta's confidence that this barrier still exists.

Lucy awaits the ghost's arrival with "the expectation of mystery breaking up: hitherto, I had seen this spectre only through a glass darkly; now was I to behold it face to face. I leaned forward: I looked" (562). The allegorical tableau shifts and Justine Marie arrives—not, however, the dead nun, but Justine Marie Sauveur; and with her arrives, to the junta's surprise, the victim of the recent sacrifice they were just celebrating. The arrival of Paul *Emanuel* in the company of Justine Marie *Sauveur* is thus both advent and resurrection, but Lucy, thinking she now sees Truth "face to face" (562) and has handled the veil of "the goddess in her temple," misreads the advent as loss and the resurrection as burial. Paul, she thinks, loves Justine Marie Sauveur and so is lost to her forever: "[T]he blooming and charming Present prevailed over the Past, and at length his nun was indeed buried" (565). This description turns out to be true, but not in the sense Lucy imagines. Paul said earlier that he felt no passion because his passion lay buried in a grave many winters old (433). Now that the object of that passion is finally buried once and for all, his passion itself is released from its grave. Thus when Lucy says of Justine Marie Sauveur, "scarce would you discredit me, reader, were I to say that she . . . looks like the resurrection of the flesh, and that she is a risen ghost" (562–63), the image is not the "falsity" or "figment" Lucy thinks it is.

Lucy in these scenes does see Truth face to face, but she misapprehends it completely. She thinks that confronting Truth helps free her from Fear (564), but in fact her fear is merely eclipsing the truth with a projected image of itself.[37] The scene of this false revelation is one of Charlotte Brontë's pictures of the mystery of knowledge—of the strange fact that even in a confrontation, seemingly face to face, with the demons of our private selves, we may grotesquely mistake their meaning. For what Lucy does is to misread a triumph over the grave as a triumph of the grave. The original Justine Marie has stood both for Paul's loss and the danger that he will never be able to lose his loss by giving up his worship of a "pale dead nun," who will always "rise, an eternal barrier" to prevent love. When Lucy sees "Justine Marie" in the park, she thinks she is seeing her own loss, because she thinks she sees an eternal barrier between her and Paul. But this is Justine Marie Sauveur: emblem of the revival of M. Paul's capacity for love—of passion rescued from its grave, saved from burial. Unbeknownst to Lucy, Justine Marie Sauveur is at the picnic as Paul's accomplice against the junta, his accomplice in saving Lucy from the convent and giving her a place of her own in alien Villette.

VII

Lucy returns to the convent thinking she has won "freedom and renovation," and that is true, but not in a sense she is yet able to recognize. These facts are represented in her discovery in her bed of yet another version of the ghost that has haunted her throughout the book. In a scene that surely has no parallel in Brontë's Gothic predecessors, the heroine, in a fit of anger rather than fear, attacks the ghost, rips it to shreds, and tramples it under her feet (569).

The significance of this act is manifold. Lucy's struggle against the haunting of a ghost is the central symbolic struggle against all the Gothic perils of her inner and outer worlds, and the ghost, simultaneously a version of the Other Woman of Gothic romance, is the central "barrier" Lucy must get beyond in order to find transcendence. The brilliance of Brontë's use of the ghost is revealed in its multiple identities: as a symbol of passion and the lack of it, rebellion and acquiescence, sexuality and repression, the necessity for burying the past and the danger of doing so, deadly iteration, the return of the familiar as the alien, the impulse toward immanence, and the struggle for transcendence.

The first reference to the ghostly nun was in the context of Mme. Beck's disappointed efforts to attract Graham: having failed, she "turned darkly from" (170) her mirror in a gesture recalling Lucy's own recognitions, at various times, that her appearance is unlikely to attract love. One response to that recognition is the attempt to bury passion. The consequences of that response are related in the passage immediately following Mme. Beck's scene at the mirror: the legend of the nun, buried alive "for some sin against her vow"—a sin that in the Gothic tradition evoked here is always a sin of passion. This nun, it is said, does not remain quiet in her tomb. Not only does she haunt the old convent; the apparently dead tree above her grave persists in remaining alive, putting out its "perfumed snow in spring" and "honey-sweet pendants in autumn" (172). After the scene in the park, Lucy takes her "freedom" home to bed to see what she can "make of it" (566). She is free from the illusion of being loved and seems to think this knowledge can free her from love itself. But in her bed is the ghostly nun, the old rebellious passion that she can not get rid of simply by knowing it is not reciprocated. Here, as in the original legend, the nun's haunting represents the eternally defiant life of the sexual passion that cannot, in fact, be buried; its persistent triumph over all who would lock it away. In this context, Lucy's attack on the ghost is yet another in a long series of attempts to destroy her own irrepressible passion—an angry act of violence against herself that provides momentary relief but, as usual, will not work, as evidenced in the fact that fragments of the ghost remain and must be hidden under her pillow.

The ghost, however, has been associated not only with the irrepressible passion embodied in the sinful nun but also with the repression[38] embodied in the saintly, "acquiescent" Justine Marie, of nunlike "inactive passions." [39] Thus the ghost is at the same time an image of the passionate impulses that Lucy cannot "keep down" and the repressive impulse that motivates her attempts to bury them. This apparently contradictory double meaning is Brontë's final defiance of the Gothic tradition that sees the Good Other Woman as separate from the Evil Other Woman, the buried saint as separate from the buried sinner. Brontë sees these two false images not as binary opposites but as two mystifications of the same reality: discovering the impossibly good, obedient, sexless, and victimized woman is in fact the same as discovering her impossibly bad, sexual (and also victimized) counterpart. This fact is implicit in the narrative structure of *The Mysteries of Udolpho,* in which the story of the nun, Sister Agnes, turns out to be the story of the passionate Laurentini and in which this story of the Bad Other Woman itself is uncovered during the same narrative sequence that uncovers the secret of the Good Other Woman, Emily's victimized aunt. Brontë makes more obvious the meaning of the necessary connection between these two false images of women by identifying the haunting nun both with the saintly Justine Marie and with the passionate sinner nun of the convent legend. Lucy must exorcise both these mystifications of woman's true nature in order to end her own self-division. With the end of that division, the disjunction between Lucy's own faculties of thought and feeling breaks down: her attack on passion in this scene is itself passionate, not "studious" or matter-of-fact like the earlier attempts to paralyze her own energies, not cold and reasonable like the attempt to bury her love for Graham with his letters—an attempt that resulted merely in the resurrection of the ghost, which burst out to haunt her moments after the letters were interred. Her angry assault on the passion that so torments her is, paradoxically, a release of passion and an assault on the forces of repression from which she has suffered so long, a rejection of the inactivity and acquiescence into which the junta would like to lure her by making her like the nun whose image she here rejects so violently.

This rejection is the first step in the explication of the supernatural in this Gothic tale and, as such, once more shows Brontë's genius as a revisioner of the Gothic tradition. With Lucy's attack on the nun, the supernatural that has haunted her begins to be explained—not, however, in the access of reason and reestablishment of daylight logic that a reader of Radcliffe or Sleath or Mackenzie would expect, but in a fit of anger, a wild release of the irrational. This is only logical in the context: Lucy's assault on the nun marks the climax of the long scene of her revolt against her own timid "acquiescent habits" as an inmate of Mme. Beck's convent, and the consequent liberation of her own "inactive passions." The nun, lying in Lucy's own bed, is an image of herself. That is, Lucy comes home to find in her bed the other self who was susceptible to Mme. Beck's devices of paralysis and "dead trance"—the self she left behind by leaving the convent; the nun self, in fact, that she now, in a final liberation of passion, destroys completely. This non-self had no life, anyway; it was a fiction created by the attempt to disguise passion, as the final explication of the "ghost" makes clear. The "nun" was Ginevra's lover de Hamal, so dressed in order to keep their passion a secret. It is left lifeless on her bed because they will need this concealment for passion no more; Ginevra has fled the convent through the door Lucy left ajar (568, 572).

The final explanation of the ghost in Ginevra's letter casts yet another light on the meaning of Lucy's scene of passion, because Ginevra's flight has an interesting double meaning. Ginevra, the very personification of the capacity to speak "I," is liberated as an aspect of Lucy's escape from self-enclosure: that is, Lucy's own capacity to assert herself has finally been freed. But Ginevra is also the personification of a tendency *only* to speak "I," and so her departure from Lucy's own place of residence is also an exorcism of the torment of "unsparing selfishness" (118), "the whole burden of human egotism" (450). The paradox is explained by the picture Lucy and Ginevra have constituted together of the way an incapacity for self-assertion results in self-absorption. After Ginevra departs, Lucy is free to assert her ego and so to escape the egotism of self-enclosure.[40]

Brontë's portrayal of the ironic identity of obsessive self-abnegation and obsessive self-absorption has been, throughout the book, an implicit attack on Victorian ideals of womanhood, an attack that Lucy's assault on the ghostly nun enacts literally. In the same scene in which he extolled selflessness as a female virtue, M. Paul recommended for Lucy's contemplation a series of pictures entitled "La vie d'une femme," which Lucy found most revolting. The women in this series were "cold and vapid as ghosts. . . . bloodless, brainless nonentities" (278). That is, one of the dangers of living out the conventional life of a woman is that it will render one spectral, unreal, nobody. This association of proper and conventional womanhood with ghostliness makes Lucy's destruction of the nun an enraged assault on those ideals that render women "bloodless, brainless nonentities." Unlike Dacre's Victoria, and gratifyingly so, Lucy is not punished by the author for the act. Instead, in her own act of exorcism, Brontë replaces the heroine's usual terror of the ghost with an explosion of that anger of which women Gothicists were themselves so afraid.

Thus the ghost represents on the one hand the irrepressible passion Lucy tries so hard to keep down and, on the other, the "specter of her powerlessness" to free that passion to bear fruit in the world—to liberate it from the spectral "vie d'une femme." Lucy defies Mme. Beck in the sequence leading up to this scene; thus it is appropriate that she "defie[s] spectra" (569) here. No longer will she be haunted by Mme. Beck in her ghostly aspect: she has escaped the constant surveillance of Modesty and of Reason severed from emotion, and the fear that produced her constant retreat from knowing and being known.

In addition, ghosts are an emblem of what is irrevocably lost but cannot be exorcised. The ghost in Lucy's bed recalls Paulina, image of haunting loss, creeping like a little ghost into her bed at Bretton. Thus Lucy's attempt to destroy the ghost in her bed is yet another in a long series of attempts to vanquish the specter of loss. Specifically, her rage at the ghost is an expression of anger at the other woman whom she at this moment perceives as the cause of her most recent loss. The ghost has been identified with "Justine Marie," and it is (another) Justine Marie who is apparently taking Paul away from her, just as the ghostly Justine Marie, because of Paul's own inability to bury his loss forever, threatened to do earlier. Like Victoria's attack on Lilla in *Zofloya,* Lucy's attack on the image of true womanhood (in all her "nonentity") is at the same time a jealous attack on the woman she perceives as her rival in love.

The junta kept alive this ghostly rival in the house of the Rue des Mages. In this they resemble all the Gothic "Archimages" that rely on the manipulation of ghostly apparitions to terrify their victims from seeking to know too much. Fear has been the junta's key tactic in keeping Lucy and Paul apart: Paul remarked that his friends counseled him to fear Lucy (512), and Lucy has been perversely afraid sometimes of even the most ordinary social contacts with Paul—a result of the inhibiting inner forces that the junta represents allegorically: fear of being known, modesty, perverse self-reliance, a tendency to answer desire with repression and retreat, the temptations of privation. The explosion of anger in Lucy's destruction of the nun, symbol of what the junta would like her to be, is thus an exorcism of fear, a means of exorcism not ordinarily available to Gothic heroines. Only the villainess may rant and rave. Significantly, in her furious attack on the ghost, Lucy resembles Vashti, who, like Dacre's Victoria, has been associated with the wild, unfeminine,

280 / Boundaries of the Self in Women's Gothic

passionate sublime of action and power, represented metaphorically in the force of a "deep, swollen, winter river, thundering in cataract, bearing the soul, like a leaf, on the steep and steely sweep of its descent" (341). Indeed what Lucy does here is described in the earlier description of Vashti: "I have said that she does not *resent* her grief. No; the weakness of that word would make it a lie. To her, what hurts becomes immediately embodied: she looks on it as a thing that can be attacked, worried down, torn in shreds. Scarcely a substance herself, she grapples to conflict with abstractions. Before calamity she is a tigress; she rends her woes, shivers them in convulsed abhorrence" (340).

Such an aggressive response to one's woes is hardly feminine. Thus, like Victoria's sublime attack on the (merely) beautiful Lilla in Dacre's *Zofloya,* Lucy's attack on the ideal of feminine passivity reveals what Dacre would have called a "masculine spirit." On the other hand, the object of the attack is itself the masculine spirit that has haunted Lucy for so long; the ghostly nun is really a man disguised in the acquiescent habit of a woman. Thus, just as the attack on the nun is both an effort at repression and an outburst against repression, so it is both an assault on the feminine ideal that threatens to bury Lucy's masculine spirit and an effort to destroy that very spirit: the source, after all, of Lucy's woe—of the fact that she belongs to a "class of natures" for whose transcendent longings "the world has no satisfaction" (234). This man who played the nun is the lover of Ginevra, for whose love Lucy herself, as his dramatic counterpart in the play, competed with the rival Graham figure while at the same time, like her rival for Graham, Ginevra, making her part into a flirtation with their audience, Graham himself.[41] And yet the "man" Lucy played that night—the man who himself has played the part of a nun, de Hamal—is himself "womanish" (281): small, "smooth," "pretty" (216), not rugged and sublime. Thus in the end, Lucy's attack on de Hamal's costume is both an assault on and an expression of what really haunts her: the androgynous nature that deprives her of satisfaction in a world that has no name for legitimating such a nature and no language in which such a nature can explicate the mystery it has therefore become. For the nun does not speak; its masculine voice would reveal the feminine nun self for what it is: none, no one, a mystification.

In Lucy's defiance of spectra, we see her anger at her own tormenting passion; her anger at the repressive forces that have tormented that passion; anger at her loss; anger at the familiar nunlike self she thought she had left behind but now finds confronting her once more; anger at the rival who has apparently left her a victim of passion and deprivation, once again in danger of succumbing to catalepsy, acquiescence, nonentity. Her attack on the ghost is her assault on her apparently inescapable destiny as "none"; on the masculine spirit she has been able neither to give voice to nor to exorcise; on the passive feminine ideal that spirit has rebelled against—the inert woman Modeste had wanted to put in Lucy's place. It is her assault on the woman who has taken her man; on the man who has taken her woman; on the androgynous self that, because it is Lucy's true nature in a world with no name or place for such a nature, is only "the specter . . . of her powerlessness." The sum of all these meanings is the sum of those woes that Lucy, like Vashti, "rends . . . in convulsed abhorrence." The reality of these woes, which others have failed to see at all or, like Graham, have thought a mere spectral delusion, is validated in this discovery that there was, after all, a "ghost."

Once again, as in *Jane Eyre,* Brontë's *surnaturel expliqué* is a clever solution to the usual problem of contradiction and anticlimax it involves in Gothic romance. In her predecessors, the explained supernatural functions to blank out what has gone before, projecting over the earlier nightmares of mystery and illogic a wish that, after all, the inexplicable phenomena of the heroine's own tortured mind do not exist. Irrational forces only appeared to disrupt the civilized decorum of her inner life; it was all an illusion. Brontë's explained supernatural is a clever variation on its predecessors. As Lucy stands over the ghost, she realizes that this thing that has haunted her for so long, embodiment of all the terrors she has suffered from so pathologically, really was nothing. She is alive; these terrors, in contrast, have no substance. "In a moment, without exclamation, I had rushed on the haunted couch; nothing leaped out, or sprang, or stirred; all the movement was mine, so was all the life, the reality, the substance, the force; as my instinct felt" (569). This is a striking rendition of the moment of psychological triumph when the walls of repression come down and the fearful thing behind them loses its reality altogether while its long-time victim discovers suddenly that she, on the other hand, is fully alive. As Johnson says, "Lucy is here treading on more than the flimsy props of a silly hoax; she is rending the whole fabric of make-believe that has swathed her private world of fantasy . . ." (335). In that sense, the explication of the supernatural here serves, as such explications always do, to drain the terrors of their reality. But unlike the traditional explication, this one does not thereby back away from the psychological insights represented in the terrors themselves. On the contrary, Brontë's explained supernatural functions precisely to validate the heroine's experience of the irrational. The specter did exist; the "materialist" Graham was wrong to see Lucy's suffering as her own fault, a figment of her imagination rather than a response to, and a creation of, the world outside her.

But there is another twist as well. Graham failed to cross the threshold of Lucy's haunted mind because his misapprehension of her as calm, passionless, "inoffensive and shadowlike" prevented him from knowing her true inner state. The ghostly nun itself is an image of that misapprehension of the heroine's nature: a coercive misknowing that has haunted almost all her dealings with other people and has helped shut her into the self-enclosure symbolized by her status as "nun(none)" in the convent. De Hamal once compared Lucy herself with a nun (178); thus his haunting of Lucy was a repeated enactment, on her own private stage, of the world's false image of her nature. The great danger of this haunting was that Lucy might follow Graham in mistaking an external mystification for an aspect of her own mind. Her ripping apart of the false image puts an end to that danger by validating her own experience of her inner life: both by proving the "reality" of her suffering and by asserting, through a passionate outburst of anger, the unreality of the self-concept that the world—in great part with her collaboration—has tried to impose on her.

"Was the picture of a pale dead nun to rise, an eternal barrier?" (491) Lucy asked earlier. Lucy's destruction of the nun is a destruction of one of the barriers between her and Paul: her tendency to submit instead of rebelling, her tendency to be afraid instead of angry, her collusion in the world's false image of her inner self. The whole adventure of the night, in fact, has been a destruction of that obstacle: a liberating transgression of the rules of decorum and decency, an end to the division between Lucy and her passionate inner life, and an escape from the walled enclosure of the self. Mme. Beck had wanted Lucy to be the nun in this bed, lost to herself and the world in a death-like trance. With the recognition that "all the movement was mine, so was all the life, the reality, the substance, the force," Lucy ends the deadly iteration of the nun's haunting and recovers, through the destruction of the mystery, what has been lost for so long in this Gothic convent: Lucy herself.

But the meaning of Lucy's true "freedom and renovation" are not yet obvious to her. The next morning, like many a Gothic heroine after her escape, she finds herself back in the prison she just fled. "After a short and vain struggle, I found myself brought back captive to the old rack of suspense, tied down and strained anew" (578). Leaving the convent, entering the park, and vanquishing the ghost were a great internal victory, but in the morning, nothing has changed. In one sense this is an example of the bitter psychological realism that makes *Villette* so deeply pessimistic: this experience of repetition is an account of the soul's susceptibility to the illusion that it is powerful where it is most weak, and of the ephemeral nature of self-transcendence. The passage suggests, too, that vanquishing a private ghost in one's own room is not enough: freedom and renovation for women like Lucy depend on events in the outside world as well as on psychological events. Lucy wins a great victory in the dead of night, but she wakes in her customary place and even in her customary state of mind. The rack she has returned to is the old rack of "suspense": once again, after her excursion and "adventure" (555), she is back in the convent in woman's fated role. "In song and story the young man is seen departing adventurously in search of woman; he slays the dragon, he battles giants; she is locked in a tower, a palace, a garden, a cave, she is chained to a rock, a captive, sound asleep: she waits" (de Beauvoir 328).

She waits, and her rescuer arrives. What happens next reveals the extent to which Lucy misunderstood the real freedom and renovation she won in her adventure beyond the convent walls. Paul appears, but Mme. Beck intervenes to get him away from Lucy. "[M]ade now to feel what defied suppression, I cried—'My heart will break!' " And indeed, a barrier gives way: "What I felt seemed literal heart-break; but the seal of another fountain yielded under the strain: one breath from M. Paul, the whisper, 'Trust me!' lifted a load, opened an outlet. With many a deep sob, with thrilling, with icy shiver, with strong trembling, and yet with relief—I wept" (580). Paul, too, is "roused"; he sends Mme. Beck from the room and the door shuts behind her; then he leads Lucy out of the convent into the city. This is Lucy's rescue: traditional in that it is rescue by a man, but a departure from tradition in the extent to which Lucy herself is its agent. She has already prepared it herself the night before, by escaping, on her own initiative, from the restraints of Mme. Beck.

Before this, Paul opened doors to burst in on Lucy, peered into her desk, violated her space, looked in her window, shut her into an overheated room with him, locked her into the garret. These are images of violence, but perhaps only in that Lucy reacted with fear to Paul's siege of her soul. He intruded on her to love her; he shut her in to bring her close to his own "flamme à l'âme"—and, once, in the garret, to give her the privacy she would need to find a voice to serve her later in public. Now he becomes the opener of doors in a different sense: first "ushering" Lucy through the front door of a little house, "opening an inner door" to the parlor, giving her a tour of the rooms, finally "halt[ing] with a certain ceremony before a larger door than had yet been opened" (585)—the door to the classroom that reveals this to be Lucy's own private house and her public place of business.

This experience, in which what was an unknown place turns out to be Lucy's own house, is alive with resonance. It is a final reversal of the spell of not knowing from which Lucy has suffered, in which the familiar changed to the alien and what was full of meaning became completely drained of it. Lucy's waking at La Terrasse in part had the same effect: there, what seemed a strange place turned out to be her old place of refuge, filled with things she had made with her own hands. But the refuge had never been her home. La Terrasse was still Bretton translated into a foreign place, and the things she had made belonged to somebody else. Here, instead of going home from the foreign country to a lost childhood paradise, the heroine finds a new home—and adult responsibility—in the place of her exile.

This discovery is linked to a new ability to speak "I," as Lucy, deciding to ask the truth about Justine Marie, announces, "I want to tell you something . . . I want to tell you all." The passage that follows is the climax of Lucy's Gothic drama of confinement and release: "I spoke. All leaped from my lips. I lacked not words now; fast I narrated; fluent I told my tale . . ." (590–91). To this confidence, Paul reciprocates with his own. By finally making her love known, Lucy can finally know Paul's real motivation: he wants to marry her.

It is significant in the context of this climactic episode that the most dramatic scene of release in *Villette* consists not of a bursting of metaphysical bounds to escape into infinite space "beyond and above" but of that moment when Lucy opens a door and walks out into an ordinary city. True, she is going forth "to view the night"; she has seen the moon "supreme, in a element deep and splendid" (547); the incident is imbued with the unreality of an opium haze; there are allusions to a ghost and the expectation of seeing one; a severed head appears on a heap of jewels; the evening ends in a wild frenzy in which Lucy rips apart her spectral rival. Her exit from the "convent" is charged with the symbolism of escape from external oppression and internal repression. But the place into which she is thus liberated is in the end the real world, a social one. And in this realm she has entered with such wild sense of boldness and abandon, she is calmly recognized by M. Miret as someone entitled to a certain position and esteem. It is characteristic of Charlotte Brontë's Gothic that Lucy's escape from the perils of the night leads her into the communal life of a city. In both *Jane Eyre* and *Villette,* the longing for transcendence, despite impassioned hymns to Imagination or ecstatic visions of the moon rising into "fathomless" depths of space (*Jane Eyre* 148), amounts in the end to the "modest hope" of getting beyond the boundaries of the self to commune with other people—most intensely with one special person—and, without fear, take a meaningful place in society.

In *Villette* the novel, the visit to the Faubourg Clotilde shows Lucy's discovery of a place of her own in a foreign city, which is, by definition in a social and economic world, the discovery of a means of economic self-sufficiency. She does not receive a vast unexpected fortune, as do the heroines of romance, but an unexpected hundred pounds does come her way. "I asked no questions, but took the cash and made it useful" (593), says the heroine of the novel. In *Villette* the romance, the cityscape of the novel is an allegorical topography of Lucy's soul. The end of the romance shows Lucy, in what was once the alien city of her inmost self, finding herself, with some surprise, at home. The conjunction of the novel and romance meanings of Lucy's little house shows the interdependence of psychological and economic freedom, just as the junta Lucy vanquished were the external forces of violence internalized as inhibitions.

But the junta is not fully vanquished externally. Although Lucy escapes Mme. Beck's convent and Père Silas's attempts to lure her into another one, the attempt to separate her from Paul succeeds in the end. "We walked back to the Rue Fossette by moonlight," Lucy says, "such moonlight as fell on Eden—shining through the shades of the Great Garden. . . . Once in their lives some men and women go back to these first fresh days . . . taste that grand morning's dew—bathe in its sunrise" (591–92). "Once in their lives": this is not a happy Gothic romance in which the heroine recovers fully her childhood bliss; already the announcement is made that Lucy's recovery of paradise is temporary. Lucy gains her independence, but the beginning of the last chapter of the novel juxtaposes her new activity, running a business in Villette, with the old curse of waiting, and finally with a last instance of repetition: her loss, once again, of the prospects of finding something "higher" (450) than self-sufficiency.

Lucy comes to know herself and to be known in the social world outside her. But recovering the lost paradise of home means more to Lucy than being known by a local bookseller as the director of a pensionnat in his town or even being known to herself. It means, as it did for Jane

Eyre, knowing and being known in an intimate relationship. "Courage, Lucy Snowe!" the heroine exorted herself long before, when it seemed her hopes were to be unfulfilled;

> be content to labour for independence until you have proved, by winning that prize, your right to look higher. But afterwards, is there nothing more for me in life—no true home—nothing to be dearer to me than myself, and by its paramount preciousness, to draw from me better things than I care to culture for myself only? Nothing, at whose feet I can willingly lay down the whole burden of human egotism, and gloriously take up the nobler charge of labouring and living for others? I. . . . see that a great many men, and more women, hold their span of life on conditions of denial and privation. I find no reason why I should be of the few favoured. (450–51)

Lucy has escaped the torment of selfishness, but "home" in all the resonance it has in this passage is never hers.[42]

Lucy wins temporarily, but then M. Paul is lost, and the victorious junta returns in the last paragraph: "Mme Beck prospered all the days of her life; so did Père Silas; Madame Walravens fulfilled her ninetieth year before she died. Farewell" (596). This final paragraph announces at once the death and long life of the junta, Lucy's victory and her defeat. On the one hand it sounds like the triumph of the conspiracy; it speaks, just after the revelation of Paul's death, of the prosperity and longevity of those who, in essence, killed him. But it is also implicitly their epitaph, and Lucy is still alive, the survivor. Lucy's manner of saying that her enemies finally died by saying that they lived and prospered reflects the nature of her victory over them: they lost, but they also won. The end of complicity with oppression, in other words, does not end oppression itself. Of women's special problems in Victorian society, Brontë once wrote Elizabeth Gaskell, "They say, however—and to an extent truly—that the amelioration of our condition depends on ourselves. Certainly there are evils which our own efforts will best reach; but as certainly there are other evils—deep-rooted in the foundations of the social system—which no efforts of ours can touch; of which we cannot complain; of which it is advisable not too often to think" (*Shakespeare Head Brontë* 3: 150. Letter of August 27, 1850).

In one sense, the conclusion of Lucy's story repeats again the repetition she experienced earlier when, thinking she had achieved a great victory, she woke to the same oppressive reality that had been hers for so long. The sober end of *Villette* is in keeping with the sober way, throughout the book, that Brontë has set the Gothic drama of confinement and release in the context of the limited possibilities for transcendence available to women in her society. Such transcendence as Lucy finally achieves is long in coming, agonizingly hard won, and painfully modest after all. It manifests itself not in a sublime flight of rhetoric like that with which Jane overpowers St. John in the grandest tradition of Gothic heroines, but in a brief, explosive verbal attack on Mme. Beck; an outburst of weeping; and, finally, the "fluent" telling of her tale. The reader of *Jane Eyre* can exult in every word of the passionate speech in which the heroine vanquishes her enemy forever and takes full, responsible possession of the undisciplined potential for "fierce speaking" (*Jane Eyre* 70) she demonstrated as an "untaught child." The reader of *Villette* cannot even hear what Lucy says to Paul; her great achievement is that she brings herself to speak at all. The scene in which Lucy weeps, like that in which she finally speaks, is one of enormous intensity, all the more explosive for the extraordinary restraint that precedes it. In a book full of images that associate water with relief, paradise, and the rush of life restored, the image of this release as the bursting of the seal of a fountain is significant. It is not just that Lucy weeps but that the sources of life deep within her are liberated, despite her own and others' attempts to lock them away. Even so, this moment of self-transcendence is different from that when, as at the earthquake that freed Paul and Silas, the doors of Jane Eyre's prison flew open and her soul communed, "independent of the cumbrous body" (447), with that of Rochester.

Jane Eyre's triumph takes place in the realm of pure spirit with all the energies of her soul in full play. At her great moment of release she transcends herself, her enemy, space, time, history, nature, even mortal flesh. Lucy's great moment is just the walking out of a door into a city; a bold, heroic venture into a public park where everyone else has gone as a matter of course. In the context these are monumental victories, charged with as much intensity as anything in *Jane Eyre*. But from a more objective distance they are sadly limited, in tune with the insistently realistic tone of the novel itself. Whereas the poor orphan Jane Eyre attains a fortune, a home, a marriage of perfect communion in which she can "talk . . . all day long" (*Jane Eyre* 476), Lucy attains a job, a house in a foreign city, and three years of correspondence with a lover who is thousands of miles away and never comes back.

Lucy's victory over Gothic horrors, her escape from the "fear-spent, spectre-ridden life," is nonetheless a great victory, more convincingly real than the ending of *Jane Eyre*. There is no La Vallée for Lucy to go back to, but she makes a place for herself in the city of her exile; no fortune is suddenly revealed to be rightfully hers, but she finds a way to earn a living. She escapes being walled up and being intruded upon; she learns to know and make herself known. Such is the extent of her soul's "reconcilement" with a world in which she will always be a foreigner. But this partial victory is not her greatest triumph; her real victory lies in the reconcilement of her soul with its own depths, despite the world's attempt to keep them apart.

Such reconcilement had long been a problem posed in Gothic romance written by women, but posed as an aspect of the narrative's struggle against itself and so always unresolved, the overt ideology of the narrative form being in perfect collusion with the social ideology that sorted women into the angelic and demonic, saintly and sexual, decorous and bad, and shut them out from the knowledge of their own hidden selves. *Villette* confronts these issues directly, portraying a woman's difficult victory over her internal collusion with the social forces—the "forces of violence"—that would separate her from her own emotional capacities and even her own practical capacities. Even so, the world she lives in continues to be one in which the full unfolding of faculties that Mary Wollstonecraft dreamed of for women is not possible. Like the capacity for loving Graham Bretton, which can never be put to use because of his own limitations, much of Lucy's potential resembles the tent of Peri-Banou:[43] "All my life long I carried it folded in the hollow of my hand—yet, released from that hold and constriction, I know not but its innate capacity for expanse might have magnified it into a tabernacle for a host" (555).

The drama of longing to be "beyond and above" in *Wuthering Heights* is played out in the vast natural setting of the open moors, where society itself, represented by Lockwood, is laughably out of place. In *Jane Eyre*, it is given a social context, but the happy ending belongs to a setting removed from the world. Indeed, as Gilbert and Gubar observe, "[T]he physical isolation of the lovers [at Ferndean] suggests their spiritual isolation in a world where such egalitarian marriages as theirs are rare, if not impossible" (369) In *Villette*, the drama of a woman's confinement and transcendence is played out in the social world of a city. Confronted with the pettiness of this world—even its name is a diminutive—the soul in its immensity is all the more lost, its capacities all the more constricted and constrained. Here there is only the very smallest room for women like Lucy to "unfold their faculties"; this is not a world in which their "innate capacity for expanse" can be fully realized or one that can afford to accommodate their special Imagination, whose temple is "too wide for walls," and "whose floors are space . . ." (308).

Epilogue

Charlotte Brontë's importance as an artist in the Gothic tradition cannot be overestimated. It was she, among nineteenth-century writers, who saw most clearly the confusion of me and not-me in women's most terrifying experience of themselves—who saw the hidden identity of the ghostly other selves that haunt the female mind and the forces of oppression whose violence shapes those ghosts in its own image, making them at the same time both self and fearful Other. She saw the realism of women's Gothic fantasies, the real meaning of Gothic repetition in women's lives, and the sinister identity of domestic horrors and the final domestic "transcendence" exalted by women Gothicists. She saw the Good Other Woman and the Evil Other Woman as equally false versions of the heroine's true self; the villain as the hero's other face. She saw too the identity, in women's lives, of mystery and loss: the spiritual, intellectual, and psychological loss created by women's exclusion from a "masculine" sphere of knowledge; the self-loss that results when the "forces of violence" combine with the collusion of their victim to make woman's "authentic self" a mystery even to her. She saw the mystification of woman as a loss both to her and society, making her the eternal voiceless Other in a world of alien institutions that deprive her of the power to name both them and herself.

Such is the vision produced by Brontë's final, most audacious demystification of women's Gothic. And yet even more audaciously, she made this bleak vision the context for a vision of woman's freedom: one woman's hard-earned freedom at least not to be Other to herself—a limited freedom, but perhaps the only one attainable without the power to change those evils, "deep-rooted in the foundations of the social system," of which Brontë herself needed courage even to speak obliquely in the troubled voice of Lucy Snowe.

The insecurities of that voice continue to make *Villette,* despite its dazzling illumination of the long-obscured meanings of women's Gothic, one of the most opaque works of nineteenth-century literature. "Fast I narrated, fluent I told my tale," Lucy says of her liberating outburst to Paul. Yet the tale she tells in *Villette* is anything but fluent, blotted as it is by that tendency to self-erasure over which even at the end, she has triumphed only in part. The ending itself—a tragedy limned only by allusion to the comedy "sunny imaginations" would place in its stead—reveals the blanks that result when a woman like Lucy Snowe attempts self-expression in a medium that can only end by making a mystery of the self it cannot make known.

For it stands to reason that in a world in which language itself defines women as the fearful Other, the most revealing stories they tell about themselves are mysteries. The writer's self-transcendence through the act of writing, simultaneously an act of knowledge and of self-defense, was the only kind of transcendence in which the Gothicist finally believed. Even so, for nineteenth-century women writers the escape from private nightmare into public art envisioned by Henry James was itself a mode of transcendence fraught with perils. Not the least of these was the fact that for women, the very passage from the haunted mind to the palace of art was a dangerous act of transgression. Even the modest escape of storytelling presented special problems for women writers, who lacked equal access to education and the literary marketplace and who, because of female decorum and the ideology of woman's sphere, lacked the equal freedom to exploit the language in which they were working or, often, the full resources of their own imaginations.

That is why, although women's Gothic is passionately ambitious for the sublime, embedded in its extravagant striving "to speak somewhere without bounds" is a deep consciousness of the restraints that bound women's discourse in special ways. And that is why it is so appropriate that the constraints of female discourse, from the beginning a subject of women's Gothic, should be at the very center of Charlotte Brontë's work as she unlocks the subversive potential of the genre and liberates the anger implicit in Gothic fear. For Lucy Snowe is herself the prototypical woman Gothicist, struggling for self-transcendence through the process of telling a ghost story but encountering in the struggle a set of conventions and taboos that threaten at every turn to paralyze her faculties as a narrator.

It is appropriate, too, that in Brontë's work, the fullest realization in nineteenth-century fiction of the potential the Gothic romance offered women for speaking "I," at least one reviewer recognized "the whole hedge of immemorial scruple and habit broken down and trampled upon."[1] Destroying such barriers had from the beginning been the project of women's Gothic, but most often a timid, secret one. It was Brontë's scandal and triumph to place her art so boldly in that long and rich history of transgression.

Notes

Introduction

1. Thus, for example, Nathan Drake refers to "the late favourable reception" of "two or three publications" that use "Gothic" superstitions to incite terror ("On Gothic Superstition" 88). Maturin's preface to *Montorio* refers to "the present style of novels," bewailed by many as *"Diavolerie, tales fit to frighten the nurs-ery, German horrors"* (1: iii). Coleridge's review of *The Monk* refers to a "species of composition" associated with "fiends, incomprehensible characters . . . shrieks, murders, and subterraneous dungeons" (*Miscellaneous Criticism* 370). *The Criti-cal* in 1796 remarked that "since Mrs. Radcliffe's justly admired and successful romances, the press has teemed with stories of haunted castles and visionary terrors" (*Critical Review* 16: 22, quoted in Lévy 251). Anna Maria Mackenzie associates the new type of romance with Radcliffe and with Walpole, their "great original" (*Mysteries Elucidated* xv). In other such characterizations of the new genre, T. J. Horsley Curties refers to the jealousy of novel writers, who will not suffer those humble architects, romance writers, "to build our airy castles, or mine our subterranean caverns, unmolested" (*Ancient Records, or The Abbey of St. Oswythe, A Romance* [London, 1801], quoted in Tarr [3].) Mrs. Bullock, author of *Susanna: or, Traits of a Modern Miss, A Novel* (London 1795) refers to "a species of novels, lately very much in fashion, which possess (in addition to the usual folly of such works) all the improbabilities of antient romance; books, that tell of *beautiful* damsels, who have been confined *twenty* years in caverns; of murders, ghosts and ruined castles" (2: 191, quoted in Tarr [3]).

2. "Walpole's decorator's temperament did reign over a good deal of later Gothic fiction . . ." (Kiely 32). "His antiquarian's mentality . . . prompted him

to write with the too-inclusive instinct of the collector rather than with the selective imagination of the artist" (33).

3. Such designations are often intended, of course, to refer to what Fowler calls the "mode" rather than the genre (92). Nevertheless, more and clearer distinctions would often be useful in discussions of particular works. What does it mean, for example, to call both *The Mysteries of Udolpho* and *Moby-Dick* "Gothic romance"? Melville's novel makes some use of the Gothic tradition, but to say that it participates in the genre of Gothic romance unnecessarily dilutes the meaning of the term. Hence the aptness of Novak's protest that "works like *Moby-Dick* may utilize certain Gothic effects, but they are not essentially Gothic." As he says, the critic of Gothic fiction who finds "skeletons, shrieks, old castles and trap doors . . . an embarrassment" should find another subject (51). For a different view, see Keech, who argues that a definition of the Gothic should be based not on its "trappings" but on the response it attempts to effect.

4. The most significant characterizations of Gothic romance before Lévy's massive study were by Killen (1915), Scarborough (1917), Birkhead (1921), Railo (1927), Tompkins (1932), Summers (1938), Sadleir (" 'All Horrid?' " 1944), Varma (1957), Roudaut (1959), Nelson ("Night Thoughts," 1962). Since Lévy's study the most significant examinations of the Gothic are Hume's "Gothic Versus Romantic" (1969), the subsequent exchange between Platzner and Hume in PMLA (1971), Thompson, ed., *Gothic Imagination* (1974), Moers (1978), Doody (1977), Holland and Sherman (1977), Wolff (1979), Kahane (1980), Sedgwick (*Coherence* 1980), and Day (1985).

5. See, for example, the discussions of the Gothic in Nelson ("Night Thoughts") and Porte ("In the Hands").

6. For evidence of the immense popularity of British Gothic romances in America in the 1790s, based on numerous catalogues of libraries and booksellers, see Ringe (13–17). By 1800, the Gothic romances of such writers as Ann Radcliffe, Sophia Lee, Clara Reeve, Charlotte Smith, M. G. Lewis, Regina Maria Roche, Eliza Parsons, Stephen Cullen, Richard Warner, Francis Lathom, and Eleanor Sleath "represented a substantial part of the offerings" listed in book catalogues (Ringe 14–15).

7. Such as Malin's discussion of Southern "Gothic" (1962); Nelson's discussion of *Moby-Dick* (1962); Fiedler's discussion of the American novel (1966); and Porte's discussion of *Wieland* ("In the Hands," 1974).

8. Guillén's description of genre in "On the Uses of Literary Genre" (109).

9. Frederick S. Frank's "Aqua-Gothic Voyage" looks at "clever transpositions" of Gothic terror to "watery terror" in Poe's "A Descent into the Maelström."

10. That is, most notably Walpole, *The Castle of Otranto* (1764); Reeve, *The Old English Baron* (1778, originally published 1777 as *The Champion of Virtue);* Radcliffe, *The Castles of Athlin and Dunbayne* (1789), *A Sicilian Romance* (1790), *The Romance of the Forest* (1791), *The Mysteries of Udolpho* (1794); Lewis, *The*

Monk (1796); Radcliffe, *The Italian* (1797). Most critics of Gothic would also include Godwin, *Things as They Are; or, The Adventures Of Caleb Williams* (1794); Mary Shelley, *Frankenstein* (1818); and Maturin, *Melmoth the Wanderer* (1820).

11. As in Thompson, ed., *Gothic Imagination*. My objection to giving such tacit primacy to Maturin is that he himself was so self-consciously using an already-established pattern for his own purposes. In the preface to *Montorio,* for example, he defends as his own subjects "the present subjects of novels and romances" (1: iii), and the preface to *Melmoth* anticipates the criticism that he is imitating—or, as he says, attempting a "revivification"—of "Radcliffe-Romance" (5).

12. Thomas Love Peacock, "Essay on Fashionable Literature," quoted in Blakey (2).

13. Raddin provides an account of the library and a list of the novels and romances in the 1804 catalogue.

14. ". . . Melville—who, incredibly enough, seems actually to have fancied that *Pierre* was 'calculated for popularity'—may have thought that his novel would succeed as *The Monk* had done sixty years earlier, and partly for similar reasons" (Arvin, "Melville and the Gothic Novel" 44).

15. Thus, for example, it leads to such bizarre contortions as Day's image of the canon as a place that James could temporarily step "out" of in order to locate himself in a popular tradition while writing *The Turn of the Screw*. It can also lead to the blanking out of a whole female literary tradition, as in Day's statement that Emily Brontë uses the Gothic tradition but is not "of it," because *Wuthering Heights* does not "feed back into the genre, becoming part of its development" (2). It would be puzzling if Emily Brontë's version of the Gothic villain had had no influence on Charlotte Brontë, whose version of the Gothic in *Jane Eyre* is indubitably the ancestor of mass-market women's Gothic in the twentieth century, beginning with Du Maurier's *Rebecca*.

16. This is the opinion of many critics, for example, Tompkins (243), Kiely (65), and Lévy (246).

17. Indeed, as Fowler says, "The three phases . . . may interpenetrate chronologically and even be in doubt within a single work" (91).

18. For example, Talfourd said of her in 1826, "Mrs Radcliffe may fairly be considered as the inventor of a new style of romance . . ." (105).

19. Of the hundreds of romances on which Lévy based his study, he found only twelve that seemed to be direct descendants of *The Monk* (418). He classifies most of the romances he read as imitations of Radcliffe, with the intrigue constructed around a heroine (403).

20. At least this seems to have been the opinion of Anna Maria Mackenzie in her preface to *Mysteries Elucidated,* in which she refers to Radcliffe as "another modern genius" (x) and "that truly ingenious author" (xi) but explains in a foot-

note that the author she has referred to as the "great original" of the modern romancers who "have dyed their walls in blood" is "Walpole, in his Castle of Otranto" (xv).

21. In a *Roundabout Paper* in 1860 (no. xxiv), quoted in Dobrée (xiii).

22. For a discussion of the ways in which female Gothic typically is and is not quest romance, see Chapter 5.

23. The view of this search as "the central preoccupation of English novelists" (5) Wilt takes from Raymond Williams, *The English Novel from Dickens to Lawrence* (New York: Oxford University Press, 1970).

24. The differences between my version of this model and Sedgwick's will become evident as my interpretation of the Gothic unfolds, especially in Chapter 5.

25. For Sedgwick's own use of this term, see *Coherence* (37). Other critics whose interpretations of the Gothic focus explicitly on the dividing line between self and Other are Miyoshi, Day, Holland and Sherman, and Kahane. Sedgwick looks at the arbitrary creation of boundaries between self and world. Day's focus, in contrast, is on the disintegration of these boundaries and "the dialectic of fear and desire" associated with the consequent fragmentation of identity. Holland and Sherman apply to the Gothic a model of reader response that includes fantasy (which defines "what we project from within onto the outer world") and defense (which defines "what we let into ourselves from that outer world") as two of its primary terms and thus involves very centrally "the boundary between self and other" (281). In their reading, the experience of being in the castle, by evoking "that earliest stage in human development when the boundaries between inner and outer, me and not-me, are still not sharply drawn," creates the anxiety of "nonseparation" (283). The castle also, however, allows for the assertion of a separate identity through sexual desire (285). Kahane reads the anxiety of non-separation more specifically in terms of the heroine's encounter, at the "secret center of the Gothic structure" (50), with a mother figure: "a mirror image who is both me and not me" (48), in terms of whom, and in battle against whom, the heroine must engage in her "struggle for a separate identity" (48). Thus the Gothic concerns "the mysteries of identity, which turn on discovering the boundary between self and a mother-imago archaically conceived who threatens all boundaries" (52). The true Gothic fear, in her view, is that being a woman is "threatening to one's wholeness, obliterating the . . . boundaries of self" (59).

26. Most notably Birkhead, Kiely, Killen, Lévy, Lundblad, Railo, Sadleir, Summers, Tompkins, and Varma.

27. In this I agree with Lévy, not in reference to the whole genre, but to the works of what, in Fowler's terms, would be its "primary" phase.

28. For example, at the entrance to the Castle of Udolpho, "One of those instantaneous and unaccountable convictions, which sometimes conquer even strong minds, impressed [Emily] with its horror" (*Mysteries of Udolpho* 228). Lévy

provides a number of the many examples of the heightened significance Gothicists attribute to the crossing of the threshold (404–6).

29. The villains, respectively, of Ann Radcliffe's *The Italian, The Castle of Otranto, The Mysteries of Udolpho;* Mary-Anne Radcliffe's *Manfroné, or The One-Handed Monk;* Curties's *The Monk of Udolpho;* and Maturin's *Montorio.*

30. Lévy says of the architecture in Gothic romance, "Comme sur les dessins de Piranèse, le fantastique nait de la disproportion entre ces vastes halls, ces porches gigantesques, ces escaliers sans fin, ces voûtes démesurément amples et hautes, ces perspectives de colonnes qui se perdent dans les ténèbres, et les chétives personnes qui s'y meuvent. L'architecture oppresse, accable, étouffe, elle n'est pas à la mesure de l'homme" (270–71).

31. As Day points out, "The [Gothic] fantasy defines its world as a place where there exists one self; everything else in that world is Other; an enemy to the desires and integrity of the self, whether that self wishes to become a god or simply to escape and get married" (19).

32. "Praise of the active life and disapproval of the contemplative life are ever present in discussions of the religious state [in Gothic romance]. 'The selfish apathy of a secluded life' is contrasted unfavorably with 'that divine philanthropy, whose amiable effusions constitute the charm of social life' " (Tarr 49).

33. Compare Carnochan on "the dialectical interchanges between limit and limitlessness" in Piranesi's *Carceri* (9) and on the "image of infinitude rendered in its most claustrophobic terms" in Beckford's *Vathek* (135).

34. On the relation of the Faust myth to Gothicism, see Hume ("Exuberant Gloom").

35. Especially relevant to my angle of vision here is Wilt's emphasis on "the terrors of the separated one" (19) as the subject of Gothic and on the way that separateness and merging in Gothic romance (23–24) are integral to its development of a "mystic theoretic of the topic" central to the English novel (see Raymond Williams)—"the search for a community of individuals" (5). The fact that her emphasis on the double *desire* for separateness and community (24) rather than the double fear of them is in a sense the reverse of mine points to an important difference in our focus. Among the contexts behind my use here of the term Other is Varnado's interpretation of the Gothic, in terms he takes from Otto Rank's *The Idea of the Holy* (1917), as concerned with the "numinous feeling" (16) associated with a sense of the "wholly other" (15).

36. I take the distinction from Emerson's *Nature* (22) for reasons discussed in Chapter 4.

37. MacAndrew sees "devices of reflection" as "the mainstay of Gothic fiction from the beginning" (155; see also 214).

38. The term is Peckham's ("Toward a Theory of Romanticism.")

39. Our approaches differ also in that whereas my central aim is to see what Gothic conventions are "about," showing ways that the important Gothic conven-

tions are about the same thing is part of Sedgwick's procedure but not her aim (*Coherence* 5–6). There is a difference, too, in the kinds of content we focus on: she looks at three kinds of content: "the phenomenological, which deals with spatial and temporal proprioception; the psychoanalytic, which deals with the repression of sexual energy; and the structuralist, which deals with the way language treats itself and the relation between signs and meanings." The content of the conventions I am looking at is more accurately defined as the psychological and social content in interrelation, with "the repression of sexual energy" as only one aspect of the psychological context. The fact that Sedgwick's three areas of interest omit the question of what sorts of social relationships, especially relationships of power, the primary Gothic conventions stand for, means that our conclusions are very different.

Chapter 1

1. As in Radcliffe, *The Romance of the Forest, The Mysteries of Udolpho;* Smith, *Emmeline;* and Roche, *Clermont,* respectively.

2. My reading of *Clarissa* is especially indebted to Kinkead-Weekes, *Samuel Richardson.*

3. Parallel examples can be found in Musgrave, *Solemn Injunction* (3: 280) and *Cicely of Raby* (3: 4).

4. The doctrine is stated in numerous works: for example, in Sleath's *Nocturnal Minstrel,* Edgar says that innocence is "a shield . . . always . . . impenetrable" (153); in *A Northumbrian Tale,* Emmeline tells Beatrice, "Thou art, indeed . . . beset with dangers: still persevere, innocence will be thy guard . . . " (167); in *Mort Castle,* Maurice tells how in a moment of danger, "conscious innocence clad her armour round my soul to shield it from assault" (120).

5. See, for example, Braudy (195).

6. For his view of Radcliffe, see "On a Taste for the Picturesque," in which, through the mouthpiece of a gentleman friend of excellent taste, he commends her as "without doubt, the most illustrious of the picturesque writers" and criticizes those who "limit the attention, as is usually done, to her human figures" instead of recognizing the "lasting excellence of her works" (he mentions "Travels on the Rhine," *Udolpho,* and *The Italian)* to be the presentation of "affecting pictures." "Yet," he concludes, "Mrs. Radcliff's [*sic*] narrative is beautiful and interesting" (165). These comments suggest, among other things, that Brown had read not only "her two last romances" (165) but perhaps others as well; that he saw his comments as part of a general context of critical appreciation for Radcliffe's work; that he regarded the usual views of her as overemphasizing character (that eighteenth-century concern) at the expense of setting (the aspect of Radcliffe that leads most strikingly toward nineteenth-century Romanticism); and that he found her plots, though not her greatest merit, to be "interesting"—a word much stronger in his day than in ours. McNutt quotes the relevant passage (198).

7. On his acquaintance with the Gothic fiction of his day, and the role of Gothic romance in "the cultural environment from which [*Wieland*] emerged," see Ringe (13–17, 37–39).

8. Of Radcliffe's heroines, Tompkins says, "They have no enemy within; they are sure that innocence will be divinely shielded, and they never doubt their innocence. Those pits of agony into which Maturin cast a glance, where lie the souls of those who feel an involuntary pollution darkening their minds and dread lest their natures should conform to those of their persecutors, were beyond their scan" (259).

9. As is Antonia's case in *The Monk*.

10. As in the case of Agnes (*The Monk*), Ellena (*The Italian*), and numerous others.

11. As in *A Sicilian Romance*, in which the villainness poisons the villain and stabs herself; or in *The Italian*, in which Schedoni poisons both Nicola and himself.

12. As in *The Italian* and *A Sicilian Romance*.

13. About *The Wings of the Dove*, William wrote, "You've reversed every traditional canon of story-telling (especially the fundamental one of 'telling' the story, which you carefully avoid) . . ." (William James to Henry James, October 25, 1902, quoted in Matthiessen 338).

14. An ingenious attempt to attribute the villainy to Mrs. Bread reveals little about Mrs. Bread but much about James's elusiveness even on the simplest level of plot. Compare the opportunities James gives us for wondering whether Milly Theale was really ill.

15. For two other perspectives on the Gothicism of *The Portrait of a Lady*, see Nettles and Banta, both of whom read the whole plot as in some sense Gothic and discuss the Gothic metaphors in the scene of the midnight vigil.

16. Citing Vincent Blehl, who says that Isabel would be affirming Osmond's values if she yielded to Caspar's approval, Schriber adds, "Flight with Goodwood would confirm Osmond's values, but return to Rome confirms and redeems Isabel's own: the sanctities and solemnity of marriage, of forms, of promises" (454). But the situation is more complicated than this indicates, as Osmond himself values "forms" so highly.

17. See the many examples in Lévy (404–6).

18. On the Calvinism of the Gothic in *Wieland*, see Porte, "In the Hands of an Angry God."

Chapter 2

1. Lévy points out that Radcliffe's use of *surnaturel expliqué* does not represent the whole of her attitude toward the supernatural and cites Adeline's dream in *The Romance of the Forest* as an example of the unexplained supernatural (280–81). A contemporary of Radcliffe's also commented on the fact that not all

of her mysteries are explained. Anna Maria Mackenzie, in her preface to *Mysteries Elucidated,* remarked that the mysteries in romance should be elucidated at the end "without the intervention of super, or preternatural appearances. Dreams and apparitions savour too much of the superstition which ought never to be encouraged, and indeed I was happy to see, in that author's last voluminous publication [presumably *The Mysteries of Udolpho*], an amendment of this error" (xii).

2. "The ruins of these once magnificent edifices, are the pride and boast of this island. We may well be proud of them; not merely in a picturesque point of view: we may glory that the abodes of Tyranny and Superstition are in ruin." Uvedale Price, *An Essay on the Picturesque, as Compared with the Sublime and the Beautiful* (Hereford, 1798), 300, quoted in Lévy (220).

3. The description of the Scottish commonsense philosophers' position on this issue is from Terence Martin (112).

4. Murray provides an excellent analysis of the way Radcliffe lures her readers, through their very confidence in the "circumspect rationality" of the heroine, into irrational leaps of imagination (95–99). Murray's view of Radcliffe's final position is a sensible one: "Mrs. Radcliffe pressed at the bounds of Rationalism without yielding to Romantic idealism on one hand or to Humean skepticism on the other. She left the door open to feelings she was not willing to indulge . . ." (161).

5. "Le fantastique radcliffien a moins pour source l'intrusion, réelle ou supposée, de l'insolite dans le quotidien, que le climat d'angoissant mystère qui pèse sur les personnages et leurs gestes, et que ne détruisent pas les peu convaincantes 'explications' finales" (Lévy 281). Many readers have found the life of Radcliffe's work to lie outside its ostensible moral and philosophical center. Kiely says, for example, "She may preach prudence, moderation, and universal harmony, but the potential fertility of that irrational state remains the most original and convincing aspect of Mrs. Radcliffe's art" (71). See also Haggerty (382–83).

6. Howells offers a compelling account of the competing claims of reason and imagination in *The Mysteries of Udolpho* (52–61).

7. Of her explanations of ghosts, Kiely explains, we are skeptical: "She has shown all too well that there are crucial moments when neither reason nor faith in cosmic order is the central factor in the experience of an individual" (80).

8. The title of a romance by Anthony Frederick Holstein (Blakey 68).

9. As Durant says, Radcliffe's "heroines enter the fallen world simply because their protectors disappear. God finds no one eating the apple; He simply disappears, taking the garden with Him" (521).

10. Of Radcliffe's Gothic edifices, Tompkins says, "[N]one of [them] are ever fully known, even to their inhabitants . . ." (257).

11. "In the Gothic view . . . individual identity . . . is social and relational rather than original or private; it is established only ex post facto, by recognition" (Sedgwick, "Character" 256).

12. Lévy sees usurpation as a central crime in two of the plot types he finds most prevalent in Gothic romances and as an aspect of the third type (394ff).

13. For example, Thorslev: "[T]here is a very real sense in which the only love possible for the Romantic hero . . . is an incestuous love. First, it symbolizes perfectly this hero's complete alienation from the society around him; and second, it symbolizes also what psychologically speaking we can call his narcissistic sensibility, or, more philosophically speaking, his predilection for solipsism" (50). Thorslev describes a dilemma of Romanticism: "If the Scylla of Romantic poetry, theory, and practice is a loss of all sense of personal identity in some absolute outside the self, then surely the Charybdis of Romantic theory and poetry is solipsism, the illusion that one's own mind and its ideas are the only reality. And as the loss of personal identity is often symbolized in the dissolution of the poet-hero in the west wind, or in the waves of the dark blue ocean, or in the image of a passive Eolian harp strummed by the impersonal Life Force of the universe, so the other possibility, or the other danger—that of solipsism— is often symbolized in an incestuous brother-sister love" (55). I would argue that certain Gothic romances, like *Montorio,* present both dilemmas simultaneously. I do not argue that Annibal is a victim of the illusion that his own mind is the only reality, but that he and Ippolito become bounded by the darkness of their own consciousness, despite their realization that there is a world beyond them from which they have been cut off.

14. Similarly, Hawthorne's Aylmer aspires to the "infinite" ("The Birthmark" 1028), but he begins his experiment on Georgianna by enclosing her in an apartment whose curtains are designed to "shut in the scene from infinite space" (1025).

15. Axton's reference to Immalee's "growing love for the man she knows to be the worst of sinners" (xviii) seems to me to be based on a serious misreading of the plot. Melmoth's true spiritual state as "the worst of sinners" is precisely what Immalee-Isidora does *not* know until he finally reveals it to her in the prisons of the Inquisition. Maturin insists again and again on this essential gap in her knowledge, and it is central to the subtleties of the moral issue he investigates by means of her relationship with Melmoth.

16. On "mediated narration" as a device of Gothic enclosure, see MacAndrew (10, 48, Chap. 4), and Sedgwick (*Coherence* 21–22).

17. The thematic centrality of knowledge in this sense is revealed by what Berthoff describes as the book's "insistence on explaining in minute detail every inflection of motive in Pierre's mind, and every new position and rhythmic phase in the mechanics of his responsiveness"—a method that, "at its most effective . . . gives us with considerable cogency something like an affective, not to say dramatic, theory of knowledge; it provides, that is, a working display of the process by which thoughts are formed and the commitments of feeling actually entered into within the human mind" (52).

18. Lévy associates the "verticality" of the Gothic world in general with the Fall: "Par essence le rêve 'gothique' est un rêve de l'expérience verticale, auquel

s'attachent les images de la pureté ethérée, comme les angoisses du vertige et le désespoir de la *chute:* le thème Faustien, si cher à Lewis et à Maturin, prend dans ce contexte, toute sa pesanteur" (8). See also Tracy's comments on the fall in Gothic (3–5, 10, 195) and her list of Gothic references to falling ("Index" 199).

19. Furrow associates Lucy with Claude's landscapes and Isabel with Salvator's, but my discussion is intended to show that Melville is mixing pastoral and sublime landscapes more ambiguously than that distinction suggests.

20. Kearns has shown how in *Pierre* the question of the continuity, or discontinuity, between the self and the world is part of Melville's criticism of the idealistic psychology of his day, which asserted a "physical connection between the human mind and the external world" that was "divine, harmonious, magnetic": a "solid and nearly inescapable primary harmony." Melville, in contrast, saw this connection "as functional and developmental," influenced by the specific psychological history of the perceiver (49). The experience of the sublime was "one of the standard touchstone situations of idealistic psychology" (47), because it seemed to prove an exact correspondence between mind and world (41). Kearns demonstrates how both Isabel's and Pierre's experience of the sublime illustrates, instead, the very opposite: "the fragility of human relationships with the world outside . . ." (48). Pierre's reading of the scene at the casement window, therefore, is a mistake: "[I]t is a mistake to read any sensations, especially sensations of the moral and passionate faculties, as caused by some external 'preternatural' stimulus, especially when there are internal causes (such as the sexual urge) just as powerful. Making this mistake, Pierre is all too willing to be guided by the 'phantoms' created by his mind, believing them to represent a supernatural realm with which he has a direct connection" (47).

21. As Dimock says, "At the rupture between mother and son, one kind of confidence replaces another as Pierre withdraws his 'perfect confidence' to become a 'confidence man' embarked on what he calls an act of 'pious imposture' " (399).

22. Thorslev's comments on the Romantic hero are relevant here, especially since he makes them in the context of incest as a Romantic symbol: "For the Romantic hero, as for many Romantic poets, the mind is its own place. . . . It is not a very long step from the assertion that the mind is its own place to the awful feeling that perhaps it is the *only* place, and this is a feeling that haunted . . . a good many . . . Romantic poets and heroes" (54–55). Thompson refers to the Dark Romantics' "suspicion that the external world was a delusive projection of the mind" ("Introduction" 5) and says that "in part, Gothic themes represent a quest for a theory adequate to world perceived as mind. . . . the Gothic tale could at least embody the world felt, if not perceived, as mind" (6). As I have indicated, the problem of knowledge in Gothic romance seems to me more complicated than this view acknowledges, and the applicability of Thompson's generalization depends on the particular romancer. Strictly speaking, a "suspicion

that the external world does not exist" is not a characteristic of Radcliffe's romances. It is true that she portrays the mind's private world so vividly that, at
times, the external world seems less relevant or important. However, it does seem
to be true that Pierre more than flirts with an epistemology that perceives the
world as mind. Certainly he experiences the "world felt . . . as mind" since,
knowing nothing about Isabel aside from what he "knows" intuitively, he makes
his consciousness the measure of the world and so becomes imprisoned in the
mind.

23. Kiely is describing Emily's experience in *The Mysteries of Udolpho:* "Like
all romantic heroes and heroines, she is gradually separated from the world and
imprisoned within her own consciousness."

24. This dilemma was Melville's own, as Arvin describes it in *Herman Melville:* ". . . *Pierre* is the work of a man who has acquired a terrible knowledge
of human motives, a terrible insight. . . . If Melville's constructive and expressive power, when he wrote *Pierre,* had been equal to this knowledge, the book
would have been the great book it so signally fails to be" (224).

25. Although not uniformly convincing with regard to *Frankenstein,* much of
what Swingle says about problems of knowledge in that work is applicable to
Pierre. Swingle discusses the Stranger figure in Romantic literature, who poses
the "fundamental question" of "the human mind's ability to know things" (57).
The "true nature" of "second-generation Romantic Strangers" like Keats's Por-
phyro and Frankenstein's Monster is "never revealed" (60). "Mary Shelley's novel
is a study of the mind in the process of trying to come to terms with the
Stranger. . . . *Frankenstein* is a drama of man's mind struggling with the awareness that the Stranger is a stranger and yet being forced, nevertheless, to deal
with it as if it were a known quantity" (61). The statement that "in creating the
monster, Frankenstein unwittingly exposes himself to the essential unknowableness of things . . ." (63) could apply as well to the consequences of Pierre's
relation with Isabel. Swingle's point about Frankenstein as a "modern version of
the myth of transgression" is also applicable to *Pierre:* "Mary Shelley seeks to
show through Frankenstein and Walton that the mind's dangerous attempt to reach
out beyond established boundaries may result in a sort of mental suicide" (63).

26. In this Isabel resembles the sisters of Lee's *The Recess.*

27. My discussion of pastoral, here and elsewhere, has greatly benefited from
conversations with Susanne Wofford.

28. As Alicia does in *The Solemn Injunction.*

29. As Emily does in *The Mysteries of Udolpho.*

30. For example, Olavida's near-revelation of Melmoth's identity, cited previously, and the many passages like that in which a dying stranger attempts to
warn Rosalina of her peril: "The signora Rosalina has a secret enemy; bid her to
beware of—of—" (Mary-Anne Radcliffe, *Manfroné* 1: 34).

31. I think here not only of the "heartless voids and immensities of the universe" of which Melville says the "white depths of the milky way" remind us,

but also of the description of the "awful lonesomeness" of the "open ocean": "The intense concentration of self in the middle of such a heartless immensity, my God! who can tell it?" (*Moby-Dick* 263, 529).

32. For other discussions of the Gothic elements in *Moby-Dick,* see Arvin ("Melville and the Gothic Novel"), Nelson, and Boudreau.

33. See, for example, Hough's discussion of the dreamlike quality of *The Faerie Queene* (95–99), for which he relies substantially on Chapter 6 of *The Interpretation of Dreams.*

34. As C. S. Lewis says of allegory, its proper function is to reveal "that which cannot be said, or so well said, in literal speech. The inner life, and specially the life of love, religion, and spiritual adventure, has therefore always been the field of true allegory; for here there are intangibles which only allegory can fix and reticences which only allegory can overcome (*Allegory of Love* 166).

35. Rose gives a reading of *Pierre* based on Melville's admiration, expressed in *White-Jacket,* for Walpole's play (" 'The Queenly Personality' ").

36. See, for example, Arvin (*Herman Melville*) and Berthoff (40–41).

37. For a different view, however, see Paul Lewis, "Melville's *Pierre* and the Psychology of Incongruity."

Chapter 3

1. See, for example, Aikin, "Bertrand" (127–37), and Drake, "Henry Fitzowen."

2. Hurd, for example, insists that *The Faerie Queene* be criticized as "a Gothic, not a classical poem" (56).

3. Thomas Holcroft, Preface to *Alwyn, or The Gentleman Comedian* (London: Fielding and Walker, 1780), quoted in Allott (46).

4. Arnold Hauser, *The Social History of Art,* trans. Stanley Godman. New York: Knopf, 1952), 1: 272–73. Quoted in Muscatine (167).

5. On reflection as a characteristic Gothic device, see MacAndrew (155, 214) and Malin (77). Wilt discusses a special aspect of repetition in the Gothic: the "fear of automatism" present in such characters as Melmoth, with "his eternal ineffectual dream of closure" (60), and in Dracula, "the greatest of automatons," "fettered by those dozens of rules . . . that make an undead's life scarcely worth living" (89).

6. This passage is cited in Porte ("In the Hands" 48) and Praz (19–20). Praz, picking up Andersen's suggestion that "there is a passage still unexplored leading from the *Carceri* into the strangely echoing vaults of the English Gothic novels," discusses Piranesi's influence on Walpole and says of the De Quincey passage, "So much had Piranesi's *Carceri* penetrated the spirit of the Gothic tales, that when De Quincey evoked them in a famous passage of the *Confessions of an English Opium-eater* he gave them a 'Gothic' character" (19).

7. Carnochan uses Plate 9 of the *Carceri* as an example of "the dialectical interchanges between limit and limitlessness" (9). He discusses the "resonant doubleness of feeling" resulting from "the demolition of the closed world and its replacement by the infinite universe. The seventeenth-century intuition of infinitude and the invigoration of its paradoxes brought to a pitch the double feelings of wanting to soar and not wanting to, of hating confinement and cherishing it, of being fixed in place and being lost in a great nowhere with nothing to hang on to. . . . The record of eighteenth-century thought is one of strategies and adjustments brought on by this new recognition of our nature" (8).

8. "[A]t the heart of many a Gothic wandering," Carnochan says, lies "the fear Kepler had expressed, early in the seventeenth century, at the prospect of an infinite universe—'This very cogitation carries with it I don't know what secret, hidden horror; indeed one finds oneself wandering in this immensity, to which are denied limits and center and therefore also all determinate places' . . ." (10)

9. The distinction, when it is made, tends to derive from Radcliffe's distinction between terror, which "awakens" and "expands" the faculties, and horror, which "contracts" and "freezes" them.

10. It is interesting, with regard to the theme of the boundaries of the self, that Freud identifies the "animistic stage in primitive men" and the corresponding stage in each individual as "a time when the ego had not yet marked itself off sharply from the external world and from other people" ("The 'Uncanny' " 236, 240).

11. MacAndrew uses a version of this image to describe the Gothic world (155).

12. Malin ascribes the flat quality of Gothic characters to the "concern with narcissism" in Gothic and quotes Ihab Hassan: "The Gothic insists on spiritualization, the spiritualization of matter itself, and it insists on subjectivisim" ("Carson McCullers: The Alchemy of Love and Aesthetics of Pain," *Modern Fiction Studies* 5: 312). Malin continues, "It seeks, in other words, to demonstrate how weaklings read meanings into matter, meanings that reflect their own preoccupations. *Reality becomes a distorted mirror*" (6).

13. My thinking about the relation between the perceiving subject and the perceived object in the Gothic tradition has been influenced by Malin's discussion of narcissism in the Gothic, Nuttall's discussion of the "solipsistic fear" resulting from "the sealing of the [mind's] doors" by Lockean epistemology, and Carnochan's discussion of metaphysical and epistemological "prisons" in eighteenth-century literature.

14. Newlin discusses three of Hawthorne's supernatural tales, using the framework of Freud's remarks on the "uncanny," especially emphasizing the importance of repetition.

15. I do not want to imply by this that Hawthorne was therefore a realist in the strict sense in which the Scottish commonsense philosophers were realists. Both Martin and Pancost have shown how complicated was the relation between

these philosophers' epistemology and Hawthorne's. Nor do I want to imply that Hawthorne's epistemology was identical to Radcliffe's—on the contrary, as the conclusion to this chapter should indicate. On the other hand, Hawthorne's perception of the dangers of self-absorption seems clearly to be based on an assumption that there is something "out there" from which it is tragically easy to become cut off but to which the perceiving mind (or heart) acquires access in rare moments of illumination. Such is the moment in which Miriam and Donatello are united beneath the image of the bronze pontiff: "There is a singular effect oftentimes when, out of the midst of engrossing thought and deep absorption, we suddenly look up, and catch a glimpse of external objects. We seem at such moments to look farther and deeper into them, than by any premeditated observation; it is as if they met our eyes alive, and with all their hidden meaning on the surface, but grew again inanimate and inscrutable the instant that they became aware of our glances" (*Marble Faun* 777).

16. Relevant to Hawthorne's understanding of distorted perception are Sir David Brewster's comments on "spectral illusion" in his *Letters on Natural Magic*. The book was charged to Hawthorne at the Salem Athenaeum, September 19, 1837 (Kesselring 45). Brewster pays special attention to "those singular illusions of sense by which the most perfect organs either cease to perform their functions, or perform them faithlessly; and where the efforts and the creations of the mind predominate over the direct perceptions of external nature" (17–18). In a passage clearly related to Dimmesdale's extraordinary mental state during his vigils, Brewster says, "In darkness and solitude, when external objects no longer interfere with the pictures of the mind, they become more vivid and distinct; and in the state between waking and sleeping, the intensity of the impressions approaches to that of visible objects. With persons of studious habits, who are much occupied with the operations of their own minds, the mental pictures are much more distinct than in ordinary persons; and in the midst of abstract thought, external objects even cease to make any impression on the retina" (55). I am indebted to Buford Jones for calling my attention to Brewster's book.

17. These issues are discussed more fully in chapter 5.

18. From his *History of Morals* 1869 (London: Longmans, 1911), 359. Quoted in Tomalin (309).

19. Porte cites this scene as the one passage in which "Emily's innocence is subjected to its most profound threat—intimations of universal sinfulness and the reality of damnation" and sees the scene itself as a probable influence on Hawthorne's portrayal of the relationship between Miriam and Hilda ("In the Hands" 44). See also Kahane's discussion of Emily's relation to Laurentini (51).

20. In a lecture at Odense University, Denmark, 1981.

21. For a fuller discussion of this issue, see Chapter 5.

22. Richard Sickelmore, *Osrick; or, Modern Horrors, a Romance* (London: Lane, 1809), quoted in Summers (363).

23. Brombert explores this aspect of Romantic prisons. He speaks, for ex-

ample, of the "expansion towards infinity" implied in Hugo's view of solitude (112) and associates Pascal's "elating imprisonment" with the *felix culpa* (24). Important for my discussion is his whole consideration of the "importance . . . for the Romantic imagination" of the paradox of "Salvation through enclosure, insight into darkness": a paradox "rooted in the age-old symbol of the captive soul, in the religious notion of a happy captivity" (17).

24. *Les Plaisirs et les jours* (Gallimard 1924) (13), quoted in Brombert (17).

Chapter 4

1. In this sense it heralds what Abrams calls the "natural supernaturalism" of the Romantic movement.

2. The racism and xenophobia of *Zofloya* are characteristic of the Gothic, which so often implicitly or explicitly equates the boundaries of the self with racial, class, or national boundaries. The title of Radcliffe's *The Italian* is a case in point: even though the intrigue is set in Italy and both the hero and heroine are Italian, "the" Italian of the title is clearly the exotic and evil Schedoni, who is somehow Italian in a way that the hero and heroine, with whom the English reader is supposed to identify, are not. (The extent to which this ploy works is revealed in the fact that readers even today almost never recognize the illogic of the title.) The anxiety to keep "us" separate from "them" is one of the motivating anxieties of the Gothic: Poe's racism, for example, comes through, in inverted form, in the terror with which the black Nu-Nu regards the white curtain at the end of *Pym*.

3. "More and more, as the [eighteenth] century draws to its close, readers of all kinds . . . groped towards the colossal, the impassioned, the dark sublime. They wanted to see great forces let loose and the stature of man once more distended to its full height, even if it were stretched on the rack" (Tompkins 287). Tompkins points to the signs, even in the 1780s, of the Romantic heroes to come: "[T]he conventional moral ending [of repentance] wholly fails to cover (it was probably not intended to cover) the sympathetic excitement caused by the aspect of uncontrolled passion. It was exhilarating in a circumspect world to feel that the human mind was after all capable of this abandon, that it had something to show akin to the destructive glories of those storms in which amateurs of the picturesque delighted" (287–88).

4. My understanding of the sublime aesthetic comes from Nicolson; Boulton, Elizabeth McKinsey's lectures at Harvard (1982), and of course Burke.

5. The term comes from Miyoshi, who sees the creators of this myth as having found much that was "powerfully attractive" in Gothic tales, especially their portraits of Gothic villains, "their sensationalism, their introspectiveness" (xiv–xv).

6. Abrams discusses this passage (*Mirror and Lamp* 53).

7. I am especially indebted to the articles by Hume and Porte, which suggest

that as Thompson says in his introduction, "the apprehensions that there was a dark substratum to the rock of Romantic faith obsessed those Romantic writers who turned to the Gothic mode of terror and horror in an effort to express a complex vision of the existential agony confronting man since the Age of Faith" (5).

8. Porte remarks that the staircase in this passage is "reminiscent of Piranesi's nightmarish engravings" and notes that Emerson listed De Quincey as one of the writers he wanted to meet in Britain on his first trip (*Representative Man* 181, 346).

9. "The central form of Dark Romanticism is essentially an acute perception of evil with little move toward either solution or escape" (Hume, "Exuberant Gloom" 123). Similarly, Platzner says it is "the singular quality of *evil* that distinguishes the *Gothic* vision from all other types of fantasy literature . . ." ("Rejoinder" 267) and identifies "the pathology of the spirit all Gothic fiction exhibits" with "an obsessive apprehension of evil that demands expression or deliverance" (*Metaphysical Novel* 70). See also Nelson, "Night Thoughts"; Le Tellier, *An Intensifying Vision of Evil;* and MacAndrew, who correlates the trajectory of the Gothic with changing ideas about "the place of evil in the human mind." Her reading is particularly interesting for the way it locates in Benevolism the roots of the Gothic approach to evil.

10. The central place of the Fall in the Gothic vision is emphasized in Thompson's anthology, in which each essay, as he says, "revolves in some manner around the breakdown of a stable Medieval world order, paralleling the mythic expulsion of man from Eden" (3). Porte's version of this is particularly relevant here: "Victim and victimizer, hound and hare, the terror-stricken sinner and his awful deity, are one because they represent the divided halves of what was once a primal moral unity from which things have sadly and perversely declined. The ruined world of Gothic fiction is a dramatization of this separation, of the sinner in flight from his God-consciousness, or—as Jung might say—of man pursued by his soul" ("In the Hands" 63).

11. Any discussion of *Wuthering Heights* in these terms must be profoundly indebted to Miller's long and subtle analysis of the novel in *The Disappearance of God*. After his investigation, it would be unnecessary to attempt any complicated analysis of the relations among self, other selves, and God in *Wuthering Heights*. I want here only to indicate how striking an example the novel is of a Romantic's Gothic use of boundaries and barriers to explore the theme of the boundaries of the self and to point to the close proximity in *Wuthering Heights* of Gothic despair and exultant Romantic transcendence in the context of this theme. Miller uses the term "boundaries of the self" in his discussion of the novel. Much of his language, in its use of metaphors of boundaries, is suggestive in regard to the present chapter.

12. For the use of this term in the context of the Gothic, see Varnado's "The Idea of the Numinous." Other critics who set Gothic mysteries in a mystical or

theological context are Porte ("In the Hands"), Summers, Varma, and, most provocatively, Wilt.

13. As Kiely says, the novel "is filled with transformations, the fusion of opposites or the interchange of aspects, until there are fewer and fewer clear distinctions and more and more newly realized continuities" (237).

14. The term is from Abrams's book of the same name.

15. As Miller says, "The otherness of nature is replaced by the more frightening otherness of a ghost, and the stormy moors are established as the expressions of a supernatural as well as a natural violence. The spiritual powers are immanent in nature, and identified with its secret life" (169).

16. It is not specifically in his persona of priest that Orazio offers Ippolito access to this Other realm; nevertheless it is logical that Orazio's relations to the two brothers are to be taken together as parts of an allegorical whole. What is significant is that both of them become involved with him because of their thirst for the knowledge of what cannot be known.

17. The term is from Summers, whose study of Gothic romance is devoted to the thesis that Gothicism has its origin in mystical aspiration.

18. In "Exuberant Gloom," Hume implies that *The Monk* is ambivalent in this respect, although his emphasis is different from mine: "Living in a mental hell, one very natural response is to burlesque it. M. G. Lewis' *The Monk* is a perfect example of a work which shuttles uneasily between the serious *Schauer-Romantik* and the devaluative mode" (124). For an interpretation of the relations of humor and fear in the Gothic in the context of incongruity theory, see Paul Lewis, "Mysterious Laughter."

19. Van Ghent comments that "the technical *displacement* of Heathcliff's and Catherine's story into past time and into the memory of an old woman functions in the same way as dream displacements: it both censors and indulges, protects and liberates" (165).

20. Van Ghent makes the same point and explains its significance: "Even in the weakest of [the characters'] souls there is an intimation of the dark Otherness, by which the soul is related psychologically to the inhuman world of pure energy, for it carries within itself an 'otherness' of its own, that inhabits below consciousness" (171). This point is relevant to my whole discussion of the novel, as is Van Ghent's fine reading of the window scene. She relates this scene to the immediately succeeding scene in which Heathcliff and Cathy as children look in through the Lintons' drawing room window, to the final scene at Heathcliff's deathbed, and to the scene in which Cathy "Literally . . . 'catches her death' by throwing open the window" (165–69). She sees the window as "a separation between the soul's 'otherness' and its humanness" (169).

21. As Daiches says, "There is a recurrent and disturbing suggestion [in *Wuthering Heights*] that the depths of man's nature are in some way alien to him" (27).

22. Relevant here is Van Ghent's comment that the novel "is profoundly in-

formed with the attitudes of 'animism,' by which the natural world—that world which is 'other' than and 'outside of' the consciously individualized human—*appears* to act with an energy similar to the energies of the soul; to be permeated with soul energy but of a mysterious and alien kind . . ." (171).

23. Miller points out that sadism "is a way of breaking down the barriers between oneself and the world" (195), although he makes this comment not with reference to Cathy and Heathcliff's relationship but with reference to Heathcliff's cruelty to everyone except Cathy.

Epilogue (I)

1. James's account is from "A Small Boy and Others," as quoted in Edel, *The Untried Years* 67–79.

Chapter 5

1. The best discussion of these difficulties is to be found in Showalter, Chaps. 1–3. More generally, on women's problem in speaking "in the language of the self," see Rabuzzi (176). Portions of this chapter first appeared in *Legacy: A Journal of Nineteenth-Century American Women Writers* ([Spring 1988]: 3–13) and are reprinted here with the permission of the editors.

2. Tompkins discusses the decorum expected of female authors in this period (125–26).

3. This is slightly different from saying, as Doody says, that "the 'real world' for characters in a Gothic novel is one of nightmare. There is no longer [as in earlier novels containing Gothic dreams] a common-sense order against which the dream briefly flickers. . . . There is no ordinary world to wake up in" (553). This seems to me technically inaccurate as a description of many of the most famous Gothic romances (e.g., *Mysteries of Udolpho* and *Children of the Abbey*) when one considers their structure, although it may be affectively true when one considers their general atmosphere. The distinction is important, because there are many significant and interesting relations, still for the most part unexplored, between the realistic and romance sequences in Gothic works of fiction. Nonetheless, what Doody says of the historical subject matter of *The Recess* seems strikingly true: "This Gothic story about sixteenth-century characters is a judgment of the real world. . . . Institutions, power, political activities are the nightmarish cruel realities from which no one can escape" (560). ". . . Ellinor cannot be brought back to the comfort of the real world, because there is no comfort in her real world, and her madness is a simple reflection of what exists outside herself" (559).

4. Her discussion of *The Recess* is the best illustration of how Gothic romance renders "the true nightmare which is history" (562) as women experience it.

5. "The pretence at setting [*Mysteries of Udolpho*] in the late sixteenth century gives Mrs Radcliffe the freedom to choose forms which both embody and disguise contemporary neuroses, and as Emily pursues her elusive way through the terrors of a world of romance her adventures are very evidently an analogue for the predicament of the late eighteenth-century woman" (Howells 49).

6. As in Eliza Parsons, *Castle of Wolfenbach. A German Story.* 2 vols. London: Lane, 1793). This information is from Tracy's plot summary (125–26). Other examples are in Parsons, *Mysterious Warning;* Musgrave, *Cicely of Raby;* and a romance by Sarah Wilkinson: *The Spectres, or, Lord Oswald and Lady Rosa, Including an Account of the Marchioness of Cevetti who was Basely consigned to a Dungeon Beneath Her Castle by her Eldest Son, whose Cruel Avarice Plunged him into the Commission of the Worst of Crimes, that Stain the Annals of the Human Race. An Original Romantic Tale.* 31 pp. (London: Langley, n.d.). "Francisco even counterfeited his own mother's death; she is released from her dungeon at the age of seventy-one" (Tracy 188–89).

7. As in Roche, *Children of the Abbey.* See also the case of the hidden mother of Mrs. Patrick's *More Ghosts!* 3 vols. (London: Lane, 1798). Information from Tracy's summary, 128.

8. *A Sicilian Romance.*

9. Wollstonecraft, *Maria.*

10. In *A Sicilian Romance,* for example, not only is the heroine's mother hidden in the deserted wing; the hero's sister is discovered hidden in a convent. See also Roche, *Nocturnal Visit* (the case of Lady Endermay); Radcliffe, *The Italian* and *The Mysteries of Udolpho;* Lewis, *The Monk;* and Fuller, *The Convent* (the case of Agatha).

11. Lee, *The Recess.*

12. Raby's mother in Mrs. Harley, *Priory of St. Bernard. An Old English Tale.* 2 vols. (London: Lane, 1789). Raby's father had put his wife and two daughters "in the priory for safekeeping during wartime and failed to reclaim them, but he kept his infant son with him" (Tracy 68).

13. *A Sicilian Romance.*

14. For example, *Castles of Athlin and Dunbayne.* In another variant, a mother for years must conceal her identity from her son, who knows her only as his "veiled Protectress": see Mary Meeke, *The Veiled Protectress, or The Mysterious Mother. A Novel.* 5 vols. London: Newman, 1819. Information from Tracy's summary (117).

15. Compare Russ's discussion of the convention of the "Other Woman" in modern Gothics, "who is at the same time the Heroine's double and her opposite" (33; see also 34 and 47) but whom Russ identifies in the modern Gothic as always immoral and "more openly sexual" than the heroine (34). See also Radway on

the "female foil" (149) and Kahane on "the spectral presence," at the "secret center of the Gothic structure" (50), of a "dead-undead mother, archaic and all-encompassing, a ghost signifying the problematics of female identity which the heroine must confront" (47–48).

16. For example, Agnes in *Mysteries of Udolpho;* Lady Dunreath in *Children of the Abbey;* Mildred in *Solemn Injunction.*

17. Filial duty in general is one of the most piously adulated virtues in Gothic romance and the one the actual narratives undercut most outrageously. Thus to a story of the most appalling oedipal violence, the author prefaces a regret that he could not have entitled his book *Filial Piety* instead of *The Monk of Udolpho* (Curties, "Introduction" vii).

18. For example, Mary in *The Recess;* St. Aubert's sister in *Mysteries of Udolpho.*

19. Ann Ronald discusses the sexual imagery in the description of Udolpho itself, as Emily first approaches it (179). Similarly, Nina da Vinci Nichols sees place in female Gothic as a metaphor for the heroine's "most sinister enemy . . . her own awakening sexuality" (188).

20. It is for this reason, as well as for others, that I disagree with Mise's interpretation of the heroine's experience in Gothic, which sees the knowledge that the heroine gains during her confinement as sexual and identifies it with the acquisition of "a sense of her own adequacy as a woman" (247). The kind of sexual "adequacy" (249) at issue here is in my view exactly not the subject of Gothic endings, and sexual knowledge is exactly not the knowledge the heroine gains, despite the fact that sexuality is so extensively a subject of Gothic romance. Nor are the "sexual threats and assaults" on Emily portrayed as "exalt[ing] her sexuality" and so "giv[ing] her confidence in her adequacy as a woman" (123). They are, on the contrary, sources of pain and fear, and emblems of women's vulnerability. On the connection between Emily and Laurentini, see Kahane (51) and Porte (44).

21. For example, by Montoni's death and the telling of the sad story of St. Aubert's sister, which establishes her husband as having wronged her.

22. Sir William Blackstone, *Commentary on the Laws of England,* 1765, quoted in Strachey 15. Strachey discusses the legal and economic status of married women in the late eighteenth century and the nineteenth century (15–18, 34–40, and passim).

23. For example, Frank, "From Boudoir to Castle Crypt."

24. As Hough points out in his discussion of allegory (135).

25. For an example of the way this works in dreams, see Freud, *Interpretation* (350).

26. Thus, although he did gamble, "his heart was not depraved," and the other charges were not true at all.

27. See Poovey on the nature and importance of the economic exploitation at issue in the Udolpho sequences, especially her reading of "Valancourt's passion

for gambling" as an "embryonic" version "of the destructive energy Montoni embodies." Poovey's is the only reading of Udolpho that clarifies the central ideological significance of what has often been regarded as a gratuitous series of episodes designed merely to lengthen the narrative: the long sequence in which St. Aubert is suspected of promiscuity and Valancourt of gambling.

28. The difference between the old and new versions is presumably mediated by the role St. John plays in *Jane Eyre*, the novel that Russ does identify as an ancestor of such modern "Gothics" as Dorothy Eden's *The Brooding Lake* (1953), Anne Maybury's *I Am Gabriella!* (1962), Margaret Summerton's *Nightengale at Noon* (1962), Susan Howatch's *The Dark Shore* (1965), Phyllis Whitney's *Columbella* (1966), and Helen Arvonen's *The Least of all Evils* (1970).

30. As in Wolff's analysis of the male characters as projections of women's attitudes toward their own sexuality.

31. On women and class, see West.

32. For discussions of the problems of single women, see also Strachey (17) and Watt (142–48).

33. See, for example, Watt's discussion of the "crisis in marriage" in eighteenth-century England (142–48). He points out that Mary Astell, Daniel Defoe, and Samuel Richardson all were interested in some form of "Protestant nunneries" as a solution to the spinster's problem.

34. The setting of *The Children of the Abbey* is contemporaneous with its author, but the Protestant heroine takes refuge temporarily in an Irish convent.

35. See, for example, the reference in *The Female Aegis* to "prompt active benevolence" as "natural" in women (9). (*The Female Aegis, Or, the Duties of Woman from Childhood to Old Age, and in Most Situations of Life, Exemplified* (London: Sampson Low, 1798; New York: Garland, 1974.) Quoted in Poovey (309). Once again Wollstonecraft is relevant, as she brings up the question of women's supposedly greater "humanity," contending that women's "confined views" are more likely to narrow their affections than expand the heart and that "even women of superior sense, having their attention turned to little employments, and private plans, rarely rise to heroism . . ." (*Rights of Woman* 279).

36. For example, Frye: "The novelist deals with personality, with characters wearing their *personae* or social masks. He needs the framework of a stable society. . . . The romancer deals with individuality, with characters *in vacuo* idealized by revery . . ." (305). See also Chase (13–14).

37. The term is from MacCaffrey (47–49).

38. Although this pastoral ideal of education has not been recognized as an important Gothic convention, it was common enough for Barrett to mock it at the beginning of *The Heroine*: "My venerable Governess, guardian of my youth, must I then behold you no more? . . . Must I no longer wander with you through painted meadows, and by purling rivulets?" (1: 1).

39. I take the term from Jacobus, who uses it in another context (but one that,

as will be evident later, is interestingly related to this), the happy ending envisioned by Lucy and Paul in *Villette* (242).

40. See Varma on the womblike qualities of *The Recess* ("Introduction," *The Recess* xviii–xix) and Roberts on the inhibiting effects on Matilda of "being born and raised in seclusion" (72).

41. Among many other suspected heroines are Henrietta, in Elizabeth Bonhote, *The Fashionable Friend*, 2 vols. (London: Becket and Dehondt, 1773); Clarentine, in Sarah Harriet Burney's *Clarentine*, 3 vols. (London: Robinson, 1796); Adeline in *The Romance of the Forest* (suspected of an affair with Mme. de la Motte's husband); Elvina in Roche, *Houses of Osma* (her father finally exonerates her by confessing his own sins, which she knew of but did not reveal because of her desire to spare him). See also Fuller, *Alan Fitz-Osborne*, in which there are two stories of wrongly suspected women (1: 45, 2: 47). The information on Bonhote and Burney is from Tracy's summaries.

42. Mise discusses the importance of the family romance in Gothic and of evil parent figures, from whom the heroine escapes as part of her maturation. He points out that late eighteenth-century "emphasis on economic individualism," changes in family life, and "the spread of democratic ideas" were causing a reexamination of filial duty, a reexamination that makes its way into the Gothic novel (8). I do not agree, however, with some of the specific examples Mise offers of this, such as the idea that Ellena's filial piety toward Schedoni is being "ridiculed" by the author (172).

43. This kind of recasting of a story is common in Gothic. Indeed, Moers sees it even in *Mysteries of Udolpho*, when the dead St. Aubert is replaced by "what looks very like a shattered mirror image of the impossibly good father": the "severe, demanding, nasty, and perverse" father figure of Montoni (135).

44. This is, of course, true not only in women's Gothic. Wilt points out that closure is what Melmoth the Wanderer dreams of but never gets: "Or rather—supreme horror—the closure was coextensive with the quest, and all is helpless repetition" (61).

45. As she points out with reference to *The Recess*, "The villainous characters create a sort of omnipresent, hostile environment for this quest" and "The sexual identity of this environment is primarily male" (105).

46. I do not imply that Charlotte Lennox's book is Gothic but that the protagonist she introduced into English literature was the only one available for Gothic renderings of the female quest.

47. I am grateful to Jacques Lezra for pointing out the many ways in which circularity is an aspect of *Yvain and Gawain*.

48. ". . . Ellena requires the approval of the good mother figure before she can act (i.e., overcome her moral delicacy)" (Mise 174).

49. See also Amanda's convoluted reasoning in the scene in which she agonizes over whether or not to send Ellen to explain to Lord Mortimer why she is unable to meet him at the appointed time. She is tempted to do so, since other-

wise Lord Mortimer will undoubtedly think ill of her. "She thought of sending Ellen to acquaint him with the occasion of her detention at home; but this idea existed but for a moment: an appointment she concealed from her father, she could not bear to divulge to any other person; it would be a breach of duty and delicacy she thought. 'No,' said she to herself, 'I will not from the thoughtlessness and impetuosity which lead so many of my sex astray, overstep the bounds of propriety . . ." (2: 97).

50. This passage is one of several that suggest that Zofloya is the original of Frankenstein, and Victoria of Mary Shelley's Victor.

51. On the question of the conservative or revolutionary nature of the Gothic in general, see Durant, Fiedler, Paulson, Sadleir, Summers (399–401), Sypher, Tompkins (250–51), and Wilt (223). The best answer to the question of whether the Gothic is revolutionary or reactionary is Radway's article on modern women's Gothic, whose most general conclusions about the ideological function of the genre apply equally well to that of the 1790s.

52. Radway attributes this theoretical basis of her argument about the Gothic in great part to Jameson: "Reification and Utopia in Mass Culture," *Social Text* 1 (Winter 1979): 94–109, and "Ideology, Narrative Analysis and Popular Culture," *Theory and Society* 4 (Winter 1977): 135–63.

53. The exceptions tend to prove the rule: in one sense most women's Gothic is profoundly conservative, but its subversive aspects are so strong that writers like Godwin, Wollstonecraft (in *Maria, or the Wrongs of Woman*), and Charlotte Smith found them ready-made for use in works openly critical of social institutions. As Marilyn Butler says, "[B]oth Godwin and Mary Wollstonecraft were drawn to the Gothic, because it had developed powerful images for conveying the idea of an oppressive, coercive environment" (134).

54. See Gilbert and Gubar 282–83. In all of this I am much indebted to Gilbert and Gubar's discussion of heaven and hell and the "fall into gender" (225) in *Wuthering Heights* (*Madwoman* chap. 8).

55. On self-expression as a theme central to the story, see Gilbert and Gubar (89–92) and Treichler, who reads the wallpaper itself as "a metaphor for women's discourse" (62).

56. See Hedges on both contemporary and subsequent readers' blindness to the "connection between the insanity and the sex, or sexual role, of the victim . . ." (41).

Chapter 6

1. *The Recess* is a rare exception, because of the way it deliberately engages the issue of innocence and experience.

2. Thus I do not agree with Tillotson's view that "such social commentary as [*Jane Eyre*] may offer is . . . incidental" (257), although she is surely right in

her praise of Brontë's psychological realism: "The profounder explorations of *Jane Eyre* were new indeed to the novel; not before in fiction had such continuous shafts of light penetrated the 'unlit gulf of the self'—that solitary self hitherto the preserve of the poets" (260–61).

3. Homans's view, although it comes from a theoretical vantage point different from mine, is closer to the one I am presenting here: "The special horror of the Gothic is that Jane's allegiance to the plain and practical truth cannot rescue her from the dangers of subjectivity, because it is in the practical world that her fears and subversive wishes take their most terrifying form" (260).

4. The best case for the identification of Bertha and "plain Jane" is in Gilbert and Gubar's chapter on *Jane Eyre*.

5. As Gilbert and Gubar say, "[T]here is an impediment . . . despite their avowals of equality. Though Rochester, for instance, appears in both the gypsy sequence and the betrothal scene to have cast away the disguises that gave him his mastery, it is obviously of some importance that those disguises were necessary in the first place" (354). They go on to discuss Rochester's secrets as "secrets of inequality": of his greater sexual experience, a form of superiority to Jane; and of the inferiority implied in the "self-exploitation" (356) of his marriage to Bertha.

6. My reading of *Jane Eyre* is informed throughout by Gilbert and Gubar's perception that inequality is the key to the "impediment" (354ff), although my view of the sources of that inequality occasionally differs from theirs.

7. That is, not merely "a repulsive symbol of Rochester's sexual drive" and thus of "Jane's guilt about Rochester's passion" (Eagleton 32), although she is that, in part, but also Rochester's actual potential for violation.

8. As Gilbert and Gubar argue so convincingly.

9. The gloss is Gilbert and Gubar's: "The plot device of the cry is merely a sign that the relationship for which both lovers had always longed is now possible, a sign that Jane's metaphoric speech of the first betrothal scene has been translated into reality: 'my spirit . . . addresses your spirit, just as if both had passed through the grave, and we stood at God's feet, equal—as we are!' " (367).

10. Yeazell's article presents an excellent analysis of the importance of equality in Charlotte Brontë's view of love, and of the way in which the "mysterious summons" signals Jane's achievement of "that separate identity without which genuine love, in Brontë's world, cannot exist" (141).

11. Leavis points out that Jane comes here "as a penitent," "performing an act of faith"; "the episode reads like a pilgrimage and an ordeal" (25).

12. As Gilbert and Gubar point out (367).

13. Moers uses Kroeber's definition of this, "travel combined with rapture" (Kroeber 116), in her description of "traveling heroinism" (128).

Chapter 7

1. See Rowe's reading of the ending of *Jane Eyre* as in fact a rejection of fairy tale wish fulfillment, and Jane's earlier "immersion in romantic fantasy" (81) as something that "threatens her integrity" (81) and is finally overcome.

2. Treatment of the Gothic elements in *Villette* has been strangely cursory, with the notable exceptions of discussions by Heilman, Wolff, Jacobus, Burkhart, and Crosby. Hook's view that *Villette* represents a "retreat . . . from the more Gothic elements of plot and character in *Jane Eyre*" is characteristic. From this point of view the novel inevitably appears to be paying "too much attention . . . to the nun" (153). The reason for this sense that *Villette* is less Gothic than *Jane Eyre* may have to do not only with the denser social texture but also with the fact that, although the Gothic convention of the haunted family mansion still has a lively currency in novels and film, that of the escape from the convent is less familiar to contemporary readers.

3. The term is from Russ (33).

4. In addition, because, as Carlisle points out, "This quaint child takes Lucy's place" as the recipient of Louisa's attentions ("Face" 271), her arrival is a double loss: not only a displaced version of Lucy's primal loss of home, but also a signal that Lucy has in some sense lost even her replacement for home, her position as someone who is "a good deal taken notice of" (*Villette* 61) at the Brettons'.

5. Implicit in my discussion of Brontë's use of novel and romance techniques is the assumption that the obvious presence of Bunyan in her work should be taken seriously: not only was she familiar with allegorical techniques; one of the great allegories is obviously a subtext for both of her major novels. *Villette*, especially, calls attention through its many personifications to the fact that allegory is one of its central narrative procedures. There is no reason to view Brontë's use of allegory as some unhappy accident of which she was an unconscious and incompetent victim; her allegory, on the contrary, reveals her as a conscious and skillful artist in a long and rich tradition.

6. For a different reading of the convent and of Mme. Beck's role there, see Auerbach, *Communities of Women* (98–113).

7. Other readers who have seen Lucy and Ginevra as doubles are Gilbert and Gubar, who see Ginevra as Lucy's "self-gratifying, sensual, romantic side" (436), and Crosby. Crosby provides a suggestive reading of the mirror scene in terms of the Lacanian Imaginary and therefore in terms of the boundaries between self and Other. She also sees Lucy's essential project in terms of the boundaries of the self: "She must learn what are the proper boundaries between herself and other people, neither living in unhealthy isolation nor defining herself completely in terms of someone else" (52). Her perspective on this issue, however, is extremely different from the view I am proposing here. In Crosby's reading, Ginevra doubles Lucy despite the narrator's and the author's intentions. The many doublings of the text function in it as a deconstructive force, undermining Lucy's

coherence of identity, which is "the necessary condition for [the] mastery of herself and of the world" (71) that is the success story of *Villette*. "Lucy and Ginevra, seemingly so different, are constructed as doubles . . . such a conflation of characters mocks the fundamental enterprise celebrated in *Villette,* that of determining an inviolate identity" (5). In my reading, the doublings are formal aspects of an allegorical technique in which Brontë is working skillfully and consciously throughout the novel-romance and that enables her to define Lucy's complex identity with the subtle precision to which good allegory lends itself so well. For this reason, many elements that I see merely as elements in the allegory, functioning formally in ways consistent with the usual procedures of that tradition, Crosby reads as contradictions or dissonances. Nonetheless, her invaluable illumination of the many ways in which the characters in *Villette* double each other has contributed much to my reading of the novel. I am grateful to Christina Crosby for permission to quote from her dissertation.

8. Again like Mary Wollstonecraft, Lucy at one time or other tries all three of the jobs ordinarily open to women of her class: companion, governess, teacher.

9. Gilbert and Gubar point to this danger in their statement that Lucy for a time, because she is a single woman, sees herself as "nun(none)" (428).

10. For other accounts of the dynamic I am describing here, see Momberger ("Self and World in the Works of Charlotte Bronte"), Kinkead-Weekes ("Place of Love" 85), and Crosby ("Haunting of the Text").

11. Tanner makes this point: "[S]he is unaware of the real otherness of the given world and its inhabitants" (18).

12. This is a connection to which Lacan's work points, that mystery itself is a response to and a sign of loss.

13. Tanner also discusses the way Lucy's condition of being "everywhere not-at-home" produces the uncanny as Freud described it (12) and attributes Lucy's "vertigo of apprehension" in part to her "recurring sense of estrangement amidst what to other people seems the familiar . . ." (12).

14. It was not Lucy's original home from which Louisa had fetched her in Chapter 1 but "the kinsfolk with whom was at that time fixed my permanent residence" (62).

15. Tanner discusses ways Lucy herself chooses to be "a piece of furniture," "a non-person" (20).

16. Silver discusses the social context of Lucy's "difficulty in saying 'I' " (99).

17. On Lucy's " 'heretic' narrative," see Tanner (50).

18. She sees the results of this reading in the fact that unlike *Jane Eyre*, *Villette* treats "memory as a problematic function" ("Face" 264).

19. As Carlisle documents in both "Face" and "Prelude."

20. See Platt (21–22), and Millett's excellent discussion of Paul's role in the "Cleopatra" scene (143).

21. "Voilà Monsieur! had scarcely broken simultaneously from every lip when

the two-leaved door split (. . . such a slow word as 'open' is inefficient to describe his movements), and he stood in the midst of us" (415).

22. As Jacobus says, Caroline's "plea for the inalienable rights of self" in this passage is "the starting point of *Villette*" (228).

23. Gilbert and Gubar point out that the progression of Brontë's work "suggests that escape becomes increasingly difficult as women internalize the destructive strictures of patriarchy" (400). The present chapter is in great part an analysis of the formal means by which this internalization is represented in *Villette*.

24. As Auerbach says, "[T]eaching in Charlotte Brontë's novels is almost always a psychodrama, in which the pupils are less sentient human beings than they are the teacher's own rebellious urges with cahiers before them, bobbing up to be crushed down" (99).

25. The term is from Gilbert and Gubar (409).

26. In this respect, Mme. Beck's is a version of Lowood, which, as Gilbert and Gubar point out, is a "school of life where orphan girls are starved and frozen into proper Christian submission" (344).

27. Gilbert and Gubar point out that the fact that Mme. Walravens "emerge[s] *through the portrait of a dead nun*" reveals the identity of the two, which they define somewhat differently: "[T]he witch *is* the nun"; "Mme Walraven's malevolence is . . . the other side of Justine Marie's suicidal passivity" (432).

28. However, I would identify "Paul's imagination" not as "[t]he real threat to Lucy's emotional well-being" (Blom 98) but as one component of a complex threat involving, as well, Lucy's own self-image and the special perils that assail a woman of her social status.

29. The image of this intervention is strikingly clear in a frontispiece to *Otranto* which, as Wilt points out, shows the "great old one" stepping down out of his frame to scare the younger generation out of their wits (69).

30. Carlisle points out that in Lucy's waking in the underwater "cave" of the room at La Terrasse, the "lyrical qualities [of the scene] are themselves warnings against the seductive and potentially dangerous powers of memory. . . . this passage is an image of a withdrawal that is also a regression. In the womblike 'submarine home' of memory, one is protected from the storms of adult experience; there the sound of conflict is magically transformed into a lullaby. . . . Like every other retreat Lucy finds, it must be abandoned . . ." (268). See also Tanner (13).

31. "That there is a very strong element of guilt and masochism in [her] attitude to her own emotional disposition hardly needs to be pointed out. But . . . it is a habit of self-mutilation and mortification which is forced on her by her social position" (Tanner 33).

32. Brontë's ability to see what groups were oppressed was severely limited, as *Shirley* in particular makes clear. The only oppressed group she treats with insight is that of unmarriageable middle-class Englishwomen in reduced circumstances. But the limits of her horizon do not detract from the force of her percep-

tion regarding the victim's internalization of the external enemy, a perception akin to that of Paulo Freire, who says of the oppressed, "They are at one and the same time themselves and the oppressor whose consciousness they have internalized" (Quoted in Daly 48). Daly cites this passage from Freire in her analysis of the way sexism operates on and in the psychology of women: "[T]he oppressor, having invaded the victims' psyches, now exists within themselves" (48). On women's internalization of oppression, see also Donovan (136–40).

33. See Daly (4).

34. Such has been the extent of Lucy's self-alienation heretofore that as Carlisle points out, she was literally unable to recognize her own image in a mirror (283).

35. Her reading of Radcliffe is attested to in the discussion of *The Italian* in *Shirley*.

36. ". . . Lucy's tight-lipped treatment of the girl signifies the erection of a blandly rational barrier against her own coldly unacknowledged impulses. Lucy projects herself into Polly and then cooly dissociates herself from that self-image . . ." (Eagleton 63).

37. Crosby sees Lucy's "project[ion of] her own fears . . . onto the scene she secretly observes" here as a characteristic failure "to distinguish adequately between herself and others" (74): "She interposes her own projections between herself and the real truth . . ." (75).

38. Jacobus provides an excellent discussion of the nun as a symbol of repression.

39. The nun's association with repression is also indicated, as Carlisle shows, by her first appearance when upon the receipt of Graham's letter, Lucy "is trying to summon reason to restrain emotion" (284). Carlisle says that "While Dickens uses Urich to objectify the sexual impulses that David must deny, Lucy Snowe's nun projects the refusal to express such energies . . ." (284). Gilbert and Gubar, similarly, see the nun as "a symbol of [Lucy's] chastity and confinement" (435), as does Burkhart: "type of self-repression and world-denial, of the anti-sensual and austere" (114), "at the end it steals her celibate bed and becomes her" (117). However, this association of the nun with repression points only to part of her significance. Her first appearance is connected not only with an effort "to restrain emotion" but also with the sudden liberation of emotion. Similarly, when the nun appears in Chapter 26, she is an embodiment both of the repressive tendencies that helped Lucy bury the letter and the passion that will not be buried in this way and so escapes as soon as the burying is over. Her double function as passion and repression of passion is indicated in the legend itself: this is a nun (repression), but a sinful one (rebellious passion).

40. Another aspect of the paradox is illuminated in Gilbert and Gubar's reading of this scene: "We have already seen how Ginevra and de Hamal represent the self-gratifying, sensual, romantic side of Lucy. Posturing before mirrors, the fop and the coquette are vacuous but for the roles they play. Existing only in the

'outside' world, they have no more sense of self than the nun whose life is completely 'internal.' Thus, for Lucy to liberate herself from Ginevra and de Hamal means that she can simultaneously rid herself of the self-denying nun" (436).

41. My discussion of the nun as androgynous owes much to Crosby's suggestive discussion of the sexual indeterminacy of the specter and the characters related to it (113–23) and the "pervasive confusion of sexual value" (118) that reveals "a compelling tendency towards [the] subversion" of the "sexual antithesis" (120) throughout the text.

42. What Ewbank says of *Shirley* is relevant here: "It is made very clear, by digressions and by the use of the two spinsters . . . that the life of an old maid is unfulfilled, that lovelessness is the greatest form of human misery and poverty; and that the self can only be realised in mutual love" (198). In an otherwise misguided essay, Bledsoe rightly points out that Lucy's final "independence" must be read in the context of its frequent pre–twentieth-century associations with narcissism and "destructive isolation from humanity" (214). However, it is clear from the context in which independence and marriage are actually discussed in *Villette* that Lucy's move out of the convent and into a business of her own is a move out of the self-pitying isolation that Bledsoe sees as characteristic of her even at the end of the novel. Independence is clearly good in this passage, but there is something "higher," which Lucy finally misses in the end.

43. "Lucy reveals that she has that within which would transcend and traverse the bourgeois boundaries. It is her 'innate capacity for expanse' . . ." (Tanner 15).

Epilogue (II)

1. Anne Mozley, "Review," *The Christian Remembrancer* 15 (June 1953): 404–43. Quoted in Ewbank (44).

Bibliography

Bibliographies

Fisher, Benjamin Franklin IV. "Ancilla to the Gothic Tradition: A Supplementary Bibliography." *American Transcendental Quarterly* 30 (1976): 22–36.

Frank, Frederick S. "The Gothic Novel: A Checklist of Modern Criticism." *Bulletin of Bibliography.* 30.2 (1973): 45–54.

———. "The Gothic Novel: A Second Bibliography of Criticism." *Bulletin of Bibliography.* 35.1 (1978): 1–14, 52.

———. Crawford, Gary W., and Benjamin Franklin Fisher IV. "The 1978 Bibliography of Gothic Studies." *Gothic* 1.2 (1979): 65–67.

Lévy, Maurice. "Bibliographie chronologique du roman 'gothique,' 1764–1824." In his *Le Roman "gothique" anglais, 1764–1824.* Series A 9. Toulouse: Association des Publications de la Faculté des Lettres et Sciences Humaines de Toulouse (1968): 661–83.

———. "Bibliographie générale." *Le Roman "gothique"*: 683–708.

McNutt, Dan J. *The Eighteenth-Century Gothic Novel: An Annotated Bibliography of Criticism and Selected Texts.* New York: Garland, 1975.

Articles and Books

Abel, Darrel. "Hawthorne, Ghostland, and the Jurisdiction of Veracity." *American Transcendental Quarterly* 24 (1974): 30–38.

Abel, Elizabeth, Marianne Hirsch, and Elizabeth Langland, eds. *The Voyage In: Fictions and Female Development.* Hanover, N.H.: Univ. Press of New England, 1983.

Abrams, M. H. *The Mirror and the Lamp: Romantic Theory and the Critical Tradition.* London: Oxford Univ. Press, 1953.

———. *Natural Supernaturalism: Tradition and Revolution in Romantic Literature.* New York: Norton, 1971.

Aikin, John, and Anna Laetitia Aikin. "An Enquiry into Those Kinds of Distress Which Excite Agreeable Sensations, with a Tale." *Miscellaneous Pieces in Prose.* London: J. Johnson, 1773. 190–214.

———. "On Monastic Institutions." *Miscellaneous Pieces.* 88–116.

———. "On the Pleasure Derived from Objects of Terror, with Sir Bertrand, a Fragment." *Miscellaneous Pieces.* 119–37.

Allen, M. L. "The Black Veil: Three Versions of a Symbol." *English Studies* 47 (1966): 286–89.

Allen, Walter. *The English Novel: A Short Critical History.* 1954. Harmondsworth, Eng.: Pelican, 1958.

Allott, Miriam. *Novelists on the Novel.* 1959. London: Routledge & Kegan Paul, 1965.

Anderson, Jørgen. "Giant Dreams: Piranesi's Influence in England." *English Miscellany* 3 (1952): 49–59.

Arnaud, Pierre. *Ann Radcliffe et le fantastique: Essai de psychobiographie.* Paris: Publications de l'Université de Paris, 1976.

Arville Castle: An Historical Romance. 2 vols. London: B. Crosby and T. White, 1795.

Arvin, Newton. *Herman Melville.* The American Men of Letters Series. 1950. Westport, Conn.: Greenwood Press, 1972.

———. "Melville and the Gothic Novel." *New England Quarterly* 22 (1949): 33–48.

Auerbach, Nina. *Communities of Women: An Idea in Fiction.* Cambridge, Mass.: Harvard Univ. Press, 1978.

Austen, Jane. *Northanger Abbey.* In *Northanger Abbey and Persuasion.* Ed. Mary Lascelles. 1818. London: Everyman, 1962.

Axton, William F. Introduction. *Melmoth the Wanderer: A Tale.* By Charles Robert Maturin. Lincoln: Univ. of Nebraska Press–Bison, 1961.

Bachelard, Gaston. *The Poetics of Space.* 1958. Trans. Maria Jolas. Boston: Beacon Press, 1969.

Ballin, Rosetta. *The Statue Room: An Historical Tale.* 2 vols. London: Symonds, 1790.

Banta, Martha. "The House of the Seven Ushers and How They Grew: A Look at Jamesian Gothicism." *Yale Review* 57.1 (1967): 56–65.

Barrett, Eaton Stannard. *The Heroine, or Adventures of a Fair Romance Reader.* 3 vols. London: Colburn, 1813.

Benton, Richard P. "The Problems of Literary Gothicism." *ESQ* 18.1 (1972): 5–9.

Bercovitch, Sacvan. "Of Wise and Foolish Virgins: Hilda *Versus* Miriam in Haw-thorne's *Marble Faun.*" *New England Quarterly* 4 (1968): 281–86.

Berthoff, Warner. *The Example of Melville.* New York: Norton, 1972.

Bird, John. *The Castle of Hardayne: A Romance.* 2 vols. Liverpool: J. M'Creery, 1795.

Birkhead, Edith. *The Tale of Terror: A Study of the Gothic Romance.* London: Constable, 1921.

Blakey, Dorothy. *The Minerva Press, 1790–1820.* London: Oxford Univ. Press, 1939 for 1935.

Bledsoe, Robert. "Snow Beneath Snow: A Reconsideration of the Virgin of *Villette.*" *Gender and Literary Voice.* Ed. Todd. 214–22.

Blom, M. A. "Charlotte Brontë, Feminist Manquée." *Bucknell Review* 21 (1973): 87–102.

Boswell, James. *The Life of Samuel Johnson.* Ed. Bergen Evans. New York: Modern Library, 1965.

Boulton, J. T. Introduction. Edmund Burke, *A Philosophical Enquiry into the Origin of Our Ideas of the Sublime and Beautiful.* xv–cxxvii.

Boudreau, Gordon V. "Of Pale Ushers and Gothic Piles: Melvilles's Architectural Symbology." *ESQ* 18.2 (1972): 67–82.

Braudy, Leo. "Penetration and Impenetrability in *Clarissa.*" *New Approaches to Eighteenth-Century Literature: Selected Papers from the English Institute.* Ed. Phillip Harth. New York: Columbia Univ. Press, 1974. 177–206.

Brewster, Sir David. *Letters on Natural Magic Addressed to Sir Walter Scott.* 1832. New York: Harper, 1843.

Broadwell, Elizabeth P. "The Veil Image in Ann Radcliffe's *The Italian.*" *South Atlantic Bulletin* 40 (1975): 76–87.

Brombert, Victor. *The Romantic Prison: The French Tradition.* Princeton, N.J.: Princeton Univ. Press, 1978. Originally published as *La Prison roman-tique.* Paris: José Corti, 1975.

Brontë, Charlotte. *Jane Eyre.* Ed. Q. D. Leavis. 1847. Harmondsworth: Penguin, 1982.

———. *Shirley.* 1849. Ed. Andrew and Judith Hook. Harmondsworth: Penguin, 1981.

———. *Villette.* 1853. Rpt. and Ed. Mark Lilly. Introd. Tony Tanner. Har-mondsworth: Penguin, 1981.

Brontë, Emily. *Wuthering Heights.* 1847. Ed. David Daiches. Harmondsworth: Penguin, 1965.

Brown, Charles Brockden. "Advertisement for 'Sky Walk.' " *Weekly Magazine* 1.8 (March 17, 1798): 228–31. Rpt. in *The Rhapsodist and Other Uncol-lected Writings by Charles Brockden Brown.* Ed. Harry R. Warfel. New York: Scholar's Facsimilies and Reprints, 1943. 135–36.

———. *Edgar Huntly; or Memoirs of a Sleepwalker.* 1799. Ed. David Stineback. Masterworks of Literature Series. New Haven, Conn.: College and University Press, 1973.

———. *Ormond; or the Secret Witness.* 1799. Ed. Ernest Merchand. The Hafner Library of Classics 24. New York: Hafner, 1937.

———. "On a Taste for the Picturesque." *The Literary Magazine and American Review* 2.9 (1804): 163–65.

———. "Walstein's School of History, From the German of Krants of Gotha." *The Monthly Magazine and American Review* (August–September 1799): 335–38, 407–11. Rpt. in *The Rhapsodist and Other Uncollected Writings.* 145–56.

———. *Wieland; or The Transformation, Together with Memoirs of Carwin the Biloquist.* 1798. Ed. Fred Lewis Pattee. New York: Hafner, 1926.

Brownson, Orestes. "Victor Cousin." *The Christian Examiner* 21 (1837). Rpt. in *The Transcendentalists: An Anthology.* Ed. Perry Miller. Cambridge, Mass.: Harvard Univ. Press, 1950. 106–14.

Burke, Edmund. *A Philosophical Enquiry into the Origin of Our Ideas of the Sublime and the Beautiful.* 1757. Ed. James T. Boulton. Notre Dame, Ind.: Univ. of Notre Dame Press, 1958.

Burkhart, Charles. *Charlotte Brontë: A Psychosexual Study of Her Novels.* London: Gollancz, 1973.

Butler, Marilyn. "The Woman at the Window: Ann Radcliffe in the Novels of Mary Wollstonecraft and Jane Austen." *Gender and Literary Voice.* Ed. Todd. 128–48.

Calhoun, Thomas O. "Hawthorne's Gothic: An Approach to the Four Last Fragments: 'The Ancestral Footstep,' *Dr. Grimshawe's Secret, The Dolliver Romance, Septimus Felton.*" *Genre* 3 (1970): 229–41.

Campbell, Joseph. *The Hero with a Thousand Faces.* 1949. Cleveland: Meridian-World, 1969.

Carlisle, Janice. "The Face in the Mirror: *Villette* and the Conventions of Autobiography." *ELH* 46 (1979): 262–89.

———. "A Prelude to *Villette:* Charlotte Brontë's Reading, 1850–52." *Bulletin of Research in the Humanities* 82 (1979): 403–23.

Carlyle, Thomas, trans. *German Romance: Specimens of Its Chief Authors, with Biographical and Critical Notices.* 4 vols. Edinburgh: William Tait and Charles Tait, 1827. Vols. 1 and 2.

Carnochan, W. B. *Confinement and Flight: An Essay on English Literature of the Eighteenth Century.* Berkeley and Los Angeles: Univ. of California Press, 1977.

Rev. of *The Castle of Otranto. The Critical Review* 19 (1765): 50–51.

Rev. of *The Castle of Otranto,* 2nd ed. *The Critical Review* 19 (1765): 469.

The Cavern of Death: A Moral Tale. 2nd ed. London: J. Bell, 1794.

Rev. of *The Champion of Virtue. The Critical Review* 44 (1777): 154.

Charney, Maurice. "Hawthorne and the Gothic Style." *New England Quarterly* 34 (1961): 36–49.

Chase, Richard. *The American Novel and Its Tradition.* Garden City, N.Y.: Doubleday, 1957.

Coad, Oral Sumner. "The Gothic Element in American Literature Before 1835." *JEGP* 24 (1925): 72–93.

Coleridge, Samuel Taylor. *Biographia Literaria.* 1817. Ed. J. Shawcross. London: Oxford Univ. Press, 1973. Vol. 2.

————. Rev. of *Hubert De Sevrac: A Romance of the Eighteenth Century.* By Mary Robinson. *The Critical Review* 23 (1798). Rpt. in *Coleridge's Miscellaneous Criticism.* Ed. Thomas Middleton Raysor. Cambridge, Mass.: Harvard Univ. Press, 1936. 382.

————. Rev. of *The Italian.* By Ann Radcliffe. *The Critical Review* August (1794). Rpt. in *Miscellaneous Criticism.* 378–82.

————. Rev. of *The Monk.* By M. G. Lewis. Rpt. in *Miscellaneous Criticism.* 370–78.

————. Rev. of *The Mysteries of Udolpho.* By Ann Radcliffe. Rpt. in *Miscellaneous Criticism,* 355–70.

Crosby, Christina. "The Haunting of the Text: The Case of Charlotte Brontë's *Villette.*" Diss. Princeton Univ., 1982.

Curran, Ronald T. " 'Yankee Gothic': Hawthorne's 'Castle of Pyncheon.' " *Studies in the Novel* 8 (1976): 69–80.

Curties, T. J. Horsley. *The Monk of Udolpho: A Romance.* 4 vols. 1807. Ed. Devendra Varma. Gothic Novels 3. New York: Arno Press–New York Times, 1977.

Dacre, Charlotte ("Rosa Matilda"). *Confessions of the Nun of St. Omer: A Tale.* 3 vols. 1805. Introd. Devendra P. Varma. New York: Arno Press–New York Times, 1972.

————. *The Libertine.* 4 vols. 1807. Foreword John Garrett. Introd. Devendra P. Varma. New York: Arno Press–New York Times. Vols. 1 and 2.

————. *Zofloya: or, The Moor, a Romance of the Fifteenth Century.* 3 vols. 1806. Foreward G. Wilson Knight. Introd. Devendra P. Varma. New York: Arno Press–New York Times, 1974.

Daiches, David. Introduction. *Wuthering Heights.* By Emily Brontë. 7–29.

Daly, Mary. *Beyond God the Father: Toward a Philosophy of Women's Liberation.* Boston: Beacon, 1973.

Day, William Patrick. *In the Circles of Fear and Desire: A Study of Gothic Fantasy.* Chicago: Univ. of Chicago Press, 1985.

de Beauvoir, Simone. *The Second Sex.* 1949. Trans. H. M. Parshley. 1953. New York: Vintage–Random House, 1974.

De Quincey, Thomas. *Confessions of an English Opium Eater.* 1821. Ed. Alethea Hayter. Harmondsworth, Eng.: Penguin, 1973.

Dickinson, Emily. "One need not be a Chamber—to be Haunted—." *Final Harvest: Emily Dickinson's Poems*. Ed. Thomas H. Johnson. Boston: Little, Brown, 1961. 168–69.

Dimock, Wai-chee. "*Pierre:* Domestic Confidence Game and the Drama of Knowledge." *Studies in the Novel* 15.4 (1984): 396–409.

Dobrée, Bonamy. Introduction. *The Mysteries of Udolpho*. By Ann Radcliffe. World's Classics. Oxford, Eng.: Oxford Univ. Press, 1980. 5–14.

Donovan, Josephine. *Feminist Theory: The Intellectual Traditions of American Feminism*. New York: Ungar, 1985.

Doody, Margaret Anne. "Deserts, Ruins and Troubled Waters: Female Dreams in Fiction and the Development of the Gothic Novel." *Genre* 10 (1977): 529–72.

Doubleday, Neal Frank. "Hawthorne's Use of Three Gothic Patterns." *College English* 7 (1946): 250–62.

Drake, Nathan. "The Abbey of Clunedale, a Tale." No. 6 in *Literary Hours; or Sketches Critical and Narrative*. By Drake. Sudbury, Eng.: J. Burkitt, 1798. 325–46.

———. "On Gothic Superstition." No. 20 in *Literary Hours*. 87–96.

———. "Henry Fitzowen, a Gothic Tale." Nos. 7, 8, and 9 in *Literary Hours*. 97–136.

———. *Rochester Castle; or Gundulph's Tower, a Gothic Tale, Extracted from Dr. Drake's Literary Hours*. London: J. Roe and Anhe Lemoine, 1810.

Durant, David. "Ann Radcliffe and the Conservative Gothic." *SEL* 22.3 (1982): 519–30.

Eagleton, Terry. *Myths of Power: A Marxist Study of the Brontës*. New York: Barnes & Noble, 1975.

Edel, Leon. *1843–1870: The Untried Years*. Vol. 1 of *Henry James*. 5 vols. Philadelphia: Lippincott, 1953.

———. *The Life of Henry James*. 2 vols. 1953. Harmondsworth, Eng.: Penguin, 1977. Vol. 1.

Edwards, Jonathan. "Sinners in the Hands of an Angry God." *Jonathan Edwards: Representative Selections*. Ed. Clarence H. Faust and Thomas H. Johnson. American Century Series. 1935. New York: Hill & Wang, 1962. 155–72.

Eliot, George. *The Lifted Veil*. 1859. Rpt. Edinburgh: Blackwood, n.d.

Emerson, Ralph Waldo. *Selections from Ralph Waldo Emerson: An Organic Anthology*. Ed. Stephen E. Whicher. 1957. Boston: Houghton Mifflin, 1960.

Engel, Leonard. "The Role of the Enclosure in the English and American Gothic Romance." *Essays in Arts and Sciences* 11 (1982): 59–68.

Ewbank, Inga-Stina. *Their Proper Sphere: A Study of the Brontë Sisters as Early-Victorian Female Novelists*. Cambridge, Mass.: Harvard Univ. Press, 1966.

Fairclough, Peter, ed. *Three Gothic Novels: The Castle of Otranto, Vathek, Frankenstein.* Harmondsworth, Eng.: Penguin, 1973.

Fiedler, Leslie. *Love and Death in the American Novel.* Rev. ed. 1966. Briarcliff Manor, N.Y.: Stein & Day, 1975.

Fleenor, Juliann, ed. *The Female Gothic.* London: Eden Press, 1983.

Flexner, Eleanor. *Mary Wollstonecraft: A Biography.* New York: Coward-McCann, 1972.

Fowler, Alastair. "The Life and Death of Literary Forms." *New Directions in Literary History.* Ed. Ralph Cohen. Baltimore: Johns Hopkins Univ. Press, 1974. 77–94.

————. "From Boudoir to Castle Crypt: Richardson and the Gothic Novel." *Revue des Langues Vivantes* 41 (1975): 49–59.

Frank, Frederick S. "The Aqua-Gothic Voyage of 'A Descent into the Maelström.' " *American Transcendental Quarterly* 29 (1976): 85–93.

————. "From Boudoir to Castle Crypt: Richardson and the Gothic Novel." *Revue des Langues Vivantes* 41 (1975): 49–59.

Freud, Sigmund. *The Interpretation of Dreams.* Trans. James Strachey. 1900. New York: Discus-Avon, 1965.

————. "The 'Uncanny.' " Trans. James Strachey. *Standard Edition.* Vol. 17. 1919. London: Hogarth Press, 1955. 217–56.

Frye, Northrop. *Anatomy of Criticism: Four Essays.* 1957. Princeton, N.J.: Princeton Univ. Press, 1971.

Fuller, Anne. *Alan Fitz-Osborne: An Historical Tale.* 2 vols. Dublin: P. Byrne; London: Rpt. for the Author, 1787.

————. *The Convent; or History of Sophia Nelson,* by a Young Lady. 2 vols. London: T. Wilkins, n.d.

Furrow, Sharon. "The Terrible Made Visible: Melville, Salvator Rosa, and Piranesi." *Emerson Society Quarterly* 73 (1973): 237–53.

Gabrielle de Vergy: An Historic Tale. 2 vols. London: T. Wilkins, 1790.

Gilbert, Sandra, and Susan Gubar. *The Madwoman in the Attic: The Woman Writer and the Nineteenth-Century Literary Imagination.* New Haven, Conn.: Yale University Press, 1979.

Gilman, Charlotte Perkins. "The Yellow Wallpaper." 1792. Old Westbury, N.Y.: Feminist Press, 1973.

Godwin, William. *St. Leon: A Tale of the Sixteenth Century.* 1799. Foreword Devendra P. Varma. Introd. Juliet Beckett. New York: Arno Press–New York Times, 1972.

————. *Things as They Are; or The Adventures of Caleb Williams.* 1794. Ed. David McCracken. New York: Norton, 1977.

Grant, Aline. *Ann Radcliffe: A Biography.* Denver: Alan Swallow, 1951.

Gregor, Ian. *The Brontës: A Collection of Critical Essays.* Englewood Cliffs, N.J.: Prentice-Hall, 1970.

Guillén, Claudio. "Toward a Definition of the Picaresque." *Literature as System.*
    71–106.
———. "On the Uses of Literary Genre." *Literature as System: Essays Toward
    the Theory of Literary History.* Princeton, N.J.: Princeton Univ. Press,
    1971. 107–34.
Haggerty, George E. "Fact and Fancy in the Gothic Novel." *Nineteenth-Century
    Fiction* 39.4 (1985): 379–391.
Hart, Francis Russell. "The Experience of Character in the English Gothic Novel."
    Experience in the Novel: Selected Papers from the English Institute. Ed.
    Roy Harvey Pearce. New York: Columbia Univ. Press, 1968. 83– 105.
Hawthorne, Nathaniel. *The American Claimant Manuscripts: The Ancestral Foot-
    step, Etheredge, Grimshawe.* Ed. Edward H. Davidson, Claude M. Simp-
    son, and L. Neal Smith. Centenary Edition. Colombus: Ohio State Univ.
    Press, 1977. Vol. 12.
———. "The Birthmark." *The Complete Novels and Selected Tales of Nathaniel
    Hawthorne.* 1021–33.
———. *The Blithedale Romance. The Complete Novels and Selected Tales of
    Nathaniel Hawthorne.* 439–585.
———. *The Complete Novels and Selected Tales of Nathaniel Hawthorne.* Ed.
    Norman Holmes Pearson. New York: Modern Library, 1937.
———. "The Haunted Mind." *Selected Tales and Sketches.* 410–14.
———. *The House of the Seven Gables. The Complete Novels and Selected Tales
    of Nathaniel Hawthorne.* 243–436.
———. *The Marble Faun. The Complete Novels and Selected Tales of Nathaniel
    Hawthorne.* 589–858.
———. "The Minister's Black Veil." *The Complete Novels and Selected Tales
    of Nathaniel Hawthorne.* 872–82.
———. *The Scarlet Letter. The Complete Novels and Selected Tales of Nathaniel
    Hawthorne.* 85–240.
———. *Selected Tales and Sketches.* Ed. Hyatt H. Waggoner. 3rd ed. New
    York: Holt, Rinehart, and Winston, 1950.
———. "Wakefield." *The Complete Novels and Selected Tales of Nathaniel
    Hawthorne.* 920–26.
Hedges, Elaine R. Afterword. "The Yellow Wallpaper." By Gilman.
Heilman, Robert B. "Charlotte Brontë's 'New' Gothic." *From Jane Austen to
    Joseph Conrad: Essays Collected in Memory of James T. Hillhouse.* Ed.
    Robert C. Rathburn and Martin Steinmann, Jr. Minneapolis: Univ. of
    Minnesota Press, 1958.
Holcroft, Thomas. Preface to *Alwyn: or The Gentleman Comedian.* London, 1780.
    Rpt. in *Novelists on the Novel.* Ed. Miriam Allott. 1959. London: Rou-
    tledge & Kegan Paul, 1965.
Holland, Norman N., and Leona F. Sherman. "Gothic Possibilities." *NLH* 8 (1977):
    279–94.

Homans, Margaret. "Dreaming of Children: Literalization in *Jane Eyre* and *Wuthering Heights*." *The Female Gothic*. Ed. Fleenor 257–79.

Hook, Andrew D. "Charlotte Brontë, the Imagination, and *Villette*." *The Brontës: A Collection of Critical Essays*. Ed. Gregor. 137–56.

Hough, Graham. *A Preface to The Faerie Queene*. 1962. London: Duckworth, 1968.

Howells, Coral Ann. *Love, Mystery, and Misery: Feeling in Gothic Fiction*. London: Athlone, 1978.

Hume, Robert D. "Charles Brockden Brown and the Uses of Gothicism: A Reassessment." *ESQ* 18.1 (1972): 10–18.

———. "Exuberant Gloom, Existential Agony, and Heroic Despair: Three Varieties of Negative Romanticism." *Gothic Imagination*. Ed. Thompson. 109–27.

———. "Gothic Versus Romantic: A Revaluation of the Gothic Novel." *PMLA* 84 (1969): 282–90.

Hurd, Richard. *Letters on Chivalry and Romance*. 1762. Ed. Hoyt Trowbridge. Augustan Reprint Society, Publication No. 101–2. Los Angeles: William Andrews Clark Memorial Library, 1963.

Ireland, William Henry. *The Abbess: A Romance*. 4 vols. 1799. Foreword Devendra P. Varma. Introd. Benjamin Franklin Fisher, IV. New York: Arno Press–New York Times, 1974. Vols. 1, 2, and 3.

Jacobus, Mary. "Villette's Buried Letter." *Essays in Criticism: A Quarterly Journal of Literary Criticism* 28 (1978): 228–44.

James, Henry. Preface to *"The Altar of the Dead," "The Beast in the Jungle," "The Birthplace," and Other Tales*. Vol. 17 of *The Novels and Tales of Henry James*. 26 vols. New York Edition. 1909. New York: Scribner, 1937.

———. *The American*. 1877. New York: Signet, 1963.

———. *The Portrait of a Lady*. 1881. New York: Signet, 1963.

———. *The Turn of the Screw*. 1898. Harmondsworth, Eng.: Penguin, 1971.

Jameson, Fredric. "Magic Narratives: Romance as Genre." *New Literary History* 7 (1975–76): 135–63.

Johnson, E. D. H. " 'Daring the Dread Glance' ": Charlotte Brontë's Treatment of the Supernatural in *Villette*." *Nineteenth-Century Fiction* 20.4 (1966): 325–336.

Johnston, Arthur. *Enchanted Ground: The Study of Medieval Romance in the Eighteenth Century*. London: Athlone, 1964.

Kahane, Claire. "Gothic Mirrors and Feminine Identity." *The Centennial Review* 24 (1980): 43–64.

Kearns, Michael S. "Phantoms of the Mind: Melville's Criticism of Idealistic Psychology." *ESQ* 30.1 (1984): 40–50.

Keech, James M. "The Survival of the Gothic Response." *Studies in the Novel* 6 (1974): 130–44.

Kendall, A. *Tales of the Abbey: Founded on Historical Facts.* 3 vols. London: C. Whittingham for H. D. Symonds, 1800.

Kermode, Frank. *The Sense of an Ending: Studies in the Theory of Fiction.* 1966. London: Oxford Univ. Press, 1967.

Kesselring, Marion L. *Hawthorne's Reading, 1828–1850: A Transcription and Identification of Titles Recorded in the Charge-Books of the Salem Athenaeum.* New York: New York Public Library, 1949.

Kiely, Robert. *The Romantic Novel in England.* Cambridge, Mass.: Harvard Univ. Press, 1972.

Killen, Alice M. *Le Roman "terrifiant" ou roman "noir" de Walpole à Anne Radcliffe et son influence sur la littérature française jusqu'en 1840.* Bibliothèque de la Revue de Littérature Comparée 4. Ed. Baldensperger and Hazard. 1915. Paris: Librairie Ancienne Edouard Champion, 1924.

Kinkead-Weekes, Mark. "The Place of Love in *Jane Eyre* and *Wuthering Heights.*" *The Brontës: A Collection of Critical Essays.* Ed. Gregor. 76–95.

———. *Samuel Richardson, Dramatic Novelist.* London: Methuen, 1973.

Kroeber, Karl. *Styles in Fictional Structure: The Art of Jane Austen, Charlotte Brontë, and George Eliot.* Princeton, N.J.: Princeton Univ. Press, 1971.

Kuhn, Annette, and Ann Marie Wolpe, eds. *Feminism and Materialism.* London: Routledge & Kegan Paul, 1978.

La Regina, Gabriella. " 'Rappaccini's Daughter': The Gothic as a Catalyst for Hawthorne's Imagination." *Studi Americani* 17 (1971): 29–74.

Leavis, Q. D. Introduction. *Jane Eyre.* By Charlotte Brontë.

Lee, Sophia. *The Recess; or, a Tale of Other Times.* 3rd ed., corrected. 3 vols. London: Cadell, 1787.

Leland, Thomas. *Longsword Earl of Salisbury: An Historical Romance.* 1762. Ed. and Introd. John C. Stephens, Jr. New York: New York Univ. Press, 1957.

Le Tellier, Robert Ignatius. *An Intensifying Vision of Evil: The Gothic Novel (1764–1820) as a Self-Contained Literary Cycle.* Salzburg: Institute für Anglistik & Amerikanistik, Univ. of Salzburg, 1980.

Levin, Harry. *The Power of Blackness: Hawthorne, Poe, Melville.* 1958. New York: Knopf, 1970.

Levine, George, U. C. Knoepflmacher, and Peter Dale Scott. *The Endurance of Frankenstein: Essays on Mary Shelley's Novel.* Berkeley and Los Angeles: Univ. of California Press, 1979.

Lévy, Maurice. *Le Roman "gothique" anglais, 1764–1824.* Series A 9. Toulouse: Association des Publications de la Faculté des Lettres et Sciences Humaines de Toulouse, 1968.

Lewis, C. S. *The Allegory of Love: A Study in Medieval Tradition.* 1942. London: Oxford Univ. Press, 1971.

———. *A Preface to* Paradise Lost. 1942. London: Oxford Univ. Press, 1979.

Lewis, M. G. trans. *The Bravo of Venice: A Romance.* 1805. Introd. Devendra P. Varma. New York: Arno Press–New York Times, 1972.

———. *The Monk: A Romance.* London, 1796. Rpt. New York: Avon, 1975.

Lewis, Paul. "Melville's *Pierre* and the Psychology of Incongruity." *Studies in the Novel* 15.3 (1983): 183–201.

———. "Mysterious Laughter: Humor and Fear in Gothic Fiction." *Genre* 14.3 (1981): 309–27.

Lippard, George. *The Quaker-City; or The Monks of Monk Hall.* 1844. Introd. Leslie Fiedler. New York: Odyssey Press, 1970.

Lippit, Noriko Mizuta. "Tanizaki and Poe: The Grotesque and the Quest for Supernatural Beauty." *Comparative Literature* (Eugene, Ore.) 29 (1977): 221–40.

Lovejoy, Arthur O. "The First Gothic Revival and the Return to Nature." *Modern Language Notes* 27 (1932): 414–46.

Lundblad, Jane. *Nathaniel Hawthorne and the Tradition of Gothic Romance.* Cambridge, Mass.: Harvard Univ. Press, 1946.

MacAndrew, Elizabeth. *The Gothic Tradition in Fiction.* New York: Columbia Univ. Press, 1979.

Macaulay, Rose. *Pleasure of Ruins.* London: Weidenfeld and Nicolson, 1953.

MacCaffrey, Isabel G. *Spenser's Allegory.* Princeton, N.J.: Princeton Univ. Press, 1976.

Mackenzie, Anna Maria. *Mysteries Elucidated: A Novel.* 3 vols. London: Lane, Minerva Press, 1795.

Malin, Irving. *New American Gothic.* Carbondale: Southern Illinois Univ. Press, 1962.

Marchand, Ernest. "The Literary Opinions of Charles Brockden Brown." *Studies in Philology* 31 (1934): 541–66.

Martin, Terence. *The Instructed Vision: Scottish Common Sense Philosophy and the Origins of American Fiction.* Indiana University Humanities Series 48. Bloomington: Indiana Univ. Press, 1969.

Matthiessen, F. O. *American Renaissance: Art and Expression in the Age of Emerson and Whitman.* Oxford: Oxford Univ. Press, 1974.

———. *The James Family: A Group Biography.* 1947. New York: Vintage–Random House, 1974.

Maturin, Charles Robert. *The Albigenses: A Romance.* 4 vols. 1824. Foreword James Gray. Introd. Devendra Varma. Gothic Novels 2. New York: Arno Press–New York Times, 1974.

———. *The Fatal Revenge; or The Family of Montorio, A Romance.* 3 vols. 1807. Foreword Henry D. Hicks. Introd. Maurice Lévy. Gothic Novels 2. New York: Arno Press–New York Times, 1974.

———. *Melmoth the Wanderer: A Tale.* 1820. Rpt., Ed., and Introd. Douglas Grant. London: Oxford Univ. Press, 1968.

Meeke, Mary. *Count St. Blancard; or The Prejudiced Judge, A Novel.* 3 vols.

1795. Foreword Devendra P. Varma. Introd. John Garrett. New York: Arno Press–New York Times, 1977.

Melville, Herman. *Moby-Dick; or The Whale.* 1851. Ed. Charles Feidelson, Jr. Indianapolis: Bobbs-Merrill, 1964.

———. *Pierre; or The Ambiguities.* 1852. New York: Grove Press, 1957.

Miller, J. Hillis. *The Disappearance of God: Five Nineteenth-Century Writers.* New York: Schocken, 1963.

Millett, Kate. *Sexual Politics.* Garden City, N.Y.: Doubleday, 1970.

Milton, John. *Comus: A Mask Presented at Ludlow Castle, 1634.* Rpt. in *The English Poems of John Milton.* The World's Classics 182. London: Oxford Univ. Press, 1971.

Mise, Raymond W. *The Gothic Heroine and the Nature of the Gothic Novel.* Diss. Univ. of Washington, 1980. New York: Arno Press–New York Times, 1970.

Miyoshi, Masao. *The Divided Self: A Perspective on the Literature of the Victorians.* London: Univ. of London Press, 1969.

Moers, Ellen. *Literary Women.* 1976. London: The Women's Press, 1978.

Momberger, Philip. "Self and World in the Works of Charlotte Brontë." *ELH* 32.3 (1965): 349–69.

Mort Castle: A Gothic Story. London: J. Wallis, 1798.

Murray, E. B. *Ann Radcliffe.* Twayne's English Author Series 149. New York: Twayne, 1972.

Muscatine, Charles. *Chaucer and the French Tradition: A Study in Style and Meaning.* Berkeley and Los Angeles: Univ. of California Press, 1964.

Musgrave, Agnes. *Cicely; or The Rose of Raby, an Historic Novel.* 4 vols. London: Minerva Press, 1795.

———. *The Solemn Injunction: A Novel.* 4 vols. London: Minerva Press, 1798.

Mussell, Kay J. " 'But Why Do They Read Those Things?': The Female Audience and the Gothic Novel." *The Female Gothic.* Ed. Fleenor. 57–68.

Nelson, Lowry, Jr. "Night Thoughts on the Gothic Novel." *Yale Review* 52 (1962): 236–57.

Nettles, Elsa. " 'The Portrait of a Lady' and the Gothic Romance." *South Atlantic Bulletin* 39 (1974): 73–82.

Newlin, Paul A. " 'Vague Shapes of the Borderland': The Place of the Uncanny in Hawthorne's Gothic Vision." *ESQ* 18.2 (1972): 83–96.

Nichols, Nina da Vinci. "Place and Eros in Radcliffe, Lewis, and Brontë." *The Female Gothic.* Ed. Fleenor. 187–206.

Nicolson, Marjorie Hope. *Mountain Gloom and Mountain Glory: The Development of the Aesthetics of the Infinite.* Ithaca, N.Y.: Cornell Univ. Press, 1959.

A Northumbrian Tale. Written by a Lady. London: S. Hamilton, 1799.

Norton, Rictor. "Aesthetic Gothic Horror." *Yearbook of Comparative and General Literature* 21 (1972): 31–40.

Novak, Maximillian E. "Gothic Fiction and the Grotesque." *Novel: A Forum on Fiction* 13 (1979): 50–67.

Nuttall, A. D. *A Common Sky: Philosophy and the Literary Imagination.* London: Chatto & Windus for Sussex Univ. Press, 1974.

Pancost, David W. "Hawthorne's Epistemology and Ontology." *ESQ* 19 (1973): 8–13.

Parsons, Eliza. *The Mysterious Warning: A German Tale in Four Volumes.* 1796. 4 vols. The Northanger Set of Jane Austen Horrid Novels. London: Folio Press, 1968.

Paulson, Ronald. "Gothic Fiction and the French Revolution." *ELH* 48.3 (1981): 532–54.

Peckham, Morse. "Toward a Theory of Romanticism." *PMLA* 66 (1951): 5–23.

Peterson, Jeanne M. "The Victorian Governess: Status Incongruence in Family and Society." *Suffer and Be Still.* Ed. Vicinus. 3–19.

Phillips, George L. "The Gothic Element in the American Novel Before 1930." *West Virginia University Bulletin: Philological Studies* 3 (1939): 37–45.

Platt, Carolyn V. "How Feminist Is *Villette?*" *Women and Literature* 3 (1975): 16–27.

Platzner, Robert L., and Robert D. Hume. " 'Gothic Versus Romantic': A Rejoinder." *PMLA* 86 (1971): 266–74.

———. *The Metaphysical Novel in England: The Romantic Phase.* Diss. Univ. of Rochester, 1972. Gothic Studies and Dissertations. New York: Arno Press–New York Times, 1980.

Poe, Edgar Allan. "The Fall of the House of Usher." *Selected Prose, Poetry, and Eureka.* 1–21.

———. "Narrative of A. Gordon Pym." *Selected Prose, Poetry, and Eureka.* 150–336.

———. *Selected Prose, Poetry, and Eureka.* 1838. Ed. W. H. Auden. New York: Holt, Rinehart and Winston, 1950.

———. "William Wilson." *Selected Prose, Poetry, and Eureka.* 39–60.

Polidori, John William. *The Vampyre: A Tale.* 1819. Tring, Hertfordshire, Eng.: Gubblecote Press, 1974.

Poovey, Mary. "Ideology and *The Mysteries of Udolpho.*" *Criticism* 21.4 (1979): 307–30.

Porte, Joel. "In the Hands of a Angry God: Religious Terror in Gothic Fiction." *Gothic Imagination.* Ed. Thompson. 42–64.

———. *Representative Man: Ralph Waldo Emerson in His Time.* New York: Oxford Univ. Press, 1979.

———. *The Romance in America: Studies in Cooper, Poe, Hawthorne, Melville, and James.* Middletown, Conn.: Wesleyan Univ. Press, 1969.

Praz, Mario. Introduction. *Three Gothic Novels: The Castle of Otranto, Vathek, Frankenstein.* Ed. Fairclough. 7–34.

Punter, David. *The Literature of Terror: A History of Gothic Fictions from 1765 to the Present Day.* London: Longmans, 1980.

Rabuzzi, Kathryn Allen. *The Sacred and the Feminine: Toward a Theology of Housework.* New York: Seabury, 1982.

Radcliffe, Ann. *The Castles of Athlin and Dunbayne: A Highland Story.* London, 1789. Rpt. in *The Castles of Athlin and Dunbayne and A Sicilian Romance.* Chiswick, Eng.: C. and C. Whitingham, 1827.

―――. *Gaston de Blondeville; or The Court of Henry II Keeping Festival in Ardenne, a Romance; and St. Alban's Abbey, A Metrical Tale, with some Poetical Pieces. To which is prefixed a memoir of the author, with extracts from her journals.* London: Henry Colburn, 1826.

―――. *The Italian; or The Confessional of the Black Penitents, a Romance.* 1797. Ed. Frederick Garber. London: Oxford Univ. Press, 1968.

―――. *The Mysteries of Udolpho.* 1794. Rpt. and Ed. Bonamy Dobrée. Oxford: Oxford Univ. Press, 1980.

―――. *The Romance of the Forest.* 3 vols. 1791. Ed. Devendra P. Varma. Gothic Novels 2. New York: Arno Press–New York Times, 1974.

―――. *A Sicilian Romance.* 1790. Rpt. in *The Castles of Athlin and Dunbayne and A Sicilian Romance.*

―――. "On the Supernatural in Poetry." *New Monthly Magazine and Literary Journal.* N.S. 16 (1826). "Original Papers," Part 1. London: Henry Colburn, 1826. 145–52.

Radcliffe, Mary-Anne. *Manfroné; or The One-Handed Monk.* 1809. Foreword by Devendra P. Varma. Introd. Coral Ann Howells. New York: Arno Press–New York Times, 1972.

Raddin, George Gates, Jr. *An Early New York Library of Fiction, with a Checklist of the Fiction in H. Caritat's Circulating Library, No. 1 City Hotel, Broadway, New York, 1804.* New York: H. W. Wilson, 1940.

Radway, Janice. "The Utopian Impulse in Popular Literature: Gothic Romances and 'Feminist' Protest." *American Quarterly* 33.2 (1981): 140–62.

Railo, Eino. *The Haunted Castle: A Study of the Elements of English Romanticism.* 1927. New York: Humanities Press, 1964.

Rank, Otto. *The Double: A Psychoanalytic Study.* Trans. and Ed. Harry Tucker, Jr. 1925. Chapel Hill: Univ. of North Carolina Press, 1971.

Reeve, Clara. *The Old English Baron: A Gothic Story.* 1778. Ed. James Trainer. Oxford: Oxford Univ. Press, 1977. Originally Published in 1777 as *The Champion of Virtue: A Gothic Story.*

"Review of *Rimualdo; or, The Castle of Badajos.*" *The Monthly Review* 34 (February 1801): 203–04.

Richardson, Samuel. *Clarissa; or The History of a Young Lady.* 4 vols. 1747–48. New York: Everyman-Dent, 1976.

Ridgely, J. V. "George Lippard's 'The Quaker City': The World of American

Porno Gothic." *Studies in the Literary Imagination* 7.1, *Sources of Terror to the American Imagination* (1974): 77–94.

Ringe, Donald A. *American Gothic: Imagination and Reason in 19th-Century Fiction*. Lexington: Univ. Press of Kentucky, 1982.

Roberts, Bette B. *The Gothic Romance: Its Appeal to Women Writers and Readers in Late Eighteenth-Century England*. Gothic Studies and Dissertations. Advisory Ed. Devendra P. Varma. New York: Arno Press–New York Times, 1980.

Roche, Regina Maria. *Children of the Abbey: A Tale*. 5 vols. 1796. Paris: 1807.

———. *Clermont: A Tale*. 4 vols. London: Minerva Press, 1798.

———. *The Houses of Osma and Almeria; or Convent of St. Ildefonso, a Tale*. 3 vols. London: Newman, Minerva Press, 1810.

———. *Nocturnal Visit: A Tale*. 4 vols. London: Lane, 1800.

———. *The Tradition of the Castle; or Scenes in the Emerald Isle*. 4 vols. London: A. K. Newman, 1824.

Ronald, Ann. "Terror-Gothic: Nightmare and Dream." *The Female Gothic*. Ed. Fleenor. 176–86.

Rose, Edward J. " 'The Queenly Personality': Walpole, Melville, and Mother." *Literature and Psychology* 15.4 (1965): 216–29.

Roudaut, Jean. "Les Demeures dans le roman noir." *Critique* (August-September 1959): 713–36.

Rowe, Karen E. " 'Fairy-born and human-bred': Jane Eyre's Education in Romance." *The Voyage In*. Ed. E. Abel et al. 69–89.

Russ, Joanna. "Somebody's Trying to Kill Me and I Think It's My Husband: The Modern Gothic." *The Female Gothic*. Ed. Fleenor. 31–56.

Sadleir, Michael. " 'All horrid?' Jane Austen and the Gothic Romance." *Things Past*. London: Chiswick Press, 1944. 167–200.

Scarborough, Dorothy. *The Supernatural in Modern English Fiction*. New York: Putnam, Knickerbocker Press, 1917.

Schiller, Friedrich von. *On the Sublime*. In *Naive and Sentimental Poetry and On the Sublime: Two Essays by Friedrich von Schiller*. 1801. Trans. Julius A. Elias. Milestones of Thought Series. New York: Ungar, 1980.

Schriber, Mary S. "Isabel Archer and Victorian Manners." *Studies in the Novel* 8 (1976): 441–57.

Sedgwick, Eve Kosofsky. "The Character in the Veil: Imagery of the Surface in the Gothic Novel." *PMLA* 96 (1981): 255–70.

———. *The Coherence of Gothic Conventions*. Gothic Studies and Dissertations. New York: Arno Press–New York Times, 1980.

Shelley, Mary Godwin. *Frankenstein; or The Modern Prometheus*. London, 1818. Rev. ed., 1831. Rpt. in *Three Gothic Novels: The Castle of Otranto, Vathek, Frankenstein*. Ed. Fairclough.

Showalter, Elaine. *A Literature of Their Own: British Women Novelists from Brontë to Lessing.* 1977. London: Virago, 1979.

Sickels, Eleanor M. *The Gloomy Egoist: Moods and Themes of Melancholy from Gray to Keats.* Columbia University Studies in English and Comparative Literature. New York: Columbia Univ. Press, 1932.

Silver, Brenda R. "The Reflecting Reader in *Villette.*" *The Voyage In.* Ed. E. Abel et al. 90–111.

Sleath, Eleanor. *The Nocturnal Minstrel; or the Spirit of the Wood.* 1810. Ed. and Introd. Devendra P. Varma. Gothic Novels 1. New York: Arno Press–New York Times, 1972.

Smith, Charlotte. *Emmeline: The Orphan of the Castle.* 1788. Ed. Anne Henry Ehrenpreis. London: Oxford Univ. Press, 1971.

———. *The Old Manor House.* 1793. Ed. Anne Henry Ehrenpreis. London: Oxford Univ. Press, 1969.

Sprague, Allen B. *Tides in English Taste (1619–1900).* Cambridge, Mass.: Harvard Univ. Press, 1937.

Sten, Christopher W. "Bartleby the Transcendentalist: Melville's Dead Letter to Emerson." *MLQ* 35 (1974): 30–44.

Strachey, Ray. *"The Cause": A Short History of the Women's Movement in Great Britain.* 1928. London: Virago, 1978.

Summers, Montague. *The Gothic Quest: A History of the Gothic Novel.* 1938. New York: Russell and Russell, 1964.

Swigart, Ford H., Jr. "Ann Radcliffe's Veil Imagery." *Studies in the Humanities* (March 1969): 55–59.

Swingle, L. J. "Frankenstein's Monster and Its Romantic Relatives: Problems of Knowledge in English Romanticism." *Texas Studies in Literature and Language* 15.1 (1973): 51–65.

Sypher, Wylie. "Social Ambiguity in a Gothic Novel." *Partisan Review* 12 (1945): 50–60.

Talfourd, Thomas N. "Memoir of the Life and Writings of Mrs. Radcliffe." *Gaston de Blondeville.* By Ann Radcliffe. 1826. 62–132.

Tanner, Tony. Introd. *Villette.* By Charlotte Brontë.

Tarr, Sister Mary Muriel. *Catholicism in Gothic Fiction: A Study of the Nature and Function of Catholic Materials in Gothic Fiction in England (1762–1820).* Washington, D. C.: Catholic Univ. of America Press, 1946.

Thompson, G. R., ed. *The Gothic Imagination: Essays in Dark Romanticism.* Olympia: Washington State Univ. Press, 1974.

———. "Introduction: Romanticism and the Gothic Tradition." *The Gothic Imagination.* Ed. Thompson. 1–10.

Thoreau, Henry David. *Walden.* 1854. In *Walden and Other Writings of Henry David Thoreau.* Ed. Brooks Atkinson. New York: Modern Library, 1965.

Thorslev, Peter L., Jr. "Incest as Romantic Symbol." *Comparative Literature Studies* (Univ. of Maryland) 2 (1965): 41–58.

Tillotson, Kathleen. *Novels of the Eighteen Forties*. London: Oxford Univ. Press, 1956.

Todd, Janet, ed. *Gender and Literary Voice*. *Women and Literature* 1 (new series). New York: Holmes and Meier, 1980.

Tomalin, Claire. *The Life and Death of Mary Wollstonecraft*. 1974. New York: Penguin, 1977.

Tompkins, J. M. S. *The Popular Novel in England, 1770–1800*. 1932. Westport, Conn.: Greenwood Press, 1961.

Tracy, Ann B. *The Gothic Novel 1790–1830: Plot Summaries and Index to Motifs*. Lexington: Univ. Press of Kentucky, 1981.

Treichler, Paula A. "Escaping the Sentence: Diagnosis and Discourse in 'The Yellow Wallpaper.' " *Tulsa Studies in Women's Literature* 3 (1984): 61–77.

Turner, Arlin. "Hawthorne's Literary Borrowings." *PMLA* 51 (1936): 543–62.

Tymmes, Ralph. *Doubles in Literary Psychology*. Cambridge, Eng.: Bowes and Bowes, 1949.

Van Ghent, Dorothy. "On *Wuthering Heights*." In *The English Novel, Form and Function*. By Van Ghent. New York: Holt, Rinehart, and Winston, 1953. Rpt. in *Wuthering Heights: An Anthology of Criticism*. Ed. Alastair Everitt. New York: Barnes & Noble, 156–71.

Varma, Devendra P. *The Gothic Flame, Being a History of the Gothic Novel in England: Its Origins, Efflorescence, Disintegration, and Residuary Influences*. 1957. New York: Russell and Russell, 1966.

Varnado, S. L. "The Idea of the Numinous in Gothic Literature." *Gothic Imagination*. Ed. Thompson. 11–21.

Vicinus, Martha, ed. *Suffer and Be Still: Women in the Victorian Age*. Bloomington: Indiana Univ. Press, 1973.

Wadlington, Warwick. *The Confidence Game in American Literature*. Princeton, N. J.: Princeton Univ. Press, 1975.

Walpole, Horace. *The Castle of Otranto: A Gothic Story*. 1765. Rpt. in *Three Gothic Novels*. Ed. Fairclough.

Wasserman, Renata R. Mautner. "The Self, the Mirror, the Other: 'The Fall of the House of Usher.' " *Poe Studies* 10.2 (1977): 33–35.

Watt, Ian. *The Rise of the Novel: Studies in Defoe, Radcliffe, and Fielding*. 1957. Berkeley and Los Angeles: Univ. of California Press, 1967.

Weiten, Alida Alberdina Sibbellina. *Mrs. Radcliffe: Her Relation Towards Romanticism, with an Appendix on the Novels Falsely Ascribed to Her*. Amsterdam: H. J. Paris, 1926.

West, Jackie. "Women, Sex, and Class." *Feminism and Materialism*. ed. Kuhn and Wolpe. 220–53.

Whitman, Walt. *Song of Myself*. In *Complete Poetry and Selected Prose of Walt Whitman*. 1891. Ed. James E. Miller, Jr. Boston: Houghton Mifflin, 1959. 25–68.

Wilde, Oscar. "English Poetesses." *Queen* 84.2189 (December 8, 1888). Rpt. in *Miscellanies by Oscar Wilde.* Ed. Robert Ross. London: Dawsons of Pall Mall, 1969. 110–20.

Wilt, Judith. *Ghosts of the Gothic: Austen, Eliot, and Lawrence.* Princeton, N.J.: Princeton Univ. Press, 1980.

Wise, Thomas James, and John Alexander Symington. *The Shakespeare Head Brontë: The Brontës: Their Lives, Friendships and Correspondence.* 4 vols. Vol. 3: 1842–1852. Oxford, Eng.: Blackwell, 1932.

Wollstonecraft, Mary. *Maria, or The Wrongs of Woman.* 1798. Rpt. with Introd. Moira Ferguson. New York: Norton, 1975.

————. *A Vindication of the Rights of Men, in a Letter to the Right Honourable Edmund Burke; Occasioned by his Reflections on the Revolution in France.* 2nd ed. London, 1790. Gainesville, Fla.: Scholars' Facsimiles and Reprints, 1960.

————. *A Vindication of the Rights of Woman.* 1792. New York: Norton, 1975.

Wolff, Cynthia Griffin. "The Radcliffean Gothic Model: A Form for Feminine Sexuality." *Modern Language Studies* 9.3 (1979): 98–113. Rpt. in *The Female Gothic.* Ed. Fleenor. 207–26.

Woolf, Virginia. "Professions for Women." 1925. Rpt. in *Collected Essays by Virginia Woolf.* 4 vols. London: Hogarth Press, 1966. Vol. 2.

Yeazell, Ruth Bernard. "More True Than Real: Jane Eyre's 'Mysterious Summons.' " *Nineteenth-Century Fiction* 29 (1974): 127–43.

Ziff, Larzer. "A Reading of *Wieland.*" *PMLA* 77 (1962): 51–57.

Zweig, Paul. *The Adventurer.* New York: Basic Books, 1974.

Index

Accusation, as motif, 173–76
Activity
  acceptance of boundaries and, 270
  interpretation as, for protagonist, 48
  transcendence and, 195, 220–22
  vs. passivity, 171–72
Adventure, and decorum, 178–81
Alcott, Louisa May, 152
Alienation. *See also* Separation; Unity in
    separateness paradox
  illicit knowledge and, 61–63
  knowledge and, in *Pierre,* 74–77
  loss of knowledge and, 240
  male-female relationships and, 166–67
  moral estrangement and, 99–108
  not knowing and, 83
  place in society and, 231
  of Romantic hero, 301*n*13
  search for knowledge and, 56–58
  from self, 135–37
  sin and, 98–99, 103
  women's education and, 167–73
Allegory, 304*n*34, 317*n*5, 317*n*7
American literature, and definition of
    Gothic genre, 7–8
Anger, 189, 279–81
Anxiety. *See also* Fear; Terror
  about boundaries, 19–21
  about physical violation, 29–32

Architecture
  at center of Gothic romance, 15
  danger of fall and, 72
  forces of violence and, 17–18
  soul's "voyage out" and, 121
Ariosto, 90–91, 94
Art
  as access to the sublime, 144–45
  as act of knowledge, 115–16
Arvin, Newton, 303*n*24
Auerbach, Nina, 319*n*24
Austen, Jane, 11, 36, 149–50

Bachelard, Gaston, 64
Ballin, Rosetta, 51, 121, 173, 180
Barrett, Eaton Stannard, 3–4, 51, 173,
    179, 271, 313*n*38
Barriers
  inequality of meaning of, 26
  metaphors for breaking of, 67–75
Berthoff, Warner, 301*n*17
Blackstone, William, 157, 312*n*22
Bledsoe, Robert, 321*n*42
Blom, M. A., 261
Bondage, 21
Boundaries
  anxiety about, 19–21
  critical focus and, 296*n*25
  in Hawthorne, 99

341

perceptions inspired by, 45–46, 47
readers and, 132–33, 141

Dacre, Charlotte, 278, 279–80
   Zofloya, 184–85, 280, 307*n*2
Daiches, David, 136, 309*n*21
Daly, Mary, 27, 265, 320*n*32
Dark Romanticism, 308*n*9
Day, William Patrick, 12, 295*n*15, 296*n*25
Deadly iteration, 97–117, 230
Death, ambiguity in tableaus of, 137–38
De Beauvoir, Simone, 148, 172–73, 175–
   76, 185, 187, 200, 267
Decorum
   adventure and, 178–81
   convent as symbol of, 162
   internal barriers and, 234–35
   recognition of, as barrier, 271–72
   as restraint, 178–89, 271–72
   violation of, in *Jane Eyre,* 214, 219
Defense, against the self, 163, 213–14,
   230. *See also* Self-defense
Delusion, 46, 263
De Quincey, Thomas, 94–95, 304*n*6
Dickinson, Emily, 38, 126, 138
Dimock, Wai-chee, 302*n*21
Discontents of women, Gothic as voice for
   domestic monotony and, 177–78
   domestic relations and, 151–60
   longing for security and, 185–86
   social status of women and, 160–65
Displacement, 309*n*19
Divine intervention, 221–22
Domestic confinement
   Gothic spaces as metaphor for, 191–92,
     205–6
   immanence and, 206
   marriage and, 211
   as peril, 200-201
   as theme, 151–53
   women's impulse to transcendence and,
     191–92, 224–26
Doody, Margaret Anne, 151, 160, 310*n*3
Door. *See also* Threshold, crossing of
   closing of, 101, 125, 126
   opening of, 271, 283–84
Doubling, 317*n*7
Drake, Nathan, 20, 51

Dreams, 160
Durant, David, 187–88

Eagleton, Terry, 256–57
Education. *See* Women's education
Edwards, Jonathan, 96, 98
Egotism
   delusions of, 263
   and self-abnegation, 235–37, 238, 278
Eliot, T. S., 97
Emerson, Ralph Waldo, 24, 121–22, 124–
   26, 195
Emotion. *See also* Feelings, expression of
   reason and, 256–57, 263–64
   restraint of, 231–32
Enlightenment, Gothic subversion of, 48
Equality
   of access to outside world, 26–28
   love and, 316*n*10
   transcendence and, 218–19, 223–26
Escape
   in Charlotte Brontë's work, 252, 266–75
   constraints against, 178–89
   relation between terror and sublime tran-
     scendence and, 140–41
   from self-enclosure, 266–67
   through sense of equality, 218–19
   through sublime experience, 181–82
Evil
   goodness of God and, 126–27
   Hawthorne's view of, 110–14
   in human mind, 308*n*9
   problem of, in Gothic romance, 108–9,
     110–11
   sublime action and, 184–85
   within self, 108–9, 120–21, 163
Evil Other Woman
   discovery of, as convention, 153–54
   function of, in *Jane Eyre,* 212–13
   happy endings and, 156
   as heroine's self, in *Villette,* 264–65
   relation to, 154–56
Ewbank, Inga-Stina, 321*n*42

Fall, the, 301*n*18
   bounding of knowledge and, 171
   in Gothic vision, 308*n*10
   imagery of, 72, 73

Self-expression (*continued*)
  problem of, in women's Gothic, 24–25,
    166, 173–76
  restraint in, as convention, 149–51
  self-defense and, 166, 173–76, 196–98,
    268–69
  in *Villette*, 24–25, 244–45, 284, 291
Self-image, 26–28. *See also* Identity;
    Personal littleness
Selfishness. *See* Egotism
Self-knowledge
  danger of, as Gothic theme, 91
  repressions and, 75–77
  women's education and, 168–73
Selfless woman, 236–37
Self-scrutiny, 253–57
Self-transcendence
  focus on, 237
  social forces against, 252–66
  in *Villette*, 287
Separation. *See also* Alienation; Unity in
    separateness paradox
  fear of, 22–23
  sin as, 98–99
  terror of, 238, 249–52
Sexuality
  in *Jane Eyre*, 214
  in *The Portrait of a Lady*, 41
  projection of woman's feelings of, 155–
    56
  sexual knowledge and, 312n20
  in *Villette*, 269, 276
Shakespeare, William, 110
Shelley, Mary, 24, 25
  Frankenstein, 10, 190–91
  hero-villains in, 211
  stranger figure in, 303n25
  theme of knowledge in, 56–58, 90,
    190–91
Sherman, Leona F., 27–28, 296n25
Showalter, Elaine, 195–96
Sin, and alienation, 98–99, 103
Skepticism, and the supernatural, 132–35
Smith, Charlotte, 46
  Emmeline: The Orphan of the Castle,
    158, 252
  An Old Manor House, 53
Social relations, in *Pierre*, 71

Social status
  in Charlotte Brontë's work, 232, 233–37
  economic position and, 237–48, 254–55
  homelessness as theme and, 242
  human relationships and, 265
  intelligence and, 248
  lack of, and forces of violence, 230–32,
    233–37
  perils in work relations and, 232, 237
  women's discontent and, 160–65
Society
  escape into, 284–86
  social institutions as forces of violence
    and, 16–17
  transcendence and, 288–89
Solipsism, 301n13
Soul
  ambivalent struggle of, 134–37
  haunted, 134–35, 136, 138
  immensity of, 119–21
  "voyage out" of, 121–22
Spenser, Edmund, 90–91, 94, 159
Stein, Gertrude, 125
Strachey, Ray, 312n22
Stranger figure, 303n25
Sublime, the. *See also* Curiosity;
    Transcendence
  action and, 184–85
  association of men with, 182–84
  experience of, as escape, 181–82
  in *Jane Eyre*, 210
  repression and, 263–64
  transcendence and, 139–43, 215–16
Summers, Montague, 133
Supernatural
  boundaries and, 21
  explanation of, as failure of Gothic
    quest, 133
  Gothicists's ambivalence toward, 132–
    35
  role of, in Gothic, 120
  unexplained, 133–34
Surnaturel expliqué
  in Charlotte Brontë, 221, 277, 281–
    82
  confusion of mortal and immortal and,
    119–20
  narrative dilemmas and, 64